Writing Postcolonial Histories of Intercultural Education

INTERKULTURELLE PÄDAGOGIK UND POSTKOLONIALE THEORIE

Herausgegeben von Heike Niedrig und Louis Henri Seukwa

Band 2

PETER LANG

Frankfurt am Main · Berlin · Bern · Bruxelles · New York · Oxford · Wien

Heike Niedrig / Christian Ydesen
(eds.)

Writing Postcolonial Histories of Intercultural Education

PETER LANG
Internationaler Verlag der Wissenschaften

Bibliographic Information published by the Deutsche Nationalbibliothek
The Deutsche Nationalbibliothek lists this publication in the Deutsche Nationalbibliografie; detailed bibliographic data is available in the internet at http://dnb.d-nb.de.

Cover Design:
© Olaf Gloeckler, Atelier Platen, Friedberg

Gratefully acknowledging financial support
by the Danish School of Education
at the University of Aarhus
and by iMiR - Institut für Migrations- und
Rassismusforschung e.V., Hamburg

ISSN 1867-626X
ISBN 978-3-631-60904-0

www.peterlang.de

Preface and Acknowledgements

The idea for this book has its roots in a symposium titled "Writing Histories of Intercultural Education", held at the European Conference on Educational Research (ECER) in Vienna in September 2009. Susanne Spieker and Christian Ydesen, both members of the European Educational Research Association's (EERA) Network 17, "Histories of Education", had invited members of the EERA Network 7, "Intercultural Education and Social Justice", to convene a joint symposium in an effort to explore the historical dimensions of current concepts, theories and practices of Intercultural Education.

The experimental attempt to intermarry these two educational subdisciplines – the 'historians' and the 'interculturalists' – proved to be more of a challenge than anticipated. The reactions to the eight contributions by members of the two different EERA networks ranged from interested openness and mild bemusement to the sceptical question of whether what these 'others' were doing really qualified as science. One may conclude that the historically developed and ingrained differences between 'scientific cultures' should not be underestimated. In the metaphorical terms of courtship patterns, the symposium was certainly not a marriage, but rather a first date. However, even though many participants did not experience 'love at first sight', others were intrigued by the encounter and decided to create an anthology in order to follow up on the interesting issues that arose from these initial discussions.

Only three of the contributions to this volume (Baquero Torres, Niedrig, Ydesen) are based on papers presented at the symposium. Since, for personal reasons, Susanne Spieker could not embark on such a project, Heike Niedrig (Intercultural Education) took her place, joining Christian Ydesen (History of Education) as co-editor of the anthology. Through our various scientific networks and connections, we invited additional contributions. Many positive responses came from a 'new' generation of educational researchers not yet firmly established in the institutionalised structures; thus to some extent, this anthology has also evolved into a platform for up-and-coming young researchers.

With few exceptions, the contributions were written in English by non-native speakers or had to be translated into English. Since we had limited financial resources, we could not afford professional translation services. Proofreading the final text versions was, therefore, a particularly challenging task. We were extremely fortunate to have our two English speaking authors from the United States helping us in this endeavour, and would like to express our special gratitude to *Adrea Lawrence* and *Christopher J. Frey* who tirelessly provided valuable input that far exceeded our expectations for the proofreading process.

Many messages crossed the ocean in order to negotiate the finer nuances of meaning. Their commitment to the anthology project was truly priceless.

We gratefully acknowledge the financial support from the Danish School of Education, University of Aarhus, for funding the proofreading, and from the "Institut für Migrations- und Rassismusforschung e.V. (iMiR)" (Institute for Research about Migration and Racism) in Hamburg, Germany, for subsidising the publication costs. We are further indebted to Prof. Dr. İnci Dirim, University of Vienna, for providing financial aid as well as linguistic assistance in translating the Turkish contribution to this anthology.

Heike Niedrig and Christian Ydesen, June 2011

Contents

Writing Postcolonial Histories of Intercultural Education – An Introduction

Heike Niedrig and Christian Ydesen

1. "Intercultural Education" – an educational concept with a "short history"...

Even though our report of the dynamics at the symposium from which this anthology originated (see preface) might suggest it, we do not claim that a historical accounting of the development of "multicultural education" is completely new. In fact, almost any academic publication that provides an introduction to issues of multi- or intercultural education/pedagogy starts with a short review of the different stages of its development. As a rule, however, this educational development is located in the context of mass migration after World War II, and the scope of historical research is rather limited (cp. the comprehensive critical review by Myers 2009). This might not be so very surprising when considering European nations. But as far as we know, the discussion about intercultural or multicultural education does not reach further back than the 1970s, even in countries with a long history of immigration that define themselves explicitly as immigration countries such as Australia, Canada and the United States (see e.g., Kasinitz, Waters & Mollenkopf 2002; Levitt & Waters 2002). For a long time, the dominant cultural identity in Australia and Canada was – due to their Commonwealth membership – British; and their "native populations" were not perceived as cultural collectives of equal standing. Therefore, a new orientation in education globally only came about as a result of post-war immigration from Southern and Eastern European and from Asian countries; and in the case of Canada, was assisted by demands of the self-assertive francophone minority. In the U.S., before the 1960s, the "melting-pot-ideology" had prevented any serious educational interest in ethnic and cultural differences, even though Steiner-Khamsi (1992) reports about a first multicultural movement in education in the 1920s and 1930s. But it was the Civil Rights Movement in the 1950s and 1960s against 'racial segregation' in schools that proved to be the decisive impulse to make cultural differences and conflicts subjects of study in the formal school system, along with the public acknowledgement of minority cultures and their political rights. Other ethnic minorities followed the example of African Americans; and the Ethnic-Revival-Movement instigated according developments in pedagogy in the 1970s, which was labelled as "multicultural education" (Auernheimer 2007: 26f.).

2. … but with a "long past"

The dominant view in Western Europe that "multicultural" issues in education are recent phenomena that date back no further than the labour immigration after World War II has been challenged by a group of educational historians in Germany since the late 1980s (e.g. Krüger-Potratz 1989; Krüger-Potratz, Jasper & Knabe 1998, Knabe 2000). Their historical research of the educational policies in the German Empire (*Kaiserreich;* 1871 – 1918) and during the Weimar Republic (1918-1933) shed light on early patterns of constructing differences along the lines of nationality, ethnicity, culture and language, and a number of educational responses that have been – unconsciously – revitalized after 1945 in dealing with immigrant children. This research has, therefore, given valuable insights into the "long past" of the "short history" of intercultural education in Germany, and into the many unnoticed continuities of patterns in educational responses by the German national education system to the presence of "other" children – to children who are perceived as not really belonging to the 'German national collective' which is imagined as culturally homogeneous (Krüger-Potratz 2005: 62ff.). Only very recently, though, since about 2005, German colonialism was included in the investigation of the "long past" of multicultural discourses in education.

As recounted by Goodman, McCulloch & Richardson (2009: 696f.), the International Standing Conference for the History of Education (ISCHE) turned its attention to these questions a decade earlier at a conference in Lisbon 1993 under the heading of "Education Encounters Peoples and Cultures: The Colonial Experience (16th – 20th Centuries)". The subsequent publication of selected papers included an inspiring, programmatic historiographical essay by António Nóvoa who proposed *rethinking history and history of education* in an interdisciplinary manner, drawing on the insights of postcolonial theory and related critical theory traditions in order to "bring multiple and diversified points of view into the historical narrative" (Nóvoa 1995: 25).

In this spirit, the contributions to our anthology give insights into the (pre)-history of intercultural issues in education across a vast range of historical, national-geographical and political contexts – from medieval Japan via colonial India to post-Apartheid South Africa and post-Holocaust Germany. In the words of Cornel West, we may say that this anthology is a veritable attempt

> To thrash the monolithic and homogeneous in the name of diversity, multiplicity, and heterogeneity; to reject the abstract, general, and universal in light of the concrete, specific, and particular; and to historicize, contextualize and pluralize by highlighting the contingent, provisional, variable, tentative, shifting and changing (1990: 93).

Yet, from these diverse accounts a number of patterns do emerge that transcend the historically specific and the contingent. We will try and outline some of these more general issues.

3. The history of the terminology of "culture"

One of the most contested conceptual issues in the recent internal debates in the field of "multicultural/intercultural education" has been the term "culture" itself – as well as its derivatives. There are plenty of attempts to differentiate, for instance, between the most common terms "multicultural" and "intercultural." In his first introductory textbook for teacher education students in 1990, Auernheimer, one of the most renowned German educational scholars in the field of "intercultural education", summarized the conceptual discussions of the time around this term in German, English and French discourses: Some authors suggested, for instance, that "multicultural" was a descriptive term to denote the fact that Western immigration societies were made up of a multitude of 'cultures', whereas "intercultural" should be used as normative or prescriptive term to discuss appropriate educational responses to the multicultural reality. Other authors saw "intercultural" as a term that helped to overcome some of the shortcomings of the 'multicultural perspective' because the prefix "inter" underscores the idea of interaction and exchange as opposed to the idea of a mere neighbourhood of self-contained 'cultures' (Auernheimer 1990: 1ff.). The more recent terms "transcultural" and "cross-cultural" have been promoted on similar grounds; in fact, they go beyond the idea of a simple exchange by implying mixture and hybridization.

The debate around the most appropriate prefix already hints at the core of the problem, which actually resides in the basic notion of "culture". The term "culture" in its ethnographic sense has been traced back to Sir Edward Burnett Tylor (1832–1917), considered by many as founding figure of British Social Anthropology. Tylor used the elitist German term "Kultur" which was based on Hegelian philosophy and 'democratized' it, so to speak, by shifting its meaning from the purely 'spiritual sphere' into social and practical domains, including tools and weapons, dress and food production, as well as beliefs, art, morals, and the laws and customs of any human society. However, Tylor spoke of "culture" in the singular and had an evolutionary view of a comprehensive human culture or civilization according to which differences were due to different stages of development (Tylor 1873; also see Wax 1993).

The notion of culture on which the political and educational multiculturalism of the 1970s was based goes back to the 'Boas-Benedict'-concept of culture

(Boas 1911, Benedict 1934). These anthropologists promoted the idea of a plurality of 'cultures', and their approach laid the foundation for so-called 'cultural relativism', or the claim that each 'culture' is organized according to a unique pattern profoundly distinct from other cultural collectives, thereby negating a universalistic socio-cultural development culminating in (Western style) modernity. Murray Wax, the first president of the "Centre of Anthropology and Education" in Washington (D.C.), speaks of the "irony" that this notion of culture started to become the central concept of debates in pedagogy and educational policy in the U.S. (as well as in other Western immigrant countries) at precisely the time when influential cultural anthropologists began to question the validity of this concept (Wax 1993: 99). As Carrither argues in the section "Culture" in the Dictionary of Anthropology (1997), the concept of culture – regardless of its theoretical and empirical merits – has promoted a number of problematic views, such as the perception that the world is segmented into relatively autonomous societies with homogeneous 'cultures', each rooted in their own traditions: "Yet societies are hardly autonomous; they exist in relations of commerce, of mutual dependence and (above all) in relationships of dominance and subjections with others" (Carrither 1997: 101).

And indeed, most of the recent contributors to the field of "intercultural education" agree about the dangers of an essentialist concept of culture, and tend to adopt a constructivist approach when dealing with issues of 'culture', taking into account the "relationships of dominance and subjection". This view may be called one of the 'common denominators' of the contributions to this anthology, even though the implications of this view are spelled out in decidedly different ways.

4. Pioneer research into the pre-history of educational research

Susanne Spieker, one of the original convenors of the symposium (see preface), who is currently writing her Ph.D. dissertation examining the influence of the 'discovery of America' on European educational thought, has presented pioneering historical work on the issues we wish to address in this volume. In her article, "An early researcher in the field of education: Bernardino de Sahagún in sixteenth-century Mexico" (Spieker 2008), she writes about the life and work of the Franciscan friar Sahagún (1499/1500 – 1590) who travelled to New Spain [Mexico] in 1529 to work as a missionary amongst the Nahua, and has since become famous for his ethnographic work on the late Aztec Empire before 1519 and his historiography of Meso-American pre-Columbian cultures (General History of the Things of New Spain; 1578/79). In her final comments, Spieker focuses on the fact that Sahagún's work, which was undertaken in the service of the Catholic mission in New Spain, can be perceived as an example of early educational research practice:

> Though Sahagún is rooted in Renaissance humanism, his methods of research are surprisingly valid in today's empirical educational research; for example using questionnaires, expert interviews, representative surveys. Like many researchers even today, he retained his own and his former pupils' bias – the language of the upper classes was adopted by the priests as model for their own use; common people, on the other hand, were not questioned (ibid. 771).

Spieker also concludes, based on Dussel's philosophical approach, that Sahagún's educational research is "part of a process of simplification in which the mainly Spanish missionaries of sixteenth-century New Spain managed centrality through hegemony of an integrating culture", and that therefore, "Sahagún stands at the beginning of a very ambiguous process which led to the integration of the Indians into the (European) story of mankind" (ibid.).

Another insight, however, emerges from Spieker's account of Sahagún's research motivation, which we consider of great importance for a postcolonial historiography of "intercultural educational research", but which is not taken up in the conclusion to the text. Spieker recurrently refers to Sahagún's research motives: In one instance, his conclusion that it was necessary to explore pre-Hispanic Aztec culture because "'idolatrous things' happened in the presence of priests without their understanding" (ibid. 761); in another instance, Sahagún's observation "how metaphorical language was openly mixed into Christian song texts without the priests even realising it" (ibid. 762); and yet in another example, "Sahagún cites several examples […] how Aztec festivities continued under the guise of Catholic Saints" (ibid. 763). "The knowledge of Aztec gods is explained as important in combating the Nahua's religious beliefs" (ibid. 764), as Spieker notes, and from this follows the "necessity to understand the 'exact and metaphorical meanings', 'their way of speaking, and most of their [the Nahua's] ancient practices, the good and evil'" (ibid. 765).

Apparently, the perceived need for an "improvement of intercultural understanding" (ibid. 771), which in terms of research practice meant to embark on an endeavour to better *understand the cultural 'Others'"*, arose as the need to better *control these colonized Others* as objects of missionary zeal.

5. A postcolonial perspective on "intercultural education"

A notable change of the original symposium title in naming this anthology is the insertion of the term "postcolonial". We suggest that an explicitly postcolonial perspective in retracing the pre-history of the current debates about "interculturality" is needed to decentre the hegemonic accounts in order to focus on issues that tend to be sidelined (see also Nóvoa 1995). This view can be spelled out with respect to the three central terms of this anthology:

First, we wish to point out the specific historical contexts in which the anthropological concept of *culture* has been conceived and developed. European anthropology is rooted in European exploration, expansion and colonialism. As Spieker's historical research has made visible, the desire for ethnological knowledge about the 'culture' of the 'others' cannot be separated from the context of colonial domination and subjection. Postcolonial theorists, therefore, understand knowledge production about the colonized Others as part of a power-knowledge-complex (e.g. Spivak 1984).

Second, postcolonial theory is a decentred approach to *history*, undermining the European master narrative. As Stuart Hall points out, the postcolonial retelling of the past offers an alternative narrative, which presents colonialism not as a local or marginal sub-plot within a 'greater history', but as a central, comprehensive world-historical event that fundamentally altered all existing structures. Postcolonialism perceives 'colonisation' as a global transformative process; and the globalised world, including the current global migration movements, is, basically, a postcolonial phenomenon. Since 1492, European explorations, 'discoveries', expansion and colonisation processes have transformed the world irrevocably, and ethnic essentialism has become an increasingly impossible strategy (Hall 2006: 249f.).

Third, *education* as a science is part of the development of the modern Human Sciences (such as sociology, history, anthropology, psychology, pedagogy, human biology and medicine etc.), which is closely connected to the development of natural sciences and their quest for classification as well as scientific race theories of 18th and 19th century, particularly in the era called "Enlightenment". Much has been said and debated regarding the question of the extent to which the prominent philosophers of the Enlightenment, such as Immanuel Kant and Georg F. W. Hegel, and their philosophical world views and views of humankind can be called "racist", e.g., Kant's lecture (1775) "*Von den verschiedenen Racen der Menschen: Von der Verschiedenheit der Racen überhaupt*" (On the different races of men: On the diversity of races in general). By introducing the concept of 'race' into the German discourse of Enlightenment, Kant laid the foundation for the concept of racial hierarchy, in spite of assertions that his race concept was actually 'neutral' or even 'progressive' because he proclaimed an equality of the human origin, regardless of the diversity of 'races' (Piesche 2005: 31f.). A similar debate revolves around the question whether it is possible to dismiss openly racist assessments of "the Africans" in Hegel's writings as irrelevant for the truth of his universalist philosophy of history (Farr 2005: 147ff.). From a postcolonial perspective, the essential point, however, is the observation that like other European intellectuals, Kant and Hegel wrote about the world and about 'mankind' from a White European male perspective, and that the discourses of European Enlightenment constructed "women" as the emotional or irrational Other of male rationality and "savages" as the primitive antithetical Other of European progress (Weigel 1987). The concept of "Othering" is probably one of the most powerful analytical tools of postcolonial criticism. Therefore, we have dedicated the first contribution to this anthology to an exploration of this term and its theoretical history (Thomas-Olalde & Velho).

From the point of view of educational research, equally important as explicit race theories are the implicit allusions and influences of the colonial context on pedagogical thinking and writing. Of all 'human sciences', pedagogy, in particular, is a project of European Enlightenment in the service of human and social progress. In fact, even contemporary writers have spoken of the 18th century as the "pedagogical century" (Tenorth 2000: 79). In his lectures "On Pedagogy" at the University of Königsberg in the semester 1776/77 (published 1803), Kant proposed to establish pedagogy as a science based on knowledge and reflection with the objective to improve 'humanity'. In the course of his arguments he describes four stages of education: 1) disciplining or "taming of wildness/savagery", 2) cultivation, 3) civilisation, and finally 4) moralisation. The crucial question arises of how to balance freedom and constraint in an educational process that aims at 'autonomy' and the acceptance of moral principles based on free will; and Kant pleads for utmost freedom in education, only to be constrained within certain limits, which he outlines and justifies. Morality, he argues, cannot be imposed or enforced by means of punishment and reward, but can only be instilled by addressing the pupil as a reasonable being. What is notably lacking in Kant's idealist proposition of enlightened pedagogy, however, is any reflection on the power differential between educator and pupil, as well as the emotional dependency of the child on her/his caregiver (for a detailed discussion cp. Koller 2004: 25-47).

But power is, of course, at the centre of any educational situation; in the context of 'multicultural' or 'intercultural education', in educational contexts where historically ingrained majority-minority-relations are at stake, the relevance and merit of a postcolonial perspective of analysis is evident. As postcolonial thinkers assert, the 'European history' of Enlightenment and its ideals of progress and perfection of humanity cannot be separated from the history of exploration, 'discoveries' and colonialism. Referencing Godinho (1992), Nóvoa explains that "the Portuguese and the Spanish discoveries brought the consciousness of humankind its unity, thus making both the knowledge of the world and the knowledge of oneself possible" (Nóvoa 1995: 24); they are at the same time at the origin of master narratives that place Europe at the centre of history and 'civilisation'. In a similar way, Spieker argues that Sahagún's ethnographical and historiographical work in the 16th century integrated the Nahua into the story of mankind – from the point of view of the Spanish Empire, that is, to use a postcolonial turn of phrase, he fixated them in the "imperial gaze" (Spieker 2008: 759). He thus took part in preparing the grounds for discourses of Enlightenment philosophy referred to above: "Later in the eighteenth century, when evolutionary anthropology and universal conceptions of history developed, this seemingly benevolent integration led to the perception of the indigenous Americans as in a state of childhood compared to the civilized Europeans" (ibid.). To transform children, "little savages", into civil, cultivated adults whose actions are guided by sound moral judgements based on universally acceptable principles can be and has been described as a colonial project; just as colonialism has always been perceived and legitimised as an educational project.

6. Writing Postcolonial Histories of Intercultural Education

To sum up our editorial perspectives and the framework of this anthology, we refer to the different terms assembled in the anthology's title which starts with the verb *writing*: The "history of intercultural education" can be written from different perspectives. Therefore we do not presume that this anthology could present "the" history of intercultural education; rather we wish to underscore that these *histories* – in the plural – are produced in the process of writing. As our readers will find, there are many different angles from which to embark on such a writing process.

By adding the *postcolonial* perspective, we have tried to emphasis that the three central notions – history, culture, education – are not 'neutral' concepts: They can and, in our view, should be discussed with respect to postcolonial power-knowledge-complexes. As Nóvoa points out, more than three-quarters of the people living today have had their lives shaped by the experience of colonialism (Nóvoa 1995: 26, cp. Ashcroft et al. 1989). Yet critical voices have challenged the idea of "postcoloniality" on the grounds that it was a "homogenizing" and a-historical concept in so far as this label is conferred to regions and nations with vastly different historical backgrounds and contexts (e.g. Shohat 1992,

McClintock 1992): Are Britain, Canada, Nigeria and Jamaica equally postcolonial? Is Britain postcolonial in the same sense as the U.S.? Is it useful at all to think of the U.S. as 'postcolonial'? Stuart Hall accedes that it is indeed important to carefully observe the different social and ethnical contexts: "Australia and Canada, on the one hand, Nigeria, India and Jamaica on the other, are certainly not 'post-colonial' *in the same way*. But this does not mean that they are not 'post-colonial' *in any way"* (Hall 2006: 246). This observation includes the quarter of the people whose lives might not have been *directly* shaped by colonial experiences. In order to challenge a simplifying binary view of the global condition of postcoloniality, we have included a number of studies that do not fit into the traditional perspective of 'Europe' vs. 'its colonies', e.g., the cases of Japan (Frey) and Turkey (Çapar) and their 'internal others'.

Some of the contributions expressly deal with the concept of ***history***: Messerschmidt, for instance, refers to Walter Benjamin in outlining her understanding of history, which assumes the lack of closure of historical experiences of violence. "In the practice of remembrance we attempt to enter into a relation with history in order to understand ourselves [...] and in order to become aware of our own involvement in the effects of this history" (Messerschmidt in this volume, p. 76). Therefore the term postcoloniality should not be interpreted as indicating a successful break with colonialism and neither as a mere descriptive term of chronological succession, but rather as a marker of the present-day effects of colonial history. Other contributions also emphasis the ambiguity which the post-terminology is meant to convey: The terms post-colonial, post-National-Socialist, post-Apartheid all imply that what is considered 'past' is not past in the sense of 'done with' and concluded, that there is never just a historical rupture, but continuity, even though it proceeds in different forms. While many contributions in this volume focus on the underlying continuities of the experiences of violence and oppression, there are also more optimistic perspectives on 'historical heritages' and their empowering potentials (e.g., Dei's contribution on moral education in Ghana and Nigeria, Jakobsen on the recognition of indigenous Sami culture in Norway).

The term *education,* finally, is also filled with different meanings in the various contributions. When we conceived the idea of this anthology, we had in mind that "intercultural education" was a field of discourse, theory and practice with respect to formal and to some extent non-formal educational settings. But several of the contributions (most notably those of Frey and Lawrence) made us aware that what qualifies as 'education' in general, and in the context of (post)-colonialism in particular, goes far beyond that which happens inside of schools and even that which happens outside of schools in a planned manner as Kant's concept of pedagogy implies.

So editing this anthology was, in itself, an educational project, in terms of interdisciplinarity, but also in terms of international or maybe even 'intercultural' exchange. Writing about colonialism, racism and education is always embedded in specific (post)-colonial contexts that are structured by racism (and other relations of power) and shaped by particular educational experiences in- and outside of institutions. The contributions in this anthology are therefore heterogeneous in their perspectives and approaches; they are also clearly *written from different subject positions* within social structures, which became particularly evident in the use of the collective pronouns "we" and "our" in some of the contributions, e.g., one of the texts written about Germany (Messerschmidt), on the one hand, and the contribution about Ghana/Nigeria (Dei), on the other hand. These pronouns and the identification of the authors they implied were challenged by our two U.S.-American proofreaders and accordingly amended or clarified. On closer observation, it is interesting to note that these pronouns have different functions in the different contexts: The "we/our" in the text by Messerschmidt express a self-reflective, critical reference to the constructed White German hegemonic collective; for instance, when she explains that anti-Semitic projections are used to "avoid dealing with our own (German) racism and our own (German) colonial history". Dei, on the other hand, uses these pronouns as an affirmative reference to a collective postcolonial Black African identity he shares, e.g., when he refers to an African history of struggles and resistances to design "our own futures", when he demands that the African learner must be strengthened in order to design new futures "of which we can collectively be proud", or that African culture and knowledge must be included in formal education as "essential aspects of our African identity and personality."

As Laclau (1990) points out, there is no *outside* of power discourse structures; even the grammar of writing indicates that the authors of this anthology are all part of the hegemonic discourses and corresponding power-knowledge-complexes, which each of us tries to analytically dissect, undermine and shift, if only a little, from our different subject positions *within* these very structures.

7. About the contributions

Our first contribution by *Oscar Thomas-Olalde & Astride Velho* provides a theoretical introduction into the concept "Othering" as a key concept of postcolonial theory and as an important conceptual tool of critical analyses of racism, which informs a number of the analytical approaches combined in this anthology. The authors outline the complex theoretical history of the concept, from psychoanalytical concepts developed by the French poststructuralist Jacques Lacan via Edward Said's Orientalism to the re-coining of the term Othering by the postcolonial Indian thinker Gayatri Chakravorty Spivak. The theoretical explorations include postcolonial writings by Stuart Hall and Homi K. Bhabha as well as discourse analytical approaches by Michel Foucault, Ernesto Laclau, Chantal Mouffe and Judith Butler. Based on an analysis of Othering as a discourse and as a dispositive, the authors finally look into experiences and strategies of those who are forcefully 'Othered' in racist contexts. With Laclau they conclude that there is no *outside* of hegemonic discourse structures. The *inside* of these powerful social structures that all of us are part of, however, is not monolithic and unchangeable, but dependent on discursively-constructed, antagonistic divisions, and it is precisely here that anti-hegemonic practices can take effect – by blurring dichotomous distinctions.

The next three chapters deal with the history and controversies around Intercultural Education in Germany. A postcolonial perspective on German history in general is very recent and rather tenuous, and for decades the notion of 'racism' has been almost taboo in German political discourse and social analysis alike. Even critical German social researchers have tended to avoid the term 'racism', and phenomena which would be defined as cases of racism in any other national context, were usually labelled as "hostility to foreigners" (*Ausländerfeindlichkeit*) in Germany until the 1990s and even beyond (see footnote 5 in the Messerschmidt contribution). The fact that overt German involvement in colonialism was cut short due to the defeat of the German Empire in World War I and the subsequent losses of all colonies in 1918, on the one hand, the close association of 'racism' with the atrocities of the National-Socialist regime (1933-1945) in the German historical consciousness, on the other hand, are two explanations for the peculiarities of the German discourse. Those educational researchers who have started to apply postcolonial and racist-critical perspectives to analyse German issues of "Intercultural Education" are still met with a lot of scepticism and resistance.

Against this background, *Patricia Baquero Torres* presents us with new insights into the *long past* of the *short history* of Intercultural Education in Germany by examining how basic discourse structures and racist perceptions that were developed in the context of German colonialism have survived the official end of colonialism and continue to impact the construction of the "migrant-Others" in the context of post-war labour immigration to Germany. In addition, Baquero Torres strongly promotes an approach known as 'intersectionality' to do justice to the complex issues at stake in 'intercultural' negotiations of subject positions such as taking into account the interplay of social categories like 'race', 'class' and 'gender' in the critical analysis of hegemonic discourse and political practices. In particular the category 'gender' is, in her view, indispensable for an adequate understanding of the multi-layered processes of Othering in the German colonial and post-war-migration contexts.

The two contributions by *Astrid Messerschmidt* and by *Rosa Fava* share an approach to the question of "Intercultural Education" in Germany by focussing on the fact that the Federal Republic of Germany is a post-National-Socialist and post-Holocaust society. *Messerschmidt*'s text dissects the issues of postcoloniality and post-National-Socialism in present-day Germany, the different forms of Othering involved in colonial racism and in anti-Semitism, and how they relate to each other. She analyses the variety of defence mechanisms which structure the processes of remembrance in Germany and demonstrates how the hegemonic collective of 'ethnic Germans' manages to consolidate a self-image as an enlightened people who have come to terms with their history by accusing migrant-Others (in particular, "Muslim immigrants") in Germany of anti-Semitic tendencies and of being unable to deal appropriately with 'German history'. Messerschmidt concludes with a brief outline of how to structure historical education with a multi-perspectival approach, which targets a heterogeneous student group without being based on the binary distinction between "Germans" and "migrant-Others."

While Messerschmidt provides us with a bird's eye view of the theoretical issues at stake, *Fava*'s contribution deals with a case study based on the report of an incident of verbal aggression among a student group visiting a Holocaust memorial and the subsequent educational interventions by the school administration and by mediators from the educational unit of the memorial. Though Fava is not so much interested in the individual case as in general discourse structures, her discourse analytical approach can only be performed on concrete discourse material; and she chooses to illustrate her analysis using an article by Bernhard Fechler, who produced an article from his position as an educator of the Anne Frank Community Youth Centre where the case study incident occurred. Fechler's objective was to present the mediation programme he had developed in the service of the Youth Centre, recommending a new, less morally-laden approach to "Education after Auschwitz." In so doing, however, he uses a conflict between a group of politically right-wing boys of (ethnic) German descent and their classmates, who have an immigrant background; Fechler interprets this conflict as a case of "intercultural conflict" rather than as a case of racism, as Fava would deem far more appropriate. Her detailed analysis of Fechler's line of argumentation shows how the definition of the conflict as a "multicultural" issue combined with the ingrained perception of a 'cultural' division between "Germans" and "non-Germans" form a substructure in Fechler's analysis, which leads to highly problematic interpretations and ascriptions of motives. In fact, Fava is able to show how Fechler's article, inadvertently, reproduces a number of the "rejection of guilt"-mechanisms which Fechler himself outlines and criticizes elsewhere. Fava concludes that the "multicultural" perspective is not the most adequate to analyse educational conflicts in racist contexts.

The next two contributions, dealing with relations of dominance and subjection in Northern Japan and in the Southwest of the United States, provide a very different approach to the connection between history, colonialism and education and challenge a more conventional understanding of education. Colonialism has educational effects far beyond the school house and official curricula.

Christopher Frey interprets the development, deployment and reception of a popular medieval Japanese legend as an example of "intercultural education", dealing with the history of the colonial expansion of Japan and justifying the dominance of the majority-Japanese over the Ainu minority and their core area on Japan's now northernmost island of Hokkaidō. He introduces us to the mythic hero Minamoto no Yoshitsune (1159 – 1189 CE), an exceptionally famous Japanese prince, who according to the legend, overcame a tragic death and escaped to live among the Ainu. Analysing different versions, transformations, adaptations, and re-interpretations of this legend, Frey takes us on a fascinating journey through 800 years of Japanese colonial history. In the quest for legitimacy as (dominant) residents of the Ainu lands of Ezo, Japanese officials and other agents planted and cultivated the legend of "Yoshitsune in Ezo" among the Ainu, even appropriating the Ainu legend of Okikurumi, an Indigenous mythic hero, in order to fuse these heroes and make Yoshitsune appear indigenous to the Ainu island. What little is known about the (reticent) reception of the Yoshitsune legends among the Ainu, however, seems to suggest that the legend's success in shaping the popular imagination was largely limited to the colonizing majority who readily identified with the hero. The legend of "Yoshitsune in Ezo" is, in essence, the story of the colonizers.

In contrast, *Adrea Lawrence* shows how colonialism functioned as an 'educational project' amongst Pueblo Indian communities and influenced their strategies vis-à-vis representatives of (post)-colonial authorities, as the representatives of the colonial order, with few exceptions, resisted 'intercultural learning'. Her source material consists of documents and letters produced by a number of officials, teachers and superintendents, in the service of the Bureau of Indian Affairs (BIA) in the Rio Grande Valley of New Mexico between 1902 and 1912. On first view, surprisingly, the documentary record of the BIA tells us little about what went on inside the schoolhouse of the reservation day schools. Instead the documented correspondence and reports indicate which issues were apparently of importance to the writers and to their host communities. Using two ongoing conflicts – one around land use and management on the reservation, the other around liquor sale to members of the Pueblo communities – Lawrence illustrates the strategies of Pueblo community representatives, who, instead of fighting the colonial system in ongoing opposition, used to learn the hegemonic parameters of previous colonial regimes since the late 17th century and the legal structures of the U.S. colonial regime. As the documentary evidence reveals, Pueblo Indian communities were able to use their learning to advance their own objectives; however, many of the U.S. colonial officials who were new to the region were unable to take into account the experiences of the colonized groups they were in charge of, thus potential lessons were "lost" on them.

The following article by *Catriona Ellis* deals again with discourse in the arena of formal education in the colonial setting of Southern India in the 1930s; her interpretation specifically highlights the particular interests of the colonized elite. In accordance with global trends in educational philosophy of the time, a small group of Indian educational experts propagated "New Education" in opposition to both pre-colonial Indian and colonial education, both of which were criticised as authoritarian and teacher-centred educational approaches. This educational initiative was accompanied by a call for a "more scientific" and simultaneously "more socially and culturally effective" curriculum and way of teaching. From Ellis' analysis of these discourses around progressive and child-centred education emerge certain normative assumptions about the 'normal' child and childhood development. Of particular interest in this context is the construct of the 'Indian child' as simultaneously 'modern' (like the 'Western child') and in need of a 'culturally specific' education. The reference to 'culture' in these discourses turns out to be linked to social stratification as well as gender constructs. While the (urban) Indian elite positioned themselves through these expert discourses as on a par with educational experts internationally, the rural poor were 'culturalised' (presented as 'culturally different') and perceived as deviating from (masculine) 'normality'. By Othering the non-elite children, Indian pedagogues staked their own claims to modernity and universalism.

Mustafa Çapar provides us with insights into the historical backgrounds of present-day educational policy, curricula and textbook content in the Turkish national education system and how these different types of educational texts construct the "Turkish norm(ality)" in contrast to the internal minoritized Others of Turkey. The particular historical background for minority policies in Turkey is the *millet* system of the Ottoman Empire, a system based on religiously defined 'confessional nations'. Thus, Turkish nationality is conflated with religious Muslim identity in spite of the paradox it produces in a nation-state that avows secularism. Çapar's analysis reveals many more contradictions and complexities in the official perception of minorities who are either supposed to be non-existent or else dangerous elements threatening the national collective from within, the latter perception being bolstered by historical narratives of hostility and treason. Çapar argues that the nationalist system of education in Turkey leaves little, if any, room for alternative views of minority issues and fosters ignorance, on the one hand, and hostile and fearful attitudes amongst the ethnic and religious majority on the other hand. Such an attitude often turned into open violence on little provocation in the past.

The following two contributions deal with minority education policies in Scandinavia. *Jonas Jakobsen*'s article is probably the most optimistic in outlook within our collection, particularly when contrasted with the assessment of the Turkish minorities' situation outlined above. Jakobsen describes the history of Sami minority policy in the North of Norway as a "success story." He analyzes the postcolonial struggle of the Sami to overcome 300 years of forced assimilation in favour of rights, influence and a positive self-image by drawing on the German philosopher Axel Honneth's concept of recognition. Against a more critical view of postcolonial thinkers like Talal Asad, who have examined the 'Western project' of modernity and the according human rights discourse, Jakobsen affirms Honneth's assertion that there is a universalistic potential in the very idea of equal rights with the Sami case. In order to achieve equal opportunities, however, special provisions might be necessary, particularly in education, and Jakobsen briefly sketches the tension between the ideal of equality and the right to cultural recognition since "culture" is a vague, shifting and contested issue as can be illustrated with respect to the question what "Saminess" implies.

Christian Ydesen presents results of a historical comparative analysis of Danish educational policy towards two rather different minority communities: the Inuit of Greenland, a former Danish colony and later part of the Danish Commonwealth, and the Germans in Southern Jutland, a border territory between Denmark and Germany. Danish educational policies in both cases aimed at assimilation. But the different historical and political contexts resulted in rather different educational provisions and controversies from 1945 – 1970. The comparative perspective highlights the specificity of each of these 'intercultural relations': On the one hand, Greenland is a neo-colonial setting where assimilation aimed at granting Inuit children access to 'modernity', and the policy was, to a considerable extent, endorsed by the colonialized subjects themselves, while assimilative ends were, in fact, contradicted by a racialised identification of the Inuit. On the other hand, southern Jutland is a context marked by the recent occupation of Denmark by NS-Germany, where assimilation aimed at neutralising a potentially powerful minority; here, German identity was a matter of choice and self-identification. Danishness was constructed in relation to both alterities – as White modern universal identity in relation to the colonialised Others; as democratic, creative, liberal in relation to a post-fascist national minority.

The last two contributions dealing with African educational contexts discuss the role of 'traditional African culture' in education from very different perspectives. *George J. Sefa Dei* argues for the adoption of local cultural resource knowledge, such as proverbs, folktales and other forms of folkloric production, into formal teaching contexts as an important educational tool to advance moral education in African contexts. His suggestions are firstly supported by an extensive literature review of the role of indigenous education in moral education and violence prevention. Secondly, results from a qualitative study in Ghana and Nigeria, involving interviews with African educators and elders, demonstrate that proverbs do, indeed, play a substantial role in different teaching contexts inside and outside of schools. Dei argues that resuming cultural knowledge handed-down from past generations does not imply taking recourse to a romanticised past, as no tradition is immune to criticism. In fact, from the narratives of the interviewed teachers emerge a number of contested issues in the employment of traditional proverbs in modern, postcolonial contexts, as Dei illustrates using the example of gender issues. Dei understands (re)claiming African identities and cultural knowledge as an exercise in decolonization that recognizes the authenticity of African identity and experience; and though "authentic", in his reading, he does not imply that they are "pure" or "uncontaminated"; rather, he suggests that such identities should be seen as authentic and valid in their own right.

The last text by *Heike Niedrig* provides insights into educational conflicts in South Africa after the end of Apartheid. Due to the cultural and educational policies and discourses of the Apartheid-regime, in the South African context "multicultural education" is strongly associated with Apartheid ideology and its essentialist and racialised notions of "culture" and "language". Based on two different case studies involving different issues of "culture" – the protection of "White Afrikaner culture" on the one hand and the adoption of elements from "traditional African culture" into the school context on the other – the author discusses the multi-layered and contradictory South African discourse on "multicultural education" in order to explore ambivalences in this discourse which are particularly obvious in the South African context, but most likely just as relevant in other contexts as well.

The discourse of "Intercultural Education" can serve to bolster and legitimise hegemonic power relations as not only the Afrikaans-school-conflict in Niedrig's presentation demonstrates, but also many of the other contributors to this anthology argue. At the same time, acknowledging cultural resources of disempowered communities has an empowering potential, as the Sami-case in Jakobsen's presentation appears to confirm and as Dei firmly argues. The quest for "Africanising" the South African curriculum, however, is a controversial issue as the concrete case study illustrates. Niedrig's analysis of this conflict is based on Stuart Hall's claim that it is not possible to resume a pre-colonial African identity untarnished by colonial oppression. Educators working in "multicultural contexts", therefore, need to be aware of the ambivalences involved in "understanding the Others", and to explore educational strategies to address the histories of power relations and to deconstruct hegemonic subject formations.

Literature

Ashcroft, B., Griffiths, G. & Tiffin, H. (1989): The Empire Writes Back – Theory and practice in post-colonial literatures. London/New York.

Auernheimer, G. (1990): Einführung in die Interkulturelle Erziehung. Darmstadt.

Auernheimer, G. (2007, 5th ed.): Einführung in die Interkulturelle Pädagogik. Darmstadt.

Benedict, R. (1934): Patterns of culture. Boston, MA.

Boas, F. (1911): The mind of primitive man. New York.

Carrither, M. (1997): Article »Culture«. In: Barfield, T. (ed.): The Dictionary of Anthropology, 98 – 101.

Farr, A. (2004): Whiteness Visible: Enlightenment Racism and the Structure of Racialized Consciousness. In: Yancy, G. (ed.): What white looks like: African-American philosophers on the whiteness question. New York/London, 143 – 158.

Godhinho, V. M. (1992): L'essor de l'Europe aux XVe et XVIe siècles – Les grandes découvertes et la formation d'une civilisation plurielle. In: Cadmos, Vol. 58-59, 89 – 125.

Goodman, J., McCulloch, G. & Richardson, W. (2009): 'Empires overseas' and 'empires at home': postcolonial and transnational perspectives on social change in the history of education. In: Paedagogica Historica, 45: 6, 695 – 706.

Hall, S. (2006): When was 'the postcolonial'? Thinking at the limit (orig. 1996). In: Chambers, I. & Curti, L. (eds.): The Postcolonial Question: Common Skies, Divided Horizons. London, 242 – 260.

Kant, I. (1803/1983): Über Pädagogik. In: Kant, I.: Werke in 10 Bänden, ed. by W. Weischedel. Vol. 10 (5th ed.), Darmstadt, 693 – 761.

Kasinitz, P., Waters, M. C. & Mollenkopf, J. H. & Anil, M. (2002): Transnationalism and the Children of Immigrants in Contemporary New York. In: Levitt, P. & Waters, M.C. (eds.): The Changing Face of Home. The Transnational Lives of the Second Generation. New York, 96 – 122.

Knabe, F. (2000): Sprachliche Minderheiten und nationale Schule in Preußen zwischen 1871 und 1933. Eine bildungspolitische Analyse. Münster/New York.

Koller, H.-C. (2004): Grundbegriffe, Theorien und Methoden der Erziehungswissenschaft. Eine Einführung. Stuttgart.

Krüger-Potratz, M. (1989): Die Ausländerpädagogik versichert sich ihrer Geschichte: Plädoyer für eine historische Minderheitenbildungsforschung. In: Unterrichtswissenschaft 17: 3, 223 – 242.

Krüger-Potratz, M. (2005): Interkulturelle Bildung. Eine Einführung. Münster.

Krüger-Potratz, M., Jasper, D. & Knabe F. (1998): 'Fremdsprachige Volksteile' und deutsche Schule. Schulpolitik für die Kinder der autochthonen Minderheiten in der Weimarer Republik. Münster/New York.

Laclau, E. (1990): New Reflections on the Revolution of Our Time. London.
Levitt, P. & Waters, M. C. (eds. 2002): The Changing Face of Home. The Transnational Lives of the Second Generation. New York.
McClintock, A. (1992): The Myth of Progress: Pitfalls of the Term Post-colonialism. In: Social Text, No. 31/32, 281 – 298.
Myers, K. (2009): Immigrants and ethnic minorities in the history of education. In: Paedagogica Historica, 45: 6, 801 – 816.
Nóvoa, A. (1995): On History, History of Education, and History of Colonial Education. In: Nóvoa, A., Depaepe, M. & Johanningmeier, E. V. (eds.): The Colonial Experience in Education: Historical Issues and Perspectives, Vol. 1 of Paedagogica Historica Supplementary Series, 23 – 61.
Piesche, P. (2005): Der 'Fortschritt' der Aufklärung – Kants 'Race' und die Zentrierung des *weißen* Subjekts. In: Eggers, M. M., Kilomba, G., Piesche, P. & Arndt, S. (eds.): Mythen, Masken und Subjekte. Kritische Weißseinsforschung in Deutschland. Münster, 30 – 39.
Shohat, E. (1992): Notes on the Postcolonial. In: Social Text, No. 31/32, S. 101 – 109.
Spieker, S. (2008): "An early researcher in the field of education: Bernardino de Sahagún in sixteenth-century Mexico", in: History of Education, Vol. 37, No. 6, 757 – 772
Spivak, G. C. (1984): The Rani Of Sirmur. In: Barker, F. et al. (1985): Europe and its others. Vol. 1: Proceedings of the Essex Conference on the Sociology of Literature July 1984. Essex.
Steiner-Khamsi, G. (1992): Multikulturelle Bildungspolitik in der Postmoderne. Opladen.
Tenorth, H.-E. (2000): Geschichte der Erziehung. Einführung in die Grundzüge ihrer neuzeitlichen Entwicklung (3rd ed.). München.
Tylor, E. (1873/1958): Primitive Culture. New York: Harper.
Wax, M. (1993): How Culture Misdirects Multiculturalism. In: Anthropology and Education Quarterly, 24: 2, 99 – 115.
Weigel, S. (1987): Die nahe Fremde – das Territorium des ‚Weiblichen'. Zum Verhältnis von ‚Wilden' und ‚Frauen' im Diskurs der Aufklärung. In: Koebner, T. & Pickerodt, G. (eds.): Die andere Welt. Studien zum Exotismus. Frankfurt/M., 171 – 199.
West, C. (1990): The New Cultural Politics of Difference. October, 53, 93 – 109.

Othering and its Effects – Exploring the Concept

Oscar Thomas-Olalde and Astride Velho,
University of Innsbruck, Austria

Othering has been established as key concept of postcolonial theory, and as such it has also found entry into critical analyses of racism. In this context, *Othering* is defined as a process in which, through discursive practices, different subjects are formed, hegemonic subjects – that is, subjects in powerful social positions as well as those subjugated to these powerful conditions. To arrive at such an analytic description, however, some measure of abstraction is required, because *Othering* denotes simultaneously both the features of discourse structures and processes, and the formation of subjectivity engendered by such discourse. Our contribution focuses on ways in which these two moments constitute each other.

In specialised discussions, but increasingly within everyday communication as well, the term *Othering* is used to refer to phenomena of stereotyping and racialisation. This incorporation of the term into everyday language runs the risk of diminishing the analytic precision of the concept. Therefore we have embarked on a quest for theoretical insights and connections that have been fundamental in the development of the concept *Othering*. Our objectives are, first, to delineate a number of relevant theoretical approaches, and second, to ponder the analytical potential and effects of the concept. Based on the psychoanalytical concepts of Jacques Lacan, the term *Othering* was re-coined by Gayatri Chakravorty Spivak in the context of postcolonial theory, and since then it has been widely applied, in particular within anthropology. Edward Said and Homi K. Bhabha are both prominent writers who have dealt with discursive and political practices that can be described as *Othering*. As to the analytical potential of the concept *Othering*, we will explore several questions: To what extent can the term *Othering* help us to better grasp and understand hegemonic practices and processes of subject formation in Western migration societies, where encounters and conflicts are labelled "intercultural" and where racialisation and ethnification are part of social normality? Further, we will discuss the structural and political effects of an analysis of ethnification and racialisation processes based on the concept of *Othering*. Are the insights which the concept of *Othering* inspires useful for a critical analysis of power structures in migration societies?

1. Theoretical references

1.1 Being (constitutionally) dependent on others: Jacques Lacan

At the 16th congress of psychoanalysis 1949 in Zurich, the French psychoanalyst Jacques Lacan presented for the last time his paper "Le stade de mirroir" [The mirror stage]. This and other writings by Lacan contributed substantially to changing perspectives about the development of the subject and its identity, moving beyond a solipsist process of a (however-defined) Self, toward consideration of the self as a continuous "dynamic of reflection" in interaction with the environment. Lacan thus created a new reading of the unconscious which in his view was organised like a language – "as discourse of the Other" (Mertens 2000: 26 ff., translated by ed.). He postulated that there can be no a-social desire, but that any desire is engendered by the desire of an Other and thus also through social structures (ibid.).

His concept of the subject, the imaginary structure of the I or the Self, has become a leading concept in (poststructuralist anthropology of) postmodernism, in post-Freudian psychoanalysis, and also in postcolonial approaches which, among other things, deal with processes of *Othering*. The theoretical and analytical core of this concept consists in the constitutive "dependency" of the subject, since the construction of Self and non-Self is only possible via the reflection in the "Other".

According to Lacan (1973), the mirror stage, which he theorises from the point of view of developmental psychology, is the stage in which a symbolical matrix of subjectivity is developed, an ontological structure of the human world, which remains of lifelong significance: Between the ages of six and 18 months, children first recognise their specular image as reflected in the mirror as a total form of the body, which elicits a jubilant response (ibid.: 63). The infant anticipates in this *Gestalt* (shape/form), in the mirror "outside" the maturation of her/his body and her/his agency, even though s/he is in fact still in a state of motor incapacity, lacking bodily control, completely dependent on the caregiver (ibid.: 64), and without yet the physical sensation of completeness as perceived in the mirror. The mirror stage, which in Lacan's view is an indispensable stage in the development of the Self, thus fixates the Self in the area of the imaginary. That is to say, the self-image as whole and independent always remains, to some extent, an illusion:

> This development is experienced as a temporal dialectic that decisively projects the formation of the individual into history. The *mirror stage* is a drama whose internal thrust is precipitated from insufficiency to anticipation – and which manufactures for the subject, caught up in the lure of spatial identification, the succession of phan-

> tasies that extends from a fragmented body-image to a form of its totality that I shall call orthopaedic – and, lastly, to the assumption of the armour of an alienating identity, which will mark with its rigid structure the subject's entire mental development. Thus, to break out of the circle of the *Innenwelt* into the *Umwelt* generated the inexhaustible quadrature of the ego's verifications (ibid.: 67).[1]

Considered from an interaction theory perspective, the act of reflection described by Lacan takes place between the child and her/his caregiver or social environment. The image which is transported through facial expressions and other reactions of the person opposite at the sight of the child is transformed into the self-image of the child. A consciousness of the Self thus develops as one that is alienated, dependent on the opposite person. The images which are thus adopted create an illusion of wholeness, which the individuals as vulnerable beings can never achieve, and which must be defended in order to negate the actual imperfection of the Self.

Based on this concept of the subject as produced in Lacan's writing (which we could only briefly sketch here), we will discuss in more depth the dynamics of subject formation in the context of *Othering* in the third section of our contribution. We will deal with the effects of constituting hegemonic subjectivity through practices of *Othering* as well as with the psychic form which power takes in the context of *Othering* and racism for those subjected to these experiences (Butler 1997).

1.2 Othering or being made the "Other": Edward Said's Orientalism[2]

Another scientific perspective deals with those discursive practices which render others into "Others" and thereby engender a *collective* self-image. This perspective became widely known through the influential work of Edward Said about the construction of the "orient" as the antithesis of the "occident". In his oeuvre "Orientalism" (Said 2003, orig. 1978), which has been acknowledged as a founding document of postcolonial theory (Castro Varela & Dhawan 2005: 29), Said analyses the discursive practices which produce "the Orient" and "the Oriental" and positions them in a constitutive relationship with the self-image of the "West" – without actually using the term *Othering*; this term was coined as theoretical term by Spivak only in 1985.[3]

---

1 English translation: http://www.acsu.buffalo.edu/~erikconr/courses/DMS_259/readings/05_LacanMirrorStage.pdf, p. 4

2 This part of the text is based on an article about religious Othering (co-authored with Paul Mecheril): Mecheril & Thomas-Olalde 2011.

3 Said himself does not use the term Othering. In the postcolonial reception of his work, however, his analysis of "Orientalism" has been interpreted as an analysis of a paradig-

According to Said, the mechanisms and the effectiveness of these practices need to be understood in the context of European imperialism and thus as practices of legitimisation and stabilisation of claims to power with respect to the constructed Others. From this perspective, *Othering* can be described as a double process: the "Others" are constructed through certain practices of knowledge production which legitimise domination; at the same time, however, this (political, economical and cultural) hegemonic intention makes the resulting epistemological practices appear "plausible" and "useful".

Said analyses the practices of knowledge production which serve to orientalise the "Orient"[4]. Historically, the establishment of Oriental Studies as an officially recognised academic discipline correlates with the European policy of expansion into the so-called orient (the region labelled "Middle East", but also Northern Africa and India) in the 19th century. Based on the administrative structures of colonialism, an "obsessive study of the Orient" (Castro Varela & Dhawan 2005: 33, translated by ed.) is nurtured in Europe which purports to strive to understand the 'others'. With this attitude, European researchers set out to collect 'information' about 'the others' and to create a body of knowledge which explains 'the others', a process through which Europe seized epistemic possession and thus claimed the right of domination. Of course, this explanation requires that *the Others* be constructed, in an essentialising process, as a homogeneous group. Collectivisation (constructing a homogeneous collective) and essentialisation are the two moments of one and the same epistemological operation. From this point of view, epistemology (interpreted as the study of those knowledge formations which determine the development of world concepts) is never neutral, but always a social and political study. Therefore, Said claims that knowledge (which is always produced within a particular social position) and relations of power are closely interconnected.

Essentialising practices turn heterogeneous 'bodies of knowledge' into a compact 'mantle of knowledge' which makes it possible to turn socially produced 'information' into dominating and power-laden assertions about the 'essentiality' of the Others. This construed 'essentiality' is, according to Said, always characterised by an ambivalence, for it represents *the others* in the sense of

matic practice of Othering, and has been used as a starting-point for further theory development.

4 When Said speaks about the "Orient", he does not refer to a geographical region, but to a European (colonial) imaginary construct. In Europe, the term "Orient" has been used to denote different regions such as the "Middle East", Northern Africa and India, but also other Asian regions like China and Japan.

the Other as *a-historical, quasi-metaphysical subjects*, while at the same time arguing with the historicity of the own produced knowledge.[5]

When essentialising practices become dominant discourses, or in other words absolutely plausible discourses without any alternatives, they give rise to such epistemological practices that are able to abstract from individual traits in an absolute and unchallenged manner. That which is specific or unique, which belongs to the lifeworld and to individual biographies is negated and only acknowledged within the generalized discourse. The epistemological knowledge production, Said argues, legitimises that "no matter how deep the specific exception, no matter how much a single Oriental can escape the fences placed around him, he is first an Oriental, second a human being, and last again an Oriental" (Said 2003: 102).

Essentialism and homogenisation as discursive practices have one effect in particular: They produce a self-image via the construction of an antagonism. This formula contains the essence of Said's theoretical assertions. By constructing a (negative, antagonistic) Other, a self-image emerges that contrasts with the 'negative image', and thus can be approved of. As Said claims, an equally homogenised image of the West emerges against the background of the construed image of the Orient. In the process of *Othering*, negative attributes are ascribed to the construed collective. Said sketches such attributions by quoting literary and scientific texts: "The Oriental is irrational, depraved (fallen), childlike, 'different'…" (Said 2003: 40). This external attribution makes the construction of a particular self-image possible: "… thus the European is rational, virtuos, mature, normal'" (ibid.).

It would be inadequate, however, to reduce the postcolonial theory concept of *Othering* to constructions of others and self. The formula of *constructing a positive self-image via the construction of a negative image of the other* could be used to explain most phenomena of stereotyping by means of a catchy terminology. Postcolonial theories, however, do not suggest that this is automatic either in terms of psychological or in terms of social processes. According to Said, the effectiveness of Orientalism (as a historically concrete and politically effective form of *Othering*) can only be understood in the context of formation and exercise of dominance. Dominance and essentialised knowledge depend on and con-

5 "According to the traditional orientalists, an essence should exist – sometimes even clearly described in metaphysical terms – which constitutes the inalienable and common basis of all the beings considered; this essence is both 'historical' since it goes back to the dawn of history, and fundamentally a-historical, since it transfixes the being, 'the object' of study, within its inalienable and non-evolutive specificity, instead of defining it as all other beings, states, nations, peoples, and cultures – as a product, a resultant of the vection of the forces operating in the field of historical evolution..." (Said 2003: 97).

stitute each other. Castro Varela and Dhawan describe this interconnection as follows: "In consequence of concept formations within Orientalism, the Occident presents itself as separate and different from the Orient – as enlightened, civilised, and emancipated, and thus legitimises the violent territorial dominance over colonies and so-called protectorates" (Castro Varela & Dhawan 2007: 31; translated by ed.).

If we assume this constitutive interdependence between essentialised knowledge production and dominance, we must draw important conclusions for any analysis of phenomena that can be described in terms of *Othering*. One of Said's central theses is that Orientalism occurred neither by accident nor – in a general sense – unconsciously. Rather this construction is based on a decision rooted in power politics (Said 2003: 96ff.).

The *orientalisation* of the Orient is the consequence of an intention of dominance. Precisely this assumption has been criticised as monocausal, oversimplified, and even essentialist. In reply, Said explained that he did not intend to create a new enemy stereotype of the West, but wanted to analyse discursive practices. On the level of such a discourse analysis, however, it is possible to interpret *Othering* as a practice of objectification by and through domination. Objectification is a relational operation, which produces *Others* as subjects in flexible relationships, but always under the condition of one's own *positional superiority* (Said 2003: 7). Objectifying practices are discursive practices, forms of speech and interactive forms of positioning, which turn subjects into 'specimen'. Said has pointed out that practices of objectification use description in order to produce facts. Corresponding discursive devices are, for instance, the use of the "ethnographical present tense" (Fabian 1983), which is a tool of objectifying observations and has the effect of 'freezing' individuals (and collectives) within a particular temporal and political context. Objectifying practices do not only elevate momentary and subjective experiences or observations onto the level of objective knowledge, they solidify at the same time the power differences that are the foundations for these observations and their articulations. These practices materialise and perpetuate relations between observers and observed, between those who describe and those who are described.

According to this perspective, essentialism and collectivisation are the results not only of particular hegemonic and imperial exercise of domination, but these forms of knowledge also have legitimising effects on power relations and even form the very foundations of hegemonic rule. *Othering* is always a political practice.

1.3 Random Examples of Othering: Gayatri C. Spivak

In her article "The Rani of Sirmur" (1984), Gayatri C. Spivak reconstructs the dialectical process of *Othering* that produces the colonising subjects who occupy the hegemonic position as well as the colonised, marginalised Others.[6] Similarly to Edward Said, her analysis shows that the reports and practices of British colonial rule in India established a relationship between the "natives" and colonial masters, which produced the former as the Others and made them appear as 'specimen', whereas the latter occupied a position of superiority. Spivak uses examples from official correspondence of the British colonial era, the times of the East Indian Company in the Indian Simla-Hills in the early 19th century.

Captain Geoffrey Birch (an assistant agent of the governor whose letters are conveyed by a resident in Delhi to the governors secretary in Calcutta) describes riding through the mountains with no more than a single "native escort", much like a romantic figure of a novella. Birch's notes illustrate the process of "Worlding", which is based on processes of *Othering* and can be defined as „inscribing of imperial discourse upon the colonized space" (Ashcroft et al. 2007: 226), like the marking of colonies on maps. The process of fixating the colonies and inscribing upon the colonised space goes hand in hand with an act of naming that engenders hegemonic knowledge and results in control.

"Worlding" can, however, also take place in more subtle ways (ibid.): "[Birch] is worlding *their own world,* which is far from mere uninscribed earth, anew, by obliging *them* to domesticate the alien as Master" (Spivak 1984: 133). Birch consolidates the European Self by prevailing upon the "native" to recognize him, Birch, who is in fact a foreigner, as the "master", and thus to position himself as the "Other". Mirrored in the colonised Other, in the "native", Birch recognises himself as "Master", whilst the "native" – although being located on his own "home ground" – recognises himself as the colonised subject. The "na-

---

6 Contrary to Spivak who coined the term in this theory context, we use the term "Other" with capital O to refer to those subjects who have been produced and marked as different subjects by means of discursive power. Spivak follows Lacan's convention and therefore differentiates between "Other" and "other" in order to mark the different positions within the hegemonic order of dominance. Some critiques of Spivak argue for an elimination of this differentiation and for an interchangeable use of these terms, because the "Other" can be both, the hegemonic as well as the minoritised subject: "...the Empire's construction of its 'others' is often referred to as the construction of 'the Other' (perhaps to connote an abstract and generalized, but more symbolic representation of Empire's 'others')" (Ashcroft, Griffiths, & Tiffin 2007: 156). When writing Other (often without quotation marks), then this should not be interpreted as an "identification" with the Othering-operation itself, but rather as marker of its discursive and hegemonic effectiveness and power of subject formation.

tive" is made into the colonised through dominant discursive practices of the colonial *centre* and in dependency on them (Spivak 1996).

> Birch on horseback passing through the country sees himself as a representative image. By his sight and utterance rumor is being replaced by information, the figure of the European on the hills is being reinscribed from stranger to Master, to the sovereign as Subject with a capital S, even as the native shrinks into the consolidating subjected subject in the lower case. The truth value of the stranger is being established as the reference point for the true (insertion into) history of these wild regions (Spivak 1984: 133).

Spivak points out that the „agents of this cartographic transformation" not only bear names like Vincent van Gogh or those of the "policy makers", but also insignificant ones like Birch, since the colonial power is not a monolithic, but a rather heterogeneous power, composed of different social classes and positions (ibid.).

In another example, Spivak refers to a letter from Major-General Sir David Ochterlony to the Governor's secretary. In contrast to Birch, Spivak labels Ochterlony a gentleman; he is a man of higher social rank who hates the "hill people" and describes them as possessed by „brutality, perfidy, depravity and treachery" (ibid.: 134). In Ochterlony's words, the local ruler has no right to land ownership, but rather an obligation to surrender the land into the ownership of the British crown. The consequences of this „reinscription of rights as being-obliged" (ibid.: 135), of the transformation of the subject position from native to a colonised, subjugated position are formulated by Spivak as follows: „ ...the `native´ (Kings`) subject-position rewrote itself as the position of the object of Imperialism" (ibid.: 134).

Spivak (1984) points out the crucial connection between knowledge and power, and we will continue to deal with this connection in the next sections, because interpretational sovereignty and definatory power are fundamental for discourse practices as well as for processes of subject formation.

2. Analytical explorations for the migration society

2.1 Othering and discourse

Following Said's work, *Othering* can be interpreted as institutionalising the 'objective' hegemonic knowledge about the Others in political power relations. Such bodies of knowledge can be used in contemporary postcolonial social relations to recognise and analyse processes that maintain colonial figures of thinking that produce Others. For an analysis of *Othering*, we need to look into specific practices of subject formation in particular contexts; in this article we will deal with the context of European migration societies.

The discursive production of "migrants" or – since 9/11 more common – of "Muslims" in the Western world is not exercised by a central "authority of power". A rash application of analytical terminology could tempt us to discursively construct "migrants" and "non-migrants" as monolithic collectives, and to detect a linear and locatable hegemonic intention of the majority society vis-à-vis minoritised groups. This kind of dichotomous division would, at the very least, underrate complexity and – particularly from the postcolonial theory perspective –essentialise. The analytical perspective opened up by the concept of *Othering* must not lead us to tie subjects down to certain categories, but rather to better understand the power of language practices and of discourses on which those categories are based, in order to grasp their entanglement in the dynamics of knowledge production and dominance.

Any approach to these issues which assumes that hegemonic practices of *Othering* are the result of politically orchestrated campaigns not only fails to understand the complexity of practices of subject formation, but it plays down their importance altogether. For certain subjects, such practices impact on every aspect of their everyday lives and therefore need to be observed with analytical instruments that take account of everyday life discourses, dominant 'knowledge' as well as the political dimensions of the former.

How *Othering* as a discourse and as a practice that produces subjectivity are interconnected can be illustrated by means of an example.[7] Ahmet T., a German adult education trainer of Turkish descent, traces the processes of subject formation through discursive practices as follows: "In the 1980s, I was invited to panel discussions again and again in order to speak about the Turks. Social workers, in particular, wanted to better understand the 'way of life' of the Turks to be able to better work with them. There I was a Turk. In the 1990s, I was then invited to talk about migrants. Municipal politicians, educators and teachers all wanted to know more about the 'culture', the family structures, the 'mentality' of migrants. There I was a migrant. Since 2001, I have been invited to local TV broadcasters and panel discussions at universities to speak about Islam. Since then, I am not only privately, but also professionally a Muslim." This personal report attests to the 'epistemic power' of discursive practices, which produce subjects through attribution and discrimination.

---

7 The following is an extract from an informal conversation as quoted in: Mecheril & Thomas-Olalde 2011. The name was changed. The quotation was translated from German by the editor H. N.

Discourses produce subjects. That is the vanishing point in which the discourse analytical writings by Michel Foucault and by Ernesto Laclau converge. According to Laclau, the subject is not the producer of discourses, but a historically specific product of "subjectivisation" through discourse (Reckwitz 2006: 341). In the case of discourses about Islam and Muslims, we are dealing with a dominant discourse which legitimises and at the same time constitutes social, cultural and political practices of subject formation and attribution which appear as plausible and without alternative, as 'normal'.

Hegemonic discourses constitute discursive, but also structural totalities which are continuously involved in a process of interaction with social systems. Discourses form part of a certain – dynamic and polysemous – *order of things*. At the same time, they constitute the condition of the possibility of this order, since only discourses are, according to Laclau, able to produce relatively stable orders. Their construction of difference makes the radical distinction between *inside* and *outside* of the social system a plausible part of the repertoire of normality. Only by constructing *social antagonisms*, cultural antitheses and epistemic dualities, it is possible to achieve discursive stability and thus stability of power.

According to Laclau (1990), hegemonic discourses require a radical Other, a rejected non-identity, a *constitutive outside*. This *outside* first makes possible the demarcation of the *inside of society,* and makes appear as factual and given a "We" that – though void of meaning and as such unfathomable – is seemingly incontestable. Starting from this analytical terminology, the assumption seems plausible that speaking about the "culture" and the "religion" of the Others represents a hegemonic discourse. Examples are supplied by ever-present dominant practices of discourse and representation (in academic discourse, in the mass media, in literature, in public debates, etc.), which present, for instance, the "migrants" or "Muslims" as a homogeneous and en bloc group; a group whose localisation (whose definition and naming, whose identification with certain subjects) appears to be a matter of course.

A paradox of hegemonic discursive practices consists in the way that they interweave *foreignness* and *familiarness* in a constitutive manner: *Everyone* is familiar with who the *foreigners* are. The foreigners are never foreign in the real sense of the word. They are much rather familiar intimates: *Everyone* knows them. This "knowing" means two different things in our context: *Everyone knows who belongs to the Others* and *everyone knows everything essential about them.*[8] This 'essential knowledge' about 'the Others', which is at everyone's

8 The term „everyone" is used here as code for discursive figures to be met in everyday discourse, in the media and in political discourse.

disposal, is reduced to an epistemic minimum – or one may say to the minimal epistemic value that is politically required: The 'essential knowledge', further substantiated and confirmed in scientific procedures, is the knowledge about the 'Otherness of the Others'. That is the core of the minimal and simultaneously constitutive *knowledge morpheme* of hegemonic discourse practices. Founded on this binary knowledge morpheme, different, variable and even contradictory discursive practices can develop; these can range, for instance, from a caring, attentive epistemic attitude with respect to "migrants" or "Muslims" (*we want to understand them*) via the continuous call for "differentiation" to open cultural racism. The common denominator of these practices is the fact that they produce *particular subjects* through epistemic dominance, and that they turn those, through certain practices of representation, into a subjectified *"constitutive outside"* (Laclau 1990), into *radically different subjects*.

To be able to adequately describe the *epistemological grammar* of these (subjectifying) practices on which the establishment of a hegemonic discourse about the others is based, the recourse to the concept of *Othering* seems obvious. Discursive *Othering* produces different subjects – Others – onto which "difference" is ascribed as an attribute. Those who are *made Others* are first of all characterised by being "different". In practices of *Othering*, "Otherness" is not a category that needs to be specified, but rather an intrinsic quality. Its effectiveness derives precisely from its un- or underdetermindedness. The Otherness *must* stay undetermined; on this foundation it is possible to make use of the discursively produced difference as a dispositive.

2.2 *Othering as dispositive*

The division of people into natural members who belong to 'us' and 'Others' who do not belong, into the West and the rest, is a powerful colonial way of thinking that is still with us today. Spivak has analysed it on the basis of historical examples of British colonialism in India, and Said with reference to Orientalism. Stuart Hall, as well, refers to this radical and basic dichotomy in his writings. Homi K. Bhabha (1994) identifies "fixity" as the most important characteristic of colonial discourse in constructing Otherness:

> „Fixity, as the sign of cultural/historical/racial difference in the discourse of colonialism, is a paradoxical mode of representation: it connotes rigidity and an unchanging order as well as disorder, degeneracy and demonic repetition. Likewise the stereotype, which is its major discursive strategy, is a form of knowledge and identification that vacillates between what is always 'in place', already known, and something that must be anxiously repeated" (ibid.: 66).

Lacan, on the other hand, differs in his approach from authors who adopt his ideas of subject formation as specular dynamic in order to advance postcolonial studies, in that he refers to the question of power only insofar as that he localises subject formation within a social context. "According to Lacan, identity bears always traces of narcissistic self-delusion" (Haubl 2000: 671, translated by ed.). He interprets the mirror stage as identification, as a transformation of the subject triggered by the reception of an image (ibid.).

Images of people and groups that may become self-images via identification, or negative images via rejection, are produced within social relations of power and discursive practices. In the following we will deal with both, with 'images' that are interwoven with 'knowledge' or produced through 'knowledge', and with processes of identification, in Lacan's approach, as fundamental psychodynamics in the context of subject formation. Eickelpasch and Rademacher propose,

> "that any form of racism consists of at least two elements: knowledge and practices of exclusion. Only the ensemble of specific forms of knowledge and of specific practices of exclusion ensures the *construction of Otherness* which characterises all versions of racism, *the Othering*. Racism is, therefore, something which Foucault [...] has called a 'dispositive', meaning a *power-knowledge-complex*, in which no power relation exists without the constitution of a corresponding field of knowledge, and no knowledge which does not simultaneously require and constitute relations of power" (2004: 79, translated by ed.).

What analytical benefit can be derived from an approach which describes *Othering* as a dispositive of postcolonial and racist relations of power, and which thus highlights "knowledge" and "practices of exclusion" as fundamental parameter?

Foucault (1978: 119ff.) defines dispositive "first, as a thoroughly heterogeneous ensemble consisting of discourses, institutions, architectural forms, regulatory decisions, laws, administrative measures, scientific statements, philosophical, moral or philanthrophical propositions – in short, the said as much as the unsaid. Such are the elements of the apparatus. The dispositive itself is the system of relations that can be established between these elements." Second, he wants "to make use of the dispositive to explain the nature of the connection which can be formed between these heterogeneous elements" (ibid.). Third, Foucault defines dispositive as a kind of "formation which has as its major function at any given historical moment that of responding to an *urgent need*. Thus the dispositive has, above all else, a strategic function" (ibid.).[9]

---

9 There is no official English translation from the original French, cf. Le jeu de Michel Foucault. In: Ornecar No. 10, Paris, July 1977. Translation from the German version by the ed. (H. N.) supported by the following sources: http://www.kunstverein-

From an analytical perspective, we can define *Othering* as some kind of constant, as a connecting "net" between the contradictory "elements" of racism that demonstrates the "nature of these connections", and as Spivak has shown, the substantive quality of these acts. Birch as a romantic figure on horseback in the Simla hills, next to him the "native", or Ochterlony who despises hill-people and thus legitimises the annexation of the country: The power of colonialism, as differing as its appearances may be, and the knowledge about the Others, the "natives" and the "Master", produces the positions of colonial Master and colonised in a dialectical process and solidifies it.

Current racisms whose manifestations might be very diverse (that is why the plural of racism is the more adequate, even though not perfect term) – racisms are not a mere over-simplification or false representation of those "made to be the Others", but they are founded on power, desire and defence (Bhabha 1994: 75).

Racist discrimination appears as a "heterogeneous ensemble" of differing and contradictory practices. Exotism, admiration, integration, culturalisation, biologizing, contempt, marginalisation, exclusion, deportation, violence and extinction are regular experiences of people who, due to hegemonic knowledge, become racialised Others – in personal interactions as well as mediated by structures, institutions and media. In most cases, these acts of *Othering* are not perceived as acts of injustice, discrimination or violence, but as unquestioned normality, as natural realities which are legitimately voiced, cast into legislation or turned into actions. Foucault's "urgent need" can be interpreted in terms of psychodynamics à la Lacan, or else in the context of historical and current social developments.

To categorise *Othering* as a dispositive, similarly to the dispositive of sexuality introduced by Foucault (1998, orig. 1976), underscores the effects that the discursively-produced and mediated orders of knowledge have on practices, as well as the repercussions of these practices on knowledge formation, which is always imbedded in a specific historical and social situation (Bührmann & Schneider 2008: 55). To analyse *Othering* as a dispositive and as a strategy of power enables us to point out the connection of discourses, practices and power in the context of Western migration societies, which can be defined as postcolonial, postholocaust societies structured by racism. The dispositive of *Othering* is productive, for it produces certain forms of subjectivity, just as the dispositive of sexuality produces the subject of desire (ibid.: 54). That is what we will discuss more in depth in the following section. We will present a perspective on the

---

muenchen.de/01_programm_programme/dispositive_workshop/01_en_general_ information.pdf and http://foucaultblog.wordpress.com/2007/04/01/what-is-the-dispositif/

constitution of social existence in ethnifying and racialising relations of power and discursive practices that are mediated by knowledge.

3. Dynamics of subjectivation

3.1 Hegemonic formations and sacrifices

As already mentioned, Lacan deals with the symbolic matrix of subject formation as a specular dynamic, as identification, and as transformation of the subject triggered by the reception of an image (Haubl 2000: 671). "Images", on the other hand, though this view is not part of Lacan's reflections, may be perceived as socially constructed in the context of orders of knowledge and of social power relations. They are not representations of reality (ibid. 673). Rather, they themselves produce realities.

The concept of identification describes the appropriation of characteristics and functions of an object by a subject (Seidler 2000: 325). Lacan discusses the developmental-psychological process of "primary identification" which becomes a lifelong matrix. In the context of "secondary identification", the differentiation between *inside* and *outside* – or between subject and object – already exists.

From a psychoanalytical point of view, identifications can be seen as processes of defence against the outside reality. They occur not only as internal processes of individual psychic development, but also in the interpersonal realm – for instance in order to enhance the self-image, to assure the self or to face outside stimuli that are confrontational or ask too much of the individual. In processes of identification, the person opposite may constitute the Self in two different ways, either through (positive) identification, but also through dissociation. "Any influence on the individual that might endanger his integrity and his consistent bio-psycho-social balance will be mentally modified, restricted or repressed by means of defence" (Ehlers 2000: 12, translated by ed.).

As Eske Wollrad argues, "White subject formations are based on the construction of Whites as a group that is represented as 'normal' and homogeneous and as situated outside of racialising dynamics" (2007: 41, translated by ed.). Identification, the adoption of norms, values, qualities and positions, and membership in the hegemonic group (whether we call it White, colonisers or the majority) safeguards, creates and assures the Self. However, as Noah Sow writes, "racism injures our whole society, and on strict observation, we will find that in every racist system all people are affected in different ways. White people lose their dignity if they exercise racism or allow it to happen" (2008: 272, translated by ed.). Following this view, Wollrad writes: "Actually we know that – even those of us who are White. We know that racism is a structural form of violence which affects *all* subjects within a racist society, that is to say, both people of Colour as well as Whites. Only, this knowledge is mostly lost as if someone had erased it" (2007: 39, translated by ed.). Racist knowledge produces an order in which processes of identification and appropriation seem to imply that we are invulnerable, and that we possess a natural, incontestable right to exist and to live. The options of having a share in the power conceal the deprivations and losses concomitant with the identification and subject formation processes of the hegemonic subject.

The psycho-social defence mechanism of projective identification means that parts of the Self and of the internal object are split off and are projected from the Ego onto the external object so that these parts can be controlled, destroyed and disposed of outside of the Self (Ehlers 2000: 19). In this process of externalisation, unacceptable parts of the Self are concealed and denied. They enter forcibly into the object. "This happens as a rule through subtle or openly manipulative behaviour. In this way, the opposite person is prevailed upon to perceive himself and to behave according to the projections" (Reich 2000: 573, translated by ed.).

According to Karen Horney, a Freud critical psychoanalyst who practiced between 1920 and 1940, however, externalisation can also label a defence process which is not so much projective, but rather identificatory, because "many people identify so strongly with norms and ideal images that, in extreme cases, they can only experience their own self in and through the others" (Mentzos 2000: 183, translated by ed.). Based on this view, the self-constitutive dynamics of hegemonic subjectivity can be explained as identification with norms and ideal images which Wollrad labelled as "White".

The normality of *Othering* first creates and classifies those who are considered to be abnormal. Stuart Hall puts it like this: "The English are racist not because they hate the Blacks but because they do not know who they are without the Blacks" (Hall 1996: 345). In constructing, for instance, the "uncivilised, barbarian or exotic Others", the Self is set up through a narcissist and aggressive process of defence as a hegemonic Self, an unquestioned member of the dominant majority and its "normality".

> "My anatomy of colonial discourse remains incomplete until I locate the stereotype, as an arrested, fetishistic mode of representation within its field of identification, which I have identified [...] as the Lacanian schema of the Imaginary. The Imaginary is the transformation that takes place in the subject at the formative mirror phase, when it assumes a *discreet* image which allows it to postulate a series of equivalences, sameness, identities, between the objects of the surrounding world.

> However, this positioning is itself problematic, for the subject finds or recognizes itself through an image which is simultaneously alienating and hence potentially confrontational. This is the basis of the close relation between the two forms of identification complicit with the Imaginary – narcissism and aggressivity. It is precisely these two forms of identification that constitute the dominant strategy of colonial power […]" (Bhabha 1994: 76f.).

The externalisation gives rise to an image of the Other(s), a stereotype, which forms a hegemonic subject via aggressive or idealising distinctions, just as it feeds narcissism. Practices of control and subjugation are manifold in everyday life of European or Western societies that are marked by *Othering* and constitute hegemonic subjectivity. Some possible effects these processes of externalisation and of projective identification may have on those who are "made-to-be-Others" will be shown in the following section.

3.2 Experiences of Othering: the psychic operations of power[10]

According to Butler, the psychic effects of power are among "the most insidious of its productions" (Butler 1997: 6). To approach the question of how these effects subordinate people in the context of racist experiences in Germany, we reference *Othering* as a precondition of the normality of experiences of very diverse forms of racism. The normality of racist experiences produces precarious living conditions which put subjects potentially in a state of crisis, even while they retain agency and the ability to resist.

If we assume that these subjects not only experience subjection and denigration, but that their very subjectivity is created in part through these conditions, and if we follow Stuart Hall's assessment that racist experiences can lead to "the internalization of the self-as-other" (Hall 1992: 256) and the desire to assimilate, then the question must be raised: What is the psychic form that power takes (Butler 1997: 2) in the context of racist experiences?

Othering, being made the Other in the context of racist experiences, produces a continuous visibility – a visibility of those who are thus minoritised, while the 'majority' who produce and construct these minoritised Others remain unmarked. Foucault (1995, orig. 1975), by means of the panopticon, shows how modern and discursive power can affect people, often without the exercise of overt violence and control. This "generalisable functional model" (Foucault, quoted by Dreyfus et al. 1987: 220, translated by ed.), an exemplary model of the possible effects on those who are 'Othered', demonstrates how external control turns into self-control, since the blueprint of the panoptical prison subjects

10 This section is based on an article published by Astride Velho (2010).

the prisoners to continuous visibility and potential observation which very effectively influences their behaviour.

> "He who is subjected to a field of visibility, and who knows it, assumes responsibility for the constraints of power; he makes them play spontaneously upon himself; [...] he becomes the principle of his own subjection" (Foucault 1995: 202f.).

The German discourse of integration demands that the "foreigners" assimilate. Assimilation implies invisibility. Actual invisibility, however, is not tolerated by the majority society. Based on hegemonic knowledge about the Others, which ascribes to them attributes that carry either positive or else openly negative connotations, the Self as a member of the majority is constituted in contrast to the "Others". The drab monotony of everyday life is made interesting by the entertainment value of the multicultural flavour of mass culture (hooks 1994). Exoticism, idealisation, and sexualisation are the counterpart to negatively-charged ascriptions of traditional and patriarchal backwardness, directed in particular against women and men who are identified as Muslims, and to the resulting contempt and open exclusion. These fixed definitions coupled with assimilatory pressures produce paradox messages like "stay as different as you are, but become invisible".

Othering uses norms and normalities, as already mentioned, often without the open exercise of violence and control. Foucault's concept of gouvernmentality differentiates between technologies of dominance and technologies of the self. Processes of subject formation do not only take place by means of disciplining and subjection, but also by means of techniques of the self (Foucault 1988). One of the historically-developed technologies of the self discussed by Foucault is the confession. Let us imagine a person within the virtual discourse of integration who has been defined as the Other. The discriminatory reality in which this person lives defines people as aberrations based on a racist order of knowledge, then criticises those considered as abnormal for their Otherness and insists on assimilative practices in order to become a "good migrant" willing and able to integrate. In particular those who are considered non-Western or even Islamic are localised as "absolutely different" and as very distant from concepts of modernity (Castro Varela 2008). They are continuously in danger of being judged as unwilling to integrate. It is within this discourse that a person confesses to being assimilated. The admission of a hegemonic concept of complete adaption and self-abandonment is based on an implicit confession within a situation of permanent visibility: "Yes, I am an Other." This acknowledgement of being Othered and the consequent assimilative confession is a form of self-representation which, resuming Foucault's or Lacan's propositions, effects a transformation of the minoritised in the sense of an identification.

Thus, a subject is created and grows up which confirms her/his visibility, perceives her-/himself as an Other and pursues assimilation. This is a subject who continuously strives to prove her/his modernity and belonging to the phantasm of German or Western culture in order to achieve recognition. By identifying with that what has been called "German mainstream culture" [*deutsche Leitkultur*], the Self looks for protection from further experiences of *Othering*. This phenomenon has been called identification with the aggressor (Kühner 2008, Seidler 2000: 326; Reich 2000: 574). In traumatising constellations this can lead to a complete role-taking, but at other times also to a partial identification, which is accompanied by self-humiliation and self-denigration.

What emerges is a self-image of a subject that presents itself according to its own truth as willing and capable of integration, though when it is marked male and Islamic, cannot escape the suspicion of being a "sleeper" (Castro Varela 2008) and thus can at any time be rebuffed and repositioned as an unassimilable migrant.

But that is not all. At the same time, minoritised are expected to add an 'exotic flavour' to the monotony of German everyday life, for instance through their outward appearance, in the form of culinary or artistic contributions, in love relations or perhaps as the exotic children of majority members. Here again the self-technology of the confession can result in processes of identification and thus to self-ethnification or self-culturalisation, which in turn reinforces the internalization of the self-as-other. It is rather a paradox, moreover, that in the context of racist discourses in which the Others are continually exposed and made visible, confessions of ambivalent practices are extracted from these minoritised subjects while at the same time they are expected to create a coherent Self because, if not, they would be "sitting between the chairs".

People who are minoritised are not only subjected to the demands of assimilation and ethnification, but they are "in equal measure objects of fear and hope", because the discussion around integration is connected to "questions of security and to questions of demographic change" (Castro Varela 2008: 83, translated by ed.). "In consequence, they are subjected to a burden of proof of successful integration", and from this follows for many again an "unbearable double-bind" (ibid.). Within the paradoxical German normality, their own usefulness must incessantly be proven anew. As Foucault (1988: 48) put it, "disclosure of self is the renunciation of one's own self."

The confessions of people who are minoritised made in the context of *Othering* (as discourse and as dispositive), the imperative of integration and the discourse of utility, as well as the dynamics of identification are self-technologies which form the awareness of being an Other. The renunciation of one's self amounts to an internalisation of the self-as-other, to an identification with the demands of assimilation, to a symbolic extinction.

4. Perspectives

Our brief explorations of *Othering* should not be taken as a determinist perspective on processes of subject formation. We have conceptualised human existence as interwoven with dynamics of *Othering*, while being aware that there are other ambivalent power relations that occur simultaneously with racism. Human vulnerability results from the dependency of human existence on others, for "no subject emerges without a passionate attachment to those on whom he or she is fundamentally dependent" (Butler 1997: 7). Forms of subjectivity arise as hegemonic formations, as psychic forms of power that are intimately involved in orders of power and knowledge, in discourses and dispositives, and that thus provide differing positions for subjects. What should be added is that – as Foucault (1984: 319) has put it – there is "no relationship of power without resistance, without resort or escape, without possible reversal" (translated by ed. from the French original)[11]. This text has been written in the awareness of the inventiveness, the agency, the resilience and the vigorously anti-hegemonic positioning in many different social domains, e.g. against racism, anti-Semitism and anti-Islamism.

Mark Terkessidis (2004: 201f.) emphasises in his concept of subject formation the unique manner in which those who are Othered encounter experiences of *Othering* and racism. In the German context, which is dominated by demands of assimilation and the imperative of integration, he perceives subject formation that de-identifies with "Being-German" and with the ascribed identity of the Other as creating new spaces for experience. "The space is an independent creation, but it is always inhabited as well by the images of the local residents" (ibid., translated by ed.). The concept of subject formation applies to individuals, but it has also a collective quality, because "the individuals react to the very 'We' whose image is localised within them" (ibid.), and in this way, something communal always remains.

---

11 French version: „…, il n'y a pas de relation de pouvoir sans résistance, sans échappatoire ou fuite, sans retournement éventuel" (Foucault 1984: 319). The two articles which make up "The Subject and Power" were first published as an afterword to Dreyfus & Rabinow (eds. 1982) where the above phrase is translated as follows: „…there is no relationship of power without the means of escape or possible flight" (translated from French by Leslie Sawyer).

Collective practices, like uniting in antiracist initiatives or migrant organisations as well as artistic, professional and even individual forms of non-compliance, the refusal to accept and reproduce without question the positions which are assigned through *Othering*, should be multiplied. The central question of our exploration of *Othering* is: How far are we involved in keeping the power relations so very stable?

If we look at the most common forms of resistance, we find that there are antiracist initiatives which rightly point out that government measures and legislation as well as the European border regime exercise violence and have thus, for instance, transformed the Mediterranean Sea into a mass grave. Moreover, antifascist groups have committed to fight right-wing violence which so far has cost 143 lives in re-united Germany (Amadeu Antonio foundation 2009). And in education, there are 'intercultural approaches' that wish to promote acknowledgement of differences. As commendable as these efforts are, many of these practices only locate racism on the *outside*. Intercultural programmes in education, moreover, tend to concentrate on cross-cultural understanding, but often neglect or even ignore the multiple dimensions of power which play a role in educational settings, as well as the dangers of new forms of stereotyping through educational approaches that focus on "culture".

As Mark Terkessidis (2004) sums up in his study "Die Banalität des Rassismus" [The banality of racism], many second-generation migrants he interviewed lack a general knowledge about racism – and we think that this finding applies to many people in Germany who experience *Othering* and racism. Their attempts to counter discriminatory living conditions, to develop resistance, or to safeguard their own mental and physical survival are manifold, but isolated and not always constructive.

Astrid Messerschmidt (2010) has set forth that racism in Germany is, due to post-NS patterns of defence, usually presented as a right-wing phenomenon at the margins of society or attributed to National-Socialism which is perceived as a concluded epoch. Since this perspective does not completely deny the existence of racism, but seemingly deals with it, it is particularly efficient in preventing a deeper examination of the problem. Even approaches which expressly adopt an antagonist position vis-à-vis racism may to be involved in this kind of defence mechanism.

Our brief exploration could not take account of the specificity of anti-Semitic or other particular processes of *Othering*. Astrid Messerschmidt (in her contribution to this volume) explains that racism operates primarily as an instrument of discrimination which dis-empowers those who are racialised, while anti-Semitism involves a reversal of the power paradigm. From a postcolonial perspective, we would like to underline the importance of a thorough analysis of the historical and the current anti-Semitism. "…anti-Semitism and racism are connected to the extent that anti-Semitic projections are used to avoid dealing with our own (German) racism and Germany's colonial history because the anti-Semitic repertoire provides an aggressor figure with which global problems can be explained" (ibid.: p. 85).

Racist experiences are contradictory experiences, "the game of sweet and bitter words *is* a form in which racism is produced. The difficulty of identifying racism is not only a function of racism, it rather makes up a part of racism itself" (Ferreira 2003: 156, translated by ed.; emphasis in the original). That is what makes it difficult to become aware of it and to resist. When *Othering* is dealt with and scandalised as a dispositive of racist power, this holds the potential to make visible the "nature of the connections" of everyday experiences and one's own entanglement therein, as well as the subjectivity bound to it. General knowledge about the contradictory qualities of racisms which are all based on the logic of *Othering* can serve as a cognitive resource for dealing with racist experiences and as a source of agency and resistance. Foucault puts an end to the search for an outside of the power. He marks a starting place, because agency and resistance can only exist within relations of power (Muhle 2008).

At this point, a question arises about the usefulness of the analytical instrumentarium of *Othering*. We do not at all intend to deny the importance of direct and expressly political practices. But the recourse to *Othering* serves to refine the analysis of our involvement in power relations. *Othering*, furthermore, opens up an analytical perspective which takes into account the ambivalences of actions (also of actions intended to be counter-hegemonic) within dominant discourses. We deal with practices of subject formation in the context of *Othering* to extend our abilities, to reflect, and to act in order to multiply practices of resistance.

> "The subject might yet be thought as deriving its agency from precisely the power it opposes, as awkward and embarrassing as such a formulation might be, especially for those who believe that complicity and ambivalence could be rooted out once and for all" (Butler 1997: 17).

Critical readings of postcolonial theory and its analytical terminology warn us about the danger that concepts like "*Othering*" might themselves have an essentialising effect on subjects and might tie them to a certain discourse position. Thereby these concepts would, in the end, stabilise exactly those discursively constructed relations which they criticise. In addition, the *Othering*-perspective may over-generalise experiences of discrimination, exclusion and racism. If all these experiences are subsumed under the concept of *Othering*, then concrete and variable forms of racialising and/or discriminating practices might be misjudged as the "usual manifestations" of the dynamics of *Othering* and finally ignored altogether. We agree that a certain sceptical distance with respect to totalising and over-generalising terminology is appropriate, and therefore also with regard to the term *Othering*. Our exploratory (and partial) examination of the term is by no means intended as a systematic proposition. Rather, we wanted to explore the analytical potential and the perspectives with regard to reflection and action contained in the concept.

To provisionally sum up our findings, we think that the analytical benefit of the concept of "*Othering*" consists mainly in the option to perceive hegemonic discourses and political dispositives in all their heterogeneity, to examine their power of subject formation, and to deal with subject positioning, subject articulation and corresponding strategies – including their ambivalence – in the same discursive context.

We have sketched a reading of discourse and dispositive which followed the works of Foucault, Laclau, Mouffe as well as postcolonial thinkers like Spivak and Said. In this reading, dichotomous lines of division are lifted – for instance, the division between pre-discursive and discursive elements, but also between hegemonic and non-hegemonic factors. Following Laclau, cultural and political dominance can only be explained in terms of a contradictory discursive 'logic'; hegemony is always based in the simultaneous dynamics of opening and closure. Hegemonic discourses are not monolithic and unchanging, quite to the contrary: they are absolutely dependent on counter-discourses. In reversal of this perspective, anti-hegemonic practices function as policy options only when they dock with dominant discourses – subversively, strategically, ironically. If hegemony can only be sustained – as Ernesto Laclau and Chantal Mouffe claim (Laclau & Mouffe 1991) – based on a discursively-constructed, antagonistic division of society into an Inside and an Outside, then the lifting of this dichotomous division is the first element of anti-hegemonic practice.

Othering is an important category for the analysis of subject formation, but also of political formations in a migration society. The analytical benefit can be recognised at precisely those places where dominant discourses and dispositives form an Inside and an Outside, and where subjects position themselves and are positioned within this divided field: There is no Outside. This finding can be read differently and in the final analysis only in an ambivalent manner. A first reading may sound fatalist: There is no escape from the Inside of society which forms hegemony. A second reading may be formulated like this: There is no Outside (except as a construction in the sense of *Othering*), but it is exactly from the inside of the dominant discourses that anti-hegemonic strategies may be designed and put into practice. The position of subjects who have been minoritised, de-privileged and ruled by practices of *Othering* appears, from this perspective, as one that is extremely vulnerable. But precisely in this vulnerable positioning and in full awareness of it, we find anti-hegemonic resources of action. To put it in the words of Maria do Mar Castro Varela and Nikita Dhawan (2004: 220), vulnerability calls to mind not only the risk of injury, but also "the resources which a subject may manage to summon up – or not – in order to protect themselves from these risks, in order to withstand these conditions" (translated by ed.).

Translated from German by Heike Niedrig (ed.)

Literature

Amadeu Antonio Stiftung (2009): Online available at: http://www.mut-gegen-rechte-gewalt.de/news/meldungen/2009-rekordjahr, date 04-12-2009.

Attia, I. (2009): Die „westliche Kultur" und ihr Anderes. Zur Dekonstruktion von Orientalismus und antimuslimischem Rassismus. Bielefeld.

Ashcroft, B., Griffiths, G. & Tiffin, H. (2007): Post Colonial Studies. The Key Concepts. Oxon.

Bhabha, H. K. (1994): The Location of Culture. London/New York.

Bührmann, A. D. & Schneider, W. (2008): Vom Diskurs zum Dispositiv. Eine Einführung in die Dispositivanalyse. Bielefeld.

Bukow, W.D. & Heimel, I. (2003): Der Weg zur qualitativen Migrationsforschung. In: Badawia, T., Hamburger, F. & Hummrich, M. (eds.). Wider die Ethnisierung einer Generation. Beiträge zur qualitativen Migrationsforschung. Frankfurt, 13 – 40.

Butler, J. (1997): The psychic life of power. Theories in Subjection. Stanford.

Castro Varela, M. & Dhawan, N. (2004): Horizonte der Repräsentationspolitik – Taktiken der Intervention. In: Roß, B. (ed.): Migration, Geschlecht und Staatsbürgerschaft. Wiesbaden, 205 – 226.

Castro Varela, M. & Dhawan, N. (2005): Postkoloniale Theorie. Eine kritische Einführung. Bielefeld.

Castro Varela, M. (2008): „Was heißt hier Integration?" Integrationsdiskurse und Integrationsregime. In: Dokumentation der Fachtagung „Alle anders – alle gleich?". Landeshauptstadt München, Sozialreferat. Stelle für interkulturelle Arbeit. München, 77 – 87.

Dreyfus, H., Rabinow, P. & Foucault, M. (1987): Jenseits von Strukturalismus und Hermeneutik. Frankfurt a. M.

Ehlers, W. (2000): Abwehrmechanismen. In: Mertens, W & Waldvogel, B. (eds.): Handbuch psychoanalytischer Grundbegriffe. Stuttgart.

Eickelpasch, R. & Rademacher, C. (2004): Identität. Bielefeld.

Elwert, G. (1989): Nationalismus und Ethnizität. Über die Bildung von Wir-Gruppen. Kölner Zeitschrift für Soziologie und Sozialpsychologie, 41, 440 – 464.

Fabian, J. (1983): Time and the other. How Anthropology makes its Object. New York.

Ferreira, G. (2003): Die Kolonisierung des Selbst – Der Platz des Schwarzen. In: Steyerl, H. & Gutiérrez Rodriguez, E. (eds.): Spricht die Subalterne deutsch? Migration und postkoloniale Kritik. Münster, 146 – 165.

Foucault, M. (1978): Dispositive der Macht. Michel Foucault Über Sexualität, Wissen und Wahrheit. Berlin.

Foucault, M. (1982): The Subject and Power. In: Dreyfus, H. & Rabinow, P. (eds.): Michel Foucault: Beyond Structuralism and Hermeneutics, Chicago, 208 – 226.

Foucault, M. (1984): Deux essais sur le sujet et le pouvoirs. In: Dreyfus, H. & Rabinow, P. (eds.): Michel Foucault, un parcours philosophique. Paris, 297 – 321.

Foucault, M. (1988): Technologies of the Self. In: Martin, L., Gutman, H. & Hutton, P. (eds.): Technologies of the Self. A Seminar with Michel Foucault. University of Massachusetts Press, 16 – 49.

Foucault, M. (1995): Discipline and Punish. The Birth of the Prison (orig. 1975). Translated from French by A. Sheridan. New York.

Foucault, M. (1998): The History of Sexuality, Vol. 1: The Will to Knowledge (orig. 1976). London.

Foucault, M. (2005): Subjekt und Macht. (German translation by M. Bischoff). In: Defert, D. & Ewald, F. (eds.): Analytik der Macht. Frankfurt a. M., 240 – 263.

Hall, S. (1992): New Ethnicities. In: Donald, J. & Rattansi, A. (eds.): Race, Culture and Difference. London, 252 – 259.

Hall, S. (1996): Ethnicity: Identity and Difference. In: Eley, G. & Suny, R. (eds.): Becoming National. A Reader. New York/Oxford, 339 – 349.

Haubl, R. (2000): Spiegeln. In: Mertens, W. & Waldvogel, B. (eds.): Handbuch psychoanalytischer Grundbegriffe. Stuttgart.

Hooks, b. (1994): Black Looks. Popkultur – Medien – Rassismus. Berlin.

Kühner, A. (2008): Trauma und kollektives Gedächtnis. Gießen.

Lacan, J. (1973): Das Spiegelstadium als Bildner der Ich-Funktion. In: ders.: Schriften I. Oltzen: 61 – 70. [Orig.: *Le stade du miroir comme formateur de la fonction du Je (telle qu'elle nous est révélée dans l'expérience psychanalytique)*. Engl. translation: *The mirror stage as formative of the function of the I (as revealed in psychoanalytic experience)*. Delivered at the 16th International Congress of Psychoanalysis, Zurich, July 17, 1949; Engl. quotation from: http://www.acsu.buffalo.edu/~erikconr/courses/DMS_259/readings/05_LacanMirrorStage.pdf]

Laclau, E. (1990): New Reflections on the Revolution of Our Time. London: Verso.

Laclau, E. & Mouffe, C. (1991): Hegemonie und radikale Demokratie. Zur Dekonstruktion des Marxismus. Wien.

Mecheril, P. & Thomas-Olalde, O. (2011): Die Religion der Anderen. Anmerkungen zu Subjektivierungspraxen der Gegenwart. In: Allenbach, B., Goel, U., Hummrich, M. & Weißköppel, C. (eds.): Jugend, Migration und Religion. Interdisziplinäre Perspektiven. Baden [in press].

Mentzos, S. (2000): Externalisierung. In: Mertens, W. & Waldvogel, B. (eds.): Handbuch psychoanalytischer Grundbegriffe. Stuttgart.

Mertens, W. (2000): Psychoanalyse. Geschichte und Methoden. München.

Messerschmidt, A. (2010): Zwischen Entnormalisierung und Distanzierung – vier Muster im Umgang mit Rassismus. In: Broden, A. & Mecheril, P. (eds.): Rassismus bildet. Subjektivierung und Normalisierung in der Migrationsgesellschaft. Bielefeld, 41 – 57.

Muhle, M. (2008): Eine Genealogie der Biopolitik. Bielefeld.

Reckwitz, A. (2006): Ernesto Laclau. Diskurse, Hegemonien, Antagonismen. In: Moebius, S. & Quadflieg, D. (eds.): Kultur. Theorien der Gegenwart. Wiesbaden, 339 – 349.

Reich, G. (2000): Projektive Identifizierung. In: Mertens, W. & Waldvogel, B. (eds.): Handbuch psychoanalytischer Grundbegriffe. Stuttgart.

Said, E. (2003). Orientalism. London.

Seidler, G. H. (2000): Identifizierung. In: Mertens, W. & Waldvogel, B. (eds.): Handbuch psychoanalytischer Grundbegriffe. Stuttgart.

Sow, N. (2008): Deutschland Schwarz weiß. Der alltägliche Rassismus. München.

Spivak, G.C. (1984): The Rani Of Sirmur. In: Barker, F. et al. (1985): Europe and its others. Vol. 1: Proceedings of the Essex Conference on the Sociology of Literature July 1984. Essex.

Spivak, G.C. (1996): The Spivak Reader. Edited by D. Landry & G. MacLean. New York/London.

Terkessidis, M. (2004): Die Banalität des Rassismus. Migranten zweiter Generation entwickeln eine neue Perspektive. Bielefeld.

Velho, A. (2010): (Un-)Tiefen der Macht. Subjektivierung unter den Bedingungen von Rassismuserfahrungen in der Migrationsgesellschaft. In: Broden, A. & Mecheril, P. (eds.): Rassismus bildet. Subjektivierung und Normalisierung in der Migrationsgesellschaft. Bielefeld, 113 – 137.

Wollrad, E. (2007): Getilgtes Wissen, überschriebene Spuren. Weiße Subjektivierungen und antirassistische Bildungsarbeit. Online available at: http://www.ida-nrw.de/html/Tagungsdoku_Alltagsrassismus.pdf, date 04-02-2011.

Re-Writing the History of Intercultural Education in Germany from a Postcolonial Theory Perspective

Patricia Baquero Torres, University of Education, Freiburg, Germany

This contribution deals with the academic discourse on "Intercultural Education" in Germany. The history of this debate can be told and has been told in different ways and from different perspectives. Since I will adopt a postcolonial theoretical perspective, this chapter will focus on the question how the production of (educational) scientific discourse is connected to relations of power and to formations of subjectivity.

Academic educational discourse usually links the foundation of the specialised field of Intercultural Pedagogy in Germany to work migration after the Second World War. According to this historical view, pedagogical reflection about the migration processes that resulted from 'guest worker' recruitment has triggered – or is even tantamount to – the early development of theory and controversial debates within the field of Intercultural Pedagogy. And indeed, from this time onwards, educational studies in Germany that can be labelled as "intercultural" have always focused on the consequences of work migration for the German educational system. On this basis, educational concepts such as the so-called "*Ausländerpädagogik*" (pedagogy for foreigners) and "Intercultural Education" were developed, primarily designed as concrete pedagogical responses to the presence of immigrants in German schools. But this emphasis has had the effect that scholarship on the history of Intercultural Education has ignored very relevant historical aspects of the history of education in Germany. In order to avoid a restrictive and one-sided perspective of the development of this pedagogical discourse, neglected transcultural processes in the history of education – that go far beyond the post-war work migration context – have to be included. I refer on the one hand to German colonialism and the corresponding colonial discourse on education, and on the other hand to anti-Semitism (cp. Messerschmidt in this volume). Writing the history of Intercultural Education from a postcolonial theory perspective requires an analysis of the educational discourse as an integral part of the colonial episteme[1], and to explore the ways in which this discourse contributed to legitimize and to reproduce colonial relations.

---

1 Postcolonial approaches understand colonialism as an epistemological system, as a system of representation, as a discourse which is structured by relations of power and which extends beyond the chronological conclusion of a historical era. This leads to the crucial question of how new forms of colonial discourse are articulated in the present and how they continue to effect hegemonic structures. So the topics of postcolonial reflection are both new articulations of colonial relations of power as well as new cultural formations

This article approaches the topic from three distinctive angles: First of all, I will focus on German colonialism and in particular on the role of the colonial educational discourse in the formation of a White racialised German subjectivity. In the second section, I will point out discursive continuities of the colonial episteme, its underlying patterns of perception and reasoning, in the discourse of Intercultural Education. Finally, on the basis of the first two approaches, I will reflect on the category of 'gender' and its connection to the categories 'culture' and 'cultural difference' in the discourse of Intercultural Education.

At first glance, these three sections are rather heterogeneous with respect to historical context and topic of analysis; but in combination, they highlight three important aspects of a postcolonial historiography of Intercultural Education. First of all, I intend to point out a fundamental tenet of postcolonial theory, namely the conviction that colonial patterns of perception and other colonial mental patterns extend beyond the historical era of colonial political relations. This implies a non-linear concept of history which does not interpret colonialism and post-colonialism as two successive and separate historical periods. Secondly, the focus of my analysis is the connection between the production of (scientific) knowledge and discursive relations of power. My third intention is to present the paradigm of intersectionality as an adequate approach for writing a postcolonial history of Intercultural Education.

1. The relevance of German colonialism for the history of Intercultural Education

In Germany, the history of education is primarily conceived and written as a national history (Gippert, Götte & Kleinau 2008: 16). This concept of a national history is closely connected to the idea of a homogeneous, monolingual, national and cultural identity of 'Germany'. Therefore it is taken for granted that it is possible to write about the German history of education without regard to transnational processes like colonialism and its global effects.

Thus the topic of colonialism has until now been rarely considered in educational research in general or in the history of Intercultural Education in particular. A couple of studies in the 1980s and 1990s dealt with German colonial pedagogy in Africa, focussing on the local practices and policies. These studies provide a survey of the educational system in the German colonies and explore

---

in the metropole (former 'colonial mother country') itself which developed in consequence of colonisation and migration.

its influence on social processes on the African continent (cp. Nestvogel 1987; Markmiller 1995).

The starting point for a postcolonial analysis of the subjects of colonialism and colonial pedagogy, however, is a *transnational extension* of the analytic perspective, a "move to transcend the binary divide between nation and empire, metropole and colony by placing them in one analytical frame" (Goodman et al. 2009: 700). This perspective allows a shift of focus in order to explore the interaction and the transfer between metropolitan societies and colonial areas, and to raise the question: What effects did the colonial project have on social processes in the German Reich itself? Or more to the point: In which ways did social practices "there and here" influence and determine each other? From this it follows that the history of Intercultural Education needs to deal with the colonial past, with colonial pedagogy and most importantly with the historical and discursive interrelations between colonial and postcolonial eras.

Moreover, a postcolonial theory approach implies an in-depth analysis of colonialism as a system of knowledge. Power is not simply a repressive force, but also a productive one that generates symbolic meanings such as subjectivity. From the point of view of postcolonial theory, the imposition of relations of subjugation and power does not merely rely on material, institutional and structural conditions – but also on the production of dominant subject formations. In this sense, colonialism needs to be analysed as a project that constitutes subjects and identities. Thus the question arises how colonial White subjects were produced and inscribed into social practices through education. From this perspective, the construction of Whiteness[2] and of the colonial White subject can be read as integral parts of the colonial project and as fundamental for educational processes.

If we assume an interdependence among the various social lines of differences in the context of social power relations, making our premise such that racialised constructions are always only effective *in combination* with social categories like gender and class, then we need to explore the ways in which the German colonial project developed its context-specific contours in terms of these interacting social constructions. To put it differently: How did particular social placements (based on 'race', class, gender) interact in the colonial context to produce the dominance and normality of Whiteness?

2 The category of Whiteness is one of the central analytical categories of Whiteness Studies. This interdisciplinary field of research has gained influence on different scientific disciplines in Germany these past years, contributing to a fundamental change of perspectives in the analysis of social inequalities. Its analytic approach focuses on a deconstruction of the norm (cp. Walgenbach 2008: 45ff.). Examples for Interdisciplinary publications in Germany are Wollrad (2005); Eggers et al. (2005); Tißberger et al. (2006).

Such an analytical approach consists of three levels of research, which are closely linked in social practices: the structural level of social inequality, the level of individual agency with regard to the social positioning of subjects, and the symbolic level of production and reproduction of norms.

Recent educational studies about colonialism that deal with social processes in the German Empire examine the interplay between the construction of a hegemonic White national identity with genderised and class-based processes (Walgenbach 2005; Dietrich 2007). Following the research approach of Walgenbach and Dietrich, I will select two aspects that are particularly suitable to demonstrate this interaction: the debate about the "mixture of races" and the "women's question in the colonies" in "German-Southwest Africa" [Namibia], which was the only settler colony established under the German Empire. My analysis will focus on the construction of the national identity as White, and on the role of the educational policy discourse and gender-specific educational programmes in this context.

One of the significant controversial issues of German colonial policy were marriages between White men, who constituted the large majority of the European population in the colonies, and Black women, as well as the legal status of their offspring, the so-called "Mischlinge" ("half-caste children" or "bastards"). For colonial administrators, these marriages were problematic because German citizenship had to be accorded to the German men's African wives and their children. Colonial officials strongly disapproved of this requirement because colonial legal regulations were designed to prevent the extension of German citizenship to the "native" inhabitants of German colonies. However, according to the patrilineal logic of legislation applying to bi-national marriages in Europe at the time, the wife and any children born in wedlock belonged to the *Vaterland* (father's nation). The "mixed marriages" in the colonies, therefore, effectively undermined the exclusion of colonised "natives" from German citizenship. Moreover, the existence of "mixed race" children, quite generally, brought up the question of national or rather racial identity, prompting the colonial authorities to act in order to prevent sexual relations between White colonists and African women altogether. In the course of this controversy, the increasing numbers of "Mischlinge" were perceived as a threat for the future of the colony and its White German rule. This fear was based on racial theories of the time which proclaimed the "mixture of races" as negative for human evolution (Dietrich 1007: 210), and since the "black race" was already relegated to the lowest level of the so-called "race hierarchy", "interbreeding" was bound to deteriorate the "quality" of the "white race" (Dietrich 2007: 183). For colonial policy, therefore, the existence of the "Mischlinge" endangered the imaginary German identity by subverting the neat racial compartmentalization and hierarchy in which this identity was rooted. As a result of this controversy, the colonial administration began revoking the already-conferred German citizenship of these children (Dietrich 2007: 211). In summary, the two central factors in the process of White self-affirmation that prevented "Mischlinge" from becoming Germans were the fact that "natives" could not, by law, be members of the German Reich and that "mixed marriages" were prohibited. These legal provisions clearly demonstrate the political objective to create a biological foundation for the demarcation-line between "Whites" and "Blacks", thus implying an inseparable connection between Germanness and Whiteness.

The "Mischling"-question, which at first seemed only relevant for the local colonial policy, also intruded into the discussion about the national identity of the German Empire (*Kaiserreich*) in the metropole. This discussion evolved around the concept of the "German Volk", and the question was raised whether and in what manner the definition of the German nation should be based on racial and anthropological criteria. The objective of this debate was to keep the German population – which was imagined as homogeneous – "racially pure" and White (Dietrich 2007: 228). Within the colonies, both the coloniser's identity as German and the premise of German "racial superiority" had to be stabilised. In relation to other colonial powers, it was important to hone the specificity of the so-called "*Deutschtum*" (Germanness) in order to gain a profile as colonial power.

The low numbers of German women in the colonies was perceived as the core of the problem of "miscegenation". In order to maintain "racial purity", the colonial administration at first suggested sending White prostitutes to the colonies. But this suggestion brought up a new dilemma, namely whether prostitution was, indeed, a means to safeguard "racial purity" and an attendant morality. The question of 'colonial women', therefore, became another vital aspect of colonial policy and was fiercely debated in the Reich. The participation of German women in the colonial project gained prominence through this debate, and they were attributed a central role in the stabilization and protection of colonial rule, and racialisation in the colonies.

At this point in the discussion, the construction of the image of the "German White women" abroad in the colonies, as well as at home, became of central importance. They were now presented as the carriers of German culture, and were assigned a "national duty" (Walgenbach 2005: 145). They were expected to reproduce the White collective – biologically, culturally and socially. This particular construction of the White women was intertwined with a racialising process which aimed at a radical separation between "White Germans" and "Black Africans"; at the same time it was based on an expressly bourgeois concept of women (ibid.). The discourses on gender and on Whiteness thus flow together at this point.

In 1907, the "*Frauenbund der deutschen Kolonialgesellschaft*" (Women's Association of the German Colonial Society) was founded. Its aim was to promote women's emigration to Southwest Africa, thus preventing "mixed marriages" and establishing "Germanness" in the colonies. Amongst the many activities of the Women's Association, its participation in the foundation of "Colonial Women's Schools" (*Frauenkolonialschulen*) in Germany is of particular importance. For instance, in the *Frauenkolonialschule* in Rendsburg, which was only closed in 1945, the curriculum covered both the theory and practice of home economy and agriculture, as well as aspects of population and sexual policies (Linne 2008: 34). Apart from cooking, carpentry, hygiene, and nursing, subjects of teaching included "National Political Studies", "Genetics", "Race Studies", and "Eugenics", particularly during the time of National Socialism (ibid.).

In these schools, the daughters of the "educated classes" (nobility and bourgeoisie) were to be trained in all aspects of home economics in order to prepare them for a life in the colonies (Walgenbach 2005: 96) – an intention which points unambiguously at the class interests of the Association. But since bourgeois households, as a rule, delegated such housekeeping activities to servants, this course of study was of little interest among the bourgeois women. Because of these contradictions most of the colonial schools were doomed to failure within a few years of their existence (Walgenbach 2005: 97).

Nevertheless, it is important to explore the basic idea that gave rise to the foundation of Colonial Women's Schools, namely the conviction that "educated women" married to German men, and not women from the lower strata of society, were the means to shape "Germanness" and to ensure "orderly life circumstances and a proper German family life" in the colonies (Lerp 2009: 34, translated by ed.). Noble and bourgeois women were supposed to be more suited to life in the colonies "due to their higher education, their broader outlooks and their often greater inbred ability to endure self-denial and sacrifices" (ibid.). In other words, bourgeois women were therefore prepared for their task as carriers of culture in such schools. In the domestic and private sphere of the family, the female values ascribed to White German women were to be transferred "overseas". According to this ideology, it was assumed that "each and every single housewife, out there in the foreign parts, will create a German home, and thus a small-format Germany" (Niessen-Deiters 1913: 7, quoted by Dietrich 2009: 186, translated by ed.). According to this view, good order, discipline, civilisation, cleanliness, and hygiene were the quintessence of German culture, and this was to draw a clear distinction to "lazy", "primitive" and "dirty" African housewives and the Black populace in general. Such a view legitimized German racist dominance.

The establishment of educational institutions for women and the concept of female education that developed in this context unveil an interesting entanglement between German colonial policy and the striving for emancipation of the bourgeois women's movement. While these schools were designed to encourage women's participation in the colonial project and to thus ensure its very success, they simultaneously fashioned White women as culturally and racially superior to Black women. The colonial educational programmes as part of the colonial project contributed to construct the White educated bourgeois woman as prototype of German national identity in the colonies. Addressing women in their schools' advertisements as carriers of "German education, discipline and customs" (*deutsche Bildung, Zucht und Sitte*), the Women's Association promised these women a privileged position in the colony. The objective of the Women's Association was not merely to promote women's emigration, but more particularly to establish a place for "educated women" in the colonies. In line with the aims of the bourgeois women's movement, they intended thus to strengthen social participation of women.

But the needs of female labour differed from this programmatic aim such that the efforts of the Association were reduced to finding employment for working class women in the colonies. It is important to underscore the disparate class positions and interests of the members of the Women's Association and their clients, who stemmed primarily from the lower social strata and hoped for social mobility in the colonies.

This disparity can be observed in the social structure of the colony in general. Research has shown how, with the increase of the number of White women in the colony, social distinctions developed among them. This separation of classes was combined with both racialised lines of social positioning as well as the official colonial gender construction of the "White woman", which remained a bourgeois conception despite other social processes. As a result, German maids, for instance, were accorded positions of relative privilege vis-à-vis Black servants in the division of labour. With respect to the white *Hausfrau* (housewife), however, the social class distinction remained in place. This example illustrates the extent to which the imaginary German collective, which was based on racialised categories, presented itself as homogeneous to the outside, but was at the same time internally disparate because of other social inequalities and distinctions.

Analytically this example demonstrates the intertwining of three sociocultural colonial relationships. First, there is an intersection of the hegemonic national White identity with the binary construction of Whiteness and Blackness. Second, it can be shown how gender-specific images were constructed with respect to both the differences between the sexes as well as racialised representations. Third, the interplay of three categories of differences can be illustrated in this example: race, gender and class position. Finally, the functions of the educational discourse and of colonial educational policy 'at home' are highlighted.

My brief reconstruction has traced, in a specific historical context, aspects of the articulation of the binary and hierarchic representation of own/foreign – and thereby illustrated the general European modern logic of exclusion. Characteristic for this system of representation is that it dovetails different group identities and power positions, which historically produced complex hierarchic relationships. A transnational analysis of these historical processes foregrounds the global nature of colonial history. More importantly, the little researched unmarked position of Whiteness comes into view, and dimensions that have been ignored thus far are integrated into the analysis of power relations, which arises at the intersection of social differences based on categories like gender, race, ethnicity, culture, and class. What I want to underscore in this context is the importance of taking into consideration the construction of the *norm* – which is also highly relevant for the history of Intercultural Education.[3] A historiography of Intercultural Education needs to explore the role of educational discourses and science in the production of normality as well as identities which are shaped by images produced in the colonial context.

After the Second World War, the continuity of this hierarchical system of representation is evident in discourses about migrant-Others. Postcolonial criticism of science puts into relief the close connection between knowledge production and the social context of this production. By applying this analytic perspective to the history of discussions within the field of Intercultural Education, I will deal with the question of how this specialised scientific field constructs its

3 The productivity of Critical Whiteness Studies for a historiography of Intercultural Education is already evident in the application of 'Whiteness' as an analytical category. Critical Whiteness Studies are, however, not merely relevant for research on German colonialism, but also for research on the present-day social structures in the former metropole. Even today the construction of the hegemonic White national identity cannot be separated from the exclusion of Blackness. Therefore the relevance of Critical Whiteness approaches for Germany does not depend on the degree of Black presence in the German society. Rather, the crucial argument for the importance of such a research perspective in Germany relates to the fact that the share in social privileges is, in a habitualised manner, bound to an ascription of Whiteness. For the reception of this approach in Intercultural Educational Science see Baquero Torres (2009).

subject: How does the discourse on Intercultural Education produce knowledge about the migrant-Others?

2. Intercultural Education and the colonial episteme

As mentioned above, the foundation of the specialised field of German Intercultural Education is usually located in the context of post-war work migration. In this context, a homogenizing concept of cultural and national identity is emphasised. In this first phase of dealing with migration in the German educational discussion, we can also detect the production of binary patterns of perception and action. The following example illustrates this claim.

In the educational discourse of the 1960s and 1970s, the "deficit hypothesis" was the most prominent construction of cultural difference. Accordingly, "foreign" children or "guest worker children"[4] were defined as "problems" and as deficient in comparison to the "own" ("German") children. Consequently, the "pedagogy for foreigners" (*Ausländerpädagogik*) developed compensatory programmes to address the "deficiencies" of the children of the work migrants.

The paradigm of the "*Ausländerforschung*" (research on foreigners) of the 1960s in general was inclined to perceive "fundamental" or "marked" differences between migrants and the members of the receiving society that were attributed to assumed cultural identities and modernity differences. This reading of cultural differences was based on static, essentialist and hierarchical concepts of culture and cultural identity. The "deficiencies" were analysed with regard to "culture", and localised in the psychosocial framework of the migrant families' culture of origin. This view ignored the socio-structural living conditions of work migrants in Germany and never questioned the structure of the German educational system and its demand for complete assimilation. This paradigm of a pedagogical model that targeted "foreigners" was based on a fundamentalist perception of the national receiving society as culturally homogeneous and monolingual (Gogolin 2004).

Accordingly, so-called "foreign students" were to be educated in separate preparatory and special classes in order to compensate the language and socialisation deficits that were attributed to them so that they might be integrated into

4 Editorial note: 'Guest workers' (Gastarbeiter) was the new term for post-war immigrant workers in Germany – who had been called 'foreign workers' (Fremdarbeiter) during the time of National Socialism. Apart from the attempt to mark detachment from NS labour policy, the term 'guest' was also meant to express the expectation that migrant workers would return to their 'home countries' after a limited work period in Germany within a system of labour rotation.

the extant education system, which itself was not problematised. In addition, this predominant educational paradigm was based on the assumption that migrant children lived "between two cultures". Educational concepts therefore aimed at a so-called "double strategy": on the one hand, children were to be integrated into the culture of the receiving society; on the other hand, they were to be prepared for a re-integration into the culture of their "home country". As a result, while compensatory educational programmes were supposed to prepare migrant children for "integration" (in the sense of normalisation and assimilation into the host society), they received additional "mother tongue lessons" to prepare their re-migration.

In the early 1980s, the "deficit hypothesis" was criticised and replaced by a "difference hypothesis".[5] This new argument was that foreign students and their families were not deficient in any way, but simply different because they had a different culture. Accordingly, cultural difference should be taken into consideration in educational programmes, and the host country's students should be taught to respect this difference. Moreover, commonalities were to be emphasised, as far as they existed (cp. Gogolin & Krüger-Potratz 2006: 105). Even though this second position was opposed to the first, it must be noted that a basic underlying pattern of thinking about "We and the others", about "own/foreign", was integral for both approaches, and that the assumption of a fundamental cultural difference was still in place.

While the new focus on "difference" in intercultural education discourse tried to distance itself from the interpretative paradigm of the deficit perspective, it did not overcome an emphasis of Otherness based on a culture-determinist perspective, and thus still tended to be stigmatising and culturalising in its effects. To respect 'cultural difference' implies an emphasis on differences and accordingly a construction of closed cultural identities because the seeming naturalness of cultural differences is never questioned. This discourse contributes to the fact that the question of socially and culturally *multiple* belonging (*Mehrfachzugehörigkeiten*, term coined by Mecheril 2003) remains a taboo subject – much like the issue of "mixture" in colonial discourse.

If 'culture' is given a central place in defining difference, this implies the risk of constructing social problems as culturally determined (Kiesel 1997). As a consequence, essentialist approaches are caught in a circular argument. While they attempt to define differences between people in pluralist societies as cultural differences in order to develop adequate pedagogical concepts to overcome

5 This critique implied the demand for a fundamental change of paradigm within the educational discourse. The first symbolic step was the renaming of the specialised field "Ausländerpädagogik" as "Intercultural Education / Pedagogy".

problems resulting from these differences, they actually reinforce differences (cp. Gogolin & Krüger-Potratz 2006: 117f.). Such conceptions of Interculturality continue to be based on binary constructions of *own/foreign* that are perceived as closed and unchangeable units. Similar to my analysis of colonial discourse, we can again see that definitions of the Self and the Foreign are Eurocentric and hierarchical representations which construct the culturally *Other* as the deviation of the norm for which the dominant group sets itself as the standard.

This brief outline of two different perspectives in discourses of educational science demonstrates that both hypotheses are based on the opposition between majority society and the "foreigners", between "us" and "the Others"; this opposition has been a constant factor in all discourses on migration. Thus it would seem that the binary system of representation of the colonial discourse in the early 20th century is equally effective in the discussion about migration in the second half of the 20th century. The first hypothesis defined "guest workers' children" as deficient in comparison to "German" children, and even treated them with special pedagogical programmes to remedy these deficiencies. The second hypothesis was expressly designed to counter-act such a hierarchical way of representation and the corresponding treatment of children from ethnic minorities. But despite of this objective, it did confirm the fundamental distinction between German and immigrant "foreign" children. The logic of identity constitution based on the definition of two closed groups is still in place and reinforced. Moreover, this discursive practice constructs a homogeneous, monolingual national identity by defining ethnic minorities as the cultural or ethnic Others and by treating them as a deviation from the norm.[6]

From a bird's eye view, the decisive factor is that the concept of 'culture' has become the central and singular point of reference for social categorisation in the context of immigration. Thus this concept has acquired a fundamental discursive function. Essentialist and homogenizing notions of culture and cultural belonging reinforce mental and action patterns which contribute to the concept of cultural difference as unchangeable and clearly definable. More recently, however, the critical stance of "Intercultural Pedagogy" in response to the "Pedagogy of Foreigners" (*Ausländerpädagogik*) and the questioning of the concept of 'culture' have contributed to the development of a broad range of scientific approaches which 1) are decidedly critical of *any* culturalising and ethnifying usage of the term 'culture', and which 2) point out the dangers of using this concept in an essentialising way, in particular in the context of educa-

6 This claim is founded, amongst other evidence, on research results on institutional discrimination in the German educational system, e.g., Gomolla & Radtke (2002).

tion. In the discussion of the specialised field of Intercultural Education, therefore, a dynamic conception of 'culture as process' has gained acceptance.

These new approaches can be understood as part of a basic "change of perspective" (Gogolin & Krüger-Potratz 2006) because they have contributed to a decisive modification of the point of view within educational research as well as within theory of education. The new approaches promote a "Pedagogy for All" and a "Pedagogy of Acknowledgement" (*Pädagogik der Anerkennung*). They analyse, in particular, the political and social conditions of living and learning of all members within the immigration society (Gogolin & Krüger-Potratz 2006: 105f.), and endeavour to develop adequate educational strategies that combine equality in education with an acknowledgment of "(socio)-cultural differences" in general. Research in this context focuses, for example, on mechanisms of exclusion and discrimination within the educational system and also on the construction of "normality" within schools (Gogolin & Krüger-Potratz 2006: 106).

The change of perspective as outlined by Gogolin & Krüger-Potratz deals with social and structural discrimination and – consequently – questions the conception of normality. From this follows that theory development, empirical research designs and also the writing of the history of Intercultural Education all need to take into account the close and interdependent relationship between different social categories of difference. If we conceptualise social differences in terms of interdependence, we shift the binary logic so that subject formation can be perceived beyond stable and unchangeable binary constructions like "we and the migrant-Others", that is to say, beyond an "either-or" logic. In addition, the concept of intersectionality[7] provides, in my view, an adequate approach that enables us to analyse the interplay between identity constituting categories in the social (power) relationships of the past and the present, as I have illustrated in my analysis of the discursive function of the concept of the "German White woman" for colonial power structures. What needs to be pointed out, however, is that the fixation of the discussion on the concept of 'culture' for several decades had long-lasting effects on German discourse patterns: On the one hand, it

7 In brief, the term "intersectionality" indicates that social lines of difference such as sex/gender, ethnicity, culture, class, sexual orientation are not constructed in isolation from each other and therefore should not be perceived as separate categories in social analysis. Furthermore, intersectional analyses assume that social categories or lines of difference depend on context and thus vary given different space and time. The intersectionality approach also claims that social differences should not be understood as additive categories, but rather as inter-crossing lines of social positioning, and that social differences should be treated as structural categories on the same level of relevance, rather than as primary and secondary categories in a hierarchical relationship – which is the predominant paradigm of analysis (for a detailed discussion see Baquero Torres 2009a).

has effectively contributed to avoiding the issue of racism, on the other, the theoretical impulses from postcolonial and intersectionality studies as outlined above were only hesitatingly taken up near the end of the 20th century and are still rather controversial up to today.

In the final section that follows, I will explore a different aspect of the discursive development of Intercultural Education, this time with reference to "Gender and Women's Studies in Education" as another specialisation within Educational Science. I will explore the relation between the categories 'culture' and 'gender', and the relevance of this relation for a historiography of Intercultural Education. This reconstruction of the discourse from another point of view will demonstrate that only by taking into account and critically reflecting the category 'gender' within the debate on migration, it is possible to uncover important connections between knowledge and power that so far have been neglected in theory discussions of Intercultural Education.

3. Intercultural Education – the production of knowledge and power relations

My fundamental premise is the suggestion that the discursive connections within the colonial episteme are of particular relevance for a historiography of Intercultural Education. Since the production of scientific knowledge takes place in a field of contest, discursive acknowledgment and thus the stakes of the power of knowledge are objects of negotiation and struggle. Taking as an example the production of the "foreign woman", I will discuss two central questions of the postcolonial criticism of science: How is educational knowledge produced? In which discursive power relations is this knowledge production involved? But to start with I will give a brief historical overview about the reception of postcolonial theory in Germany and about the relationship between the categories of culture and gender in German educational science.

In a recent publication, the postcolonial theorist Maria do Mar Castro Varela expresses her astonishment about the very belated reception of postcolonial theory in Germany (Castro Varela 2010: 254). While postcolonial analysis took root in Anglophone countries in the 1990s, interest and local adaptation of postcolonialism in Germany is very recent (ibid.). In my mind, one plausible reason can be traced back to the development of the specialised discourse of Intercultural Education, which from its start ignored histories of colonialism and issues of racism. One of the peculiarities of German post-war social analysis is that racism was predominantly perceived in its connection to National-Socialism and the Holocaust, making an examination of racism beyond the NS-history a marginalised undertaking.

It should also be noted, that although since the mid-1980s the connection between genderised and culturalised processes of identity construction and the close involvement with Eurocentric interpretation patterns has been pointed out, these impulses have had hardly any impact on the development of the theory of Intercultural Education. The focus on 'culture' and on the paradigm of 'cultural difference' was, apparently, an effective shield against the reception of different theoretical approaches, in particular the analysis of discursive power relations. Therefore, only now are the continuous and ambivalent effects of colonial power relations included into German educational theory developments and are the correlations between the category 'culture' and other social categories explored.

The establishment of new academic disciplines at German universities, such as "Gender and Women's Studies in Education" and "Intercultural Educational Science" as well as the increasing number of research projects and publications in these academic fields acknowledges the importance of these two (separate) categories within Educational Science. In spite of this recent development, we should not forget that gender and gender relations were long deemed completely irrelevant in the production of scientific knowledge. The fact that the gender perspective is today a matter of course in Educational Science goes to show that what is recognised as "knowledge" in a particular context is the product of struggles of power and negotiation.[8]

Historically, the integration of 'gender' and 'culture' as central categories of Educational Science came about in two separate fields of research that developed, to a large extent, quite independently from each other. On the one hand, the field of *Women and Gender Studies* with its basic category 'gender'[9], on the

8 It is remarkable that since the 1970s, the reception of the debates around difference within German Educational Science has been initiated, in particular, by fields of study such as "Special Pedagogy", "Women's Studies", and "Pedagogy for Foreigners", all of them educational fields dealing with underprivileged groups (not only in terms of education).

9 Since the early 1990s, Social Sciences have taken up this critique of Gender and Women's Studies which "Black Women", migrant and Jewish women had already put forward in the 1980s. They had criticised the assumption that 'gender' and 'gender relations' were the primary and central axis of relations of domination, and that other categories such as 'culture' and 'ethnicity' were subordinated to the category 'gender'. The lack of reflection about racism as well as the lack of interest in the interplay between 'gender' and the categories 'culture' and 'ethnicity' were a consequence of the fact that classical Gender and Women's Studies postulated 'gender' as the central relevant category of research. But not only within Gender Studies or Intercultural Studies, but in other academic

other hand *Intercultural Education*, which – as has been shown – focussed on the categories of 'culture' and 'cultural difference' while dealing with migration and the consequences of migration for education.[10] Therefore, Intercultural Education has so far mainly been preoccupied with the discussion of the term 'culture' and with the development of corresponding theoretical positions in this debate. The status of this term as a primary category and the resulting theoretical discussion, which is largely restricted to issues of 'cultural differences', implies a grievous shortcoming. Since other social categories such as 'gender' are ignored, it follows that the interdependency between these categories has not been explored. These restrictions of the analytic approach undermine an adequate theoretical understanding of the complexity of social (power) relations (for a detailed discussion see Baquero Torres 2009; 2009a).

The inclusion of 'gender' in Intercultural Education was due to a number of researchers' well-founded criticisms of various representations of the cultural Other in education and in parts of educational Migration Studies. German educational researchers such as Helma Lutz and Christine Huth-Hildebrandt have presented detailed analyses of the function of 'gender' in the description of migrants' countries of origin within Migration Studies, in particular they pointed out how 'gender', 'culture' and 'modernity' were interwoven within scientific migration discourses (Lutz & Huth-Hildebrandt 1998; Huth-Hildebrandt 2002).

From the mid-1980s until the early 1990s, the exploitation of representations – particularly of images of the "foreign woman" – in the service of establishing hierarchical relations between West German female social workers and their female immigrant clients was uncovered.[11] Critical researchers such as Lutz (1991) pointed out that the construction of an inferior (female) Other corresponded with the paternalistic attitude of many German social workers. These analyses could show how West German women were actively involved in the

disciplines as well, a significant "blank space" can be identified in German academic discourse with regard to the examination of racism.

10 Similarly to classical Gender and Women's Studies, in the early 1990s, Social and Educational Migration Studies started to deal with the criticism of feminist migrant women and to include the category 'gender' as well as its interplay with the categories 'culture' and 'ethnicity' in their research. This new perspective, however, remained a marginalised discourse, as feminist researchers in Social Sciences noted themselves (e.g. Gümen 1996, 1998).

11 The decisive impulse for a critical reflection of the German feminist movement, of the feminist oriented social work with women migrants, and moreover of Women's Studies in general can be traced back to the "First Congress of Foreign and German Women" (1. Kongress ausländischer und deutscher Frauen) in Frankfurt (Main) 1984. At this congress, women migrants themselves took the floor and criticised the ethnocentric and paternalistic attitude of German social workers and German Women's Studies.

construction of immigrant women as "*doppelte Fremde*" ["double Outsiders"], i.e., as members of a "foreign" cultural environment, and in that environment, as women who were subdued by patriarchal relations of power, which implied that such gender hierarchies were 'foreign' to German society in principle. This critical examination of intercultural discourse thus sheds light on the mechanism of Othering and its functions, e.g., the implicit and explicit binary opposite of the constructed imaginary "oppressed Turkish woman" was the "emancipated German woman" (Diehm & Radtke 1999: 76).

The image of the "foreign woman" was first produced in the earlier context of deficit-oriented migration research. The first sociological research projects on post-war migration had focused on working conditions and related social, demographic and political problems, and had the situation of male migrants as their centre of interest. But slowly schools and educational science started to take note of the presence of "guest workers' children" (*Gastarbeiterkinder*). By the end of the 1970s, migration had also become an issue for social work, and the specific situation of female migrants was interpreted as a *problem* relevant for social education. The conflicts experienced by immigrant women were perceived as rooted in the differences between their heritage culture and the culture of the host society. In this view, the "foreign culture" was contrasted with the "own (German) culture", and was to be judged in terms of deficits. As a result, the "foreign culture" as well as the "foreign woman" were perceived as deficient and backwards.

As Sabine Hebenstreit (1986) critically pointed out, numerous studies of this kind were characterised by such constructions of binary opposites. Both gender and the modernity dissimilarities were paradigmatic constructions of difference and connected to each other in these discourses: the difference between women and men and the difference between tradition and modernity. The first binary opposition refers to a strict ascription of gender roles and to the inferior and oppressed social position of women; the second refers to the binary opposition between a rural, traditional – and therefore backward – agrarian society, closely connected to Islam as a national culture vis-à-vis a highly industrialised, modern, thoroughly rationalised, emancipated-enlightened and individualised host culture (ibid.). By producing such binary oppositions, studies such as the widely read book "*Die verkauften Bräute – Türkische Frauen zwischen Kreuzberg und Anatolien*" (The sold brides – Turkish women between Kreuzberg[12] and Anatolia) by Andrea Baumgartner-Karabak and Gisela Landesberger (published in

12 Editorial note: Kreuzberg is a district in the Western part of Berlin. According to German mainstream media, this district has long developed into the "largest Turkish community outside of Turkey".

1978), have been crucial in constructing an image of "Turkish culture" which is currently still widely accepted as valid. This construction paints Turkish culture as a rural-traditional, patriarchal-Islamic, backward way of life in contrast to the civilised, modern, highly-industrialised and progressive German (Western) society. At the same time this image of Turkish culture reinforces and institutionalises the image of the Turkish woman as the passive, weak-willed, subdued victim. The migrant woman is presented as "foreign woman" who is firmly rooted in her original, backward cultural space which is characterised by a rigid patriarchal system of values and norms.

However, a discursive shift can be detected in the 40-year-old image of the "foreign (Turkish) woman". While a traditionalist, rural Muslim culture was constructed as a basic structure for the interpretation of differences in gender relations in the 1970s, more recently cultural-religious lines of difference (Islam versus Christianity) are emphasised in the depiction of gender inequalities (cp. Leiprecht & Lutz 2010: 251).

The impact of the category 'gender' on the discursive construction of the cultural Other[13] can be differentiated in terms of three distinct discursive functions. 'Gender' serves first of all as a descriptive axis for the differences between majority society and migrant communities. These are differences that are closely intertwined with the "modernity hypothesis" and the "culture difference hypothesis"[14] and thus produce hegemonic discursive constructions. Second, gender-specific constructions such as the "imaginary migrant woman" reinforce prototypical images that have remained structurally constant and homogeneous and continue to impact educational concepts to this day (Weber 2003). Third, such external images tend to neutralise constructs of "femininity" within the majority society and to naturalise cultural identity. While emphasising the "femi-

13 Another example is the discursive construction of a connection between male Turkish adolescents and a problem of violence rooted in 'culture' (cp. Höhne 2003: 189ff.).

14 The migration discourse in both Educational Science as well as Social Sciences has for a long time been structured by the so-called "difference hypothesis", which can be differentiated into the "culture difference hypothesis" and the "modernity hypothesis" (Bukow & Llaryora 1993). Both hypotheses postulate the existence of various and fundamental differences between migrant communities and host society. The culture difference hypothesis argues that there is a different 'cultural frame' which influences the formation of (cultural) identity in an indelible manner. The modernity hypothesis is based on the concept of evolutionary steps in social development following the example of the so-called 'progressive' industrialised societies, and it tends to equate all differences with differences of competencies. These two forms of difference hypotheses are often tied together: "In this case the migrant [or the woman migrant] appears as both, as different and as backwards, an ascription which does not complicate dealing with them, on the contrary, it seems to considerably simplify it" (Bukow & Llaryora 1993: 20, translated by ed.).

ninity of the foreign women" within the ascribed gender hierarchy of the heritage societies, it is possible to ignore the symbolic meaning of the own (German) constructions of femininity instead of critically analysing them. At the same time the ethnic ascriptions are interpreted – in analogy to gender specific constructions – as "natural" traits which cannot be questioned.

From the point of view of postcolonial theory, constructions such as the "imaginary migrant woman" in all its differing versions are not only relevant because they constitute reified collective images, but because scientific discourse contributes to the production of knowledge that informs such constructions of cultural difference which are, in turn, used to legitimise social conditions and inequalities. Even special educational programmes for particular target groups are justified on this knowledge base. Thus scientific knowledge production serves to reproduce the marginalisation and exclusion of the "cultural Other" in education.

From the early 1990s onwards, some (mainly female) educational researchers in the field of Intercultural Education started to respond to the above criticism and to amend the lack of systematic reflection of the gender category in their field of research. First attempts were made to bring together the two up to then quite separate fields of study: Intercultural Education and Gender and Women's Studies. As a result, research projects dealing with processes of ethnification analysed the production of *ethnified gender* as integral part of these processes; and the discussion about the function of 'gender' in the discourse of Intercultural Education was also intensified (cp. Baquero Torres 2009). This critical analysis of the discursive function of 'gender' played an important role in deconstructing essentialist notions of gender within constructs of 'cultural difference'. In this way, the binary hierarchical patterns of perception that informed the knowledge production about migration and culture within Educational Science could be detected. This in turn facilitated the reception of theoretical approaches that define gender, culture, and ethnicity as categories that structure social relations. As a result, the critical educational researchers not only shifted scientific discourses about 'culture' and 'cultural difference' to include 'gender'; they also pointed out that these social categories are indissolubly interwoven and intertwined, and thus promoted an in-depth discussion of the relation between diverse social lines of difference.

In summary, referring to my analysis of the image of the "foreign woman" and its function for educational discourse, I would like to highlight three aspects relevant for a postcolonial historiography of Intercultural Education: first, the production of knowledge about migrant-Others is preformed by Eurocentric patterns of interpretation; second, this knowledge production is not gender-neutral; and third, the theory development of Intercultural Education failed to take into account discursive power relations. The lack of reception of this critical perspective in the scientific discussion is, in my view, highly significant. It indicates the type of power complex in which the scientific knowledge production was negotiated, and we might ask: What was considered as relevant or irrelevant by whom and in which context?

4. Conclusion

While the first section of my contribution dealt with a gap in the historiography of Intercultural Education, the second and third sections dealt with the discourse of Intercultural Education itself. I approached the critical analysis of this discourse from different angles.

First, I scrutinised this discourse from within, focussing on the ways the notion of 'culture' is employed and the resulting theoretical difficulties: The dominant discourse structure is (1) based on a hierarchical representation of "Own/Foreign", (2) in danger of (re-)producing processes of culturalisation and ethnification, and it contributes (3) to the (re-)production of homogenizing and essentialising categories of 'cultural identity'.

Second, I examined the discourse from the point of view of Gender and Women's Studies to explore the relation between the social categories 'culture' and 'gender'. My aim was to show that the introduction of a critical gender perspective has provided a decisive impulse for a critical revision of the discourse of Intercultural Education, leading to a more thorough understanding of the connection between the production of knowledge and discursive relations of power. By reconstructing the discourse about women migrants it was possible to clearly demonstrate the power of definition inherent in the scientific production of knowledge. The crucial question from a postcolonial theory perspective is in this context: *Who* speaks in *which manner* about *whom*? – The answer is obvious: It has always been German educational researchers who defined the migrant-Others – as deficient and as deviant from normality. They reduced migrants on their 'cultural' background and ascribed to them the status of 'foreigners'. Only they had the power of definition.

The recurrent theme of this essay is the Eurocentric logic of exclusion, that is to say, the hierarchical logic of "we and the others", of the "either-or" that allows no in-between. Thus I have shown the discursive continuity of the colonial episteme which represents the colonialised Others as well as the migrant-Others in a subordinate position vis-à-vis the "German" subject. At the same time I have pointed out the normative function of the White, national-cultural German identity.

Moreover, I have endeavoured to emphasise the productivity of an interdependent theorisation of social categories for the project of writing the history of Intercultural Education, focussing in my analysis on the categories 'culture' and 'gender'. Such research must be expanded. In terms of empirical analysis this implies a shift away from dealing with 'culture' and 'cultural difference' as isolates that has characterized educational discourse until now and moving towards an analysis of the intersection of 'culture' with other social categories such as 'gender', 'race', 'sexual orientation'. Such an approach will deconstruct homogenizing categorisations such as "foreigner" (*Ausländer*) by introducing multiple aspects of the social (self-)-positioning of individuals into the social research paradigm. In addition, such an approach would allow a more complex and more adequate analysis of the interlocking social, transcultural, global processes and according power relations. Therefore, this approach opens up an extensive field of research for the historiography of Intercultural Education.

Translated from German by Heike Niedrig (ed.)

Literature

Baquero Torres, P. (2009): Kultur und Geschlecht in der Interkulturellen Pädagogik. Eine postkoloniale Re-lektüre. Frankfurt/M. et al.

Baquero Torres, P. (2009a): Postkoloniale Perspektiven zur Reflexion von Bildung in einer Einwanderungsgesellschaft: die Interdependenz sozialer Kategorien als neuer Denkansatz. In: Jahrbuch für Pädagogik 2009: Entdemokratisierung und Gegenaufklärung. Frankfurt/M. et al., 335 – 349.

Baumgartner-Karabak, A. & Landesberger, G. (1978): Die verkauften Bräute: türkische Frauen zwischen Kreuzberg und Anatolien. Reinbek bei Hamburg.

Bukow, W.-D. & Llaryora, R. (1993): Mitbürger aus der Fremde. Soziogenese ethnischer Minoritäten (2nd ed.). Opladen.

Castro Varela, M. (2010): Un-Sinn: Postkoloniale Theorie und Diversity. In: Kessl, F. & Plößer, M. (eds.): Differenzierung, Normalisierung, Andersheit. Wiesbaden, 249 – 62.

Diehm, I. & Radtke, F.-O. (1999): Erziehung und Migration. Eine Einführung. Stuttgart et al.

Dietrich, A. (2007): Weiße Weiblichkeiten. Konstruktionen von „Rasse" und Geschlecht im deutschen Kolonialismus. Bielefeld.

Eggers, M. M., Kilomba, G., Piesche, P. & Arndt, S. (eds. 2005): Mythen, Masken und Subjekte. Kritische Weißseinsforschung in Deutschland. Münster.

Gogolin, I. (1994): Der monolinguale Habitus der multilingualen Schule. Münster et al.

Gogolin, I. & Krüger-Potratz, M. (2006): Einführung in die Interkulturelle Pädagogik. Opladen et al.

Gomolla, M. & Radtke, F.-O. (2002): Institutionelle Diskriminierung. Die Herstellung ethnischer Differenz in der Schule. Opladen.

Goodman, J., McCulloch, G. & Richardson, W. (2009): 'Empires overseas' and 'empires at home': postcolonial and transnational perspectives on social change in the history of education. In: Paedagogica Historica, 45: 6, 695 – 706.

Gümen, S. (1996): Die sozialpolitische Konstruktion kultureller Differenzen in der bundesdeutschen Frauen- und Migrationsforschung. In: beiträge zur feministischen theorie und praxis, 19: 42, 77 – 90.

Gümen, S. (1998): Das Soziale des Geschlechts. Frauenforschung und die Kategorie "Ethnizität". In: Argument, 40: 224 (1-2), 187 – 202.

Hebenstreit-Müller, S. (1986): Frauenräume und weibliche Identität. Ein Beitrag zu einem ökologisch orientierten Perspektivenwechsel in der sozialpädagogischen Arbeit mit Migrantinnen. Berlin.

Höhne, T. (2003): Pädagogik der Wissensgesellschaft. Bielefeld.

Huth-Hildebrandt, C. (2002): Das Bild von der Migrantin. Auf den Spuren eines Konstrukts. Frankfurt/M.

Kiesel, D. (1997): Migration und Kultur – zur Kulturdebatte in der Interkulturellen Pädagogik. In: Gogolin, I. & Nauck, B. (eds.): FABER. Konferenz über Folgen der Arbeitsmigration für Bildung und Erziehung, March 1997, 213 – 236.

Lerp, D. (2009): Zwischen Bevölkerungspolitik und Frauenbildung. Die Kolonialfrauenschulen in Witzenhausen und Bad Weilbach. In: Bechhaus-Gerst, M. & Leutner, M. (eds.): Frauen in den detuschen Kolonien. Berlin, 32 – 39.

Lutz, H. & Huth-Hildebrandt, C. (1998): Geschlecht im Migrationsdiskurs. In: Das Argument, 40: 2, No. 224, 159 – 173.

Lutz, H. & Krüger-Potratz, M. (2002): Sitting at a crossroads – rekonstruktive und systematische Überlegungen zum wissenschaftlichen Umgang mit Differenzen. In: Tertium Comparationis, 8: 2, 81 – 92.

Markmiller, A. (1995): „Die Erziehung des Negers zur Arbeit": wie die koloniale Pädagogik afrikanische Gesellschaften in die Abhängigkeit führte. Berlin.

Mecheril, P. (2003): Prekäre Verhältnisse: über natio-ethno-kulturelle (Mehrfach-)-Zugehörigkeit. Münster et al.

Nestvogel, R. (ed. 1987): Afrika und der deutsche Kolonialismus : Zivilisierung zwischen Schnapshandel und Bibelstunde. Berlin.

Niessen-Deiters, L. (1913): Die deutsche Frau im Auslande und in den Schutzgebieten. Nach Originalberichten aus fünf Erdteilen. Berlin.

Norris, E. G. (1993): Die Umerziehung des Afrikaners: Togo 1895-1938. München.

Paseka, A. (2001): Gesellschaft und pädagogische Praxis. Dekonstruktionen am Beispiel von Sexismus und Rassismus. In: Fritzsche, B., Hartmann, J., Schmidt, A. & Tervooren, A. (eds.): Dekonstruktive Pädagogik. Erziehungswissenschaftliche Debatten unter postrukturalistischen Perspektiven. Opladen, 187 – 199.

Tißberger, M., Dietze, G., Hrzán, D. & Husmann-Kastein, J. (eds. 2006): Weiß – Weißsein – Whiteness. Kritische Studien zu Gender und Rassismus. Critical Studies on Gender and Racism. Frankfurt/M. et al.

Walgenbach, K. (2005): „Die weiße Frau als Trägerin deutscher Kultur". Koloniale Diskurse über Geschlecht, „Rasse" und Klasse im Kaiserreich. Frankfurt/M. et al.

Walgenbach, K. (2008): Whiteness Studies als kritisches Paradigma für die historische Gender- und Bildungsforschung. In: Gippert, W., Götte, P. & Kleinau, E. (eds.): Transkulturalität. Gender- und bildungshistorische Perspektiven. Bielefeld, 45 – 66.

Weber, M. (2003): Heterogenität im Schulalltag. Konstruktion ethnischer und geschlechtlicher Unterschiede. Opladen.

Wollrad, E. (2005): Weißsein im Widerspruch. Feministische Perspektiven auf Rassismus, Kultur und Religion. Königstein/Taunus.

Intercultural Education in a post-National Socialist society – Processes of Remembrance in Dealing with Racism and anti-Semitism

Astrid Messerschmidt, University of Education, Karlsruhe, Germany

Intercultural Education in the German context has until now rarely been reflected with reference to National-Socialism (NS) or to colonialism. This article outlines the educational responses to migration within the context of contemporary history; it suggests a double perspective on postcolonial and post-NS images of the Self and the other. Racism as well as anti-Semitism will be analysed with regard to their connection to colonialism and National-Socialism respectively. The historical analysis points out the differences between these two forms of discrimination and looks more closely at their present-day manifestations. This article will develop a concept for intercultural education as processes of remembrance. Within this concept, remembrance constitutes a cultural practice which enters into a relationship with histories of suffering and perpetration.

1. Remembered history in a post-National Socialist society

As we attempt to mark the present with historical characterizations, the limits of our own view of history endure, and it follows that no appropriate label can be found to accurately capture that which it attempts to name. At the same time, historical terms highlight the connection between past and present and have the potential to stimulate the reflection of these connections. If we describe contemporary society as a *postcolonial* one, we speak of the "here and now", a present day distinct from the historical time of colonialism, which itself has not simply transformed into the past. The prefix "post" in Postcolonialism does not signify only the past, but the current connection to history. This terminology points out that colonialism might be past, and yet not over. The discussion about *postcolonial* theory has produced important suggestions for the interpretation of "post" as a means to mark contemporary history. "Postcoloniality" does not indicate the past with reference to the time after decolonization; rather, it signifies the prevailing and present-day relevance of the colonial experience. It is not so much a term for an epoch, but a category of analysis, which does not evoke something that is in the past and finalised, but something that continues without definite closure (Ha 2004: 95). In order to analyse the connection between past and present, I will try to use the term without implying an unambiguous understanding of postcoloniality. With respect to colonialism, postcoloniality should neither be read as an indicator of a successful historical break with colonialism, nor as a description of a chronological succession. The term, instead, serves to direct our attention to the present-day effects of the colonial history, a history which post-colonial discourse scrutinizes as contradictory processes and not as "linear progression" (Castro Varela & Dhawan 2005: 24, translated by ed.).[1]

This perspective is based on an understanding of history which assumes the lack of closure of historical experiences of violence. Walter Benjamin has outlined the fundamental principles of this critical understanding of history in his "Thesen zum Begriff der Geschichte"[2] (Benjamin 1974). In Benjamin's view the historical events have no closure, and he therefore dismisses the suggestion that we should be done with it. As Schweppenhäuser has noted, „*Aber nichts, wollen Benjamins Reflexionen über den historischen Gegenstand bedeuten, ist unabgeschlossener als das Geschehene*" (Schweppenhäuser 1975: 7). [But nothing, as Benjamin's reflections about the historic incident mean to indicate, is less concluded than that which has happened (translated by ed.).] With that, Benjamin turns against a memory that silences the shake-ups which emanate from history and against a way of remembering which serves to legitimize present social conditions.

To 'bear in mind' [*Eingedenken*] in Benjamin's sense means to protest against the disappearance of what has been. Schweppenhäuser interprets this thought as "the right of that which has been" [*Recht des Gewesenen*], a right to a "lost future that has yet to be found" (ibid.: 8, translated by ed.). The past extends into the present. "*Unter dem Jetzt der Lebenden breitet sich eine unerledigte Jetztzeit der Toten aus*" (ibid.: 8). [Spread underneath the present of the living is an unfinished present time of the dead (translated by ed.)]. Benjamin defies the thinking along temporal sequences; he challenges us to mistrust chronological order and finished epochs, and he leads us into confusion about the past character of what is past. Remembrance injures the historic continuum, it refers to past life, to the dead of history, whose "futile hope" is that "which makes them continue to live within the living" (ibid.: 9, translated by ed.). To speak about remembrance in the sense of Benjamin means to leave behind a conception of history that assumes the closure of the past. His conception of history instead connects the knowledge of the historic events with the "lamentation" for the victims. The victims are the subjects of history, and the lamentation for them constitutes the subjectivity of history, which allows us to recognize that

---

1 Ella Shohat, for instance, states that the prefix ‚post' might indicate a rupture or a chronology of history and is therefore problematic (Shohat as referred to in: Castro Varela & Dhawan 2005: 114).

2 English: "Theses on the concept of history", by Walter Benjamin, orig. 1940 [translation anonymous]

the seemingly complete conception of an objective history of scientifically researched facts is merely a fragment. The objectivity of a science of history that blocks our access to the subjective side of history is in Schweppenhäuser's view a form of reification of the subjects, a reification of the victims (ibid.: 12). Benjamin perceives history always as a rupture of continuity. It is only within this rupture that history may briefly appear. The past cannot be appropriated like a good. It is fleeting – an "image which flashes up at the instant when it can be recognized and is never seen again" (Benjamin 1974: 695, translation anonymous). To be recognizable, this fleeting picture of the past depends on the ability of those living in the present to recognize their reflection in this image. "For every image of the past that is not recognized by the present as one of its own concerns threatens to disappear irretrievably" (ibid.). In the practice of remembrance we attempt to enter into a relation with history in order to understand ourselves (Messerschmidt 2003: 116-128) and in order to become aware of our own involvement in the effects of this history.

The starting point for the following considerations is the assumption that the social present cannot be separated from the histories of colonialism and of National-Socialism (NS). After tracing the reverberations of colonial and NS-images of the Self and the world below, I will explore options for a contemporary reflection of racism and anti-Semitism in education. My interest in stimulating a reappraisal of colonialism within the German social context must also be contextualized within a society marked by the after-effects of National-Socialism. The postcolonial present after Auschwitz is characterized by NS-constructed images of humanity and of the world that continue to resonate. Likewise, the post-NS present is characterised by the after-effects of the experiences of colonial practices of power and by images of the non-European 'Other' and of the European 'Self' produced within the colonial framework. By attempting to examine contemporary educational processes in relation to these historical after-effects, it is necessary to adopt a double perspective that distinguishes both internal connections and lines of differences (Messerschmidt 2008).

2. Practices of *Othering* (creating strangeness/foreignness)

The encounter with groups of people considered to be strangers to a dominant European perspective has been staged again and again as a history of European seizure and dominance. The suggestion that "we" (Germans) ought to learn about and from the "foreign cultures" has been popular in pedagogical discourse for quite a while by now, and, without question, has been imbued with positive connotations. Renate Nestvogel, one of the few German educational researchers who explore the colonial roots of contemporary intercultural education, has pinpointed the historic ruptures of such a discourse: "From a historical perspective the interest in foreign cultures has played an important part in the conquest and oppression of foreign peoples" (Nestvogel 2003 [1990]: 187, translated by ed.). From this point of view, the interest in the foreign cannot be perceived as innocent curiosity, but must be seen as an extension of earlier pedagogies stimulated by colonial interests. A psychological perspective that highlights the insecurities, which are sparked by encounters with the foreign, is deficient if it is not complemented by a historical analysis of the subjugation and appropriation of the foreign (Messerschmidt 2005a). "In the encounter with the foreign we are not only confronted by our own inner conflicts and individual narrow-mindedness, but also by the real history, a history of conquest, of racism and anti-Semitism, which has become inscribed in our thinking and feeling" (Rommelspacher 1995: 147, translated by ed.). The 'Others' of the European subject, having been identified as the foreigners/aliens, had to be subjugated. It was through contrasting one's Self and the nation to foreigners that allowed the development of the European self-image of the enlightened bourgeoisie.

A relief projection was needed for everything that was external to this self-image – the undisciplined, the savage and the uneducated – making the memory of the history of the European/German relations with foreigners an integral part of any analysis of our conception of "foreignness". We need a form of 'commemorative work' (*Gedächtnisarbeit*) that traces residues of colonial relations to the foreign within contemporary relations of power which continue to influence current relationships. Only on an abstract level can we speak of a relation of reciprocal dependence between the positions of the Self and the Other, because in social practice, this interdependence is superimposed by procedures of power. The one who identifies 'Others' as foreigners/strangers is the one who has the power of definition and who belongs to those who are not foreign, but are perceived as 'normal' or 'belonging'. It is from this position that the foreigner is defined as the one who is deviant. Consequently the discourse about foreignness is never just about foreignness, but is always also about inequality. Our every dealing with foreignness takes place within a complex of power relations, within structures of dominance characterised by social relations of superiority and inferiority. The ways in which foreignness is assessed, and in which the decisive difference from the dominant group is defined, are part of social patterns of order and therefore change over time. Against the backdrop of her historical reconstruction of the ways of dealing with foreignness in modernity, Renate Nestvogel suggests a "cultural self-reflection" to enable us to become aware of internalized cultural traditions. In particular she is concerned about a critical examination of "occidental convictions of superior value" (Nestvogel

2003 [1990]: 188), which have turned into a "collecting tank for a variety of projections" (ibid.: 188f., translated by ed.) and which continue to affect our dealing with diversity in an immigration society up to today.

Zygmunt Bauman (1995) analyses the ambivalent dealings with foreignness in the nation-state at the end of the 19th and beginning of the 20th century in Europe with attention to practices that contested the German Jews' national membership. Non-Jewish Germans (forcefully) ascribed foreignness to the Jewish minority, while simultaneously expecting German Jews to discard everything that might make them foreign. By demanding the cultural assimilation of the Jewish minority, the non-Jewish German majority set themselves up as the "native elite" which assumed the right "to judge whether the efforts to overcome cultural inferiority had been indeed genuine and more especially if they had been successful" (Bauman 1995: 146, translated by ed.). The majority demanded proof of successful assimilation, even though such efforts would never be granted success because any assimilatory aspirations were perceived as a subversion of national identity and roused suspicion.[3] After all, the "construction of political, economical, and cultural unity as a nation [implied] first of all and in particular a strong promotion of the collective identity of the Germans" (ibid.: 158).[4] Any effort to acquire unequivocal membership via education and self-improvement was doomed to failure due to the pervasive belief that the national community was "based on common fate and blood" (ibid.: 155, translated by ed.) – a pre-modern concept which, however, has not yet been overcome in the history of the modern nation states. In this context, the logic of nation-building requires that foreigners can only become equals by way of a self-alienation, or the loss of everything contrary to the national identity. Only after they have discarded everything that might be perceived as 'different' is belonging offered. But it would be an illusion to believe that assimilation could safe-guard against discrimination and persecution.

The current German discourse on integration still mirrors something of these practices which are simultaneously assimilationist and exclusionary. The discourse of integration demands a declaration of unequivocal affiliation, and at the same time, it marks non-belonging by casting suspicion on immigrants in general. "The notion of integration is again en vogue after more than 30 years. This

3 "The paradox result of assimilation efforts was that precisely those activities and styles of living which were adopted to cover over the differences were perceived as reasons to force the respective agents into marginalization" (Bauman 1995: 156, translated by ed.).

4 "Jewish efforts to turn the Germany which they loved into a place that was somewhat better suited for civilized, human co-existence were perceived as subversive activities, which threatened to undermine the integrity and the strength of the emerging national unity" (Baumann 1995: 158, translated by ed.).

is hardly reasonable. Because in Germany this term conceals all sorts of tacit convictions about what 'Germanness' implies, how people ought to behave at 'our' place and what they ought not to do, who possesses the right predispositions and who the deficits, for whom the institutions are put in place and who is in truth merely a visitor" (Terkessidis 2010: 7, translated by ed.). The integration discourse insists on the existence of a fundamental difference between the majority-Germans and migrant minorities while at the same time demanding that this difference should be made to disappear (Ha & Schmitz 2006: 251). In spite of the fact that only the 'migrants' are talked about, this discourse contains implicit claims about the autochthonous society, which is represented as a homogeneous system of secure convictions, even though the demand for integration manifests that the 'national' homogenized 'We' is untenable (ibid.: 248). In order to render this invisible, it is necessary to take recourse to the "image of the *Volk* as symbol of the national *Self*" and to create a "division between an affirmative *We* and an objectified *Them*" (ibid., emphasis in original, translated by ed.). If the educational preoccupation with integration does not include a critical reflection of such practices of division, pedagogic thought fails to address the social context in which integration becomes a measurement for a forced assimilation that has exclusionary effects. Moreover such education fails to address its own function and its "participation in processes of social reification and discrimination" (ibid.: 252). Educational programmes need to develop approaches that critically analyse the concept of integration. Instead of applying assimilatory practices and adhering to concepts of socio-cultural homogeneity under the premise of integration, a pedagogy that deals with the social context of migration must examine structures and attitudes which lead to discrimination. To do that, we need a historical reflection of world images and images of humanity.

3. The historical background and current manifestations of racism and anti-Semitism

The fixation on problems of integration marginalises efforts to deal with racism. In the German context, the idea long prevailed that racism was a phenomenon of the past, belonging to a different system of dominance. Even today it is exceptionally difficult to acknowledge the *existence* of racism in German society as long as the term 'racism' is tightly linked to the NS-persecution of Jews; Germans like to believe that they have left everything connected with these events firmly behind. The fallacy of this reasoning does not exist in the supposition of a connection between racism and NS-anti-Semitism aiming at extermination, but rather in the conviction that since the Holocaust is in the past, racism is also in the past. The suggestion that the democratization of society implies that the racist worldviews have been overcome is an obstacle for any attempt to examine everyday racism. It also hampers efforts to examine in depth the contemporary consequences of colonial racism on the one hand, and of images of the society as *Volk* in the NS-ideology on the other (Messerschmidt 2009: 143ff.). Both historical patterns continue to affect who can be 'German' and how much internal heterogeneity this society will tolerate (Messerschmidt 2010).

Until the 1980s, the West German discussion about racism, if it was discussed at all, was to a large extent restricted to an analysis of National-Socialism (Müller 1997: 357). Due to this historical fixation of the topic, the discussion focused only on anti-Semitism, implicitly suggesting that racism and anti-Semitism were fundamentally similar or even interchangeable. In this context, Heinz Müller points out a "German taboo around the notion of racism...which represented the historically unique inhumanity of National-Socialism" (ibid.: 361, translated by ed.). In programmes of political education the exploration of present-day racisms and their historical roots started very belatedly, accompanied by a rejection of the term "Ausländerfeindlichkeit"[5] (hostility towards foreigners) which downplayed racism. But determining the relationship between racism and anti-Semitism remains difficult. Not only has racism rarely been reflected in the German context, and when it is, it is most often a shorthand association with the NS brand of anti-Semitism. In addition, analyses of anti-Semitism are often all too quickly abbreviated as analyses of "racism". Both forms of reduction fail to recognize the specific systems of reasoning and the specific effects of racist vs. anti-Semitist discrimination. If racism is historically only examined with respect to National-Socialism, the colonial history of racist worldviews is ignored.

The history of colonial world relations has not simply been overcome, but continues to affect the present. The same is true for National-Socialism, but differs from the colonial paradigm with respect to its structures of power and its consequences. In the context of National-Socialism, anti-Semitism as ideology

5 Note of the translator: The term 'Ausländerfeindlichkeit' is very specific for German political discourse. It has been and is still widely used to denote phenomena that are labelled as 'racism' in other national contexts. One of the implications of the term is that the targets of hostility and violence are "foreigners" in Germany, so that – in analogy to the term 'xenophobia' – the hostility is presented as to some extent "natural" or "understandable" as a wariness of strangers. As a matter of fact, however, acts labelled as 'Ausländerfeindlichkeit' have as a rule not been directed against White foreigners (tourists, business people etc.) from North America or European countries; at the same time German citizenship is no protection for Germans of colour against the so-called 'hostility towards foreigners'.

and as political practice is rendered as a signature, which produces mass loyalty to the system and which achieves the integration of the "Germans" – who can no longer simultaneously be Jews – as one *Volk*. In its inception the NS-movement cultivated socially rebellious, anti-bourgeois and anti-capitalist resentment, which targeted the Jews, on whom was inscribed everything that offended and oppressed the German *Volk*. In other words, National-Socialism secured the support of the masses by offering 'ordinary people' the ability to perceive themselves as oppressed and National-Socialist partisanship as a solution to overcome their oppression. At the same time, NS-ideology constructed the idea of 'the Jews' as a negative repository for everything objectionable, combining contradictory projections of Jews' inferiority and superiority, making them seem simultaneously deficient and dangerous.

After 1945, the post-NS German nation was confronted with the fact that the vast majority of Germans had been in no position to oppose the racist *Volk* policy, aiming as it did at exclusion and extermination. They had either tolerated, accepted or even identified with this policy. This recognition, however, did not so much inspire a thorough national self-reflection, but it was the motive for the construction of a defensive collective memory. As a result, National-Socialism has been repeatedly represented as a limited episode, a "reign of terror" which rendered people incapable of agency and produced nothing but horror.

When speaking of "the Nazis" [short form for "the National-Socialists"], such defensive representations are in play; this term makes National-Socialism appear as something foreign, which can be clearly identified and compartmentalized, and whose individual representatives are easy to distance from ourselves. The identification with the system, the nationalist enthusiasm of the masses and the self-images of the majority of Germans with respect to the *Volk* have to be 'de-realised'. They are part of the objective and normative reality of a history, *after* which to live means that we can never again live *before* it, that we can never again tell a national history unencumbered by that past. In the process of de-realisation, *Deckerinnerungen*[6] are used which transform the NS into a partly heroic, partly painful narrative of war – dealing with abused soldiers and bombarded civilians. Such historic narratives are exonerating for the narrators who are represented as victims, while the historic crimes disappear behind a universal history of suffering. Those practices to occlude that which proved

6 Deckerinnerung: Remembered historic facts which are used to replace or "cover up" (verdecken) other historic events and which help to avoid talking of these other events. A good example is the history of the expulsion of German settlers from many Eastern European countries after the war which is kept alive in collective memory by politically influential groups and replaces/covers up the (memory of the) history of the German occupation policy during the war including the expulsion of persecuted groups.

most disturbing and distressing after 1945 form a two-part defensive pattern against a negative history which has not come to an end, nor aligns with the post-1945 self-image of enlightened progress. Firstly, anti-Semitism is primarily interpreted as something connected temporally with the NS-past and consequently has disappeared along with the NS. Secondly, "racism as analytic category" (Kalpaka 2003: 60, translated by ed.) to analyse social processes of segregation is rarely used in the German context because there is hardly anything more threatening to the German mind than to be diagnosed as racist.

With respect to their historic manifestations and justifications, racism and anti-Semitism differ though they are both expressions of a self-reassurance about cultural identity and of nationalist aspirations to power. The positions of the hierarchically defined 'Other' are filled by different groups, but in each case their function is to support a self-image of superiority and attendant power. Whilst colonial racism could exterritorialize the foreigner, the modern version of anti-Semitism is characterised by the idea of a domestic subversive element. The disparate power relationships that come with colonial knowledge offered the European subject the opportunity to construct itself as civilized and enlightened. Almost as a complement, anti-Semitic knowledge is helpful in shaping this self-image in a way to make it morally acceptable: "In contrast to the colonial Other, the anti-Semitically marked Other is not only inferior, but also powerful. And thus dangerous. Anti-Semitism makes it possible for us to view ourselves as victims and to imagine that we are dominated and exploited" (Messerschmidt 2005b: 139, translated by ed.). Therefore colonial and anti-Semitic images of the Self and the 'Other' correspond while being different. This process of projection functions like a mirror-image to the colonial discourse in which the European Self constructs itself as superior. In the colonial image of the Self, the Europeans do not perceive themselves as victims, but as victors who hold the colonized in contempt. Within the framework of anti-Semitism, this same Self is constructed as honest and unselfish; it works productively, and its wealth is hard-earned. It is convinced that its wealth is not based on the exploitation of 'Others', but is gained by its own labour. This Self has a clear and pure conscience because it has found a projection screen for everything impure. The exploitation of the 'Other' is judged as morally reprehensible, and can be ascribed to the Jews, who do not represent so much the contemptible, but rather the threatening. Modern European anti-Semitism can thus also be interpreted as a defence mechanism against their own colonial history of exploitation. Instead of dealing with the after-effects of colonialism, anti-Semitic world images can be employed to explain existing inequalities and continuous injustice in a manner that avoids the reflection of our own involvement.

4. Secondary anti-Semitism

What characterizes anti-Semitism *after Auschwitz* is the rejection of a remembrance of the NS-crimes, a legitimization of anti-Semitism through the denial or the playing down of the Holocaust, and finally the projection of guilt on the Jews, who are blamed for what has been done to them, and who are perceived as those who never stop bothering "us" (Germans) with the memory of Auschwitz. Moreover, in the course of this victim-aggressor reversal, Jews are made responsible for all sorts of historic and present-day atrocities, "in order to undermine the Jewish status as victims, so to speak" (Bergmann 2006: 44, translated by ed.). The basic structure of this *secondary anti-Semitism* consists in a defensive relationship with National-Socialism, and in an attempt to bring history to a closure by discrediting the victims.[7] Ilka Quindeau calls this complex a "rejection-of-guilt anti-Semitism" – "anti-Semitism not in spite of, but because of Auschwitz" (Quindeau 2007: 162, translated by ed.). This pattern reflects dealings with the NS-past which are still based on a rejection of guilt, on silence, and on repression. The practice of exoneration by keeping history at a distance was dominant in the German Federal Republic (West Germany) until the 1980s. Armin Pfahl-Traughber considers the "rejection of guilt component of secondary anti-Semitism" as being the "most widespread form of anti-Semitism in Germany" at present (Pfahl-Traughber 2007: 9, translated by ed.). The line of argument that insinuates that the Jews "exploit the memory of the genocide for their own advantages" presents the remembrance of the NS-crimes as an "act of aggression" (ibid.). Manifestations of post-NS anti-Semitism rarely occur in form of racist programmes anymore. Only "neo-Nazi parts of right wing extremism" might still resume racist anti-Semitism (ibid.). Practices of de-realising the criminal actions, of playing them down by comparing them to other historic atrocities, and also the aggressor-victim-reversal of secondary anti-Semitism predominate. The rejection of historical memory and the downplaying of historical findings with reference to other historical events are mutually constitutive within this complex of defensive practices. One very efficient instrument of diminishing the significance of these particular historical memories consists in making "the victims of the past [appear] as the aggressors of today" (Holz 2005: 59, translated by ed.). In Klaus Holz' view this "reversal of the relationship between aggressor and victim" is the "core element of anti-Semitism after Ausch-

7 "The so-called secondary anti-Semitism has become, far beyond Germany, a European phenomenon. Especially resentment against Jews as 'privileged victims' is, for instance, very strong in France, which has to do with French history, that is a lack of reappraisal of the colonial past and the Second World War, but just as much with criticism of Israel and anti-Semitism" (Eckmann 2005: 107, emphasise in the original, translated by ed.).

witz" (ibid.). Even though anti-Semitism has lost its foundation in race theory almost entirely after 1945, it has lost nothing in terms of its force of attraction (Bergmann 2004). It would be inadequate to speak of a "new anti-Semitism" with respect to how the concept is structured, rather a "displacement of the reasons and motives to raise this subject" can be observed (Bergmann 2006: 47, translated by ed.). Werner Bergmann identifies four motives for current anti-Semitisms that could be observed in the last ten years: first, a critical stance towards Israel which "approaches anti-Zionist, anti-Semitist positions" (ibid.: 33); second, a left-wing anti-Semitism, which has been revitalized by the Middle East conflicts and which replaces the "rejection-of-guilt anti-Semitism that focused on the past" by a perspective on Israel as the 'aggressor'; third, an anti-racist anti-Semitism, which perceives Israel as an embodiment of racist policies; fourth, the "development of a radical anti-Jewish attitude in the Arab world" (ibid.: 34). Anti-Israel positions have become the dominant manifestation of current anti-Semitism.

These positions are recognisable as not merely critical stances vis-à-vis the policies of the State of Israel, but as anti-Semitic, when they are characterised by the following aspects: Jews in general are identified as Israeli; Israel is denounced as being wholly responsible for manifold global problems; and the radical political forces in Israel's neighbourhood are completely ignored. A discriminating judgment of particular political parties and groups within Israel who propagate anti-Palestinian views is just as important as an awareness of tendencies that lead to a sweeping condemnation of the State of Israel.

If anti-Semitism is only perceived as a particular manifestation of racism, then the ideological elements of the anti-Semitic mindset remain unchallenged. The ideology of anti-Semitism cannot be reduced to general racist patterns. The "rumour about the Jews" (Adorno 1951: 141, translated by ed.) offers, on the one hand, a projection screen for our apprehension about modernity. On the other hand, the ways of understanding and of discussing the current problematic of racism by referencing the NS race policy promote a perception of racism as a programme of a fundamentalist *Volk* policy within a dictatorial complex of power. Against this historical background it is difficult to recognize everyday racisms within a democratic society. The problem seems to belong to a different context of power, seemingly unrelated to our present. The absorption of anti-Semitism as a form of racism, in turn, misinterprets the specific manifestation of secondary anti-Semitism and remains stuck in the history before 1945. To be able to analyse racism and anti-Semitism, it is therefore necessary to develop an approach which makes visible the differences in the present-day manifestations while examining historic connections. Racism works in the first place as an instrument of discrimination, disempowering those who are identified as 'racially different'. In everyday contexts racism implies the restriction of rights and of access to resources as well as experiences of degradation. In contrast, anti-Semitism leads to a "reversal of the paradigm of power" (Eckmann 2006: 221, translated by ed.) by creating the concept of an overpowering enemy. In the history of modern anti-Semitism, this concept of the enemy manifests itself particularly in the "class based rhetoric of anti-Semitism" (Hund 2006: 91, translated by ed.). In this discourse, Jews are simultaneously "suspected to be ruthless social climbers" as well as "the ones pulling the strings of dark and subversive machinations which destabilize the social whole in the area of both, the lower strata as well as the ruling classes" (ibid.). The bridging of class antagonism via anti-Semitism continues to this day, when anti-Semitic clichés from the left and right are employed to blame people completely unconnected to one's own life for the apprehension that one feels about social developments. "The essential aspect of this strategy is the production of the concept of an enemy – of a powerful and threatening opponent, so that we may perceive and identify ourselves as his victims" (Eckmann 2005: 109, translated by ed.). This analysis also applies to a postcolonial discourse manipulated in the service of politically questionable ends, when this discourse is combined with anti-western resentments and when Jews are perceived as "agents of Westernization and of a naturally just as 'Western' imperialism" (Loewy 2005: 56, translated by ed.).

Only if we distinguish analytically between racism and anti-Semitism, we can adequately examine the particular post-NS constellation. Next to an 'Other' who is represented as inferior and powerless, another super-powerful 'Other' appears who allows us to put ourselves into the role of the discriminated. The self-image of being blamed and accused, and subjected to a tribunal of political correctness is a resource of defence against criticism. By ascribing power to Jews as a group it is possible to exonerate the collective memory from its history of violence. On the one hand, guilt is projected onto Jews as those who burden "us" (non-Jewish Germans) with a never-ending history; on the other hand, "our" self-image is articulated as that of the victim of unreasonable accusations. At this point, racism and anti-Semitism come together again as speaking about each engenders similar defensive reflexes – "again we are to be blamed – again we are the ones who have done something wrong". That is how a national collective – 'We' – of wrongly accused is formed, and who, by a demonstrative display of their harmlessness, claim to finally be normal.

Moreover, anti-Semitism and racism are connected to the extent that anti-Semitic projections are used to avoid dealing with our own (German) racism and Germany's colonial history because the anti-Semitic repertoire provides an aggressor figure with which global problems can be explained. At present, this figure can be identified as the state of Israel, which according to the logic of this pattern, appears as responsible for the lack of peace in the world. This pattern of perception represses any analysis of the complex history of the founding of Israel and of the manifold actors involved in the Middle East conflict. Pointing out Israeli practices of power vis-à-vis Palestinians, Lebanon and other Muslim populations is a way for non-Jewish Germans to dispose of the problem of the own history of anti-Semitism by presenting the victim in the role of the aggressor. At the same time, this perspective helps to repress the memories of Germany's history of colonialism by ascribing colonial practices to 'Others'. The counterparts to such externalization are projections within the internal national order which try to locate extant anti-Semitism in Germany among its current minorities. The divisions between the ethnic German 'we' and the migrant outsider 'they' in contemporary German society can be put to use in order to reject any critical self-reflection. It is the 'Others' who are racist and anti-Semitic and not 'us', implying that ethnic Germans have already dealt with the history of anti-Semitism for many years in depth and with great success.

5. Postcolonial memory after Auschwitz

Educational work that deals with contemporary history must, firstly, open up ways for a reconstruction of historical developments, and secondly, explore how these developments are reflected in present-day practices and perceptions. In so doing, educational programmes about contemporary history can hardly ignore the complex connections between different historical events; rather, in the context of social globalisation, these programmes should enable learners to reflect the different experiences of crimes against humanity, mass murder and collective persecution in a manner that allows them to explore particularities as well as more general connections and interactions. On the basis of an analysis of racism and anti-Semitism, it will be possible to outline forms of postcolonial remembrance in the context of a society which is connected to the perpetration of the Holocaust. The integration of the colonial history into the collective memory of the Germans cannot happen additively – as addition of a neglected subject; it requires a reflection of the contemporary context *after Auschwitz*.

Every instance of historic remembrance is exposed to the forms and interests of appropriation of those who reconstruct history, who make it visible and recall it to memory. In the German context, a tendency exists to play down the particular 'monstrosity' of the Holocaust. The remembrance of the colonial crimes in the German context follows this tendency and diminishes the significance of the Holocaust. Reinhart Kößler and Henning Melber interpret this observation as an attempt "to play an historical guilt off against another" (Kößler & Melber 2004:

40, translated by ed.). A careful reflection of the inter-connections is necessary. Rivalry of memories, however, will neither do justice to the historic contexts nor to the present-day requirements of a globalising culture of remembrance. Such rivalries block the view on each specific history. To be able to perceive the present-day after-effects of both, colonialism and National-Socialism, it is necessary to analyse the two historical formations in a manner that avoids any levelling and any deduction that might imply that these histories are equivalent with each other while simultaneously keeping in mind that the wish to diminish the significance of the Holocaust is still very viable in our society.[8]

When dealing with the relationship between colonialism and National-Socialism in historic perception, it is problematic to simply assume "continuity", as if the colonial practice of power inevitably transformed into the NS policy of extermination. Birthe Kundrus interprets the "continuity hypothesis" and the hypothesis of the "exemplary function" of the German colonial wars for the NS war of extermination as a way of "coming to terms with contiguity" and as a form of denial of historical discontinuities and parallel histories (Kundrus 2006: 52, translated by ed.).[9] But I believe that a general rejection of any assumption of continuity is similarly inadequate. One starting-point for the assumption of continuity is the race policy of German colonialism which represented the colonized as racially inferior. Jürgen Zimmerer perceives "racial" segregation as a central element of the German colonial regime, as a "principle of the colonial state which was based on the binary division between 'White' and 'Black', between 'natives' and 'non-natives', between *(Herren)menschen* (members of the master race) and 'servants/slaves'" (Zimmerer 2005: 143, translated by ed.). The idea of the racial state forms also part of NS-ideology, and even today the racist ideas have effects beyond the NS complex of power. These are important aspects of postcolonial processes of remembrance. When we insist on a perspective of *either* continuity *or* break between colonialism and NS, we reduce historic complexity in favour of an unambiguous picture of the past which tends to play down either the importance of racism or the importance of anti-Semitism. Based on studies of racism and anti-Semitism, I conclude that we ought to speak of elements of continuity which can be observed in the continuous effects of racism. At the same time it is important to examine *discontinuities* which are

8 "In the discourse of cultural memory the postcolonial and the post-NS debate about how to deal with the history and with each of the histories from which these debates emerged come together. I would wish that this mutual crossing of the border might be reflected as such, instead of being discussed in terms of rivalry" (Heyl 2005: 162, translated by ed.).

9 Kundrus' statement refers to Reinhard Koselleck who assumes the simultaneity and diversity of pasts (Kundrus 2006: 53).

linked to anti-Semitic projections of an opponent superior in strength and which provide a populist element in the representation of the 'Other'.

In contrast to a narrative of continuity that negates ambiguities, we should look at crossovers *and* discontinuities as such a perspective appears suitable for processes of remembrance, which refer to colonialism and NS without neglecting the specificities of each complex of power. In my view, we can deduce two forms of dealing with colonialism and NS from these reflections: the recognition of historic discontinuities and of particular aspects of these practices of power and the exploration of simultaneously effective consequences of both historical contexts up to today. Every attempt to relate colonialism and NS to each other in terms of deduction or similarity has, in my opinion, two problematic tendencies: the tendency to give colonialism more weight by comparing it to the NS and the tendency to portrait the NS as dominant in the collective memory by implying that it is the fixation on the Holocaust that has caused German society to lose sight of other criminal histories.[10]

The second discursive pattern contrasts the debate about postcolonial memory with the commemoration of the Holocaust, a history with which Germans have presumably successfully come to terms. Both tendencies fail to do the respective historic subjects justice. The tendency to present the remembrance of the NS-crimes as dominant national memory ignores the fragility of this memory in German society and focuses only on established forms of commemoration in the public sphere (Messerschmidt 2003: 32ff.). Beyond this sphere, however, there is no collective consensus to remember the Holocaust. The private memory in the majority of German families is focused on the privation in the years of war, so that the Second World War appears primarily as a national history of suffering.[11] Since the colonial history has to a large extent been no issue at all for the collective memory, the perception of the dealing with NS history became distorted, as if this was a memory successfully anchored in the national consciousness. Ideally, the emergence of a collective memory of colonial history would accompany a consciousness about the fragile and continuously vulnerable place of the Holocaust memory. To know about the social inclination to make

10 Sebastian Conrad and Shalini Randeria note that "the central event of the Holocaust" has absorbed the attention of historical and cultural researchers "and the comparison has marginalized other alignments of German history" (Conrad & Randeria 2002: 40, translated by ed.). At the same time they leave open the question in how far "dealing more in depths with the traces of the colonial past" might "show the policy of genocide in the years of war in a different light" (ibid.).

11 "[...] the past of the exterminated Jewish Germans is taken up in non-Jewish German families only as a history of their disappearance, not even as a history of the dead, let alone as living history" (Welzer, Moller & Tschuggnall 2002: 210, translated by ed.).

the Holocaust more "bearable" by comparing it to other historic events remains an unsettling moment and a point for critical analysis when dealing with a collective postcolonial memory that has still to emerge. "A *double perspective* is therefore required which examines current reflections of colonial and NS images of the world and of the Self and which distinguishes between them" (Messerschmidt 2008: 56).

6. Intercultural education about contemporary history: reflecting the after-effects of colonialism and National-Socialism

The relationship of Germans to their NS-past is characterised by ambivalence. On the one hand, there has been the wish to get rid of the memory of these crimes for decades. On the other hand, since the 1990s a kind of pride of the successful reappraisal has emerged so that the remembrance of the NS appears almost as the trademark of political culture of the Federal Republic. This ambivalence is also obvious in dealing with the memory of NS-history within the present immigration society. Migrants in Germany are still refused unequivocal membership, but they are expected to fully identify with Germany, including how they deal with German history. In this context, the production of national self-images is complemented by the production of external images of the immigrants who are suspected of not dealing adequately with history. More especially after the reunification of the two German states "the quarrel about how to 'come to terms with the past', which has for many years been a political quarrel about different concepts of democracy, has evolved into a quarrel about national identity" (Loewy 2005: 53, translated by ed.). In Hanno Loewy's view, the Holocaust has thus been claimed to restore a national German identity which is homogenized again, and which excludes those who have already become part of the society but whose membership continues to be questioned. Loewy labels them as the "real 'Others' of the present" (ibid.).[12] Wolfgang Meseth confirms that the preoccupation with the Holocaust has a "tendency towards exclusivity" and thus a tendency to exclude "people of non-German origin qua the criterion of parentage" (Meseth 2002: 126, translated by ed.). After having "developed into an integral part of the efforts of self-enlightenment of the German society about its history", dealing with the NS needs to be reflected anew, including the exclusionary effects of these efforts, so that a historical memory of multiple per-

12 "The Holocaust, being claimed for the ideal of tolerance and integration, as well as for national defensive reactions, thus cannot help playing a role in a climate of non-recognition of experiences and histories" (Loewy 2005: 54, translated by ed.).

spectives becomes possible. Only recently has the pedagogical discourse of remembrance begun to accept involvement in the social context of immigration. But as long as the involvement is merely "accepted", a difference in power remains firmly in place – an unnamed 'We' condescends to allow others to share in its own insights.

With respect to educational approaches to contemporary history focussing on the topic of NS, there is the recognition "that adolescents with and without background of immigration do sometimes not differ in their representations of the NS-past" and that the "background of immigration" does by no means always play any role at all (Kölbl 2009: 68, translated by ed.). Nevertheless, the dualist division is continuously reproduced when, for example, the historic knowledge of "German adolescents without background of immigration" is compared to the knowledge of "adolescents in Germany with background of immigration" (ibid.: 70). Migration has become a criterion for the selection of target groups in educational research even though the category of migration is critically discussed. Though it is true that different backgrounds in terms of origin and family context are social starting points for historic remembrance, these differences are to some extent evened out within the shared social context in which adolescents (and adults)[13] deal with history. It follows that there is no either-or-decision at stake. Neither ignoring migration nor charging it as a focus of identity does justice to the social-cultural conditions. We should rather strive to contextualize migration with respect to a variety of differences and belongings and to relate it to experiences in a shared social space in which history is represented. For educational programmes aiming at historic remembrance, this translates into an approach that does not treat dealing with the NS as a matter of national belonging. Imparting knowledge about the Holocaust – its extent, the manner of its execution, and its ideological justification – cannot serve as self-assurance of the own morally sound historic consciousness or about a national collective consensus of historical reappraisal. Educational conceptions of remembrance have to contribute to a critique of community concepts which continue to transport residues of the ideology of the *Volk* and its racist and anti-Semitic foundations. They must contribute to sensitize for the breaks in democracy which become apparent in the dealings with unwanted immigration, refugees and those immigrants who do not fit into the concept of success of the active entrepreneurial Self. In other words, they are about processes of remembrance which refer to the social and cultural dynamics of the present.

---

13 In the past years, educational programmes dealing with contemporary history have vastly neglected adult education although it is mainly adults who influence how conceptions of history are formed.

Recent approaches in historical-political education deal with diversity in the ways to access history and make it possible to represent the NS-past as a European and global "history of relations" (Kux 2006). They counteract the tendency to present historical NS-memory as an exclusively German matter without weakening the specific German responsibility. Projects that recognize the social context of immigration enable participants of different national and cultural backgrounds to take up the historical reappraisal of the NS-crimes and thus to relate with historical awareness to present-day German society (Gryglewski 2006). These approaches are characterized by the effort to widen the perspectives which asks of educators in the field to reflect their own historic point of view with respect to other perspectives. In the course of such educational work, controversial conceptions of history that are charged with conflict can render multi-perspective approaches to the histories of crimes extremely demanding.

With view to practices of historic-biographical education, Ulla Kux discusses an approach which takes up the intercultural dimension of educational processes in a productive manner in order to include it in the reconstruction of history. Kux asks the agents in political education to examine their own perspective because she observes a "narrowing of perspectives" when learning processes dealing in particular with the NS-history are restricted to a national 'We' (Kux 2006: 243). If NS-history is presented as "German history", migrants can only adopt an external position in this process. The author judges such an approach as "a contrast of positions that is not suitable for educational praxis" (ibid.: 247, translated by ed.) and pleads for a "history of relations based on multiple perspectives" (ibid.: 248) to make the international dimension of the NS conceivable. Such an approach is innovative and demanding at the same time and requires great sensitivity with respect to a heterogeneous group of learners as well as extensive knowledge about the manifold historic connections between the NS and different contexts of origin. Kux's approach does not perceive the culture of remembrance in the immigration society as a means for integration into a German conception of history, but rather as a process of intercultural communication about a criminal history which has global importance and is remembered in diverse ways.

Translated from German by Heike Niedrig (ed.)

Literature

Adorno, Th. W. (1951): Minima Moralia. Reflexionen aus dem beschädigten Leben. Frankfurt/Main.

Bauman, Z. (1995): Moderne und Ambivalenz. Das Ende der Eindeutigkeit. Frankfurt/Main.

Benjamin, W. (1974): Über den Begriff der Geschichte. In: Tiedemann, R. & Schweppenhäuser, H. (eds.): Gesammelte Schriften (GS), Vol. 1.2. Frankfurt/Main, 693 – 704. Engl. transl. anonymous on http://walterbenjamin.ominiverdi.org/ date: 23rd March, 2011.

Castro Varela, M. & Dhawan, N. (2005): Postkoloniale Theorie. Eine kritische Einführung. Bielefeld.

Bergmann, W. (2006): Erscheinungsformen des Antisemitismus in Deutschland heute. In: Fritz Bauer Institut & Jugendbegegnungsstätte Anne Frank (eds.): Neue Judenfeindschaft? Zum pädagogischen Umgang mit dem globalisierten Antisemitismus. Frankfurt/Main, 33 – 50.

Bergmann, W. (2004): Auschwitz zum Trotz. Formen und Funktionen des Antisemitismus in Europa nach 1945. In: von Braun, Ch. & Ziege, E.-M. (eds.): Das ‚bewegliche' Vorurteil. Aspekte des internationalen Antisemitismus. Würzburg, 117 – 141.

Conrad, S. & Randeria, Sh. (2002): Geteilte Geschichten. Europa in einer postkolonialen Welt. In: dies. (eds.): Jenseits des Eurozentrismus. Postkoloniale Perspektiven in den Geschichts- und Kulturwissenschaften. Frankfurt/Main & New York, 9 – 49.

Eckmann, M. (2006): Rassismus und Antisemitismus als pädagogische Handlungsfelder. In: Fritz Bauer Institut & Jugendbegegnungsstätte Anne Frank (eds.): Neue Judenfeindschaft? Zum pädagogischen Umgang mit dem globalisierten Antisemitismus. Frankfurt/Main, 210 – 232.

Eckmann, M. (2005): Antisemitismus im Namen der Menschenrechte? Migration, europäische Identitäten und die französische Diskussion. In: Loewy, H. (ed.): Gerüchte über die Juden. Antisemitismus, Philosemitismus und aktuelle Verschwörungstheorien. Essen, 101 – 120.

Gryglewski, E. (2006): Neue Konzepte der Gedenkstättenpädagogik. Gruppenführungen mit Jugendlichen nicht-deutscher Herkunft in der Gedenk- und Bildungsstätte Haus der Wannseekonferenz. In: Fritz Bauer Institut & Jugendbegegnungsstätte Anne Frank (eds.): Neue Judenfeindschaft? Zum pädagogischen Umgang mit dem globalisierten Antisemitismus. Frankfurt/Main, 299 – 309.

Ha, K. N. & Schmitz, M. (2006): Der nationalpädagogische Impetus der deutschen Integrations(dis)kurse im Spiegel post-/kolonialer Kritik. In: Mecheril, P. & Witsch, M. (eds.): Cultural Studies und Pädagogik. Kritische Artikulationen. Bielefeld, 225 – 262.

Ha, K. N. (2004): Ethnizität und Migration reloaded. Kulturelle Identität, Differenz und Hybridität im postkolonialen Diskurs. Berlin.

Heyl, M. (2005): Kolonialismus und nationalsozialistische Massenverbrechen in Monumenten und Gedenkstätten. In: Lutz, H. & Gawarecki, K. (eds.): Kolonialismus und Erinnerungskultur. Die Kolonialvergangenheit im kollektiven Gedächtnis der deutschen und niederländischen Einwanderungsgesellschaft. Münster, 143 – 165.

Holz, K. (2005): Die Gegenwart des Antisemitismus. Islamistische, demokratische und antizionistische Judenfeindschaft. Hamburg.

Hund, W. D. (2006): Negative Vergesellschaftung. Dimensionen der Rassismusanalyse. Münster.

Kalpaka, A. (2003): Stolpersteine und Edelsteine in der interkulturellen und antirassistischen Bildungsarbeit. In: Stender, W., Rohde, G. & Weber, Th. (eds.): Interkulturelle und antirassistische Bildungsarbeit. Frankfurt/Main, 56 – 79.

Kölbl, C. (2009): Mit und ohne Migrationshintergrund. Zum Geschichtsbewusstsein Jugendlicher in der Einwanderungsgesellschaft. In: Georgi, V. & Ohliger, R. (eds.): Crossover Geschichte. Historisches Bewusstsein Jugendlicher in der Einwanderungsgesellschaft. Hamburg, 61 – 74.

Kößler, R. & Melber, H. (2004): Der Genozid an den Herero und Nama in Deutsch-Südwestafrika 1904-1908. In: Wojak. I. & Meinl, S. (eds.): Völkermord und Kriegsverbrechen in der ersten Hälfte des 20. Jahrhunderts. Frankfurt/Main, 37 – 75.

Kundrus, B. (2006): Kontinuitäten, Parallelen, Rezeptionen. Überlegungen zur „Kolonialisierung" des Nationalsozialismus. In: Werkstatt Geschichte, 15: 43, 45 – 62.

Kux, U. (2006): Deutsche Geschichte und Erinnerung in der multiethnischen und -religiösen Gesellschaft. Perspektiven auf interkulturelle historisch-politische Bildung. In: Behrens, H. & Motte, J. (eds.): Politische Bildung in der Einwanderungsgesellschaft. Schwalbach/Taunus, 241 – 259.

Loewy, H. (2005): Der ewige ‚Dritte' in allen Konflikten? Die Diaspora, Israel und der ubiquitäre ‚Kampf der Kulturen'. In: Loewy, H. (ed.): Gerüchte über die Juden. Antisemitismus, Philosemitismus und aktuelle Verschwörungstheorien. Essen, 47 – 66.

Meseth, W. (2002): ‚Auschwitz' als Bildungsinhalt in der deutschen Einwanderungsgesellschaft. In: Lenz, C., Schmidt, J. & von Wrochem, O. (eds.): Erinnerungskulturen im Dialog. Europäische Perspektiven auf die NS-Vergangenheit. Münster, 125 – 133.

Messerschmidt, A. (2010): Distanzierungsmuster. Vier Praktiken im Umgang mit Rassismus In: Broden, A. & Mecheril, P. (eds.): Rassismus bildet. Bildungswissenschaftliche Beiträge zur Normalisierung und Subjektivierung in der Migrationsgesellschaft. Bielefeld, 41 – 57.

Messerschmidt, A. (2009): Weltbilder und Selbstbilder. Bildungsprozesse im Umgang mit Globalisierung, Migration und Zeitgeschichte. Frankfurt/Main.

Messerschmidt, A. (2008): Postkoloniale Erinnerungsprozesse in einer postnationalsozialistischen Gesellschaft – vom Umgang mit Rassismus und Antisemitismus. In: Peripherie – Zeitschrift für Politik und Ökonomie in der Dritten Welt, 28: 109/110, 42 – 60.

Messerschmidt, A. (2005a): Befremdungen oder wie man fremd wird und fremd sein kann. In: Schreiner, P., Sieg, U. & Elsenbast, V. (eds.): Handbuch Interreligiöses Lernen. Gütersloh, 217 – 228.

Messerschmidt, A. (2005b): Antiglobal oder postkolonial? Globalisierungskritik, antisemitische Welterklärungen und der Versuch, sich in Widersprüchen zu bewegen. In: Loewy, H. (ed.): Gerüchte über die Juden. Antisemitismus, Philosemitismus und aktuelle Verschwörungstheorien. Essen, 123 – 146.

Messerschmidt, A. (2003): Bildung als Kritik der Erinnerung. Lernprozesse in Geschlechterdiskursen zum Holocaust-Gedächtnis. Frankfurt/Main.

Müller, H. (1997): Anti-rassistische Pädagogik. In: Bernhard, A. & Rothermel, L. (eds.): Handbuch Kritische Pädagogik. Weinheim, 357 – 370.

Nestvogel, R. (2003) [1990]: Interkulturelles Lernen. Ein Beitrag zum Abbau von Fremdenfeindlichkeit und Ethnozentrismus? In: Lang-Wojtasik, G. & Lohrenscheid, C. (eds.): Entwicklungspädagogik – Globales Lernen – Internationale Bildungsforschung, Frankfurt/Main, 186 – 194.

Pfahl-Traughber, A. (2007): Ideologische Erscheinungsformen des Antisemitismus. In: Aus Politik und Zeitgeschichte, No. 31 (30/07/2007), 4 – 11.

Quindeau, I. (2007): Schuldabwehr und nationale Identität – Psychologische Funktionen des Antisemitismus. In: Brosch, M., Elm, M., Geißler, N., Simbürger, B. E. & von Wrochem, O. (eds.): Exklusive Solidarität. Linker Antisemitismus in Deutschland. Berlin, 157 – 164.

Rommelspacher, B. (1995): Dominanzkultur. Texte zu Fremdheit und Macht. Berlin.

Schweppenhäuser, H. (1975): Praesentia praeteritorium. Zu Benjamins Geschichtsbegriff. In: Bulthaup, P. (ed.): Materialien zu Benjamins Thesen „Über den Begriff der Geschichte". Frankfurt/Main, 7 – 22.

Terkessidis, M. (2010): Interkultur. Frankfurt/Main.

Welzer, H., Moller, S. & Tschuggnall, K. (2002): „Opa war kein Nazi". Nationalsozialismus und Holocaust im Familiengedächtnis. Frankfurt/Main.

Zimmerer, J. (2005): Deutscher Rassenstaat in Afrika. Ordnung, Entwicklung und Segregation in „Deutsch-Südwest" (1884-1915). In: Brumlik, M., Meinl, S. & Renz, W. (eds.): Gesetzliches Unrecht. Rassistisches Recht im 20. Jahrhundert. Frankfurt/Main, 135 – 153.

'Ethnic Conflicts' or Racism? – A German Case Study about "'Problematic' ways of acquiring NS-History in Multicultural Classrooms" re-interpreted from a "racism-critical"[1] perspective

Rosa Fava, University of Hamburg, Germany

Since the mid-1990s, a discussion within the fields of Teaching Methodologies for History as a school subject, Intercultural Education, and so called "Education after Auschwitz" (learning about and from[2] National-Socialism and more especially the Holocaust) has drawn attention to the fact that Germany is an immigrant society. A number of teachers and educators perceived this either as a "problem", a "challenge" or a "chance", but in any case as a starting point to develop new methods of teaching and redefine the topics and goals of a universal Holocaust Education in the country of the perpetrators. The presence of "immigrant children" (be they off-spring from immigrants or youth who immigrated themselves) in German classrooms first initiated a process of researching the particular characteristics of this "group", of pinpointing differences between these "students with migration background" and "German" students, and of designing special educational programmes for "multicultural groups of learners" (Fechler 2000: 209). Finally, Fechler et al.'s (2000) anthology *„,Erziehung nach Auschwitz' in der multikulturellen Gesellschaft"* ['Education after Auschwitz' in the multicultural society] became one of the starting points for a more systematic discussion about how to teach about the Holocaust in a country where not everyone can be addressed as being 'ethnically German'.

This article is based on material and findings from my on-going dissertation project, which deals with this discussion and its discourse structures: its main topics, underlying concepts, diverse intentions and effects, and in particular the images of the "immigrant children" that this discourse constructs. Fechler's (2000) article "*Zwischen Tradierung und Konfliktvermittlung. Über den Umgang mit ,problematischen' Aneignungsformen*[3] *der NS-Geschichte in multikul-*

1 For an explanation of the German term „Rassismuskritik" see footnote 5.

2 Public discourse and political rhetoric in Germany both focus on the objective of learning from National-Socialism in the sense of "learning a lesson from history" in order to strengthen democracy. But a first step into this direction for young people is to first of all learn something about this historical subject.

3 In German educational theory discourse the notion of "Aneignung" (acquisition) is often employed to emphasise a pedagogy that focuses on the learning subject: Children and adolescents are seen as actively involved in their own learning processes and not as passive recipients of canonical knowledge. In this creative process of acquiring knowledge

turellen Schulklassen" [Between handing-down history and mediating conflict. How to deal with ‚problematic' ways of acquiring NS-history in multicultural classrooms] provides particularly suitable material to expound on some of the characteristics of this discussion.

1. Research context and analytic framework of my re-interpretation

My dissertation research uses literature in different fields of educational science and pedagogical practice that deals with the issue of how learning about National Socialism can be adapted to an immigration context. My central research question can be summarised as follows: How are youths of non-German parentage perceived, described and attributed in this discourse?

My interest in this question arose while working as an educator at the concentration camp memorial of Neuengamme/Hamburg. I wondered about the contrast I perceived between the almost 'excited' way of speaking about "absolute differences" between students due to their ascribed nationality and the ensuing "great teaching difficulties" on the one hand, and the normality of everyday educational work at the memorial or at school on the other. In general, only few students are interested in history and politics, but most students I got to know as an educator at Neuengamme were keen to learn something about National Socialism, about which they hear and see so much in the media.

One of the principal results of my research is that discussion about "Education after Auschwitz in a multicultural society" can be understood as a way of extending the *general discourse on multiculturalism and on migrants* to another field, including not only typical patterns of perception (like equating "migrants" with "Turks" or more recently with "Muslims"), but also the silence on the issue of racism which is typical in the discourses about immigrants in Germany.

For this contribution, I endeavour to demonstrate an analytic discourse approach and to give some illustrative insights into typical discourse patterns. This is a challenging task, because in order to render the results of my analysis plausible, I need to present some in-depth critical re-reading of these discourse patterns through one particular author even though my analysis deals with *general discourse patterns*, and not with individual peculiarities. My interpretation refers to the discourse in the sense of a socially shared system of knowledge, developed by communicating about topics, and therefore I try to uncover the epis-

---

the learning subjects attribute their own meanings to "the facts", and it is unavoidable that at times their interpretation might be seen as objectively problematic.

temic substructures of communicating about "migrants" in relation to "Germans".

My re-interpretation of Fechler's text is based on new "critical race"[4] developments within the field of Intercultural Education inspired in part from Cultural Studies. A critical race approach, often linked to postcolonial theory, deals with the discursive construction of seemingly distinct social groups based on the ascription of "biological" or mainly "cultural" traits (e.g. "racial" or "ethnic groups") and with the social functions and effects of such constructions of (non-) belonging in the context of culturally diverse, pluralist modern societies. One common feature of these dominant discourse structures is the process of *Othering*. With *Othering* I denote speaking and writing about a group in a socially subordinate position which is portrayed as the counter-image of the self-image on the basis of one central criterion of difference and by projecting onto these "Others" qualities that are negated in the Self (e.g. emotional woman/rational man; proletarian relying on physical strength/intellectual bourgeois; cp. Thomas-Olalde & Velho's contribution in this volume). The concept of *Othering* has proved useful in the analysis of the sharply dichotomous distinctions ascribed to students based on their German/non-German parentage – a binary construction which turns "Germans" and "Non-Germans" into "homogeneous groups". It is remarkable that this discourse structure, in spite of its rhetoric of "*multi*culturalism", tends to fuse the non-German "Others" into a monolithic block of individuals whose predominant characteristic is to be "different" or simply "non-German", due to their "heritage culture".

4 Note of the translator: I translate the German term "Rassismuskritik" as "critical race studies", but I do not imply that this approach should be equated with what is known as "Critical Race Theory" (which was started in the USA in schools of law). The German "critical race" approach takes up recent developments and debates within the field of Intercultural Education in Germany about an adequate understanding and analysis of racism, a debate that is to a considerable extent indebted to theory developments in the Anglophone world. In contrast to the more traditional position of "Antirassismus" (anti-racism), the term "Rassismuskritik" (critical race studies) implies, for instance, that in a society structured by racism, it is not possible to claim a position outside of racist social structures. More particularly, the "critical race" approach endeavours to counteract a certain tendency of anti-racist writings which – while challenging the inequalities attached to social positions – actually reproduce and confirm, rather than question, the binary oppositions of racist discourses as such (e.g. white vs. black; Germans vs. foreigners/immigrants). From a "critical race studies" perspective the central objective is a deconstruction of these social categories as "given entities" by making visible their social and discursive production (for a detailed introduction see Mecheril et al. 2010).

When dealing with the discourse on multiculturalism in Germany, I will analyse presentations of the migrantised[5] or the "migrant-Others"[6] as social knowledge resources that inform the self-image of Germans. Terms such as "migrant-Others" or "national-ethno-cultural Others" (Mecheril 2004: 19) have been inspired by postcolonial studies and the analysis of *Othering* as discussed above. They have been coined in order to make visible the *construction* of categorical differences in the German immigration context: Those who are referred to as "migrant teenagers" in the educational debate are actually the *children or grandchildren* of immigrants, *born in Germany*, and an integral part of the German school age population; only few of them have immigrated themselves. The labels "migrant student", "migrant children", "migrant youth" etc. are, therefore, highly problematic because they construct these students as "the Others" and as not belonging; that is what the terms "migrant-Others" or "national-ethno-cultural Others" try to critically point out.

In my view, Fechler's (2000) work and in particular its international reception (Proske 205: 129), conveys problematic knowledge about the connection between learning about National-Socialism and teenagers of non-German parentage. In order to avoid misunderstandings I would like to underscore that I am interested in these epistemic foundations, not in individual traits of particular discourse agents or institutions. Individual authors, as I see it, give their voice to individually composed social concepts and ideas. In my contribution, I will present Fechler's article and demonstrate the processes of *Othering* it employs. I will show how the text exploits conceptions of "migrant adolescents" and the

5 The term "migrantised" is borrowed from Annette Seidel Arpaci (Research Fellow in the German Department at the University of Leeds; PhD-thesis at the Centre for Jewish Studies (Leeds) in 2005: "Holocaust Memory, Migration and 'Otherness' in Renationalised Germany"). The term highlights the process of "being made a migrant", in which mechanisms known as racialisation and culturalisation take effect. Quite often, however, this process of migrantisation works with hardly any ascription of specific characteristics, simply by making a dichotomous distinction between persons without German parents or grandparents and those whose parents and grandparents are perceived and recognised as Germans. To understand this phenomenon it is important to recall that until recently, Germany had no immigration policy which acknowledged immigrants and their children as Germans so that the status of "migrant" (a recent substitute for the term "Ausländer" = foreigner) was handed down from generation to generation, almost like an inherited characteristic. [The so-called "Aussiedler", people from Soviet Union and other countries from the "Eastern Block" whose ancestors were Germans, are officially acknowledged as "ethnic Germans" and have therefore direct access to German citizenship; but this is not relevant for my general discourse analysis or for the presented case study].

6 The term "migrant-Others" is a translation of the term Migrationsandere coined by Mecheril (2004: 23).

"multicultural society" in order to argue for certain shifts in a pedagogy dealing with learning about National-Socialism, shifts that must be interpreted within the context of debates conducted in a "society based on dominance" (*Dominanzgesellschaft*)[7]. One striking aspect of Fechler's text from a critical race studies perspective is its (relative) silence on racism, while dealing with education about NS-crimes that were based in racism and anti-Semitism, but also with the perspectives of "migrantised Others". Additionally, this text is suitable for such an analysis because the ascriptions to the national-ethno-cultural Others and the ways in which "Germans" and "non-Germans" are constructed in relation to each other remain very abstract. As will become clear, the epistemic basis of "difference" is not necessarily bound to value judgements and degradation of the Other.

The term "racism" does of course appear in texts about "Education after Auschwitz", since this education aims to prevent a *return* of racism in the sense of all forms of NS-biological racism and anti-Semitism (Jäger 1992).[8] Therefore, racism is perceived as a phenomenon of right-wing extremism, alien to democracy and found at the margins of society, or it is reduced to forms of domination like slavery or apartheid. This notion of racism holds in its line of sight racist violence, and possibly racist language, but rarely includes institutional discrimination. My use of the term racism, however, refers to a way of structuring society that produces social inequality, material and symbolic hierarchies as well as inclusion and exclusion. Like sexism, racism is present at all social levels, from the economy to conditions of representation, and the development of subjectivity, including the subjective identities of "Germans" and "migrants" (Terkessidis 2004; 1998). It is not a moral notion, but refers to an instance of power that structures everyday life.

7 The term Dominanzgesellschaft ('dominance society' or 'society based on dominance') goes back to Birgit Rommelpacher's analysis of the "culture of dominance" (Dominanzkultur) (Rommelspacher 1995). The term denotes a form of dominance that goes beyond simple relations between majority and minority as the more common German term Mehrheitsgesellschaft ('majority society') suggests.

8 National-Socialism fuelled all kinds of (partly death-bringing) racisms – against Sinti and Romanies, against the population of East- and South-East-Europe as well as other enemy nations, against forced labourers from different countries, against Black Germans and also against smaller groups of people from other nations.

2. Fechler's Case Study

Bernd Fechler holds a degree in education and specialised in conflict management and mediation. When the article was published in 2000, he was in charge of educational issues at the *Jugendbegegnungsstätte Anne Frank* (a Youth Community Centre dedicated to the memory of Anne Frank) in Frankfurt, which had opened three years earlier. The Youth Community Centre (YCC) explores contemporary forms of remembrance of the Holocaust and its victims while paying attention to racism and conflicts among students, in particular by methods of mediation (Fechler, Kößler & Liebertz-Groß 2000: 17). The objective of Fechler's article is to present the educational approach of the Centre, and focuses on a classroom conflict that was addressed by the YCC's mediation program. The author aims to propagate certain methods of conflict mediation while recommending new, less morally-laden approaches to teaching about the German past. Fechler chose this case because it was in his opinion particularly dramatic, but nevertheless typical (209)[9]. My re-interpretation of the case is necessarily limited because I have no means to investigate it beyond how Fechler presented it.

2.1 Scope of Fechler's arguments

First of all, the title of the article – "Between handing-down history and mediating *conflict*. How to deal with '*problematic*' ways of acquiring NS-history in *multicultural* classrooms"[10] – conveys connotations common to mainstream discourses about the immigrant population and their descendants in Germany, namely: problems, tensions and violence. In this mainstream discourse, the term "multicultural" has two different layers of meaning: On the one hand "multicultural" is employed as a code for "foreigners", "migrants" or "Germans with migration background"; in other words people who are perceived as, in a fundamental way, "culturally different". On the other hand and closely connected to this first meaning, the term "multicultural" also conveys the idea of neighbourhoods in conflict because of distinct "cultures" or "ethnic groups" which compete for limited resources and representation. In the first case the people themselves, the "migrants", appear as problematic, whereas the second case implies an abstract incompatibility ("difference"), for which none of the groups involved are held directly responsible. At any rate, the use of the term suggests that the

9 When quoting from or referring to the analysed article, I only give the page numbers. All quotations from the German text were translated by the editor H.N.

10 The quotation marks indicate that Fechler thinks the term "problematic" not entirely adequate; but he never elaborates on this issue.

conflicts at stake would not be an issue in a supposedly 'original, mono-cultural context', so that – indirectly – "the Others" are made out to be the source of the problem after all. Thus the title suggests: The "handing-down" of the 'German' "NS-history" in "multicultural classrooms" is essentially loaded with (ethnic) "conflicts" for which "migrants" are implicitly responsible.

2.2 What happened according to Fechler's account of events?

In early 1999, a 10th grade students group (*Realschulklasse*)[11] visited the Youth Community Centre for an exhibition about the persecution of the Jewish population. In the course of this visit the group was thrown into "turmoil", as Fechler reports, when seven of the teenagers[12] were found to have written "Neo-Nazi slogans" (207) into the guestbook of the Community Centre. Other students reported this incident to the teacher, demanding that the "miscreants" (ibid.) be punished. Fechler puts the "Neo-Nazi slogan" of the "miscreants"[13] into a footnote: "*Für unser Reiches Macht, für Deine Größe und Deine Herrlichkeit, jetzt und immerdar D S H*" (207, footnote 1) [For the Power of our Reich, for Thee Greatness and Thee Magnificence, now and forever D S H]. The letters D S H are an abbreviation for "*Deutschland Sieg Heil*" (Germany Victory Hail), as the writers of the note later on revealed.

Fechler reports that he offered to mediate the quarrel and that he detected "in the course of the heated and aggressive debate a deep division between one big group of students from migrant families, on the one hand, and a minority of

11 Editorial note: The German school system has a highly socially selective, hierarchic structure. The traditional types of school are (apart from Special Schools) Gymnasium, Realschule and Hauptschule into which children are streamed after the completion of grade 4. Officially this streaming is based on "ability and achievement", of course, but in practice, as empiric research has proven, the social background of the family, including national origins, is the decisive factor of placement. The Realschule is the "middle" type of school.

12 Editorial note: All of these seven students were "ethnic Germans". Those students who were upset about the Hitler quotation and reported it to the teacher were all "of immigrant background". This is apparently the basis for the interpretation of the conflict as an "ethnic conflict" by Fechler, even though he tends to avoid national and ethnic labels. Since Rosa Fava, the author of this article, objects to this ethnifying interpretation, she, too, is reluctant to attribute the students in such a manner. Nevertheless, English speaking proofreaders suggested we add this information here to prevent misunderstandings.

13 The two somewhat outdated German terms Aufruhr (turmoil; also: revolt, unrest) and Missetäter (miscreant, culprit, wrongdoer) indicate Fechler's ironic perspective, who probably wants to point out that the situation – though momentarily rather dramatic in appearance – could have just as well been treated as a minor problem.

'ethnic Germans', on the other hand" (208). According to Fechler, the "students from migrant families" insulted "their German classmates" (who had written down the Hitler quotation) as "Nazis" and "racists.[14] Those who were called to account for their offence (in Fechler's words: "those who were attacked") were hardly able to justify what they did (as Fechler puts it: to "defend themselves"). Fechler reports finding himself in a "paradoxical situation" where he felt compelled to "support the party of the miscreants at times much more intensely" (217) because without his help they had been unable to make themselves heard. Their spokesperson "Sascha" finally accepted responsibility for what he called the "stupid slogan" (208), but then moved on to present "himself and his friends as the real victims of racist discrimination in the school class group" (ibid.). The argument ended "without reconciliation", and then the "Turkish student Murat" made a comment which more than anything else bemused Fechler: "*Die das getan haben, euch Nazis sollte man doch alle vergasen!*" (ibid.) [Those who have done this, you Nazis should all be gassed!]

After Murat's threat, Fechler was not able to maintain the role of the "all-party mediator who abstains from finding the solution". He explains how he started to give a "lecture about the specificity of the genocide of the Jews and about the killing technology of the National-Socialists as opposed to present-day forms of racism", but that he then recognised how "out of place" his explanations were. Fechler discusses his own "knee-jerk reflex" by pondering the meaning of the key notions: The remark of the student expressed an "archaic model of justice", which demands that the culprit must receive a punishment in the form of his own means of offence. The boy put this thought into words by using a "dramatic rhetoric figure" similar to figures of speech "regularly employed by adolescents in Frankfurt amongst each other."[15] His "categorical mistake", however, consisted in "equating the historical 'Nazis' and the 'Nazis' in his students group who he apparently placed on the same level". But Murat had been unaware of the "monstrosity" of the "historical topos" of "gassing (all cited passages from pp. 217-219).

Afterwards, the incident became the topic of a class conference attended by the school's headmaster and the parents of the seven sloganeers, an unusual practice for conflict mediation involving students. As a result of the conference the participants agreed that it had been the intervention of the "foreign classmates" (*ausländische Mitschüler*) that had turned the "minor incident" into a

14 As mentioned above, in Germany the term "racism" is usually applied to NS-anti-Semitism, so that the term "racist" can be interpreted as a synonym for "Nazi".

15 "Ich mach dich tot" [I'll kill you] and "Ich stech dich ab" [I'll slit your throat] are examples for this style of speaking provided by Fechler (218).

"*politically* explosive scandal" (my emphasis). From the point of view of the parents and the school administration, as Fechler critically observes, "marking the slogans as the doing of 'Nazis' had gone beyond the limits of good taste and thus injured the reputation of the school as well as the dignity of the "Anne Frank Youth Community Centre". According to Fechler, the result of the class conference was a reversal of the guilt/innocence-relation, with both parties to be punished by notes in their personal files (212f.).

A couple of days after this conflict, the three boys predominantly responsible for the incident came to the Youth Community Centre to apologize. Fechler emphasises their servility and their desire to receive an extreme punishment. He suggests that they would have been satisfied if they had been ordered to clean the toilets of the Community Centre with toothbrushes, a form of punishment they had been told about by a now-elderly witness of the Holocaust when he recalled his life at an NS-elite boarding school. Fechler presents the students' willingness to perform such a punishment as features of an authoritarian character, which studies about adolescent right-wing-extremism recognised as a central factor in the affinity to right-wing attitudes and activities. But Sascha and the others were also determined "that their classmates should realise that they were no 'Nazis'" (222).

Fechler and a colleague were invited to the school several days after the class conference in order to moderate more in-depth mediation. Upon arrival in the classroom, the mediators were greeted with outrage by students of non-German parentage at the equal punishment of both parties involved in the conflict. Thus, as Fechler reports, the students of German parentage had been at a disadvantage from the beginning and had attempted to "duck down out of sight" (223). This description of the "ethnic-German" students is the only instance where Fechler uses such a vivid verbal image bound to arouse sympathy. The discussion reached a turning point when the slogan writers were asked to explain their intentions in writing their note into the guestbook. One of them explained that the words were taken from a "motivating speech by Hitler to his soldiers" (223)[16], which he had copied from a computer encyclopaedia. Based on this in-

---

16 It is a speech that Hitler made on March 12th, 1938, in front of the local population of Linz, only a few hours before the official annexation of Austria. His final sentence was: „Sehen Sie in den deutschen Soldaten, die aus allen Gauen des Reiches in diesen Stunden einmarschieren, opferbereite und opfergewillte Kämpfer für des ganzen großen deutschen Volkes Einheit, für des Reiches Macht, für seine Größe und für seine Herrlichkeit, jetzt und immerdar! Deutschland, Sieg Heil!" (Domarus 1973: 817f). [Acknowledge the German soldiers, who in these hours come marching in from all districts of the Reich (Gauen = old term for tribal settlement areas in Germanic times, borrowed by the Nazis to denote administrative districts) as warriors prepared and willing to sacrifice their lives

formation, the "decisive argument" which calmed down the discussion was then made by an "Italian girl": She said that it was "normal" to motivate "one's own" soldiers to defend their country. This objective was accepted as universal, and independent of nationality (223). In other words, she exonerated Sascha and his group from quoting typical Nazi-propaganda. In the end, it was her argument that helped resolve the conflict.

2.3 Fechler's contextualisation of the incident

In the course of in-depths reflections, Fechler justifies his approach vis-à-vis history teachers and disseminators of the, as he puts it, morally loaded "Education after Auschwitz". The "close connection of the moral dimension with the question of identity", or in other words, the question of collective guilt which according to Fechler is barely comprehensible to young people, had the effect of pushing for quick and unambiguous positions (209) and therefore led also to polarization and a breakdown of communication (210). To illustrate his point, Fechler discusses in great detail the behaviour of the three sloganeering boys who categorised themselves politically as "rather right" (221). They had reacted with great relief to his breaking down of "guilt complexes and projections": "Nearly incredulous did they receive the news from me [as an authoritative source] that in these days and times nobody would still seriously claim that they were personally associated with guilt of the crimes of the NS-time" (221). By presenting his approach in this manner, Fechler criticises established "ritual patterns" (214) of dealing with the NS-crimes and guilt. He also interrogates his own biases and involvement in these patterns by pointing out, among other things, his emotional upset when the word "gassing" was uttered. In Fechler's view, the case analysis illustrates those characteristics of the discourse about the NS-past that help to construct "identity" in a framework of moral integrity.

By problematizing his own reaction, Fechler challenges a "generation of teachers" (himself included), "who in the spirit of the motto 'Prevent the Beginnings' (*Wehret den Anfängen*) feels obliged to adhere to a particular understanding of 'Education after Auschwitz' and who very often approaches the subject with a distinct moral impetus" (209). For this perspective would "lead – nearly unavoidably – to a wrong appraisal and to a struggle with an imaginary opponent" (209). In my opinion, however, this self-critical appraisal does not really address the 'kneejerk reflex' Fechler reports. An attitude which was obliged to the injunctions "Prevent the Beginnings" and "Never again (fascism)" would

for the unity of the whole great German Volk, for the power of the Reich, for its greatness and its magnificence, now and forever! Germany, Victory Hail!].

elect the "rather right" youths as the "imaginary opponent" in order to construct a self-image ("identity") of a morally integrated personality. But with respect to Sascha and his friends, Fechler's attitude appears remarkably relaxed. It was Murat's words that, according to Fechler's account, triggered the "red alarm button" and a "moralizing inquisition" (218).

Incidents like the one presented here, where there is resistance against the actions of "rather right" students, can occur in every classroom. There could be politically-left students who scandalize Hitler quotations. There may be students who feel threatened by "a show of support for the NS-regime", as Fechler admits at one point (208), and who are targets for conflict with "rather right" students because they fit into a right-wing concept of the enemy for a number of reasons like their choice of music, style, or leisure activities, or their sexual orientation, political views, religion or ethnicity. However, Fechler chooses to focus on the conflict between moralizing teachers and "multiculturalism": What "teenagers in multicultural groups of students make reference to" cannot, according to Fechler, "be unambiguously assigned to definite positions", but "depending on context, different meanings [could] be attached" (209).[17] In this case, says Fechler, the "slogans in the guestbook" were exploited to fuel conflicts around collective identities and to compete for victim status (225). It is this interpretation of the incident that I intend to deconstruct.

3. Controversial re-interpretation

3.1 Differences in the pedagogical responses to right-wing extremism

The quarrel among the students caused by the Hitler quotation resembles other cases discussed in the mainstream literature about pedagogical responses to right-wing youths. Fechler himself has co-edited a brochure in which similar actions of right-wing oriented students of German family background are described (Youth Community Centre Anne Frank 2003). The same brochure also mentions cases of migrantised students being threatened by others in the classroom (Kaletsch 2003: 81). But there is a marked difference between these mainstream articles about the topic and the article under discussion: The case presented here is not about *teachers* who are "no longer prepared to dismiss [racist] everyday scenes at school as merely silly remarks" (ibid.), but about *teenagers from historically non-German family backgrounds* who turn into agents of resistance against racist actions of classmates. For these reasons, Fechler seems to

17 Why references to National Socialism made in the context of "monoculturalism" would be unambiguous, regardless of context, is not explained.

deal with the case as an issue of "multiculturalism", and not "right-wing extremism". The label "multicultural classroom" shifts the problematizing gaze onto the migrant-Others. Thus the students who criticize the guestbook entry are not portrayed as guardians of democracy against the political Right as would, for example, social workers and teachers involved in preventive education against right-wing extremism. Rather, they are presented as "migrant youths" who appropriate 'German history' in a problematic manner and exploit it strategically for their own ends. From this perspective, 'classically' problematic ways of appropriating the NS-past, meaning the revitalizing use of NS-slogans, are denied relevancy. This shift of focus avoids the fact that Hitler's words were written down at a place dedicated to acknowledging NS-victims and to opposition against National-Socialism, and that they *can* therefore be read as expressing dissent against this dedication.[18] Moreover, this action of students from 'original' German families – recording excerpts from one of Hitler's speeches at a Holocaust memorial and education centre while in the presence of those who are not recognised as Germans – reveals an aggressive potential not only vis-à-vis the commemoration of the victims and the dealing with the past crimes, but also vis-à-vis the present national-ethno-cultural Others.

3.2 Culturalisation

The conflict between the teenagers is not treated as a political conflict in the conventional sense, e.g. as a conflict between revitalized nationalist attitudes and resistance against these attitudes; nor does the author relate the "deep division" of the students group into "students from migrant families" and "ethnic Germans" to the meaning of the utterances in question. Fechler ignores the fact that the interpellation[19] of "Germany" implies an interpellation of subjects that are discriminated in terms of 'nationality', so that these subjects are once again divided along the lines of 'Germanness'. Taking account of the reported "*deep* division" among the students and the attitudes of the "rather right" students within this group, it is fair to assume that this has not been the first time that the latter have expressed national chauvinism and racism. The author, however, shifts the quarrel into the sphere of "culture". In accordance with the paradigm of multiculturalism, he interprets the conflict as a struggle for limited resources by different particular groups, even though he does not explicitly define them as

18 Fechler does mention this himself at this point of his analysis, but he does not attach any importance to this observation (214).

19 The term "interpellation" is used in the sense of Louis Althusser's political philosophy. French: interpellation; German: Anrufung.

"cultures" or "ethnic groups".[20] This shift has the effect of negating the structural hierarchy between the two groups. Fechler is quite aware of the fact that his interpretation moves the conflict out of the conventional sphere of political debate, which defines this kind of conflict as a "democratic core group" struggling against "the Right", and he reasons accordingly: The "question how 'Nazi like' those entry notes" might be is expressly of no interest to him (207), and in his view, "the 'right-wing youths' were not the problem in the first place…" (216). Moreover, he does not explain why references to National-Socialism do not reinforce divisions between students from families from German and non-German origin. By dismissing the gravity of quoting Hitler, a public declaration in support of a racist German nationalism, he misses the implied threat of figurative as well as real violence against migrantised populations in present-day Germany.[21]

3.3 Projecting the problem onto the Others

In his presentation of the case, Fechler quite differently deals with four problematic references to the NS-past. First, Fechler calls the Hitler quotations written down by the "rather right" teenagers *neo*-Nazi slogans, thus interpreting them as a current phenomenon, even though they are in fact a detailed historical quotation.[22] He relegates the NS-words to a footnote, he does not analyze their "Nazi" content (207), and with respect to their effect on readers who are not

20 Fechler only uses national labels whenever he thinks them necessary to describe and explain the opposition between the students. His uses a variety of labels at different times, thus demonstrating the problems inherent in all forms of labelling.

21 In Germany, (grand-)children of immigrants grow up in a social climate which instils in them the feeling that they are perceived as members of a different nationality, as not really belonging and ultimately as people who might be disposed of, even if one of their parents is German. Not all of them possess a secure residence permit, some of them even have restricted access to basic civil rights. The students who were about 15 years old in 1999 might well have consciously witnessed the arson attacks and the pogrom like attacks of the 1990s in reunified Germany. Depending on their place of living they might be confronted on an everyday basis with a hegemony of right-wing youth culture or with the strategy of creating "nationally liberated zones" by neo-Nazis (= terrorising and attacking people identified as "non-German" until they move out of the district).

22 The term "neo-Nazi slogan" has two meanings: It may refer to a historical formula such as "Sieg Heil" re-used in present-day Germany. More adequately, however, it refers to a recent formula, created by right-wing followers themselves to make reference to the present-day context, such as "Türken raus" ('Turks out', that is: a demand for/threat of deportation). In this light, the Hitler quotation is actually a historical formula and therefore rather a 'Nazi slogan'. And in general, Fechler uses this term as well.

recognised as Germans he merely notes that "the migrant youths" might "feel threatened" by it (208). But even this potential effect is not considered relevant; rather, Fechler proposes that this is a consequence of a false equivalence: "Comparisons between the persecution of the Jews and present-day racism are (too) quickly drawn" (208). With this he suggests that the "youths from migrant families" had "quickly drawn comparisons", without mentioning what these might have been. In order to feel threatened by "neo-Nazi slogans", however, it is not necessary for migrantised people to compare themselves with anyone else, particularly not with someone from the past. Second and third are references to the "Turkish" boy's reference to "gassing" and his labelling of the "rather right" teenagers as "Nazis". These words are used by Fechler twice as subtitles (207 and 217), and he presents them in great detail within the context in which they were uttered (208, 217ff). The label "Nazi" he judges as a "categorical mistake" (218) and the term "gassing" as "blasphemous" vis-à-vis the victims (219).[23] In his view, the use of these terms places conscientious educators at the core of the dilemma. Notably, however, Fechler treats the label "Nazi" in direct contrast to the slogan of the "rather right" teenagers; instead of reading "Nazi" as a simplified form of the equally colloquial term "neo-Nazi", which he uses himself, he interprets the label as a historical term. Fourth is the reduction of the NS-war of expansion and extermination to an 'ordinary' war by the students. Fechler discusses this problematic way of dealing with history, which he tolerated in this particular situation in order to resolve the tense atmosphere.

In his presentation and analysis, Fechler constructs only the actions of the students without German parentage as a social problem in the context of a "plural immigration society". It is interesting to observe the varying importance attached to different problematic terms and quotations. On the one hand, Fechler distinguishes between the two expressions Murat uses – "Nazis" and "gassing", and on the other hand between the colloquial term "Nazis" and the words by Hitler which, at the time, could only be accessed either via specialist literature or via right-wing forums.[24]

First of all, Fechler exonerates, of all things, the use of the word "gassing" by reasoning that it does not deviate from the common way of speaking amongst adolescents. This is surprising because it can be argued that the term "gassing" (*vergasen*), a collectively organised form of systematic killing and factory-like extermination, greatly deviates from individual murder fantasies expressed in

23 More adequate might perhaps be the term "disrespectful", as "blasphemous" actually refers to dealings with a deity.

24 Today, the Hitler speech can also be found on internet sites which present the speech as a historical document.

phrases such as "*Ich stech dich ab*" [I'll slit your throat] (218). In fact, it is exactly this deviation which defines the "monstrosity" of National-Socialism. On the other hand, Fechler gives considerably more importance to the label "Nazis" than might be expected, and states that by using this term, Murat was putting the "historical 'Nazis' and the 'Nazis' in his classroom" "on the same level" (ibid.). Whether the "rather right" students had actually put themselves "on the same level" as the historical National-Socialists by writing down a lengthy Hitler quotation, which might be assessed as a more significant (self-)positioning than Murat's short invective "Nazis", is of no interest to Fechler. This is worth exploring, because in Germany the term "Nazis" is widely used, in the absence of more adequate terms, to label "rather right" youths.[25] Fechler himself does not know what else to call these teenagers, who define themselves as "rather right" and who appear to fit this category: They carry Hitler quotations with them or memorise them, they study encyclopaedia for information about National-Socialism and are so well-informed about the legal limits of right-wing activities that they do not spell out the slogan "Sieg Heil" (because in Germany the use of this slogan is liable to prosecution), they feel attracted to military life, identify with Germany, and are fascinated by the narratives of former NS-elite-students. Fechler wonders, "So, how am I to categorize the teenagers who had been outed by their classmates as 'Nazis'? In my view, the 'right-wing youths' were not the problem in the first place…" (216). By capping "Nazi" with quotation marks throughout his text, he shirks responsibility for finding a more appropriate label. This would be fine, except that Fechler blames 10th-grader Murat for the general lack of adequate terminology in Germany to refer to such (racist and post-NS) phenomena. Only by stating that Murat equated Sascha and his friends to historical National-Socialists can Fechler propose an "appropriation" of NS-history by the migrantised student rather than by the "'ethnic' German" students.

Fechler's disparate evaluation of the terms "Nazis" and "gassing" also calls for further inquiry. Reading Fechler's report of events, it is clear that it is really the term "gassing" ("killing by using poisonous gas") that he considers the "worse" expression, which "triggered" (217) his "kneejerk reflex" (218). He also identifies the term "gassing" as the one through which Murat equated Sascha and the other slogan writers with historical Nazis, and one which was mediated by an "archaic model of justice". However, Fechler then claims that the term "gassing" resembles other aggressive expressions used in everyday adolescent communication, and by decontextualizing the term from "NS-history", he considerably diminishes its importance. Interestingly, he does not suggest that

25 Fechler himself distinguishes elsewhere "so called normal teenagers" from "right oriented" ones and two categories of "right-wing extremist" youths (Fechler 2003: 44).

Murat's murderous fantasies might put himself on the same level as National-Socialists. Two points can be made with respect to this seemingly contradictory dealing with Murat's use of NS-specific language. Firstly, if Fechler put more importance on identifying with NS-methods of killing, it would be difficult to maintain his supposition that the migrantised adolescents had "subjectively" identified with the (Jewish) NS-victims (213). Though, in the face of this fantasy of agency, power and resistance against a de-humanized enemy who should be "gassed", one might conclude that if Murat identifies with anyone at all, it is with the historical murderers rather than their victims. Secondly, the point is irrelevant for Fechler, as he only accords significance as an ascription of "identity" to the insult of the "German" students as "Nazis".

3.4 "Identification with NS-victims" as an ascription to migrant-Others

By focussing on the term "Nazis", Fechler can interpret this conflict within his general criticism of identity constructions within discourses about Auschwitz, which is the main objective of this case-study. But again, in Fechler's analysis the problem is not the identification of the "rather right" adolescents with Hitler, but rather how those students who denounce the guestbook entry construct their own identities:

> [The] vacillation of aggressor-victim-relations, the struggle for the status of the victim as the status of moral integrity, seems to be characteristic for any identity forming dealings with the Holocaust. For young migrants the identification with the victims seems to be self-evident, even though it is a historically problematic response. More especially, they had a genuine interest in escalating the conflict because they had reason to hope that they might be able to make symbolic capital out of scandalizing the behaviour of their German classmates and to draw attention to their everyday experiences of discrimination (213).

Fechler does not offer any support for his claim that the "foreign students" were identifying with the Holocaust victims. Similar to his claim that "comparisons between the persecution of the Jews and present-day racism are (too) quickly drawn" (208), he again suggests that "(f)or young migrants the identification with the victims seems to be self-evident, even though it is a historically problematic response" (213). Three times, Fechler cites the "*historically problematic* responses" by "foreign students who subjectively identify with the victims of NS crimes" (ibid.) without giving examples of how they did this (208, and twice 213). He neither includes quotations nor spells out the content of the comparison or the identification. All we learn from his text is that "the foreign students" used the terms "racists" and "Nazis" (208). The lack of examples is also remarkable given that this is the only passage which clearly refers to the title of the article "'*problematic*' ways of acquiring NS-*history*". The article appears to lose its subject. For Fechler, identifications and comparisons are apparent and drawn from his 'conclusion' quoted above. There exists in his view a general mechanism of "identity forming dealings with the Holocaust" in the form of a "struggle for the status of the victim as the status of moral integrity" which produces a variety of identities which for "young migrants" may be formed by an "identification with the victims". Just because this "seems to be self-evident". However, in this context, it does not make much sense to connect the denunciation of the guest book entry with the "identification" with Holocaust victims, because the entry does not refer to NS victims. It appears to be a complicated mental operation for the migrantised youths who – when reading an interpellation of a timeless "Germany" – are supposed to identify with the former victims of former National-Socialists, rather than to feel attacked by an aggressive nationalism of their fellow students who they equate with present-day (neo-)Nazis. Fechler offers no proof for his assumption that the students claimed that their situation was on a par with the "persecution of the Jews". It is not plausible to suggest that the students need historical masks to enter into the conflict. Such a suggestion negates the current reality of racism. When speaking about the students from families of German background, on the other hand, Fechler notes that Sascha and his friends presented themselves "as the real victims of racist discrimination in the classroom" (208) without assuming an identification with Holocaust victims. This articulation is acceptable to him whereas the one put forward by the migrantised youth is wrong: When they call Sascha and his friends "racists" and "Nazis", then they supposedly compare their own situation with the Holocaust. Thus racism is made 'unspeakable'. Interestingly, the assumption that the "young migrants" were "identifying" with the Holocaust victims comes up at precisely the moment when the quoting of Hitler words expresses an identification of "ethnic German" students with the NS-aggressors which – at a place like the Anne-Frank-Community-Centre – *can* be interpreted as approval of the murdering of the Jewish population. The virtual representation of the Holocaust victims is a result of the guestbook entry of the "ethnic Germans"; Fechler projects this representation onto "the Others".

3.5 Aggressor-victim-reversal

Fechler is not only silent about the historical self-positioning of the "rather right" boys, but he even interprets their recourse to Hitler's interpellation of Germany as a form of "self-assertion". He speculates that the quoting of the Hitler speech could

> „also be interpreted as the defiant attempt of self-assertion of a group who feels inferior to their 'foreign' classmates. Their pointing out the 'power', 'greatness' and 'magnificence' of the German Reich can be read like the clandestine manifest of solemn self-enhancement" (225).[26]

There are two problems with this interpretation. First, if their aim is self-enhancement with respect to their classmates, it is difficult to see why the "group who feels inferior" does not simply write Hitler's words on the blackboard of their classroom. Moreover, it should be noted that "the group" specifically chose to write in the guestbook of an institution that commemorates the victims and is, after the hubris of the NS-vision of German world domination, a symbol for a new post-NS national humility. This is what Sascha and his friends opposed by their conjuring-up of greatness and power. But it seems that Fechler intends to remove the event by all means from this 'monocultural German' context. Second, Fechler ignores that the "self-assertion", in the view of Sascha and the other boys who signed the note, works by an interpellation of soldierdom and the idea of a 'timeless Germany'. The youth understand, at least rudimentarily, that these ideas historically implied the subjugation and destruction of everyone and everything "non-German". To understand this process as "self-assertion" or "self-enhancement" is based on a remarkable image of the Self at stake. This image of self-at-risk bolsters the assumption that the "rather right" youths imagine themselves indeed as aggressive German national chauvinists. The term "self-assertion" (*Selbstbehauptung*) – a stronger term than "self-defence" – suggests that the students saw themselves as oppressed and subjugated vis-à-vis the "Others" who threatened their existence as Germans. Fechler, however, does not report any initial act of aggression by students of non-German parentage, unless their greater number in itself constituted a kind of attack. His interpretation of the incident as "self-assertion" performs exactly the aggressor-victim-reversal which the author himself had earlier criticised: The writing down of a National-Socialist slogan is not seen as an attack (against the social acceptance of guilt), but as an expression of feeling victimised (by "foreigners")[27]. The scandalizing of the note, however, does not qualify as protest

---

26 One may wonder why – if this is supposedly a "clandestine" self-enhancement – the students use the freely accessible guestbook of a public institution for this purpose and why they sign the note with their names.

27 Ironically, this would precisely constitute an expression of German nationalism before, during and after National-Socialism. Starting with the French "foreign domination" in the beginning of the 19th century up to the "bad reputation" of Germany abroad after the arson attacks against immigrants in the 1990s, the national narrative always claimed a victim's status of Germans.

against national chauvinism, but as a "historically problematic" identification[28] with the NS-victims.

3.6 *Fashioning Germans as collective victims*

The way Fechler presents the situation in the students group it would seem that "socially and structurally, in many ways disadvantaged and discriminated migrant youths are those who have the upper hand within the classroom" (225). This perspective of migrant students having the "upper hand" is reinforced by his choice of words, when he speaks, for instance, of the "attacked students" instead of the students who were called to account for the entry into the guestbook. He does not explain what it means to "have the upper hand within the classroom". Moreover, Fechler only analyzes the situation after the quarrel, and says nothing about the situation before. Sascha and his friends see themselves as "the real victims" of racism (208), and Fechler suggests that this view is valid. He speaks pejoratively about "incessant reproaches and accusations" of the migrantised students (217), without ever quoting the content of these reproaches. In summary, the suggestion that even before the quarrel the "non-German" students had the "upper hand" is contradictory and without proof. After the quarrel, he again ascribes power to the migrant youths over the "'ethnic' Germans": Whereas before the quarrel at the Community Centre some of the students of German parentage had, according to Fechler, not categorised themselves in "ethnic terms",

> „the unrelenting attitude of the migrant youths [had] put those undecided Germans, who did not support the Nazi slogans of their classmates, in a precarious position. As 'Germans' they were forced into community with those who were labelled as 'Nazis' (225f.).

But Fechler quotes Murat with the following words: "*Those who have done that, you Nazis* should all be gassed" (208, my emphasis). With these words, Murat refers to a single act by a specified group of people. And no matter what else he claims in the course of his text (217), Fechler also notes that these words refer to the "German classmates who wrote the entry into the guestbook" (218). The qualification of the accused as "*German* classmates" is made by Fechler himself.

---

28 The question may arise in which way present-day actions should be historically problematic. This is a short-hand formulation which summarises the following thought which is central for the discourse about Auschwitz: By making comparisons, equating, and forming analogies between current forms of racism and NS anti-Semitism, in particular, the singular specificity of the annihilation of the Jewish people is negated. This mechanism is often interpreted as a form of refusal to accept guilt.

The passive construction, "they were forced into community" assumes an external "force" which affects Germans when some of them are "labelled as 'Nazis'". The "undecided Germans", however, are assumed to naturally identify with the "community" even though they "did not support the Nazi slogans of their classmates". So it would seem that they place more importance on the shared nationality with the "rather right" students than on the rejection of the Hitler quotation.

But even the fact that the "undecided *Germans*" (as Fechler labels them) identify with those Germans who wrote the Nazi slogans instead of distancing themselves from National-Socialism is blamed on "the Others". Now it is the "undecided Germans" who appear as the victims.[29] Fechler himself discusses the widespread mechanism of externalising guilt by dealing inadequately with the NS-past in the German public (212f.), but in this context he does not realise that his interpretation follows the same pattern.

3.7 Denial of racism

Fechler ascribes to the students without German parentage the power to "force a community" amongst the "Germans", although his presentation of the conflict and its consequences (the class conference and its verdict) actually demonstrates the lack of power of the migrantised students in the face of a dominant German group united against the accusations. As recounted above, after the incident in the Community Centre, a closed front of slogan writers, their parents and the headmaster – all of German origin – formed in opposition to those who had scandalised the guestbook entry. On the one hand, this mirrors the lack of power of migrantised youths in a society structured by racism, in which positions of power are rarely held by migrant-Others. Part of these structures are subtle mechanisms that result from the alienation immigrant parents often feel toward schools compared to non-immigrant parents, even though in this case, Fechler does not explain why it was only parents of German origin who felt authorised to participate in the class conference. But throughout Germany, it is rare even today to find headmasters, class tutors or history teachers who share the experience of exclusion and humiliation with the migrantised students and who, when involved in such a quarrel, might make sure that such experiences are included in the evaluation of the events. On the other hand, this demonstrates how German agents (the school administration, parents, students) form a collective which punishes Others who dare touch on a sore spot by pointing out that it is

29 Again we find traces of the narrative of German nationalism: The 'Ausland' (foreign countries) are to blame for the fact that the Germans elected Hitler, because these countries humiliated Germany in the contract of Versailles after the First World War.

still possible for some people to find it reasonable to reactivate Hitler's words, at a place dedicated to the victims of the NS-crimes no less. Again we can observe a typical reflex which Fechler himself criticises as a mechanism of rejection of guilt that has existed since the end of the Second World War (213f.).

The injustice, however, which is done to the migrantised students by their punishment, remains unnamed in Fechler's article. The "outrage" which this causes among the national-ethno-cultural Other students is merely described as a form of aggression (222f.). Fechler remains silent about the exclusion from positions of power over several generations, and he separates the microcosm of the classroom from its social context: "With respect to this, the relations within the classroom were not a direct reflection of the social power relations" (225). This assessment ignores how the class conference reflected *exactly* the social power relations.

3.8 Self-reformation as Germans via the scapegoat strategy

Fechler points out that the Youth Community Centre was generally perceived "symbolically as a memorial for the Jewish victims" and thus as a Jewish institution (215; 220f.), and that it was shameful for the headmaster and the parents to fall into disrepute with such an institution due to inappropriate behaviour (212ff.). Such a reaction is based on the imagination of a Jewish authority of control and punishment and the feeling that 'one' has to be well-behaved 'as a German' vis-à-vis that authority – a typical mental pattern concordant with anti-Semitism after Auschwitz (cp. Messerschmidt in this volume). Fechler criticises this perspective without highlighting the punch line of this critical review: "Germans" clear themselves vis-à-vis a 'Jewish supervisory authority' in the form of the Community Centre of accusations of support for NS concepts by blaming the "foreigners" in their midst. Those who are themselves threatened by the fascination with Hitler get punished for it and thus are doubly disregarded: They are scapegoats, and the fact that the revival of Hitler's words violates their well-being is not acknowledged. The members of the dominant society thus have no need to either deal with present-day racism or with the continued ties to National-Socialism.

4. Attempt at an explanation

To summarise one can say that Fechler locates the cause for the conflict – as hinted at by the title of his article – with the "young migrants" and their behaviour, even though the "'problematic' ways of acquiring NS-history" originated in the "Germans", and it was their affirmative acquisition of the past which caused the quarrel. At the same time, Fechler ascribes "blame" and wrong behaviour to the national-ethno-cultural Others even with respect to mechanisms he criticises in the Self. This is an example of how undesired qualities are eliminated from the Self and projected onto the Others, the *Othering*. It is supposedly not problematic that adolescents from German family background express national chauvinist views, but the protest against these expressions causes "turmoil". When these "Others" feel threatened by an interpellation of Germany, the concept of multiculturalism offers new options to re-move what is undesired – options that go beyond those of former discourses. What is paradoxical about Fechler's article is that he also formulates a well-founded critique of dominant society's dealings with the NS-past and of right-wing extremism, and that he acknowledges the contemporary existence of racism. To explain this seeming contradiction, I am going to deal with three issues which need to be analysed through a "critical race" perspective: the mediation method, the paradigm of multiculturalism, and the post-NS context.

4.1 Structural basis of the mediation method

The mediation method, which "abstains from (analysing) content" and strives for "impartial mediation" (226), necessitates the appearance that the conflict between the students is a conflict between two approximately equally strong groups which can be solved by mediation. From this follows a silence about social hierarchies. The mediating institution wants to solve the conflict without regard to dimensions of social criticism, which is successful in this case (225). Fechler applies this method in analogy to the concept of "ethnic conflicts" within the paradigm of multiculturalism.

4.2 The paradigm of multiculturalism

Titles which contain terms like "multicultural", "in the immigration society" or "of migrants" indicate a cognitive structure which guides the perception and interpretation of phenomena which are understood as deviant from the 'monocultural norm of Germans without immigrants' and thus as disturbing the system: Fechler's title, therefore, suggests that multiculturality changes the 'German cultural' frame of action. His line of argument can be summarised as follows:

The central problem of "after Auschwitz" pedagogies, policies of commemoration and remembrance is that these approaches serve to fashion Germans into subjects of moral integrity who deal correctly with guilt. All this evolves around "questioning the own [German, the eds.] national and family origin and identity", so that "Auschwitz [became] a focal point for identity politics" (210). In this analysis, the impact of immigration is to make more obvious the resulting contradictions of dealing with Auschwitz in terms of identity politics that lead to "polarization, forming of clichés, and fixed identities" (ibid.). Fechler strives to overcome this 'classical' problem, which can result in polarized oppositions between educators and right-wing adolescents, in the way he deals with the "rather right" boys and with respect to the term "gassing". The latter term he should have just "let pass", as he re-evaluates his reaction (219).

Fechler proceeds to connect this problem of polarization with the presence of migrant-Others by interpreting the conflict as an example for the "competition for the monopoly of the victim's status" (225) and by claiming, "history" was "exploited in the service of identity politics within the struggle for power and acknowledgement" (ibid.). Fechler needs to assume an "identification" of the migrantised youths with the Holocaust victims in order to link the event at all to "NS-history". This implies, however, the ascription of a "quality" or behavioural disposition which divides "migrants" and "Germans" in order to differentiate between "cultures". To be able to speak about the exploitation of the past in the service of identity politics within the framework of an ethnic conflict, and to invoke a collective (historic-cultural) "identity" of all those who are supposed to have no "German identity"[30], Fechler is compelled to re-interpret the conflict within NS-history and to historicize the term "Nazi". And he needs to locate the exploitative dealing with the past within the "migrant-Other" adolescents in order to treat the conflict in terms of multiculturalism. Otherwise Fechler could do nothing more than report another case of "'ethnic' German" adolescents who looked for orientation to past German "culture".

The paradigm of the "multicultural society" also adds strength to Fechler's arguments against the "ritual patterns" of many educators. Fechler basically suggests a reorientation away from moral practice and historical precision, and this suggestion may be criticised. But by justifying this educational approach as a necessary reaction to "multicultural classrooms", it appears progressive. So, one may argue that Fechler takes advantage of the migrantised students in order to advance his own educational strategy, but in doing so he does not do justice to their dispositions.

30 In the face of the heterogeneous origins of the migrantised students, one has to conclude that the only common past and present they might share in order to form a "collective identity" is the experience of racism and social subordination in Germany. But this is precisely what Fechler is not interested in. Therefore, following Fechler's argument, the migrantised students create a collective identity by appropriating part of the "German history", the victim's status, in an illegitimate manner.

The interpretation of the conflict between migrantised and "German" students as an "ethnic conflict" also suggests that these are two "closed" in-groups. A 'classical' reading of the conflict within the paradigm of right-wing extremism would see those students who criticise the guestbook entry in unison with educators as a united front against emerging right-wing tendencies. Not family or "ethnic" origins, but the individual attitude would count. Taking this as a starting point, it might be possible to explore how the division along the lines of national origin of the parents became entrenched in this students group. Again the 'classical' reading of the conflict is more helpful than the culturalising approach: In this group of students, it was not the members of the "Turkish", "Italian", "German", "Afghan" and other unnamed "ethnic groups" who stood in confrontation with one another "in the struggle for power and acknowledgement", but what emerged was a clear line demarcating the "German ethnic group" from all the other "ethnic groups". So, from this perspective, elements of German ethnicity, e.g. NS tradition-building and German nationalist chauvinism, produce the opposition between students from German family background and the Others. Therefore, even an analysis of the conflict within the paradigm of "ethnic conflict" leads to the 'classical' problem of right-wing extremism and racism, provided that whatever expression is given to cultural practice and self-images is rigorously scrutinised. Indirectly, Fechler concedes that racism does play a role in the analysed conflict, when he states that the objective of the migrantised students was "to draw attention to their everyday experiences of discrimination" (213). But he separates the concrete event categorically from this observation, almost as if "rather right" adolescents did not commit acts of racism in "everyday life" and as if a national-chauvinist slogan was not an aggressive signal for exclusion and disparagement.

4.3 The post-NS context

Ultimately, Fechler's text demonstrates how the era of National-Socialism still affects social life and impacts present-day, everyday structures. The post-NS society is predominantly composed of the NS "German *Volksgemeinschaft*" (defined as 'racial' community in terms of blood-ties, cp. the German Constitution) and their descendents[31], who maintain dominance in society by separating themselves from immigrants and by marginalising immigrants and their descendents into inferior social positions. In the conflict between the students this relation-

31 The mainstream discourse about German identity as deriving from the collectively committed crimes, paradoxically neglects once more the survivors of the crimes and their descendants, implying that they are not part of the German nation.

ship is evident: The words of a formerly worshipped and adored Hitler, quoted by young *Dominanzdeutsche* (socially dominant Germans), remind us of German National-Socialism, claims of racial superiority, and the crimes of the past, and at the same time perpetuate German nationalism that is now directed at the internal immigrant population. The dominant society tends to join together even more closely when faced with the challenge of being "no Nazis" in the eyes of an imagined authority of control. Through existing structures of segregation, "ethnic German" unity is facilitated when migrant-Others point out a continued fascination with the past, and complain about current forms of racism. As indicated in my introduction, the narrow definition of "racism" in post-NS-Germany as applying only to the version of NS-anti-Semitism which led to mass murder and systematic genocide, serves to confirm that contemporary "democratic Germany" and the according "German Self" is free from racism in general. The protest of the migrantised students, however, demonstrates that there are still people in Germany who are exposed to "ethnic German" resentment and self-aggrandizement. And that is exactly what Fechler takes up under the category of "victim's status".

One leitmotiv of Fechler's interpretation is the "struggle for the victim's status" as rooted in the multicultural context which was to be channelled by mediation. Both parties involved in the conflict claim, as Fechler reports, to be "victims of racism". But the "victim's status" is in Fechler's view so closely linked to the Holocaust that he insists on interpreting the competition for the status of the "real victim of racism" *only* in historical "disguise". He assumes that the migrantised students had, in a manner of speaking, donned the mask of the "victim" from the past in order to play the role, which in reality belonged to "the Jews". At the same time, the fact that the historical status of the victim is reserved for Jewish and other NS-victims and that "the Germans" have no claim to it is in their view a continuous offence which they try to reverse in discourse. An important discourse figure in this context is the narrative about the Germans who were never real Nazis, but instead the first victims of Hitler. "Being no Nazi" and "being a victim oneself" is one and the same in this form of discourse, and thus the victim's status of Jews and other NS-victims can be neutralised. As was demonstrated, Fechler turns both the students who signed the "Nazi slogans" as well as the "undecided Germans" into victims of their migrantised classmates, and in doing so satisfies their desire to cleanse themselves of the stain of being Nazis. Consequently, the migrantised cannot claim to be victims either. It would appear as if a masquerade was being performed with the roles reversed. Thus in Fechler's interpretation we also encounter a completely 'monocultural German' "problem of identity", which combines the effects of

National Socialism with present day racism in a complex manner that I have attempted to trace.

5. Conclusion – or: "Problematising the normality of our society" (Fechler 2003: 45)

My re-reading of Bernd Fechler's case study is based on a critical analysis of two elements of social normality in Germany: the existence of racist and of post-NS structures. I have tried to re-trace the collaboration between these two structural elements with respect to a concrete case, and to indicate where they are tangible. One important consequence of this collaboration is that those who are racially discriminated against are effectively silenced. There is hardly any form of (everyday) language in Germany to speak about racism which is not in some way linked to National-Socialism. Therefore any form of criticism of racism can easily be rejected as a comparison with the Holocaust and as an inappropriate ascription of a Nazi-identity.

To conclude, I want to point out that my re-reading refers to a concrete case study and that I do not intend to contest that there are migrant-Others who do compare their situation with that of Holocaust victims, that there are schools and kindergartens, in which teenagers and children from German family background may be consequently exposed to mobbing and violence, and that immigration changes the conditions of teaching within the field of "Education after Auschwitz".

The conflict shows how German-nationalist chauvinism that connects with National-Socialism has different effects in the presence of people who are perceived as *national Others* and who at least in part perceive themselves in this way. This is different compared to an assumed situation 'before immigration into schools' when the often forgotten Jewish Germans, German Roma and Sinti, left-oriented people or others were the only or main ones who were hurt by Hitler quotations. My suggestion is, however, that a close scrutiny of the concrete contents of German nationalism that are conveyed in each situation is more productive than the framework of an abstract multiculturalism – in order to understand the quarrels and debates between people who are subjugated and perform a subjectifying process as Germans and as national-ethno-cultural Others.

Translated from German by Heike Niedrig (ed.)

Literature

Domarus, M. (1973): Hitler. Reden und Proklamationen 1932-1945. Vol. I: Triumph, Second Part: 1935-1938. Wiesbaden.

Fechler, B. (2000): Zwischen Tradierung und Konfliktvermittlung. Über den Umgang mit „problematischen" Aneignungsformen der NS-Geschichte in multikulturellen Schulklassen. Ein Praxisbericht. In: Fechler, B., Kößler, G. & Liebertz-Groß, T. (eds.): „Erziehung nach Auschwitz" in der multikulturellen Gesellschaft. Pädagogische und soziologische Annäherungen. Weinheim/München, 207 – 228.

Fechler, B., Kößler, G. & Liebertz-Groß, T. (eds. 2000): „Erziehung nach Auschwitz" in der multikulturellen Gesellschaft. Pädagogische und soziologische Annäherungen. Weinheim/München.

Fechler, B. (2003): Pädagogische Konzepte gegen Rechtsextremismus. In: Jugendbegegnungsstätte Anne Frank (ed.): Rechtsextremismus – was heißt das eigentlich heute? Über Rechtsextremismus, Rassismus und Zivilcourage. Prävention für Schule und Bildungsarbeit. Frankfurt/Main, 41 – 50.

Jäger, S. (1992): BrandSätze. Rassismus im Alltag. Duisburg.

Jugendbegegnungsstätte Anne Frank (ed. 2003): Rechtsextremismus – was heißt das eigentlich heute? Über Rechtsextremismus, Rassismus und Zivilcourage. Prävention für Schule und Bildungsarbeit. Frankfurt/Main.

Kaletsch, Ch. (2003): Eine Schule schaut nicht weg. In: Jugendbegegnungsstätte Anne Frank (ed.): Rechtsextremismus – was heißt das eigentlich heute? Über Rechtsextremismus, Rassismus und Zivilcourage. Prävention für Schule und Bildungsarbeit. Frankfurt/Main, 81 – 85.

Kößler, G. (2004): „Anne Frank. Ein Mädchen aus Deutschland" Eine interaktive Ausstellung für Jugendliche – ein interkulturelles Projekt zur Erinnerungskultur – Ein Wagnis der Kooperation, in: Gedenkstättenrundbrief 118, 4/2004, 3 – 19.

Mecheril, P. (2004): Einführung in die Migrationspädagogik. Weinheim.

Mecheril, P., Castro Varela, M., Dirim, I., Kalpaka, A. & Melter, C. (2010): Einführung in die Migrationspädagogik. Weinheim/Basel.

Proske, M. (2005): Kommunikation im Unterricht, ethnische Herkunft und die moralische Bewertung im NS-Staat – Eine Fallinterpretation eines Schülerinnenkonflikts. In: Schlag, T. & Scherrmann, M. (eds.): Bevor Vergangenheit vergeht. Für einen zeitgemäßen Politik- und Geschichtsunterricht über Nationalsozialismus und Rechtsextremismus. Schwalbach/Taunus, 114 – 131.

Rommelspacher, B. (1995): Dominanzkultur. Texte zu Fremdheit und Macht. Berlin.

Seidel Arpaci, A. (2006): National Memory's *Schlüsselkinder*: Migration, Pedagogy, and German Remembrance Culture. In: Taberner, S. & Cooke, P. (eds.): German Culture, Politics, and Literature into the Twenty-First Century. Beyond Normalization. Rochester.

Terkessidis, M. (1998): Psychologie des Rassismus. Opladen/Wiesbaden.

Terkessidis, M. (2004): Die Banalität des Rassismus. Migranten zweiter Generation entwickeln eine neue Perspektive. Bielefeld.

Yoshitsune Legends in Ezo-Hokkaido: Myth and the Teaching and Learning of Colonialism in Japan's North

Christopher J. Frey, Bowling Green State University, USA

This chapter explores the development, deployment and reception of a popular medieval Japanese legend, "Yoshitsune in Ezo" as an example of intercultural education between Japanese and Ainu. The Ainu are a people indigenous to the land once known as "Ezo" [1], which included what is now Japan's northernmost island of Hokkaidō, as well as Russian-held Sakhalin and the Kurile Islands (see map below). The "Yoshitsune in Ezo" legend centers on the purported travels of an exceptionally famous prince, Minamoto no Yoshitsune (1159-1189CE), who to this day is the subject of films, video games, and a wide variety of Japanese visual novels (*manga*). Briefly, the "Yoshitsune in Ezo" legend paints Yoshitsune, as he is usually called, as a tragic hero who overcomes death and escapes to live among the Ainu. This particular legend is but one small part of an enormous cultural corpus devoted to Yoshitsune, but as this chapter will argue, it can also illustrate some deep historical truths about Japan's colonial expansion, and the creation of intercultural spaces and stories by the Japanese that justified their authority over Ainu people. Over many centuries, this legend of "Yoshitsune in Ezo" was carried north in the minds of Japanese officials, surveyors, sailors and seasonal laborers, who planted and cultivated it in the Ainu lands of Ezo, and appropriated the Ainu legend of another mythic hero, Okikurumi, to tell the story of Japanese dominance over the Ainu.

1 The terminology may be confusing. "Ezo" is a term that can mean "barbarian" which may refer to both the ancestors of the Ainu, and others who are not Japanese. Until 1869, "Ezo" was also the name of the lands where the Ainu (and their ancestors) lived. For the sake of clarity, I will use "Ezo" to refer to the land, and "Ainu" as the people, even though the term "Ainu" did not come into widespread use until the 19th Century. The historical lands of "Ezo" include contemporary Hokkaido, Sakhalin and the Kurile Islands. In general, "Ezo" in this paper will refer to "Hokkaido".

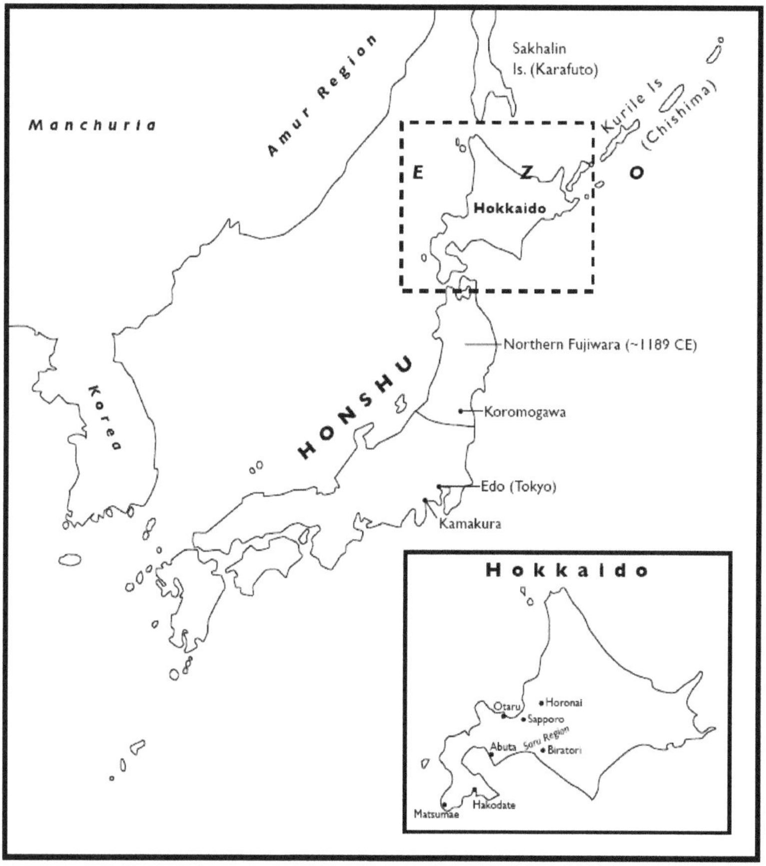

Fig. 1: Map of Hokkaido (provided by Daniel H. Schellhas)

Analysis of Yoshitsune in Ezo legend can excavate deep historical teaching and learning between the Japanese and Ainu as a way to better understand how dualistic ideologies of Japanese superiority and Ainu inferiority developed. These ideologies later influenced the structure of Ainu schooling in the 20th Century, where Ainu children were subjected to assimilationist education similar to schools for Indigenous children in the United States, Canada, and Australia (Ogawa 1997; Frey 2007). As an educational narrative, the Yoshitsune in Ezo legend teaches Japanese about their relationship with the Ainu by investing an historical Japanese hero into the heart of Ainu folklore, politics, and sacred space. Similarly, its deployment by Japanese officials among the Ainu was intended as a way for the Ainu to demonstrate their fealty to Japanese authority, promoted by the latter in the aftermath of intercultural conflicts, and planted in the Ainu landscape in the form of place names and religious architecture. Taken together, the Yoshitsune in Ezo legend emerges as form of colonial mythologizing that, in this case, places Japanese protagonists at the center of the Ainu genesis, its sacred landscape, and its political history. As we will see, the legend of Yoshitsune in Ezo has expanded and contracted to tell stories that are salient for their times and circumstances, so that, for example, once the Japanese had secured control of the Ainu and their lands in the late 1800s, the story reemerged in popular and official circles to frame Japan's expansion into Manchuria (Oguma 2002). In short, this "colonization of mythic history" is a palimpsest, an overwritten, effaced or partially erased text whose archaeology can cultivate comprehension of "the discursive, material, and psychical linkages of history and the present" (Coloma et al. 2009: 5). By reaching into the pasts of the colonized, the Yoshitsune in Ezo myth appropriates an Ainu legend in ways that justified, or at least provided historical precedent for, Japanese colonial authority.

Because of the unique setting and chronology of the Yoshitsune in Ezo legend, this analysis differs from recent scholarship on colonial education that focuses mostly on schools established by European powers in their external colonies (Nóvoa et al. 1995; Goodman et al. 2009). Much of this recent scholarship on external colonial schooling relies on post-colonial perspectives that excavate the formation of racialized, gender, religious and economic distinctions between colonizer and colonized in schooling, and the challenges to imperial epistemic dominance (Coloma et al. 2010; Hickling-Hudson et al. 2004). However, Japan as both a colonial and post-colonial subject is rarely noted in English-language scholarship on colonialism and imperialism (Young 2006). Similarly, writing on Japanese colonialism tends to follow European-American definitions that privilege external and "post-" colonialisms in ways that also separate it from "internal" settler colonialism. Thus, the attempt here is to challenge notions equating colonization with Europe, and to critique the idea that Japanese colonialism began in 1895 with the annexation of Taiwan and ended with Japan's defeat in 1945.

Finally, it is interesting to note the consistent pedagogical locus of the Yoshitsune in Ezo legend. The institutions and policies through which it was promoted are clear examples of what historian of education Donald Warren (2008) has called the "epic struggle over teaching and learning" colonialism. Beyond the broad argument that any legend must be taught and learned, and that it must find a particular meaning among its adherents and believers, this legend and its promotion is educational in three ways. First, both the Japanese "Yoshitsune" and the Ainu "Okikurumi" are "cultural instructors". In nearly all versions of these tales, both characters teach important skills like fishing and agriculture, or introduce new technologies and products such as sake and tobacco. In this sense thc "instruction" represents the creation of intercultural spaces, trade, understanding and at times, violent conflict between the Ainu and Japanese. Second, the legend was consciously spread through history texts that were used in at least one elite government school during the Tokugawa era (1603-1868). In particular, these texts were produced when the Japanese were expanding their control over the Ainu, and likely cultivated the idea among elites that the Ainu lands should be subject to Japanese control. Third, I argue that the legend is educational in that it provides a "root structure" for Japanese to claims to Hokkaido as Japanese space in ways that compete with and, perhaps, implicitly attempt to neutralize Ainu indigeneity claims. In this sense, the Japanese use the Yoshitsune in Ezo legend as a way to claim "indigeneity" for themselves in lands they have clearly colonized and taken from earlier occupants. The Yoshitsune in Ezo legend is uniquely suited for these kinds of deep, historical claims, given that its genesis and development have occurred over eight centuries.

The rest of this chapter outlines the historical development of the Yoshitsune in Ezo legend. The first section introduces the historical Minamoto no Yoshitsune. The second section explores an early example of the legend, examines the educative work of legends, and explores some early literary sources in children's books. The third section looks at the Ainu legend of *Okikurumi*, and how Japanese officials and travelers deployed the legend among the Ainu, and in their lands. The fourth section analyzes the cultivation of the Yoshitsune in Ezo legend during the colonization of Ainu lands after 1800, and how the legend served as colonial guide and inspiration as Japan expanded its empire through the mid-20th Century. The final section briefly charts the flow of the Yoshitsune legend WWII, demonstrating the persistence and malleability of the legend and shows how it was harnessed into the colonial culture of Hokkaido into the present day.

1. The Historical Minamoto no Yoshitsune

Yoshitsune is so central to Japanese literature and legend that Japan scholar Ivan Morris wrote of him: "if he had not actually existed, the Japanese might have been obliged to invent him" (1975: 67). Yoshitsune was born in 1159 CE into the Minamoto clan, who, along with the Taira, were the two dominant political families of the era. Just a year after Yoshitsune's birth, his father and most of his family were killed after they tried and failed to overthrow the ruling Taira in the

Heiji Rebellion of 1160. Yoshitsune, who was just an infant, his mother, and two half-brothers were spared by the Taira, but were separately exiled. Yoshitsune eventually was sent to the northern reaches of Japan's main island, Honshu, and raised under the protection of Fujiwara no Hidehira (1122?-1187), who reigned over a semiautonomous region as head of the Northern Fujiwara clan. At the age of 21, Yoshitsune reunited with his older half-sibling Yoritomo, and initiated another rebellion against the Taira in 1180. Yoshitsune brilliantly commanded several battles to defeat the Taira. However, it was Yoshitsune's half-brother, Yoritomo, who declared himself the first medieval "Shōgun" or military dictator, in 1185 (McCullough 1967).[2]

The new Shōgun refused his brother Yoshitsune any spoils of war, and fearing his military prowess, sent bands of soldiers to capture or kill him. Yoshitsune fled north and again sought protection under Fujiwara no Hidehira. However, Hidehira died two years later in 1187, and Northern Fujiwara could no longer resist the growing power of the Shōgun Yoritomo. Yoritomo threatened the destruction of the Northern Fujiwara if they did not hand over Yoshitsune, and they soon capitulated, sending guards to detain Yoshitsune. Realizing that his capture was imminent, Yoshitsune killed his family and committed suicide. Forty days later, Yoshitsune's severed head arrived at his brother's residence in Kamakura, as public proof of his death.

Despite their cooperation, the Shōgun Yoritomo quickly killed the leaders of the Northern Fujiwara, and took control of their domain (McCullough 1967). Interestingly, the Northern Fujiwara domain was likely a hybrid of Japanese and Ainu peoples, sometimes referred to as "Emishi", which suggests that it served as a mediating space between the Japanese to the south, and the Hokkaido Ainu to the north.

2. Four Narratives of Minamoto no Yoshitsune

The unsettled political climate of the late 12th Century, which saw the overthrow of the Taira, the establishment of the Kamakura Shogunate under Yoritomo, the death of Yoshitsune, and the destruction of the Northern Fujiwara domain, cultivated a fertile ground for the emergence of legends and tales in the following century (Ōmori 1910). Cultural anthropologist Abe Toshio (2008) argues that there are four major narratives that emerged out of Yoshitsune's historical ex-

2 The term "Shōgun" is an abbreviation of seii taishōgun, or "barbarian-subduing generalissimo". This was a term that had already been applied for several centuries to short-term military leaders charged with quelling ancestors of the Ainu and others who refused to accede to Japanese rule (Walker 2000).

ploits; the first three center on his infancy, his adolescence, and his brief adulthood. These include famous epics such as the Tale of Heike (1371), as well as short stories, kabuki dramas and many other literary forms (McCullough 1967). Accounts of the historical Yoshitsune can also be found in the Kamakura Shogunate's official chronicle, *Azuma kagami,* first published in 1266 (Ruch 2000).

The fourth narrative genre centers on the proposition that Yoshitsune escaped death, or was magically reborn after his suicide and subsequently fled even farther north to live among the "barbarian" ancestors of the Ainu in Ezo. The audiences and promoters of the reincarnation genre vary according to time and circumstances. Abe (2008) suggests that these legends are most popular among commoners. However, it may be more precise to say that children and travelers to Ezo who were looking to establish meaning in a strange land were most receptive to the idea. Government officials, meanwhile, emerge as its most consistent promoters.

2.1 The Educative Work of Legends and Myths

Though it is important to distinguish between myths, which generally focus on supernatural and timeless events, and legends, which are more often centered on exaggerated or imagined tales of heroes in historical time, the terms will in be used interchangeably to acknowledge the "mythologized legend" of Yoshitsune in Ezo, as well as its appropriation of Ainu creation epics. Myths and legends are generally considered to be outside the scope of modern, public schooling. In part, the technocratic, multicultural impetus of schooling in a democratic society has cleansed curricula of content about which a consensus cannot be reached (Sturm et al. 1996). With notable exceptions, such as when they are integral to a national or ecclesiastic identity, legends and myths tend to be taught, if at all, as metaphorical rather than factual. However, this should not suggest that legend does not have an educational impetus. Without a consensus on the veracity of a myth, or even when there is a general consensus against its authenticity, as in the Yoshitsune in Ezo myth, legends can still be educational. One reason may be that legend and myth fill spaces that official knowledge, available evidence or emotional longing fail to satisfy. Similarly, we might consider the *work* of myth rather than simply the veracity of its content, or in other words, "a lie that tells a truth" (O'Flaherty & Doniger 1988). Myths and legends find particular salience when time, distance and language make consensus on the "facts" difficult; or when the legend nestles seamlessly into established epistemologies, when it illuminates curiosities, or when the myth can undergird and give direction to youthful inspirations. The goal here is not to argue that the legend was a central or even a vitally important pedagogical tool in the intercultural space between

Japanese and Ainu; rather, it is of interest because it illuminates particular moments of teaching and learning colonialism (Warren 2008).

The Yoshitsune in Ezo legends are an aggregation of many lies that tell many truths. As Helen Parker observed about the literary spotlight on the historical Yoshitsune,

> What is of interest is that the recounting of his story, which has gradually been embellished to earn him a high profile in the Japanese tradition, reflects perceptions of history and personality in history that have appealed to audiences of different kinds in different eras (2006: 52f.).

The few contemporary declarations that the legend is true (Sasaki et al. 1972) routinely ignore the "work" of the legend, and rely on it in its "objectified state" (Bourdieu 1986: 50) in historical documents, place names, monuments, geological oddities, among others, without attention to the motivations and epistemological assumptions of the authors and creators of those objects. As we will see, this inattention to context and motivation in the creation and historical sustenance of the legend suggests that it maintains its utility among some contemporary Japanese residents of Hokkaido in ways that privilege story over evidence, and inspiration over analysis.

2.2 Children's Tales of Yoshitsune in Ezo

The earliest recorded tales of Yoshitsune in Ezo appear not in the official chronicles or epic poems, but in what are called "companion tales" (*otogizōshi*), which are short, illustrated stories that emerged as a popular literary form in the Muromachi era (1336-1568). These simple, moralistic stories were sometimes drawn from travelling storytellers, and read to children by parents or other household members. Among the fifteen or sixteen "companion tales" about heroes, Yoshitsune is featured in eight (Mulhern 1974).

One of the earliest companion tales about Yoshitsune in Ezo reveals how little most Japanese knew about the lands to the north, while illustrating some already-established tropes about its inhabitants and other "barbarians". In "Yoshitsune's Island Crossing" (*Onzōshi shima watari*), our mythic hero visits a series of islands in order to learn the "Law of Dainichi Buddha", a secret military treatise held by the Demon King of Ezo, named Kanehira. After travelling for months among islands populated with giants, dwarfs and widows, he arrives in *Kikenjō,* the capital of Ezo[3]. There, he meets the Demon King Kanehira, who is "one hundred sixty feet tall, with eight hands and feet, thirty horns, a voice au-

3 Kiken-jō is also the Japanese name for the palace of the Buddhist god Indra, though it is not clear whether this reference was intentional.

dible for two hundred fifty miles, and eyes as dazzling as the morning sun" (McCullough 1967: 51). After passing a series of tests, Kanehira accepts Yoshitsune as a disciple, but reveals nothing about the Law of Dainichi Buddha. At a banquet that evening, Yoshitsune meets the king's beautiful daughter, Asahi, and they exchange vows the next day. Yoshitsune convinces Asahi to steal the book containing the Law, but once Yoshitsune has copied it down, the text mysteriously disappears from the page. Asahi pleads for Yoshitsune to flee, and soon the skies darken, signaling to Kanehira the wrong that has been done to him. Yoshitsune rushes back to his fleet as Kanehira unleashes after him a thousand demons riding water-treading horses. Using Asahi's magical charms, Yoshitsune summons mountains of salt to evade Kanehira's demons, and rides the fair winds back to the south, where he uses the Law to once again defeat his historical rivals, the Taira clan (McCullough 1967).

The descriptions of Ezo reflect some persistent themes from earlier Japanese chronicles about the "northern barbarians" or the Ainu, who regularly fought the proto-Japanese Yamato peoples throughout the early Heian era (794-1185).[4] Beyond the fantastic, this version of the story incorporates a persistent theme of the Yoshitsune in Ezo legend, namely an explanation about why Ainu did not have a written language. According to the version above, Kanehira's sacred text disappears as Yoshitsune copies it down, though other versions suggest it was stolen. Anglican missionary John Batchelor (1854-1944) wrote that some Ainu in the late 19th Century cited Yoshitsune as the thief of their literacy. Batchelor's Ainu informants said that the name of the stolen text was the *Tora no maki mono*, though he noted that that title is "a purely Japanese name. It is, in fact, the name of a Japanese book on strategy" (Batchelor 1892: 115).

Despite these inconsistencies, the "lie" that Yoshitsune stole Ainu literacy reveals an interesting truth. Between 1670 and 1800, Japanese rulers in Ezo forbade Ainu from learning to speak or to become literate in the Japanese language. This policy of linguistic dissimilation was enacted and enforced by the Matsumae, who had been given a monopoly over trade with the Ainu in the early 1600s. The imposition of a language boundary helped the Matsumae to clearly distinguish the Ainu from the Japanese, in order to control information and movement so that the Matsumae could monopolize trade. The cultural dissimilation policies and restrictions on trade also helped to quell fighting over fishing

---

4 The fantastic physical descriptions of the Ezo in part draw on historical narratives of the barbarian Emishi from the Nihon shoki that themselves were drawn on established Chinese tropes about barbarians: "...in the winter they lodge in holes, in summer they dwell in nests. They wear furs and drink blood; eldest brothers and younger brothers are distrustful of each other. Climbing mountains they are like flying birds; running through grass they are like furry beasts in flight." See Hall et al. 1999: 29.

and hunting lands that had been exacerbated by the expanding trade with Japanese merchants to the south. Thus, it is not surprising that some Ainu would attribute their lack of literacy to a powerful Japanese like the mythical Yoshitsune, particularly if Japanese officials were telling Ainu similar stories while keeping them from becoming literate. As such, the "lie" about Yoshitsune may tell a "truth" about the dissimilation policy of the Matsumae. This theme also points to enduring tensions between Ainu orality and Japanese literacy in Ezo, particularly as a characteristic that Japanese have long used to distinguish the "barbarians" from the "civilized". It was not until the development of a series of segregated schools for the Ainu after 1901 that this language barrier was breached, and Ainu began learning Japanese in great numbers, to the ultimate detriment of their own language (Frey 2007; Ogawa 1997).

3. Yoshitsune in Ainu Epic Tales and Lands

3.1 The Ainu Legend of Okikurumi and the Yoshitsune Palimpsest

One way that the Yoshitsune in Ezo legend was cultivated among the Ainu was to argue that the Ainu demigod Okikurumi was, in fact, Yoshitsune. While this happened after Japanese began penetrating deeper into Ainu lands during the 17th Century, it is useful here to briefly summarize the Okikurumi tales to illustrate why the Japanese conflated the two heroes.

Okikurumi is the predominant character in a larger body of oral literature called *oyna* or *aeoina-kamui*, which are tales of deities and gods who take human form and reside among the Ainu (Philippi 1979). According to Kindaichi Kyōsuke (1882-1971), a Japanese scholar of the Ainu language,

> though *oyna* are conveyed in much the same way as deity legends [*kamui yūkara*], the narratives' hero is not a deity, but one who has descended from the god world (or the child of a deity who falls from the heavens) to oversee the human world. This being is [the half-god, first Ainu] *Ainurakkuru*, a slayer of demons who comes to live in the human world and teaches the foundations of Ainu life (1943: 249).

Because *oyna* center on the corporal interaction between gods and humans, these tales usually explain the origins and connectedness of Ainu culture with Nature and Land.[5] These "mythic epics", which include *oyna*, were well known among the general Ainu population, because knowledge of the interactions between

---

5 This distinguishes them from the epic oral poetry (yukar), which are centered on the gods, and short tales (u'uepeker) which deal with day-to-day human interactions. Categories of Ainu oral literature are many, and often overlap depending on the region (see Philippi 1979: 22-24; Kayano Shigeru 1984: v- vii; Kindaichi Kyōsuke 1943: 249f.).

gods and humans enabled the possessor "to obtain blessings from the good deities and drive away the bad ones" (Philippi 1979: 25). This illustrates a core Ainu understanding of the need to balance human activity with powers beyond human control, but one which also sees Nature and gods as generally benevolent and rational forces. At the same time, Ainu deities are subject to the same failures as humans; or in another turn of phrase, they are "gods you can argue with" (Fujimura 1999: 193).

Okikurumi is the protagonist in a wide variety of Ainu stories, not all of which center on his interaction with human beings (Kindaichi & Arikida 1964). It is also worth noting that the *oyna* are particularly prevalent in the Saru River area, where Japanese authorities encouraged Yoshitsune worship among the Ainu (Kindaichi 1943). One recent Okikurumi tale written by Ainu scholar Kayano Shigeru (1926-2006), himself from the Saru River area, tells of a young Okikurumi desperate to visit the beautiful human world. Scolded by his father for trying to go without permission, he is to be allowed to go conditional on passing endurance tests of heat, cold, and laughter. He passes the first two, but he fails the third because he lets out a quiet chuckle when, as two gods complete a rousing sexual performance, their "copulatory parts" become locked together (Kayano 1985: 111). Filled with regret at his failure, Okikurumi flees to the Land of the Humans with a handful of millet. Once there, he teaches the Ainu how to make fire, fashion a variety of hunting and fishing tools, and build houses. The millet he brings quickly multiplies, and from that he teaches the people to make liquor (*tonoto*) as well as shaved willow sticks (*inau*), that are said to please the benevolent gods and protect humans from malevolent deities. With these lessons complete, Okikurumi takes a human wife. But a few months later, when a man who is being helped by Okikurumi's wife tries to take her hand, Okikurumi flees back to the land of the gods with her, never to return. The story concludes with explanations of geographic and meteorological references that are meant to remind the Saru River Ainu of Okikurumi's continued presence (Kayano 1985).

The Okikurumi tales were an attractive palimpsest for Japanese reinterpretations for two reasons. First, like the tale of Yoshitsune's theft of the Law of Dainichi Buddha, the Okikurumi tale revolves around a short visit that centers on trickery, from humorous to deceptive. Second, and more importantly, Okikurumi is generally presented as a "culture god" who teaches the Ainu about fire, fishing, hunting, sewing, and other modes of survival (Kindaichi 1943: 249). The Okikurumi stories are core explanatory devices that remind one about what it is to be Ainu, and the importance of the skills, given that they were taught by a visiting deity. Kayano's telling of the story, which concludes with reminders to local Ainu that Okikurumi can still be heard in thunder, connects readers and listeners with this mythic past. The long history of trade between Ainu and Japanese, in which Ainu have usually supplied raw materials collected using skills taught by Okikurumi, in exchange for Japanese goods said to be first brought to the Ainu by Yoshitsune, suggests why these two tales were an attractive pair to conflate. Thus, Japanese were likely attracted to the Okikurumi legend as a teacher who could reorient the Ainu toward practices that would complement Japanese authority. Japanese officials turned to this teaching legend during a particularly turbulent time in Japanese-Ainu relations.

3.2 Deploying the Yoshitsune Legend among the Ainu

Political and social changes at the turn of the 17th Century brought about a deepening cultivation of the Yoshitsune in Ezo myth, particularly among Ainu who were participating in Japanese trade networks. In this case, as in many others, the deepening cognitive colonialism and more formal structures of political and social control followed periods of unrest.[6] Japanese-Ainu conflict was fueled by the trade monopoly granted in 1604 by the new Shōgun Tokugawa Ieyasu to the Matsumae, a powerful Japanese family who had lived in far southern Ezo since the 15th Century. The relatively free exchange between the Ainu in Ezo and individual Japanese domains in northern parts of the main island of Honshu was gradually closed off, and the Matsumae began exploiting individual Ainu clans in order to increase trade and enrich the domain's coffers (Harrison & Takakura 1960).

By the 1660s, intensification of trade competition among the Ainu for Japanese goods triggered skirmishes between rival chiefdoms over hunting and fishing territories. When Shakushain (1606?-1669), an Ainu headman from Saru, began attacking Japanese settlements, reports that Ainu were "pillaging Japanese territory" quickly spread throughout officialdom (Walker 2000: 63). The Tokugawa government in the Japanese capital of Edo (now Tokyo) dispatched troops from other domains in the north, though Matsumae forces alone quickly extinguished the fighting by killing Shakushain and other leaders. In the aftermath, the Matsumae tightened controls over trade, in part by banning the Ainu from learning to speak, read or write Japanese, or to trade with anyone outside their immediate area (Walker 2000). The Matsumae policy of trade monopoly and cultural dissimilation was generally successful in quelling armed uprisings and enriching the domain.

6 In the United States, for example, federal and mission schools were often established on or near decommissioned military bases after American Indians had been militarily defeated.

In order for the Matsumae officials to maintain communication with individual Ainu, bilingual Ainu and Japanese translators (*tsūji*) were dispatched to the posts to disseminate official declarations and maintain the language boundary (Mogami 1786). During this time Japanese authorities also began deploying the Yoshitsune legend among the Ainu as a means of political and social control.

The diaries of a Japanese trader and captain named Shichirōhei are an early indication of this. During a visit to Ezo in 1673, four years after the death of Shakushain, he was told by a succession of Matsumae officials of "many new developments in Ezo, among them that Yoshitsune was now being worshipped" (Kindaichi 1925: 327). Though not reflected in the official government reports, descriptions of Yoshitsune-worship appeared in a variety of official histories over the next decades, reinforcing the Yoshitsune in Ezo legend among Japanese readers. For example, one brief passage in the *Great History of Japan [Dai nihonshi]* (1706), compiled by Tokugawa Mitsukuni (1628-1701), suggested that because the Ainu worshipped Yoshitsune, the legend of his escape might be true. Kindaichi (1925) also noted that Yoshitsune worship was mentioned in several other 17th and early 18th Century texts, including *Ezo Wilderness Stories [Ezo yabubanashi]* (1712), and *Writings on Ainu Customs on Matsumae Island [Shōtoku 5-nen Matsumae shimanomai Ezo fūzoku kakiage]* (1716).

Other official histories also promoted the legend. In 1670, just a year after Shakushain's death, a new 310-volume official history called *Honganchō tsūgan* concluded, "Yoshitune did not die, but escaped to Ezo where he left heirs" (cited in Hayashi 2000). This work, written under the guidance of neo-Confucian scholar Hayashi Razan (1583-1657), became a standard of his influential private Hayashi Academy, where many government officials were educated, suggesting that the legend circulated among Japan's political elite (Backus 1979; Brownlee 1997).

Mention of Yoshitsune's heirs may have also reflected rumors that Shakushain, who had reined terror over Japanese communities in Ezo, was descended from Yoshitsune (Kindaichi 1925). This claim was likely an attempt to neutralize Ainu resistance to Matsumae rule by claiming that the strongest among them were not *purely* Ainu, but at least partly Japanese. It also may have reinforced Japanese ideas about their own superiority, by attributing Shakushain's strength to his Japanese blood. This seems reminiscent of the 19th Century American "moundbuilder myth", which held that expansive earthworks and towering mounds in the trans-Appalachia were thought to be too complex to have been created by American Indians, and thus *must* have been built by Europeans or a lost tribe of Israel (Silverberg 1986).

The idea that Ainu worshipped Yoshitsune was encouraged in official government circles in Edo [Tokyo] by the scholar and Shogunal advisor Arai Hokuseki (1657-1725), an intellectual heir to Hayashi Razan. In his innovative 1712 *Lessons from History* (*Tokushi Yoron*), as well as his 1720 *Story of Ezo* (*Ezo sōshi*), Arai maintained the legend among the official histories. In *Story of Ezo*, Arai claims that Yoshitsune was as well known among the Ainu as Japanese:

> Gods are worshipped, but although the Ezo [Ainu] do not create shrines, when someone prays over food and drink, they do so to the Imperial Officer Minamoto Yoshitsune. In East Ezo are ruins of his official residence. Loved for his tremendous bravery among the educated [Japanese] classes, among the Ezo [Ainu] he is also revered (Arai 1720: 18).

Arai goes on to explain that the Ainu had given Yoshitsune a new name, and may only recognize his real name when queried:

> In Ezo customs, as a rule when eating and drinking it is Okikurumi they celebrate. When asked, it is said that he is Hangan [Yoshitsune]. Hangan is probably thought of as Okikurumi, or that was the name applied to him during his residence. His official residence was called Hai, which among the Ezo [Ainu] became Haikuru, which became the name for people from that area (Arai 1720: 18).

At its heart, this passage clearly implies that the Ainu are ignorant of their own gods, suggesting a clear epistemological flow from Japanese to Ainu regarding the veracity of Ainu historical knowledge. Claims that Yoshitsune had constructed impressive earthwork ruins near the Shibuchari River (when archaeological evidence suggests they actually were built during the early 17th Century), and that the Ainu of the area took their names from Yoshitsune, imbue Ainu history and culture with Japaneseness. The passage also suggests how this was operationalized, for "when asked", the Ainu will admit that Okikurumi is Yoshitsune. The deep power imbalances between Ainu and Japanese during this period suggest that it was less a casual question than an imposition of Japanese historical authority onto the everyday cultural practices of the Ainu. For contemporary believers of the Yoshitsune in Ezo legend, literal readings of these historical texts are said to prove Yoshitsune's residence among the Ainu. However, when the power imbalance between the Ainu and Japanese is taken into consideration, the authenticity of the information must be called into question.

Finally, Arai introduces to his readers another extension of the legend. "It is said", he proposes, "that the Imperial officer went beyond the Northern Sea" (Arai 1720: 18). Alluding to what is most likely the 1664 *Castaway Tale of the Echizen Ship* (*Echizenbune hyōryū ki*)[7], Arai informs his readers that a group of 58 sailors bound for Ezo were blown off course to China, and there learned that

7 Nippon shomin seikatsu shiryō shūsei, v. 5 (Tokyo: San'ichi Shōbo, 1969): pp. 568-569.

Yoshitsune had visited Peking [Beijing] and raised an army there before departing for Korea. This extension of the Yoshitsune legend will gain popularity nearly two centuries later as Japan turns its attention toward Korea and Manchuria in the decades before World War II.

3.3 Investing Yoshitsune in the Ainu Landscape

Rapid changes in Japanese-Ainu relations in the late 1700s led to new deployments and interpretations of the Yoshitsune in Ezo legend, in the form of tales told to the Ainu, and stories told by Japanese to each other. Increasing Japanese pressure on Ainu lands during the 19th Century meant that the Yoshitsune in Ezo legend was deployed more deeply among the Ainu. After Japan formally annexed and encouraged Japanese colonists to settle Ainu lands after the Meiji Restoration of 1868, the legend was refashioned for Japanese settlers in ways that legitimized Japan's first modern colonial project.

3.4 Footprints of Yoshitsune and Benkei as Natural Landmarks

It is relatively easy to find sites in contemporary Hokkaido that are purported to mark the travels of Yoshitsune and his sidekick Benkei. Popular stories and reassuring tropes were projected onto the foreign land, giving familiar meaning to territory that could be easily recalled days or years later, or easily shared with those who would make similar journeys in the future. In this case, memorable places in the natural landscape were overlaid with Japanese meanings and stories as traders and laborers surreptitiously moved into Ezo across the 17th and 18th Centuries. Abe Toshio (2008) has catalogued at least 110 geographic sites in Hokkaido that refer to the Yoshitsune in Ezo legend. These include the site near present-day Matsumae City where Yoshitsune was said to have first set foot in Hokkaido and a temple Yoshitsune is said to have built there, to a wide variety of geological formations including "The Sword of Benkei", an igneous rock formation that juts out into the Sea of Japan. In the Hidaka region, which includes the Saru River, one author noted rock formations containing vague images of a seated Yoshitsune, and what he determined to be the remains of Yoshitsune's "Hai" fortress. He argued that, "there are many fans of the Yoshitsune legend" in the area, the vast majority of whom are undoubtedly Japanese (Kanazawa 1989: 79). This is likely because of the numerous "historic" Yoshitsune sites in the Saru region, but I think it may also be because the Hidaka region is home to the largest concentration of Ainu in Japan. The popularity of Yoshitsune among Japanese residents of the Saru region, coupled with the many Yoshitsune "sites" in this deeply Ainu region suggests that the Yoshitsune legend may work as a competing Japanese historical claim to the land. Contrapositive to the deep Ainu roots in the region, the Yoshistune "sites" provide local Japanese with a tale that signifies their place in the somewhat "foreign" landscape of Ainu Hokkaido, reassuringly embedded within the very land which they both claim as their own.

4. Yoshitsune as a Colonial Guide

4.1 Yoshitsune Shrine in Biratori

Similar to the promotion of Yoshitsune worship in the years after the Shakushain War, another short period of fighting between Japanese and Ainu led to a further cultivation of the legend at the turn of the 19th Century. Following violence targeting Japanese traders in eastern Ezo in 1789, and faced with increasing Russian pressure on Japan to end their policy of seclusion and open to international trade, the Tokugawa government took direct control of Ezo from the Matsumae in 1799, and embarked on a path to fortify control over the island by assimilating the Ainu. In a reversal of the Matsumae dissimilation policies that banned Ainu from learning Japanese, the new policies promoted Japanese language, clothing, and food; as well as Buddhism, and other Japanese cultural attributes (Takakura 1972).

Similar to the promotion of Yoshitsune worship in the late 17th Century, the new assimilation policies also included a renewed emphasis on the Yoshitsune in Ezo legend. Tokugawa official Kondō Morishige (1771-1829), a fervent believer in the Yoshitsune in Ezo legend, visited the Ainu village of Biratori on the Saru River in 1798. There he constructed a crude shrine on a near a hill called *Hayopira*, where Ainu believe that Okikurumi descended from the Land of the Gods. Though a recent local history of the Yoshitsune Shrine contends that Kondō built it at the behest of local Ainu (Biratori chō Yoshitsune o kataru kai 2001), there is little indication that Ainu in Biratori ever revered or worshipped Yoshitsune unless they were in the presence of Japanese.

As before, it is more likely that Japanese officials encouraged and expected Ainu to worship the Japanese prince. Matsuura Takeshirō, a Japanese official and noted chronicler of the Ainu, visited Biratori in 1856 and recorded that "near a mountain called Hayopira, there is a small shrine where Minamoto Yoshitsune is enshrined". Matsuura later wrote that Hayopira was a much more popular place of worship for the local Ainu: "the reason is unclear, but below that place their eyes become disoriented with ignorance" (Biratori chō Yoshitsune o kataru kai 2001: 177-178). Visiting the area in the 1880s, British missionary John Batchelor noted that no Ainu worship Yoshitsune, and conversely suggested that it was Yoshitsune who worshipped the Ainu, given east-facing orientation of the structure. Batchelor's unsourced Ainu voice hints at an explanation of purported Yoshitsune worship among the Ainu:

> 'You know,' says he, 'we have for a long time been subject to the Japanese *Tono Sama* [feudal lords] and *Yakunin* [officials], and it has been to our interest that we should try to please them as much as possible, so as not to bring down trouble upon ourselves. As we know that Yoshitsune did come among our ancestors, it was thought that nothing would please the officials more than for them to think that we really worship Yoshitsune, who was himself a Japanese. And so it came to pass that the shrine was asked for and obtained (Batchelor 1887: 22).

Batchelor went on to note in a wry tone that an Ainu told him that he regularly "salutes" Yoshitsune with "libations of wine...providing someone provides the sake!" In the end, he compared the "worship" of Yoshitsune in Biratori to a "London cabman worshiping [British Prime Minister William E.] Gladstone by drinking to his health" (Batchelor 1887: 22). That Batchelor and his unnamed source both believed at the time that Yoshitsune had in fact lived among the Ainu for a time suggests the extent to which the legend was embedded in Ainu lore by the late 19th Century, even though Batchelor suggested that he witnessed only a dozen Ainu ever visiting Yoshitsune Shrine in Biratori.

4.2 Locomotives and Shrines in Industrial Hokkaido

As mentioned earlier, one of the first acts of the new Meiji government (1868-1912) was to encourage Japanese settlement of Ezo. The island was renamed "Hokkaido" in 1869, and the government encouraged rapid Japanese settlement through the Hokkaido Colonization Agency, or as it more commonly known, the *Kaitakushi*. The opening of Hokkaido in the 1870s disrupted the already precarious existence of the Ainu, pushing them onto unproductive lands or onto the margins of the rapidly developing Japanese cities in Hokkaido (Ogawa 1997).

With the influx of Japanese into the interior of Hokkaido, officials again used the Yoshitsune legend to lay claim to Ainu lands. Helped by American advisors, the Kaitakushi (Hokkaido Colonization Agency) opened its first modern coal mine in the low mountains northeast of Sapporo at Horonai in 1880. In order to transport the coal from the interior mines to Sapporo and nearby ports, Kaitakushi officials also constructed the first railroad in Hokkaido from the Horonai mine to Otaru, a port city on the Sea of Japan. The Agency ordered two steam locomotives from Pittsburgh, and named Engine No. 1 "Yoshitsune" and

Engine No. 2 "Benkei", after Yoshitsune's sidekick. The locomotive operated until 1945, and since 1963 has been preserved at a museum in Horonai (Oguma 1981). With their power to collapse time and space, railroads quickly transformed societies into which they came in contact. The locomotives and the coalmines in Hokkaido could not exist without each other, in fact, one of the main consumers of coal were railroads. Railroads brought large numbers of people into cities, and concentrated social interactions among people who could afford tickets, while limiting their interactions with people along the old stagecoach lines (Judt 2010). In their new incarnation as locomotives, Yoshitsune and Benkei became symbols of modernization, hastening ecological changes and helping incorporate the old Ainu lands into the modern, industrial Japanese Empire.

Another example from this era highlights how Yoshitsune's legend was redeployed as a historical narrative for the new "Hokkaido". Inside Horonai Shrine, located near the coalmine, there are a series of votive tablets (*ema*) depicting Yoshitsune's arrival in Ezo. Like the locomotives, the tablets were commissioned directly by Kaitakushi Director Kuroda Kiyotaka (1840-1900). While the tablets depict historically accurate physical and material differences between Japanese nobility and common Ainu (*hiradojin*), including dress, facial hair, and weapons, these tablets also reveal, as so many other "Ainu images" do, the status differences between the two in Japanese eyes. In these paintings, the Ainu are hunched over, staring bug-eyed at Yoshitsune, who peers serenely yet authoritatively between perfectly manicured eyebrows and mustache. In front of Yoshitsune are small gifts of tobacco for the Ainu, though while historically inaccurate (as tobacco did not arrive in Japan until the mid 1500s), it reflects the historical trade relations between the two peoples (Hayashi 2000).

The votive images, as well as the locomotive, suggest a new phase in the use of the Yoshitsune myth. No longer used to coax Ainu submission by means of a Japanese superhero, the myth assumed an inspirational message of Japanese historical power directed at Japanese themselves. Here, Yoshitsune can be seen as a trailblazer, a pathfinder for the (now) inevitable Japanese occupation of Hokkaido. No longer was the land beneath their feet "Ezo", the "Land of Barbarians", but rather the myth of Yoshitsune gave mythical justification for the Japanese to create "Hokkaido", a modern industrial colony and an integral part of the growing Japanese Empire. The legend thus became a foundation upon which progress, strength, and modernity could be built, and encouragement for Japanese colonists who were struggling to eke out a living on the northern frontier. In this new narrative, the Ainu are secondary, disappearing characters in a story that valorizes and historicizes the Japanization of Ezo.

4.3 Oyabe Zen'ichirō and the Yoshitsune Boom of the 1920s

As Japan opened itself to the world, and expanded its colonial possessions during the Meiji Era (1868-1912), the Yoshitsune legend inspired young and adventurous Japanese. Among them was Oyabe Zen'ichirō (1868-1941), a wayward youth from the northern province of Akita. Oyabe's father had abandoned his family to join the Imperial army for an expected invasion of Korea in 1873, and when they were later reunited, the teenage Oyabe bristled under his father's Confucian ways and sought a way out. It was around that time that he read a thick tome by Shimizu Ichijirō (1886) called *The Revival of Yoshitsune [Tsūzoku Yoshitsune saikōki]*, which repeated much of the Yoshitsune in Ezo tale. But this particularly telling account does not dwell long on these established stories; most of the remaining three hundred pages detail how Yoshitsune left Ezo and then subdued the "aborigines" from the Amur River region in Siberia, three Mongolian kingdoms and finally all of China. The crux of Shimizu's tale, which had circulated in Japan since at least the 17th Century, was that the powerful Yoshitsune had taken a new name during these exploits: Genghis Khan.[8]

Inspired by Shimizu's tale of conquest, the young Oyabe determined that he would go to live among the Ainu. Turning away from his father's Confucian training, Oyabe:

> ...devoted myself wholly to the study of books adapted to my plan, such as natural and physical geographies, and some agriculture books instead of my regular lessons in philosophy and law. Of course, this all was unknown to my father (Oyabe 1898: 46).

Oyabe's focus on "Western" subjects like geography and agriculture mirrors the rapid expansion of European-inspired scientific learning taking root in Japan during the early Meiji period (Passin 1982), and helps explain some of his later efforts to educate Ainu children. Oyabe styled himself as a modern-day Yoshitsune, and set out to "follow in the track of that old, distinguished hero" (Oyabe 1898: 24). Not content to live among the Ainu for a short period of time as Yoshitsune had, Oyabe determined that he would become the new leader of the Ainu and guide them to a new homeland in Siberia. On his first day in an Ainu village, which he had entered in order to beg for food, he reports that the "chief" asked him to lecture on Yoshitsune "the Ainu's favorite and one of the supreme gods" (Oyabe 1898: 52). After he learned that Siberia was part of the Russian

8 In addition to the 1664 'Castaway Tale of the Echizen Ship', two 18th Century histories of Japan, the Kamakura Jikki (1717) and Kokugaku wasuregai (1787) claimed that Yoshitsune had left Ezo for China, see: "Yoshitsune wa Jingis Kan densetsu o ou "Ōsaka shiryō koten sekishitsu 1 kotenji 19 (May 1998).

Empire and "not without government", he was "now obliged to give up my intense desire to take the Ainu race to the Continent" and instead turned his considerable passions to seeking "true religion", which he determined to be Christianity.

Motivated by the Yoshitsune in Ezo myth, and convinced that the Ainu needed a modern education based in the "true religion" of Christianity, Oyabe made his way to the United States where he studied at two predominantly African-American schools, Hampton Institute in Virginia and Howard University in Washington D.C. At Hampton, Oyabe was mentored by Samuel Chapman Armstrong (1839-1893), the founder of the school and one of the foremost promoters of industrial education for Black and Indian students. Oyabe went on to complete a doctorate in theology at Yale University (Oyabe 1898).

Still intent on "improving" the Ainu and redeeming his country's poor treatment of them, Oyabe believed that the Hampton model of industrial training was the most suitable for the Ainu, whom Japanese officials were now referring to as "former aborigines" *[kyūdojin]* (Oyabe 1903). In general, there were few Japanese schools open to Ainu children until passage of the Hokkaido Former Aborigines Protection Act (*Hokkaidō kyūdojin hogo hō*) in 1899, which established a system of segregated, Japanese-language schools in over 20 Ainu communities in the early 1900s. In the spirit of Ainu "improvement" permeating Hokkaido, Oyabe founded the Former Aborigines Education Aid Society (*Kyūdojin kyūiku kai*) in 1900 to solicit funds and gain influence among Tokyo's social reformers (Hokkaido kyōiku kenkyūjo 1963). After raising some funds privately, and securing government monies allocated through the 1899 Protection Act, Oyabe opened his school in the Ainu village of Abuta in 1901. However, the funds were never enough to support his ambitious goals. Writing from Abuta to his acquaintances back at Hampton, his frustration is clear:

> In my young heart I thought that Hampton School came out as easily as asparagus from its root. But now I understand that the price of the Institute is the price of the heart and blood of that old soldier [Hampton President Samuel Armstrong]. If he were now living, I wonder what he would say to me, for I am doing the same line of work as the General [Armstrong] did. I am trying to save and educate the helpless race in this country (Oyabe 1903: 601).

Oyabe struggled to maintain the school, and finally resigned in 1909. He returned to Tokyo, where he struggled to find work. He apparently abandoned his interest in the Ainu, but not in Yoshitsune. After teaching for a time in Tokyo, Oyabe traveled to Manchuria as a translator for the Japanese Army in 1919, where he surveyed ruins he would later claim to be those of Yoshitsune. He published these findings in his 1924 book *Genghis Khan was Minamoto Yoshitsune*

[Chinggis Kan wa Minamoto no Yoshitsune nari] (Robinson & Yaguchi 2009). Drawing on his skewed historical sense, and on several of the Tokugawa era documents mentioned in this article, Oyabe constructed a fanciful if plodding work that attempted to rationalize his childhood imaginations of Japanese redemption and civilization of barbarian peoples. Perhaps because it provided an inspirational story and a "Japanese" history to lands already targeted for Japanese colonization, the book was a popular sensation. It went through eleven printings its first year, and was accorded special attention by the Imperial Court and Family. Oyabe's book was also singled out for praise by Amakasu Masahiko (1891-1945), an officer who helped establish the Japanese puppet state of Manchukuo in 1932 (Oguma 2002).

Oyabe's book was not without critics. The year after its publication, the literary and current events magazine *Chūō shidan* devoted a special issue to refuting Oyabe's work with contributions from linguists Kindaichi Kyōsuke and Nakamura Kyūshirō, anthropologist Torii Ryūzō, and philosopher and critic Miyake Setsugei, among others (Inoue 2008). Kindaichi, in particular, offered and extended rebuttal to Oyabe's claims that drew on the linguist's extensive study of the Ainu language and history while criticizing Oyabe's penchant for making the facts fit his theories (Kindaichi 1925).

Nevertheless, the book's success encouraged Oyabe to continue pursuing his other pet theories. He soon returned to China under the auspices of the Japanese Army to research Western influences on Japan. The result was his next book, *The Origin of Japan and the Japanese [Nihon oyobi Nihon no kokumin]* in which he posited a long-held theory that the Japanese had descended from a lost tribe of Israel (Robinson & Yaguchi 2009). This also reflected a long-held interest of Oyabe. The Japanese linguist Kindaichi wrote that when staying with Oyabe during a research visit in 1900, Oyabe claimed that the Japanese language was structured in Hebrew, an unsupportable idea that gave Kindaichi great pause. He attributed Oyabe's fanciful ideas to "the purity...of a hero who was a religious figure, an idealist, and a romantic ...all of which made it easy for him to believe in the mysterious" (Oguma 2002: 152-153). Eiji Oguma suggests that Oyabe's "demented ideas" were a product of Meiji Japan's need "to ease its sense of inferiority to the West" (Oguma 2002: 155).

4.4 Yoshitsune in the Prewar Youthful Imaginary

From the medieval *otogizoshi* to Oyabe's childhood infatuation with the Yoshitsune legend, myths such as these were adapted as inspirational and motivational teaching devices about self and others. For some, like Oyabe, the Yoshitsune myth helped structure his life's work, and set him upon an adventurous course that helped define and support Japan's expansion to the north and west with invented historical heroes. For others, the Yoshitsune story may have represented hidden or suppressed knowledge that harbored enough truth to cultivate wonder. Inoue Yasushi (1909-1971), a bestselling author of historical fiction, remarked that upon entering high school in Kanazawa just after Oyabe's book was published,

> I had a friend who passionately argued that Chinggis Khan was indeed Minamoto no Yoshitsune. During these years, then, Oyabe Zen'ichirō's bestseller was still holding its own and evidently was being read by a certain portion of Japanese youth. I got my hands on a copy of the book in college and, interested in what it was actually all about, I tried reading it but found it extremely tedious. That said…it was this book and the scholarly rebuttal in *Chūō shidan*…that sparked my own interest in the great Mongolian hero Chinggis Khan (Inoue 2008: 169-170).

This spirit of awe and mystery seems to connect prominent proponents of the legend. One myth hunter could not contain his giddiness upon reaching a rock carving said to have been etched by Yoshitsune: "The excitement and nervousness in our chests was insuppressible. Before our eyes at last was evidence of Yoshitsune in Hokkaido" (Sasaki et al. 1972: 10).

Whatever the extent of this youthful passion, it does not appear to have been promoted through formal schooling. At least one children's history textbook addressed the legend as untrue, though in very mild terms (Nishiki 1935). Despite this, the myth likely circulated through popular works, stories passed through families and communities, and finally the burgeoning print culture of late 19th and early 20th Century Japan. Historian Ōmori Kingorō noted in his *Outline of Our National History* (*Kokushi gaisetsu*) that the myth was "often believed these days" Ōmori 1910: 412f.). It seems likely that the Yoshitsune legends addressed two contrasting needs among Japan's rapidly changing society: that of grounding one's identity in a mythic and traditional Japanese hero who, at the same time, represents a historical precedent for colonial and military expansion.

5. Barbecued Mutton and the Yoshitsune Legend as Heritage

By the early 20th Century, the Yoshitsune legend had already evolved past its original intention of teaching and learning about the Ainu. In contemporary Hokkaido, where knowledge about the Ainu and their history is increasingly a two-way conversation, the legend has settled into a tourism meme grounded in "alternate history" that generally falls outside of scholarly and intercultural discourse. Nevertheless, a market for the legend persists: a quick search of a major Japanese online bookstore revealed no fewer than 13 trade books published about the Yoshitsune in Ezo legend since 1990[9], while Abe (2008) found 27 books and articles published on the tale since 1957. The small yet enduring audience for the myth suggests both its malleability in providing meaning across varying circumstances, and its continuing transmission across generations.

In the aftermath of WWII and Japan's loss of its external colonies, the Yoshitsune myth adapted to the capitalistic, democratic ethos that pervaded the country. The Yoshitsune myth was again popularized in ways that complemented new "traditions" of consumption and domestic travel.

In Hokkaido, one such tradition is a barbecued mutton dish known as "Jingis Kan". It originated in Manchuria among Japanese colonists and soldiers, who appropriated Chinese and Mongol food traditions and later brought them back to Japan. It has been said that the name for the dish came from Komai Tokuzō (1885-1961), who had studied agriculture at what is now Hokkaido University and was appointed a top advisor to Japan's Kwantung Army after the 1931 Manchuria Incident. After the war, returning Japanese colonists and soldiers helped popularize the dish, which was also facilitated by the wartime development of cheap iron grills for soldiers and colonists (Takaishi).

Today, the dish can be found all over Hokkaido, with small regional variations, and has become a standard experience for visitors to Hokkaido. In general, "Jingis Kan" is the product of grilling mutton, onions and other vegetables on a small iron dome greased with sheep fat. In a move reminiscent of "invented traditions" (Hobsbawm & Ranger 1983), a local tourist and heritage organization declared "Jingis Kan" a "Hokkaido Tradition" in 2004 (Hokkaidō isan kyōgikai). In the center of Sapporo, there is even a small restaurant called "Yoshitsune" across from the south entrance of Hokkaido University, whose deep red lantern advertises its specialty, Jingis Kan.

In addition to food, the steady publications of books, summer festivals in Biratori and Niikappu, at least a hundred place names, parks in the Hokkaido towns of Honbetsu and Higashikagura, and several restaurants around the island indicate both the persistence of the legend in Hokkaido, and the ample opportunities for teaching and learning about the myth among young Hokkaidoans, and other visiting Japanese.

9 Search of http://bookweb.kinokuniya.co.jp/, sv Yoshitsune+Ezo, +densetsu [tradition], +Hokkaido.

6. Conclusions

The influence of the legend of Yoshitsune in Ezo has ebbed and flowed for nearly eight centuries, adapting to changing relations between Japan and her colonial possessions. The legend and its deployment by historians, traders, teachers, soldiers and restaurateurs across those many centuries constitute a persistent vehicle for the teaching and learning of imagined Japanese roots in Hokkaido. For the most part, the legend has circulated not in schools or official curricula, but in collections of tales, pseudo-histories and their invented "sites", place names, and in the wild and fertile imaginations of Japanese explorers, misfits and youth.

This study of the Yoshitsune legend in Ezo also suggests a connection between Japan's internal and external colonial projects. Given that most studies of Japanese colonialism begin with the annexation of Taiwan or slightly before, research into Ainu and Hokkaido history, particularly when it connects to later colonial projects in Taiwan, Korea and Manchuria, are areas ripe for further exploration. The degree to which the legend has thrived in the historical and contemporary cultures have generally depended on the authority the Japanese have attempted to project in their historical colonial projects in Ezo and Manchuria. In addition, the legend has endured in Japanese culture not only because of its promotion by authorities, but also because the story of a Japanese progenitor in colonized lands satisfies a need by colonial settlers to give their expropriated lands a familiar, antique and glorious history. This is evidenced by the stamina of the legend in Japanese culture, in spite of its very dismissive reception by the Ainu themselves. In this sense, the legend of Yoshitsune in Ezo can be seen as an attempt by colonial authorities and settlers to plant and cultivate a Japanese historical narrative that begins long before colonization, one that reifies Japanese colonialism and undermines established Indigenous claims to time and place in an attempt to indigenize the colonial settler, and ultimately fuse colonized territories to the Japanese state.

The persistence of the Yoshitsune legend should also be seen in relation to the emerging dialogue of Indigenous rights for the Ainu, and as an example of the teaching and learning of "Hokkaido" as part of "Japan". The tensions over contemporary Ainu land and sovereignty claims are uniquely illustrated in the 2008 United Nations Declaration on the Rights of Indigenous Peoples (UNDRIP), where according to Winchester (2009), the Japanese representatives agreed to ratify the declaration only after inclusion of what became Article 46:

> Nothing in this declaration may be…construed as authorizing or encouraging any action which would dismember or impair, totally or in part, the territorial integrity or political unity of sovereign and independent States (UNDRIP 2008).

Because the Japanese government unilaterally annexed "Ezo" in 1869 without treaty with or consent of the Ainu, Japanese claims to Hokkaido and other lands historically inhabited by the Ainu, especially four of the Kurile Islands closest to Hokkaido that are currently governed by Russia, remain contested and suggest that Ainu lands remain contested colonial space.

In the end, however, the Yoshitsune in Ezo legend is drawn almost entirely from Japanese historical records (the Ainu having no written language until recently), so that the pedagogical work of the legend says more about the Japanese than it does the Ainu. This suggests that this particular legend continues to provide a deep, though unacknowledged root structure for Japanese territorial claims to Hokkaido, where settler colonialism is recent, and where debates over the assertions about place and history remain under negotiation.

Literature

Abe T. (2008 March): Hokkaidō no Yoshitsune densetsu no kōsatsu. In Hokusei ronshū, 45: 6, 198 – 218.

Arai H. (1720?): Ezo shi [History of Ezo]. Online available at: http://digicoll.library.wisc.edu/cgi-bin/EastAsian/EastAsian-idx?type=article&did=EastAsian.Ezoshi.i0001&id=EastAsian.Ezoshi&isize=M&pview=hide, date: 08-04-2010.

Backus, R. (1979): The Kansei Prohibition of Heterodoxy and its Effects on Education. In: Harvard Journal of Asiatic Studies, 39: 1, 55 – 106.

Batchelor, J. (1888 February): On the Ainu Term 'Kamui', Read November 9th 1887. In: Transactions of the Asiatic Society of Japan, 16: 1, 20 – 23.

Batchelor, J. (1892): The Ainu of Japan: the religion, superstitions, and general history of the hairy aborigines of Japan. London.

Biratori chō Yoshitsune o kataru kai (2001): Kamui Yoshitsune: Biratori Yoshitsune monogatari [The Ainu God Yoshitsune: The Legend of Biratori Yoshitsune]. Yūfutsu, Hokkaidō.

Bourdieu, P. (1986): The Forms of Capital. In: Richardson, J. E. (ed.): Handbook of Theory and Research for the Sociology of Education. Greenwood Press, 46 – 58.

Brownlee, J. S. (1997): Japanese Historians and National Myths, 1600-1945: The Age of the Gods and Emperor Jimmu. Vancouver.

Coloma, R. S., Means, A. & Kim, A. (2009): Palimpsest Histories and Catachrestic Interventions. In: Coloma, R. S. (ed.): Postcolonial Challenges in Education. New York, 3 – 22.

Frey, C. J. (2007): Ainu Schooling and Education Policy in 19th Century Hokkaido, Japan. Unpublished Dissertation, Indiana University.

Fujimura H. (1999): *Kamuy:* Gods you can argue with. In Fitzhugh, W. W. & Dubreuil, C. O. (eds.): Ainu: Spirit of a Northern People. Seattle, 193 – 197.

Goodman, J., McCulloch, G., & Richardson, W. (2009): "Empires Overseas" and "Empires at Home": Postcolonial and Transnational Perspectives on Social Change in the History of Education. In: Paedagogica Historica: International Journal of the History of Education 45: 6, 695 – 706.

Hall, J. W., Shively, D. H. & McCullough, W. H. (1999): The Cambridge History of Japan: Heian Japan. Cambridge: Cambridge University Press.

Hayashi S. (2000 March): Shiryō shōkai: Mikasa shi Horonai Jinja shozō 'Yoshitsune Ezo watari tensetsuzu ema' ["Ema (votive tablet) of the legend of Yoshitsune's coming to Yezo Island" at Horonai-jinja, Mikasa]. In: Hokkaidō Kaitaku Ki'nenkan Chōsa Hōkoku, 39, 95 – 100.

Harrison, J. A. & Takakura, S. (1960). The Ainu of Northern Japan: A Study of Conquest and Acculturation. In: Transactions of the American Philosophical Society 50: 4, 1 – 88.

Hickling-Hudson, A., Matthews, J. & Woods, A. (eds. 2004): *Disrupting Preconceptions: Postcolonialism and Education*. Post Pressed.

Hobsbawm, E. J. & Ranger, T. O. (1983): *The Invention of tradition*. Cambridge University Press.

Hokkaidō kyōiku kenkyūjo (1963): Hokkaidō kyōiku shi [History of Education in Hokkaido] v. III. Sapporo.

Inoue Y. (2008): The Blue Wolf: A Novel of the Life of Chinggis Khan (translated by J. Fogel). New York.

Judt, T. (2010): The Glory of the Rails. In: New York Review of Books LVII: 20, 60 – 61.

Kanazawa K. (1988 January 20): Hidaka no Yoshitsune densetsu [Yoshitsune Legends of Hidaka]. In: Kita no katari 3, 79 – 87.

Kayano S. (1985): Romance of the bear god: Ainu folktales. Tokyo.

Kindaichi K. (1925): Ainu no kenkyū [Ainu Research]. Tokyo.

Kindaichi K. (1943): Ainu jojishi Yūkara gaisetsu [Collection of Ainu Yukar Epics]. Tokyo.

Kindaichi K. & Arakida I. (1962): Ainu dōwa shū [Collected Ainu Children's Fables]. Tokyo.

McCullough, H. C. (1967): Yoshitsune: a fifteenth-century chronicle. Stanford.

Mogami T. (1786/1969): Ezo koku fūzoku ninjō no sata [1786]. In: Tanikawa K. (ed.): Nihon shomin seikatsu shiryō shūsei 4. Tokyo, 439 – 484.

Morris, I. (1975): The Nobility of Failure: Heroes in the History of Japan. New York.

Mulhern, C. I. (1974 Spring): *Otogi-zoshi*: Short Stories of the Muromachi Period. In: Monumental Nipponica 29: 2, 181 – 198.

Nishiki M. (1935): Kamakura jidai [The Kamakura Era]. Tokyo: Kōseikaku Shoten.

Nóvoa, A., Depaepe, M. & Johanningmeier, E. V. (eds. 1995): The Colonial Experience in Education: Paedagogica Historica, International Journal of the History of Education Supplementary Series Vol. 1. Ghent, Belgium.

O'Flaherty, W. D. & Doniger, W. (1995): *Other peoples' myths: the cave of echoes*. University of Chicago Press.

Ogawa M. (1997): Kindai Ainu kyōiku seidōshi kenkyū [Research on the Modern Ainu Education System]. Sapporo.

Oguma E. (2002): A Genealogy of 'Japanese' Self-Images. Melbourne.

Oguma Y. (1981): Yoshitsune gō. In: Hokkaidō shimbunsha (ed.): Hokkaidō daihyakka jiten [Encyclopedia of Hokkaido] Vol. 2, Sapporo, 871.

Ōmori K. (1910): Kokushi gaisetsu [Outline of Our National History]. Tokyo.

Oyabe J. (1898): A Japanese Robinson Crusoe. Boston.

Oyabe J. (1903 December): A Missionary to the Ainu. In: *Southern Workman* 32: 12, 601 – 603.

Parker, H. S. E. (2006): Progressive Traditions: An Illustrated Study of Plot Repetition in Traditional Japanese Theater. Leiden.

Passin, H. (1982): Society and Education in Japan. Tokyo.

Philippi, D.L. (1979): Songs of gods, songs of humans: the epic tradition of the Ainu. Princeton.

Robinson, G. & Yaguchi, Y. (eds. 2009): A Japanese Robinson Crusoe. Honolulu.

Ruch, B. (2000): The Other Side of History: The Search for the Common Culture of Medieval Japan. In Yamamura, K. (ed.): The Cambridge History of Japan, Vol. 3, Medieval Japan. Cambridge, 531 – 541.

Silverberg, R. (1986): The Mound Builders. Athens, Ohio.

Sasaki S., Ōmuchi K. & Higuchi C. (1972): Minamoto Yoshitsune Ezo bōmei tsuiseki no ki: Yoshitsune wa ikiteita. [An Account of the Pursuit of the Exile of Minamoto no Yoshitsune in Ezo: Yoshitsune Lived On]. Tokyo.

Shimizu I. (1886): Tsūzoku Yoshitsune saikōki [The Revival of Yoshitsune]. Tokyo.

Sturm, H., Dekker, J., Aldrich, R. & Simon, F. (1996): Education and cultural transmission: historical studies of continuity and change in families, schooling and youth cultures. In: Pedagogica Historica, Supplementary Series II. Ghent.

Takaishi K.: Yōniku ryōri 'Jingis Kan' no ikkōsatsu ["Thoughts on the Mutton Cuisine 'Jingis Kan'"]. Online available at: http://www.agri.pref.hokkaido.jp/nouseibu/zinngisukann/, date: 11-01-2011.

Takakura S. (1972): Ainu seisaku shi [History of Ainu Policy]. Tokyo.

Walker, B. (2000): The Conquest of Ainu Lands: Ecology and Culture in Japanese Expansion, 1590-1800. Berkeley.

Warren, D. (2008): What Can Happen when Histories of Education Meet American Indian Histories. In Miami, FL, October 23-26, 2008.

Weiner, M. (ed. 2009): Japan's Minorities: The Illusion of Homogeneity. New York.

Winchester, M. (2009): On the Dawn of a New National Ainu Policy: The "'Ainu" as a Situation' Today." The Asia-Pacific Journal 41, no. 3, issue 9. Online available at: http://www.japanfocus.org/articles/print_article/3234, date 24-03-2011.

Yoshitsune wa Jingis Kan densetsu o ou (1998): In: Ōsaka shiryō koten sekishitsu 1: 19.

Young, R. C. (2005): Posutokoroniaruizumu: Issatsu de wakaru [Postcolonialism: A Very Short Introduction], trans. T. Motohashi. Tokyo, v.

Lessons of Colonization: Uni- and Multi-Directional Learning in Pueblo Indian Country

Adrea Lawrence, American University, USA

At the turn of the twentieth century, the New Mexico Territory was a nexus of intercultural interaction and exchange. Pueblo Indian[1] presence along the northern Rio Grande has been rooted there from time immemorial. Pueblo Indians' early experiences with other Indigenous peoples, such as the Ute, Jicarilla Apaches, Comanches, and Diné (Navajo), and later Spanish colonists established the region as a vibrant borderland. When Spanish conquistadors and settlers moved north from their hub in what is now Mexico in the sixteenth century, they treated Native peoples as objects of conquest in order to establish colonial outposts that would generate monetary wealth through the mining of silver and gold, and spiritual wealth through the saving of souls. The Spanish colonial systems of tribute and forced labor, though, had little appeal for the Pueblo peoples who had to endure them; and in 1680, several Indian Pueblos along the Rio Grande worked together to force the secular and religious colonists out of the area.

The Pueblo Revolt, as it is now known, kept the Spanish at bay for twelve years. Upon their return – by invitation (Sando 1992: 63-69) or through reconquest (Galgano 2005: 136-141; Roberts 2004: 9-27) – the Spanish colonials and the Pueblo peoples carefully negotiated syncretic living arrangements that included new legal provisions for land grants and how they were to be used, the Spanish settlers' adoption of Puebloan irrigation techniques, a host of additional political offices within Indian Pueblos, and a firm Church presence in village life. For example, the Spanish Crown established and documented permanent land grants for each Indian Pueblo that were four square leagues (17,000 acres) and included a buffer zone of one-and-a-half leagues (3.9 miles or 6.24 km) to be free of Spanish settlement and trespass (Carlson 1975: 96). These arrangements persisted and morphed according to custom throughout the remainder of the Spanish regime and the duration of the Mexican regime (1821-1848) until

1 Pueblo Indians are an American Indian population noted for their distinctive adobe architecture and their extensive agricultural networks along the Rio Grande and its tributaries in what is now New Mexico, located in the southwestern quadrant of the United States. Each Indian Pueblo is a distinct community, or tribe. In addition to common architectural and agricultural practices, each Pueblo speaks one of three Tanoan languages (Tewa, Tiwa, Towa), Keresan, or Zuni (Shiwi'ma). For a full discussion, see (Dozier 1960; Dozier 1970; Ortiz 1969; Sando 1992).

the United States acquired sovereign, colonial right to what is now the American Southwest in 1848 at the conclusion of the U.S. War with Mexico.

By the time the U.S. officially entered the region as a colonial power, Pueblo Indians' experience with colonization had wizened them to numerous types of hegemonic efforts; U.S. officials, however, did not recognize the learning – the education – that Pueblo Indians cultivated under the two previous colonial regimes. Rather, U.S. officials, most of whom were Anglo[2] and operated through the Bureau of Indian Affairs (BIA), treated Pueblo Indians as they had treated other Indigenous peoples over the half-century: as obstacles to non-Native geographic expansion, natural resource development, and cultural progress. But the presence of two seemingly "civilized" peoples – Pueblo Indians and Hispanos[3] – confounded the colonial narrative of Manifest Destiny[4] that the U.S. had constructed for itself. Pueblo Indians offered an alternate yet clearly recognizable form of "civilized" living that adhered to both Euro-American and Indigenous standards. Pueblo Indians were sedentary farmers who lived in permanent villages, built multistoried houses, and practiced Catholicism; they also appeared "Indian" and maintained their distinctive social, political, and religious beliefs and practices that had pre-Spanish roots. Hispanos, whose roots were unequivocally European, had been in the region long enough to adopt a number of Puebloan practices such that they perplexed U.S. bureaucrats and settlers. The differences between Hispanos and Anglos were notable enough for the newcomer colonialists to regard the former as subordinate and as colonizable. And while U.S. law regarded Hispanos as legally "White", the courts and other agents of the U.S. government regularly regarded Hispanos as "Other", frequently ruling or making decisions in favor of Anglo settlers in cases of land tenure and access to limited natural resources (Gomez 2005). The longstanding colonial histories of the peoples of New Mexico thus dissolves the "colonizer-colonized" binary (Memmi 1965), offering a historical context that is endlessly complex, contested, and dependent on one's point of view in space and time.

2 "Anglo" refers to descendents of immigrants from Europe, especially from the northern and western regions.

3 "Hispano" refers to people of Spanish descent living in New Mexico. Though there are different class distinctions among the Hispano population (Dunbar-Ortiz 2007; Ebright 1989, 2008; Ebright and Hendricks 2006; Nieto-Phillips 2004), Bureau of Indian Affairs officials appear to have largely regarded this population as monolithic, making nuanced class distinctions in U.S. government documents difficult, if not impossible, to parse.

4 "Manifest Destiny" is the belief that Anglo Americans were preordained by God to occupy the whole of what is now the continental United States. John L. O'Sullivan (1845) coined the term in 1845, and it became a full-blown justification for Anglos' westward expansion, the creation of Indian reservations, and the removal of Indians to them.

Bureau of Indian Affairs (BIA) officials in the field had to navigate among these shifting colonial histories. The BIA charged school personnel – particularly teachers and superintendents – with culturally, linguistically, and economically converting American Indian children and their families to standards, norms, and beliefs that Anglo-Americans valued. Those teachers who lived and worked on reservations in day schools established for children under the ages of twelve, had especially important assignments in intercultural learning. Not only were they the eyes and ears of the BIA, they were expected to carry out policies relating to land use, citizenship, and public health, in addition to teaching lessons outlined in the *Course of Study for Indian Schools in the United States, Industrial and Literary* (Reel 1901). Superintendents oversaw the comprehensive implementation of federal Indian policy and reported back to the Bureau of Indian Affairs, often making recommendations and acting in ways that had lasting effects. Because of their proximity to and interaction with Indigenous, Hispano, and Anglo communities, BIA day school teachers and their superintendents in New Mexico acted within a nexus of colonial confrontation and bargaining. And they, like their Pueblo Indian and Hispano counterparts, sometimes learned from this. Much of the colonizing "education" policy set out by the U.S. in the late nineteenth and early twentieth centuries sifted through the schoolhouse before it made its way into local communities, transforming day school teachers and boarding school superintendents into gatekeepers, interpreters, and appropriators of federal Indian education policy. Such policy included a wide range of issues from land use and management to public health to citizenship to the traditional academic subjects taught in schools. In fact, it was through teachers and superintendents that Pueblo Indian and neighboring Hispano populations learned about official U.S. colonial policy; this learning at the periphery of the BIA school, in turn, helped create the foundation from which those populations would appropriate and subvert such policies (Lawrence in press).

This chapter considers the learning of two Bureau of Indian Affairs teachers who lived and worked in the New Mexico Territory at the turn of the twentieth century. Clara D. True and Clinton J. Crandall worked together in the Northern Pueblos District in New Mexico during the first decade of the twentieth century as the Santa Clara day school teacher and Santa Fe Indian School superintendent, respectively. Before their arrival in New Mexico, both True and Crandall had worked the BIA school circuit, serving as teachers in boarding schools across the continental United States. Previously, they had taught together at the Lower Brulé Indian School in South Dakota in the late 1890s. In 1900, Crandall was appointed as superintendent of the Santa Fe Indian School, making him both the primary supervisor of teachers at that school and at day schools in the Northern Pueblos District along the Rio Grande. His role as superintendent also meant that he was the primary Indian agent for the Bureau of Indian Affairs in that district, responsible for mitigating federal Indian policies regarding public health, land, citizenship, and schooling. Two years later, True was appointed as day school teacher at Santa Clara Pueblo, approximately thirty miles northwest of Santa Fe within the Northern Pueblos District. In this role, True lived at the Pueblo and she was to teach children under the age of twelve who enrolled at the day school; she was also responsible for interpreting and carrying out the same policies Crandall mitigated as well as serving as the eyes and the ears of the BIA (Jones 1900; "Personnel Notecard of Clara D. True's Assignments in the Bureau of Indian Affairs" n.d.).[5] Both True and Crandall, along with their Pueblo Indian and Hispano counterparts, appropriated federal Indian policies in ways that reflected their own situations, experiences, assumptions, and expectations.

Given the copious documentary record of the BIA in the National Archives and Records Administration, one might assume that learning about what went on in Indian Office schools would simply be a matter of reading the files. Little documentary evidence exists, however, from BIA teachers and superintendents about what went on inside the schoolhouse.[6] Their correspondence and reports indicate, rather, other issues they dealt with on a daily basis and what they and their host communities found to be important. These issues were instructive and often educative; yet at times, Anglo officials seem to have missed important lessons. This chapter extends research that has already been done on the years of True's tenure as day school teacher at Santa Clara Pueblo from 1902 to 1907 (Lawrence in press) and examines the lessons lost primarily on Crandall after True returned to the Rio Grande valley in 1910 after a stint as a BIA superintendent at the Potrero School on the Morongo (Malki) Reservation in southern California. Their experiences and personalities in the BIA as teachers and superintendents illustrate how two "colonizers" worked in different ways with Indigenous peoples, at times demonstrating a type of learning about colonization and the colonial enterprise that is arresting, but mostly revealing how the colonialist often and unwittingly dons blinders when considering the ways in which "Others" experience colonizing policies and actions. These lost lessons are revealed through the reports of BIA inspectors who investigated Crandall in 1911 and his successor in 1912.

5 At the time True worked as the Santa Clara day school teacher, she was Crandall's subordinate. When she returned to the Rio Grande valley in 1910, however, she left a superintendency and was Crandall's equal within the BIA.

6 Recent studies have uncovered what went on in boarding schools through first-hand student accounts. See, for example, the following seminal studies Adams 1997; Child 1998; Coleman 1993; Katanski 2005; Lomawaima 1994; Reyhner and Eder 2006; Trafzer, Keller, and Sisquoc 2006.

By looking at the day-to-day concerns of land and liquor that animated the inspection reports investigating Crandall and his successor, a discernable juxtaposition surfaces between the accumulated learning of Pueblo Indians and lessons lost on BIA officials. Beginning with an overview of schooling systems created for American Indians in the United States, this chapter contrasts what was supposed to be "learned" by Indian students through formal structures with what was actually learned, and what was lost by BIA employees through their everyday interactions of Pueblo Indians, Hispanos, and other Anglos. The analysis then proceeds with an examination of lessons lost through two vignettes: the non-Native use of Pueblo Indian land and liquor sales to and consumption among Pueblo Indians. More specifically, the documentary record reveals 1) that changing models and expectations of liquor use among Native communities reflected the disparate social and moral expectations of Anglo colonizers, like True and Crandall, as well as Native leaders; and, 2) that natural resources like prime grazing land, pitted Hispanos, Anglos, and Santa Clarans against one another.

1. Schooling American Indians

Early in the European colonization of the Americas, religious groups established missionary schools for Native children, not only to teach them how to read and write, but also to convert them to Christianity. Missionary schooling has continued ever since, but government-run schools for American Indian children emerged as the U.S. became independent from the United Kingdom at the end of the eighteenth century (Coleman 1993: 38-42; Reyhner & Eder 2006: 14-39; Szasz 2007: 5). Initially housed in the War Department, the Bureau of Indian Affairs (BIA) was established to liaise with and regulate Native peoples across the continent; this ultimately included developing and operating schools for Indigenous children. In the mid-nineteenth century, as the U.S. concluded its war with Mexico and verged on civil war, the federal government somewhat shifted its orientation toward American Indians and moved the BIA to the Department of the Interior, assuming that American Indian tribes should no longer to be regarded exclusively as foreign nations – they were to become incorporated into U.S. society eventually, or simply perish. After the U.S. Civil War (1861-1865), however, American Indian extinction was no longer a tolerable option, and federal Indian policy focused instead on assimilating Native peoples into the Anglo-American mainstream.

By the turn of the twentieth century, Progressivism with its hallmarks labor reform and scientific management pervaded the U.S. political agenda; yet federal Indian policies, particularly those oriented toward schooling, bypassed many of the child labor aspects of the reform agenda, focusing instead on an industrial model of schooling that began in day schools and extended through on- and off-reservation boarding schools. Formalized through Reel's *Course of Study for Indian Schools in the United States*, the industrial model that characterized BIA-run Indian schools split students' training between academic and vocational subjects. The goal was to resolve the "Indian problem" by transforming American Indian students culturally, morally, and, of course, economically by instilling Euro-American defined beliefs and practices, such as individualism, the English language, Christian doctrine, and capitalism. The industrial curriculum assumed a linear, progressive tendency in human development – that people adapt in an evolutionary manner and that schools can and should be institutions that accelerate such adaptations. Operating under this assumption, BIA officials, U.S. legislators, and reformers believed that through schooling and other programs like land allotment,[7] American Indian children could become part of the dominant U.S. society and would rationally relinquish their Native cultures.

BIA boarding and day schools expanded rapidly from 1880 to 1900 along with the Bureau itself. Historian David Wallace Adams writes that enrollments increased from 3598 students in 1877 to 21,568 students in 1900 in the "147 reservation day schools, 81 reservation boarding schools, and 25 off-reservation boarding schools" that the BIA operated (Adams 1988: 3). By 1900, the industrial school model was the standard for BIA schools as reflected in Reel's curriculum. In order to administer the BIA school system, which spread from coast to coast during the latter half of the nineteenth century, the Bureau became increasingly centralized and bureaucratized, relying heavily on the field reports of its superintendents (Adams 1997: 63, 70; Browning 2000: 194-195; Noble & Harrison 2000: 180; Stuart 1985: 138-139; Stuart 1987: 2, 13). Superintendents had, in fact, gained considerable power and authority within the BIA in the second half of the nineteenth century as the position became the substitute for the ubiquitous Indian Agent (Adams 1997: 60-71; U.S. Congress 2000a; U.S. Congress 2000b). This structural change consolidated the governance of the school superintendent, placing teachers, housekeepers, school matrons, disciplinarians, farmers, policemen, and assistants under his purview. BIA teachers thus served at the pleasure of their superintendents. Depending on the superintendent,

7 Land allotment is most well known through The General Allotment Act, or Dawes Act, of 1887, which broke up communally held parcels of land and redistributed 160-acre plots to individual, nuclear families to cultivate through farming. Like the Homestead Act of 1862, the Dawes Act, awarded fee simple title of the 160-acre plot after a probationary period; for American Indians under the Dawes Act, the period was twenty-five years and for non-Natives under the Homestead Act, the period was five years.

teachers, who were mostly Anglo women, might experience anything from a fruitful working environment to one that was abusive (Adams 1997: 89; Brookings Institution and Meriam 1928: 359-370; Carter 1995: 69, 73-75; Coleman 2005: 200). Unlike day school teachers – like True – and on-reservation boarding school superintendents, though, off-reservation boarding school superintendents – like Crandall – experienced a distance from the Native communities whom they served and attempted to regulate, sometimes putting these BIA officials at odds with one another. Lost were lessons U.S. agents might have learned about Native peoples and their experiences with colonization.

2. Lessons Lost – colonial conflicts as nexus points of intercultural learning

Though one might think that living near and working with Pueblo Indians might open up BIA agents' capacity to see and appreciate the "Other", this does not appear to have occurred regularly enough to create any discernable pattern. In fact, what becomes readily apparent is that BIA agents not only had to live in proximity to the "Other", but also had to be intellectually and culturally receptive to Pueblo Indians' understandings of and interactions with the physical world and peoples around them. In other words, BIA agents had to be willing to improvise and risk accepting their premises as wrong. The same disposition would hold for Pueblo Indians, effecting a form of intersubjectivity that would foster mutually recognized and appreciated modes of intercultural communication. Such a mutually constructed intersubjectivity does not appear to have happened in the Rio Grande valley from 1910-1912. Intersubjectivity and mutuality were fleeting at best, and it is in these moments – where there is an afterimage of what might have been learned – that lost lessons become visible. Part of what makes this visibility possible is the difference in experiences between Clara D. True and Clinton J. Crandall in their respective positions. True appears to have been able to receptively take part in, if not cultivate, mutually appreciated positions with Santa Clarans and other Pueblo peoples when the stakes of cultural survival were high, whereas Crandall did not. In fact, True's initial experience as the Santa Clara day school teacher coupled with her subsequent superintendency of the on-reservation Potrero Boarding School opened up the possibility for her to learn from Native peoples, even if this possibility was short-lived.[8]

8 Other historians have argued that True pushed her own agenda among Pueblo peoples, taking advantage of them to elevate her own prestige, territory, and power in the region

Evidence of this comes in an article she wrote for *Outlook* magazine in 1909, shortly before she left her post as the superintendent of the Potrero School in southern California:

> It is to be regretted that in dealing with the Indian we have not regarded him worth while [*sic*] until it is too late to enrich our literature and traditions with the contribution he could so easily have made. We have regarded him as a thing to be robbed and converted rather than as a being with intellect, sensibilities, and will, all highly developed, the development being on different lines than our own only as necessity dictated. The continent was his college. The slothful student was expelled from it by President Nature. Physically, mentally, and morally, the North American Indian before his degradation at our hands was a man whom his descendants need not despise. (True 1909: 336)

True appears to see the colonial assumptions about and attendant policies for American Indians for what they were: a political and moral strong-arm that sought to bend Native peoples into a new form, simply discarding everything "Indian" for the Euro-American "normal."

Shortly after True's article was published, she retired from the BIA and returned to the Rio Grande valley to live permanently at her ranch between the Santa Clara and San Ildefonso Pueblos. Crandall was still superintendent of the Santa Fe Indian School, though his days in that position were numbered. In the spring of 1911, the BIA sent Shelby M. Singleton, an inspector for the Bureau, to investigate Crandall for misconduct as an Indian agent. The charges against him included corruptly managing land on the Santa Clara Reservation, illegally selling liquor to Indians, and neglecting the needs of Pueblo Indian communities in his district. True, together with BIA liquor inspector William E. Johnson and the Catholic priest from the nearby Hispano village of Santa Cruz, had aligned with members of the Santa Clara Pueblo and other Pueblo Indian leaders in the area against Crandall. True's opposition to Crandall stemmed back to 1903, when diphtheria hit Santa Clara while Crandall was away in Washington, D.C. She was responsible not only for establishing a quarantine to prevent the spread of the disease, but also negotiating with the itinerant BIA physician in treating sick children and working through the two primary political factions of the Pueblo. She provided regular reports to Crandall's office. When Crandall returned in the midst of the outbreak, he accused True of exaggerating the spread of the disease and chastised her for it. True's subsequent formal communications with Crandall were significantly pared of their side commentaries, and during the remainder of True's tenure as day school teacher, she appears to have care-

---

in the 1920s (Jacobs 1996, 1999, 2002; Wenger 2009). While this might have been the case, the documentary record from 1902-1912 does not bear this out.

fully considered how Crandall might read her reports with a critical eye. In other words, she had figured out the limits of what Crandall would and would not tolerate (Lawrence in press). True's return to the Rio Grande valley in 1910, then, came with the tension of her earlier relationship with Crandall. And because she no longer worked for the BIA, but had just resigned from a position equivalent to Crandall's, she could take a firm and vocal position against him.

Though Crandall was investigated on multiple charges, two in particular had deep historical roots among Pueblo peoples in the area: liquor consumptions and the management of Indian lands. Attitudes and practices toward liquor and land over the years reflected dynamic relationships between Pueblo peoples, their Indigenous neighbors, Hispanos, and Anglos in the Rio Grande valley; and it is through the issues of liquor and land – and their historical sediment – that we are able to see lessons about Pueblo Indians that were lost on Crandall. Beginning with vignettes about liquor sales and land use found in Singleton's 1911 inspection report of Crandall, the remainder of this chapter examines three lost lessons that Crandall might have learned. The first highlights the fact that Crandall did not learn about the history of relationships between Pueblo Indians, Jicarilla Apaches, and Hispanos in the Rio Grande valley, which undermined his understanding of local customs and changing positions. The second underscores that Crandall was not mindful of the long-term education through colonization that Pueblo Indians had developed over the preceding 300 years. Finally, the third lost lesson draws attention to Crandall's lack of attention to his relationships with other BIA personnel in favor of those with local business and political figures.

2.1 Vignette 1: Liquor Consumption and the Legal Status of "Indians"

Crandall's position toward dealing with liquor and American Indians' consumption of it appears to have changed during his tenure as the Santa Fe Indian School superintendent. Shortly before True reported to her post as the Santa Clara day school teacher in 1902, Crandall attended the Feast of San Geronimo Festival at Taos Pueblo and reported to the Commissioner of Indian Affairs that neighboring Jicarilla Apaches who attended had transformed the fiesta into a drunken melee. Crandall went so far to request that the Commissioner furnish law enforcement officers at the next Pueblo festival to prevent such behavior (Crandall 1902). His request went unfulfilled. By the time Singleton investigated Crandall in 1911, it appears as though he adopted a much more relaxed position on alcohol. In fact, the BIA liquor inspector, in cooperation with Clara D. True, even accused Crandall of selling liquor to Indians from a drug store that he co-owned in Santa Fe. What precipitated this seeming change is mysterious, but both positions – curbing drinking and facilitating it – indicate a view toward Pueblo Indians, in particular, and American Indians, in general, that they were not the same as Anglos. Anglos, after all, could decide on their own whether or not they would drink.

Crandall's initial position against Indian drinking reflects longstanding colonial policy in Indian Country. The sanction for distributing and selling liquor to American Indians has a fraught genealogy in U.S. law grounded in assumptions about Native and non-Native morality. Indeed the fear and control of liquor among Indigenous populations had been a hallmark of the European colonization of North America (Ishii 2003: 676; Mancall 1995: 12-13). Sixteenth and seventeenth century Spanish colonial law stipulated that "[n]o liquor was to be sold to Indians" (Bourke 1894: 199). Similar provisions extended across the U.S. in the nineteenth century, beginning with President Thomas Jefferson's 1808 request to state and territorial governors to prohibit the sale of alcohol to Indians, to the 1834 passage of the Trade and Intercourse Act, which made such sales a federal offense, and culminating with passage of the 1897 Intoxicating Drinks to Indians Act, which established incarceration as punishment for selling liquor to Indians. Despite their venerable legal history, laws regulating liquor trade with Indigenous peoples demonstrated little regard for the historical relationships between Native groups and their use of alcohol in maintaining those relationships.

At the Taos festival, Crandall believed that the Jicarilla Apaches were to blame for the raucous behavior among Pueblo Indians, but he did not understand the long-term relationships and related drinking practices among several of the Pueblos and their Jicarilla Apache and Hispano neighbors. Though little has been written about drinking practices among Pueblo Indians and the Jicarilla Apaches, historical research has been done looking at such practices among other tribes. For example, Peter C. Mancall writes that Apache and Navajo peoples reaffirmed their social ties by consuming alcohol together (Mancall 1995: 133). By extension, it seems entirely possible that similar ties were made during the Taos festival. Crandall, however, missed this possibility. Instead, curbing Indian drinking at the northern Rio Grande Pueblos became an issue of power and authority for Crandall, reflecting his belief – at least in the early years of his tenure as superintendent – that as an Anglo representative of the U.S. government, he could and should control the behavior of Indians. In part, this had to do with Pueblo Indians' nebulous status as quasi-citizens in the New Mexico Territory and the U.S.

When the U.S. annexed the northern half of Mexico under the Treaty of Guadalupe Hidalgo in 1848, Pueblo Indians were presumed to be citizens of the territory and thus of the U.S., rather than wards of the federal government as other Indian tribes. The U.S. government took its cue from the Mexican regime, which regarded Pueblo Indians as full citizens of Mexico whether they elected to be or not. That Pueblo Indians were sedentary farmers who practiced Catholicism and built distinctive multistoried houses lent credence to the non-Native belief that Pueblo Indians were "civilized Indians", unlike their nomadic and semi-nomadic counterparts such as the Apache, Comanche, Arapaho, and Cheyenne whose ways of life had been taken as representative of "the Indian." These tribes, under U.S. law, became citizens through a probationary period of individual land ownership and cultivation, the payment of taxes, and the legal right to buy and sell alcohol. This probationary period did not exist for Pueblo peoples; rather their citizenship status took a reverse trajectory, going from full citizen to quasi-citizen to ward of the federal government. Through his annual reports to the Commissioner of Indian Affairs, Crandall, as the primary ethnographic and policy voice of the region, was instrumental in chipping away at Pueblo Indians' citizenship status in the first decade of the twentieth century.

To presume, however, that Pueblo Indians wanted New Mexican and U.S. citizenship with its attendant rights and responsibilities is a mistake. Indeed, they flatly rejected U.S. citizenship in favor of their own governance customs and procedures (Crandall 1904). Pueblo Indian leaders wanted to decide whether or not they would endorse or reject drinking in their villages. And like Crandall, they appear to have changed their positions on drinking, albeit for different reasons. Throughout True's tenure as the day school teacher at Santa Clara, there is little mention in her letters of Pueblo leaders' opposition to drinking. But upon her return, several villages, particularly Santa Clara, wanted to abolish drinking on Pueblo land. Included with Singleton's inspection report of Crandall are two letters from the All Pueblos Council in which village leaders requested that the U.S. government enforce its own laws against selling liquor to Indians and that the U.S. government recognize the centuries-old authority structure of Pueblo communities (Singleton 1911: Exhibit A, pp. 10-11; Exhibit B, p. 5). The Council found little remedy as the 1912 inspection report of Crandall's successor reveals that Pueblo leaders believed liquor consumption and drunkenness within their communities, coupled with the BIA Indian policemen who challenged Pueblo governors, and the individualism taught at BIA schools undermined governors' authority and promoted factionalism. The viability of the sociopolitical structures within each village was threatened. It is not surprising that Pueblo leaders wanted the control of liquor sales, Indian police authority, and how children should be schooled left to village leaders, not the BIA (Tipton 1912).

2.2 *Vignette 2: Grazing on Reservation Land and the Jemez Forest Reserve*

Contrary to other American Indian peoples who were placed on U.S. government created and controlled reservations in the nineteenth century, Santa Clarans remained on their centuries-long homelands and lobbied for a reservation in order to protect their land holdings and their sociocultural ways of life.[9] In addition to the 17,000 acre land grant the Spanish Crown initially recognized in the late 1690s, Santa Clara Pueblo acquired an additional land grant in 1763 that extended west of the Pueblo along Santa Clara Creek and up through Santa Clara Cañon. By the early twentieth century, these lands were continually encroached upon, and Santa Clarans sought to remedy this. By converting their land grants into a reservation the U.S. government would, in theory, be compelled to patrol and protect reservation boundaries from outsiders. On 29 July 1905, the Santa Clarans' efforts were met with success – President Theodore Roosevelt converted Santa Clara Pueblo's two Spanish land grants into an executive order reservation, a reservation created outside of treaty negotiations with the U.S. Congress.[10] Though Crandall was instrumental in pushing the case for the creation of the Santa Clara Reservation, he did not understand Santa Clarans' intent, nor did he really comprehend the extent to which they had experience with and understood colonial land policies (Lawrence in press). The circumstances under which Santa Clara had acquired the additional land grant in 1763 illuminate both their attention to colonial legal provisions that were established to protect Pueblo Indian land holdings as well as their willingness to confront colonial authorities from the eighteenth century on in order to remedy adverse situations.

Santa Clarans passed on what they learned from these episodes, and by the time the U.S. government annexed the region in 1848, the Pueblo had built a cumulative body of learning around colonial land policies under the Spanish and

9 One should not interpret this to mean that Santa Clarans and other Pueblo Indians were the only sedentary Indigenous groups in North America. Though U.S. government policies in the late nineteenth and early twentieth centuries suggest that farming Indians were an anomaly, this is not the case. Rather, Pueblo Indians' farming practices were clearly recognizable for Europeans and Euro-Americans (see, for example, Cronon 2003; Mann 2005). Through court cases and laws passed by Congress, the U.S. government helped create a narrative that Indians were nomadic; thus one of the ways in which to make them European was to teach them to farm.

10 The United States government stopped negotiating treaties with individual American Indian tribes during Ulysses S. Grant's administration (1869-1877). The "treaty" the U.S. had with Pueblo Indians was actually the Treaty of Guadalupe Hidalgo, negotiated with the Mexican government in 1848, when the northern half of Mexico was ceded to the United States. Indigenous groups did not participate in those treaty deliberations.

Mexican regimes. Two incidents during the Spanish regime highlight the fact that Santa Clarans understood the rights that came with their land grants and that they would protect those rights by working through the appropriate colonial government channels. The first incident occurred in the mid-eighteenth century when two Spanish brothers who had secured a land grant for grazing in Santa Clara Cañon just west of the Pueblo violated the terms of their grant by building homesteads on it and growing crops. Santa Claran leaders protested this, petitioning two successive local Spanish governors to resolve the problem. Their second attempt was successful – the Spanish brothers' land grant was rescinded and awarded to Santa Clara Pueblo in 1763. The second incident occurred shortly before Mexican independence in 1821. A man who was born a member of Santa Clara Pueblo became a Spanish citizen and successfully petitioned the Crown for a land grant. Santa Claran leadership found that the grant permeated the buffer zone around the Pueblo, a violation of Spanish law. Santa Claran leaders traveled to Durango in 1815 to recover the land. Again, they were successful. Each case demonstrates that Santa Claran leaders understood their land rights under Spanish colonial law, and that they worked through the colonial government to enforce colonial law. In the early 1900s, Santa Claran leaders once more attempted to work through the colonial government – this time that of the United States – to ensure that its land rights under the reservation declaration were upheld; but their efforts were foiled by the new manager of the Santa Clara Reservation: C.J. Crandall.

When the Santa Clara land grants became a reservation in 1905 with President Roosevelt stating that the land was "for the benefit of the people" (Roosevelt 1905), the management of Santa Clara lands transferred from Pueblo leaders to Crandall, the local U.S. government agent. Early in the management of the Santa Clara Reservation, Crandall did work to ensure that trespassers and squatters, particularly those who were Hispano, were routed and evicted (Lawrence in press). This did not last long, however. According to Singleton's investigation report, it appears as though Crandall was selective in the points of policy that he would enforce. Though he would work to run Hispanos squatters and trespassers off reservation land, he also issued $1 permits to Anglo and Hispano ranchers who wanted to water or graze their livestock on Santa Clara land; and Crandall did this without Santa Clarans' knowledge, a clear breach of U.S. statutory law (Singleton 1911: 13-14). As far as Santa Clarans knew, the trespassing simply continued. What the Santa Clarans did not foresee was that Crandall would work exclusively in his own interest, and their attempts to convince him to resolve the situation were unsuccessful.

As they had with the creation of the Santa Clara Reservation, members of the Pueblo were accustomed to working through the legal apparatus of the U.S.

government's colonial system to ensure their rights and maintain their relationships. But the Pueblo found that their primary liaison, C.J. Crandall, was not responsive nor were other officials who had the legal authority to help, including the U.S. attorney for the Pueblo and the Hispano justice of the peace. Santa Clarans had to improvise and take a different tack. From 1908, after True left the Rio Grande valley, through 1910, when she returned, Santa Clarans went outside colonial legal channels, seeking aid from the Bureau of Catholic Indian Missions (BCIM) to protect their land rights and deal with Hispanos who sometimes trespassed on the reservation. Not only were Santa Claran leaders worried about being able to protect their lands, they were also concerned about their relationships with neighboring Hispanos (Tafoya, Naranjo & Cajete 1910).

Crandall's priorities in looking after Pueblo lands appear to have shifted, if not in the months after the reservation was created, then shortly after True left for California. Anglo ranchers had grown used to grazing their stock on both the Jemez Forest Reserve and the Santa Clara Reservation. At the seeming threat that Pueblo land would be closed off to non-Native ranchers, one Anglo rancher wrote to both the New Mexico Territorial delegate in Congress and the Commissioner of Indian Affairs protesting such a change. At the top of his list of arguments about why non-Native ranchers should be allowed to continue to graze their stock on Pueblo lands was the premise that Pueblo Indians did not need the land as their population was diminishing, thereby decreasing their resource needs. Keeping the land in Pueblo hands would have the effect of hindering Anglo (and likely Hispano) economic development. The rancher added in a later letter to the New Mexico delegate that the nominal $1 grazing fee collected from ranchers went directly – at least in part – to the public school system, a system which Pueblo Indians did not typically use (Brook 1911b; Brook 1911a; Brook 1911c).[11] The rancher does not mention Crandall by name, but Crandall was the U.S. government agent who issued permits to graze on Santa Clara land.

11 It is not clear whether or not the Anglo rancher knew that Pueblo Indians did not participate in the public school system. It seems likely that he would have, given his proximity to several Indian Pueblos, however. His mention of the grazing fees going to public schools in New Mexico underscores the two-fold argument that schools represented "civilization" and "betterment" and that the fees were not wasted on something insignificant.

3. Lessons Lost – exploring learning options and missed opportunities

3.1 Local Histories and Relationships Matter

In placing so much importance on interpreting and carrying out federal policies, one of the central lessons lost on Crandall and other BIA officials in New Mexico was that historical relationships between peoples in the area mattered. Notably, Crandall missed the fact that Pueblo Indians had dealt with non-Native encroachment since the Spanish first settled in the Rio Grande valley. And as the Santa Clarans' 1910 solicitation of help from the Bureau of Catholic Indian Missions demonstrates, relationships between Pueblo Indians and their Hispano neighbors mattered.[12] Those relationships had long histories and were evidence of parleyed arrangements, which were sometimes broken through trespass, but worth maintaining nevertheless. The tendency toward uniformity in federal Indian law and policy, though, did not account for the possibility that local actors, namely Pueblo Indians and Hispanos, could and did attempt to appropriate U.S. policy.

In the case of land use, had Crandall been mindful of Santa Clarans' efforts to compel the enforcement of colonial law under the Spanish regime, he might not have structured a reciprocal grazing arrangement with the Jemez Forest Reserve for non-Native ranchers who wanted to graze and water their stock on the Santa Clara Reservation. Instead, Crandall's actions suggest that he recognized no limits on his authority in the Northern Pueblos District. But Santa Clarans were well aware that Crandall's arrangement did have legal boundaries, and they worked persistently to enforce them, by going to the BCIM and the Catholic priest at Santa Cruz in order for their complaints to gain traction within the BIA. By working through this alternate channel, Santa Clarans simultaneously affirmed their longstanding relationship with the Church.

Neither Crandall nor True seemed to understand that drinking practices among Pueblo Indians and their Jicarilla Apache and Hispano neighbors were centuries-old, rooted in Catholic custom, and likely grounded in practices oriented around bolstering intercommunal relationships, especially at village festivals. After all, Pueblo Indians, particularly those south of Santa Fe, had been winegrowers since the first half of the seventeenth century, when the Spanish

12 Though the BCIM was not exclusively Hispano, the Catholic church had a centuries-long presence in the Rio Grande valley, making Pueblo Indians' historical relationship to the Church and other Catholics much deeper than that of non-Catholic newcomers. While Catholicism in New Mexico was introduced by Spaniards, it had spread beyond those ethno-cultural roots by the early twentieth century.

clergy subverted colonial trade law and introduced grapes to the region (Domínguez 1956: 50-51, 59, 71, 83, 119, 151, 207; Heaston 1971: 475; Street 1997: 2-4). Instead, Crandall and True's own cultural expectations about drinking and race seem to have eclipsed the historical customs of the area, much like other non-Natives in official and unofficial capacities who attempted to regulate the behavior of Indigenous peoples (Abbott 1999: 31; Mancall 1995b: 433; Mancall 1995a: 12-13). They simply bypassed the historical roots of alcohol customs in the Rio Grande valley; Crandall opted to carry out the mandates established by the U.S. government, and True emphasized the tenets of the temperance movement that swept across the U.S. in the late nineteenth and early twentieth centuries.

3.2 Learning Colonization over the Long-Term

The non-formal education that came with centuries of intercultural exchange among Native and Hispano peoples manifested in a variety of cultural practices that changed over time and reflected the shifting interactions among Natives, Hispanos, and Anglo newcomers. There is very little evidence in the documentary record to suggest that Anglos paid much attention to the long-term learning of Pueblo Indians within their unique communities. Nor is there evidence that suggests Anglos thought they might learn much – if anything – from the Pueblo Indians' accumulation of learning within different colonial regimes. This assumption that Natives would learn from U.S. officials rather than the other way around permeated Crandall's actions and worked to encourage Pueblo Indian village leaders to unify their efforts in pushing back against him. Crandall missed the symbolic significance of such unification: when the Indian Pueblos consolidated their efforts, the effect could be dramatic, as when they expelled the Spanish from the Rio Grande valley in 1680. When issues of utmost importance, like alcohol use and land, were at stake, consideration of long-term Pueblo learning might have prevented the disintegration of trust in Crandall.

According to inspection reports and as evidenced in the lack of discussion in regular correspondence, Crandall and his successor disregarded specific Pueblo Indian land use practices and needs. In spite of – or perhaps precisely because of – their expertise in irrigation farming along the Rio Grande, Santa Clarans expressed interest in learning new farming techniques from U.S. government farmers. Thus when Santa Clarans found the BIA farmer assigned to them to be incompetent, knowing very little about farming and ranching, they were sorely disappointed and requested a capable one through the Bureau of Catholic Indian Missions and through Inspector Singleton (Baca 1908: 3; Singleton 1911: 8). Members of the All Pueblos Council were well aware of the U.S. legal obligations to them, regardless of the nebulous status as citizens, quasi-citizens, and wards. Santa Claran leaders were correct in pointing out that the use of land in Santa Clara Cañon was theirs alone because it was part of an Indian reservation that was created and governed by the federal government. But the downside of converting their land grants into a reservation was that the BIA district superintendent, C.J. Crandall, would be the primary administrator of the area. Not only did this ultimately undermine local Puebloan authority and political structures, it also permitted Crandall to create a jurisdiction akin to a fiefdom (Carter 1995; Lawrence in press).

Santa Clarans and other Pueblo Indians, however, found a sympathetic ear in Inspector Singleton. Not only did he listen to their complaints and appear to investigate each, traveling to remote sites when necessary, he clearly allied himself with Pueblo Indian authorities and Clara D. True against Crandall on issues of land use and management. Even so, his report does not indicate that he took into consideration the fact that Pueblo Indians were using the learning they had accumulated over centuries in dealing with trespassing in a colonial regime. Singleton does not mention court documents that detail how Indian Pueblos sought remedy under previous governments; and, Crandall's successor repeated Crandall's mistake by not enforcing Santa Clara Reservation boundaries and continuing to employ an incompetent farmer.

Had Crandall been mindful of the history of liquor consumption in the Rio Grande valley and why Pueblo leaders might have changed their apparent position on it based on how U.S. policy changed the internal dynamics of village life, he would have understood that self-determination and maintaining governance structures was paramount for community officials. In fact, Pueblo governors wanted to curb drinking to diminish the factional tendencies (Dozier 1966) that amplified as the U.S. government emphasized individualism at BIA schools, with land ownership, and in behavioral conduct. The letters from the All Pueblos Council included with Singleton's inspection report explain that the focus on inculcating individualism through federal Indian policy, coupled with drinking, was undermining the internal authority structure of Pueblo villages up and down the Rio Grande. To remedy this, the Council made a three-pronged request: 1) that the U.S. government and its officers recognize the authority structures that had existed in Pueblo Indian communities for centuries; 2) that the U.S. government enforce its own liquor laws which prohibited the sale of alcohol to Indians; and, 3) that the U.S. government recognize Pueblo Indians right to determine how their children were schooled (Singleton 1911: Exhibit A; Exhibit B).

The Santa Clarans' third demand emerged in part from the negative effects of a half century of US rule and schooling, which taught returned Indians that their will trumped that of their community. By deputizing Pueblo Indians to patrol the valley who had not undergone each village's political appointment process, U.S. government agents dissolved the means of investigation and punishment for wrongdoing within communities that had been held by local Pueblo officials. Added to this was the fact that each Indian Pueblo had its own governance structure, grounded in longstanding cultural beliefs and social practices that did not necessarily convey from one Pueblo to the next. And as individuals attended school, came home believing in the superiority of their individual rights, and drank, factionalism within villages escalated, undermining the local seats of power and authority. Though Singleton, alongside True, heard Pueblo Indian leaders' liquor-related complaints, what they learned did not become internalized within organizational structure of the BIA. Similar complaints were made against Crandall's successor, implying that neither he nor Crandall appeared to realize how threatening individualism and hegemonic U.S. governance policies were to official Indian leaders, or how liberating these policies might have been for individuals who wanted change on their own terms (Tipton 1912).

3.3 BIA Relationships

By not paying attention to the historical relationships among Pueblo Indians and their Indigenous and Hispano neighbors, BIA officials like Crandall and True made federal Indian policy about their own relationships, not how they could best serve Native communities in the Rio Grande valley. In part, this has to do with how Crandall, True, Singleton and others viewed their relationships with Indians, and thus their roles, differently than they did their relationships with Anglos and with Hispanos. Though each officer acted with apparently divergent intentions, each operated from an outsider position among Indian Pueblos that emphasized their insider position in relation to the BIA, and in the case of Crandall, in relation to non-Native ranchers. This had the effect of underscoring Anglos' ascribed colonizer status.

The twin – and sometimes dueling – roles of missionary and opportunist marked BIA agents' actions in the Rio Grande valley. For Crandall, attempting to enforce teetotaling behavior in the early years of his tenure as superintendent at the Santa Fe Indian School was an expression of both his perceived authority within the district and over the Indians whom he was to serve; it also expressed a missionary sentiment that Pueblo Indians and their Jicarilla Apache counterparts needed to be saved from themselves. True took on a similar missionary role when she returned to the Valley in 1910. In his inspection report of Crandall, Singleton noted that True was doing "missionary work" in expelling liquor and the liquor trade from Indian Pueblos, and in so doing sought to morally "uplift" Indigenous peoples (Singleton 1911: 30). This outlook infused federal Indian policy at the time (Tipton 1912: 46-48; Wenger 2009: 138-139). And in advocating for the Pueblos against Crandall, Singleton himself acted as a type of missionary.

But Crandall and True also acted as opportunists by taking advantage of extant circumstances. As the new administrator of the Santa Clara Reservation, Crandall bypassed Santa Claran leaders and sold grazing permits to non-Native ranchers. Though this was against U.S. statutory law, Crandall did so and bolstered the economic development of Anglo and Hispano ranchers in the area. Similarly, when True moved back to the Rio Grande valley, she found a close alliance with Pueblo Indians who wanted to get rid of liquor on Indian lands. Whether True went after Crandall because of an old grudge, because she perceived he had a history of overlooking Indian drinking, or because she believed she was fighting for the larger temperance cause is unclear in the documentary record. Each possibility, though, highlights her relationship with Crandall, her history with the BIA, and her position among other Anglos.[13]

4. Conclusion

The colonial relationships in New Mexico among Pueblo Indians, Hispanos, and Anglos – like other colonial relationships around the world – were premised on conceptions of and disparities between power and authority exercised and practices by each group. Unlike other colonizing settings in North America where a binary emerged between the U.S. government and American Indians, between Anglos and non-Anglos, Natives and non-Natives, the longstanding presence of Hispanos in New Mexico melted away any dichotomous colonial construct that might have been relevant in other places and in recent memory, even though some who perceived themselves in a dominant position, like Crandall, adhered to such a construct. Much of the colonizing "education" policy set out by the U.S. in the late nineteenth and twentieth centuries had little to do with schooling, but traveled through the schoolhouse, which became a hub of federal policy dissemination in local communities. The everyday concerns, such as land use and liquor, that enveloped Pueblo Indian communities living along the Rio Grande and the accumulated learning – the education – that developed over centuries of colonization could have been instructive for Anglo newcomers. But they were not. Rather, the examples of liquor and land use highlight the fact that several

13 Other historians have, however, argued that True regularly acted dogmatically according to her convictions and desires (Foote 2005: 140-144; Jacobs 2002).

lessons were lost on BIA officials, reflecting disjunctures in expectations and communication.

Literature and Sources

Anon. Personnel Notecard of Clara D. True's Assignments in the Bureau of Indian Affairs. n.d. National Archives and Records Administration, National Personnel Records Center.

Abbott, K.A. (1999): Alcohol and the Anishinaabeg of Minnesota in the Early Twentieth Century (Spring), 25 – 43.

Adams, D. W. (1988): Fundamental Considerations: The Deep Meaning of Native American Schooling, 1880-1900. In: Harvard Educational Review, 58: 1 (February), 1 – 28.

Adams, D. W. (1997): Education for Extinction: American Indians and the Boarding School Experience 1875-1928. Lawrence, K.S.

Baca, Pedro: Letter to Rev. Father William Ketcham 1908. Letter Regarding the Administration of C.J. Crandall. October 13. Series 1-1: Correspondence, Reel 43. Bureau of Catholic Indian Missions, Marquette University, Milwaukee, Wisconsin.

Bourke, J.G. (1894): The Laws of Spain in Their Application to the American Indians. In: American Anthropologist, 7: 2 (April), 193 – 201.

Brook, H. H.: Letter to William H. Andrews1911a. Letter Regarding the Transfer of a Portion of the Jemez Forest Land to Santa Clara Pueblo. February 24. Indians Miscellaneous Collection, Pueblo Indian Materials, Serial # 10653, Folder Santa Clara Pueblo 1911. New Mexico State Archives, Santa Fe, N.M.

Brook, H. H.: Letter to Richard Achilles Ballinger1911b. Letter Regarding the Transfer of a Portion of the Jemez Forest Land to Santa Clara Pueblo. February 12. Indians Miscellaneous Collection, Pueblo Indian Materials, Serial # 10653, Folder Santa Clara Pueblo 1911. New Mexico State Archives, Santa Fe, N.M.

Brook, H. H.: Letter to William J. Mills1911c. Letter Regarding the Transfer of a Portion of the Jemez Forest Land to Santa Clara Pueblo. February 25. Indians Miscellaneous Collection, Pueblo Indian Materials, Serial # 10653, Folder Santa Clara Pueblo 1911. New Mexico State Archives, Santa Fe, N.M.

Brookings Institution, and Lewis Meriam (1928): The Problem of Indian Administration: Report of a Survey Made at the Request of Hubert Work, Secretary of the Interior, and Submitted to Him, February 21, 1928. Washington, D.C. http://www.alaskool.org/native_ed/research_reports/IndianAdmin/Indian_Admin_Problms.html.

Browning, D. M. (2000): Extension of Civil Service Rules, September 15, 1896. In: Documents of United States Indian Policy, ed. F. P. Prucha (3rd ed). Lincoln, N.E, 194 – 195.

Carlson, A. W. (1975): Spanish-American Acquisition of Cropland within the Northern Pueblo Indian Grants, New Mexico. In: Ethnohistory, 22: 2 (Spring), 95 – 110.

Carter, P. A. (1995): 'completely discouraged': Women Teachers' Resistance in the Bureau of Indian Affairs Schools, 1900-1910. In: Frontiers: A Journal of Women Studies, 15: 3, 53 – 86.

Child, B. J. (1998): Boarding School Seasons: American Indian Families, 1900-1940. Lincoln.

Coleman, M. C. (1993): American Indian Children at School, 1850-1930. Jackson.

Coleman, M. C. (2005): The Symbiotic Embrace: American Indians, White Educators and the School, 1820s-1920s. In: The RoutledgeFalmer Reader in History of Education, ed. G. McCulloch. London/New York, 195 – 213.
Crandall, C.J.: Letter to William A. Jones1902. Letter to the Commissioner of Indian Affairs requesting law enforcement for the San Geronimo Fiesta at Taos. September 18. RG 75, Entry 34, Volume 3, Press Copies of Letters Sent to the Commissioner of Indian Affairs, p. 120. National Archives and Records Administration, Rocky Mountain Region.
Crandall, C.J.: Letter to William A. Jones1904. Letter to the Commissioner of Indian Affairs Regarding Pueblo Indians' Status as Citizens, 03/28/1904. March 28. RG 75, Entry 34, Volume 4, Press Copies of Letters Sent to the Commissioner of Indian Affairs p. 323 – 324. National Archives and Records Administration, Rocky Mountain Region.
Cronon, W. (2003): Changes in the Land, Revised Edition: Indians, Colonists, and the Ecology of New England. Revised. New York.
Domínguez, F. A. (1956): The Missions of New Mexico, 1776; a Description, with Other Contemporary Documents. Albuquerque.
Dozier, E. P. (1960): The Pueblos of the South-Western United States. In: The Journal of the Royal Anthropological Institute of Great Britain and Ireland, 90: 1 (June), 146 – 160.
Dozier, E. P. (1966): Factionalism at Santa Clara Pueblo. In: Ethnology, 5: 2 (April), 172 – 185.
Dozier, E. P. (1970): The Pueblo Indians of North America. New York.
Dunbar-Ortiz, R. (2007): Roots of Resistance: A History of Land Tenure in New Mexico. University of Oklahoma Press, September 30.
Ebright, M. (1989): Spanish and Mexican Land Grants and the Law. Sunflower University Press, June.
Ebright, M. (2008): Land Grants and Lawsuits in Northern New Mexico. Santa Fe, N.M.: Center for Land Grant Studies Press.
Ebright, M. & Hendricks, R. (2006): The Witches of Abiquiu: The Governor, the Priest, the Genizaro Indians, and the Devil. Albuquerque, N.M.
Foote, Ch. J. (2005): Women of the New Mexico Frontier, 1846-1912. Albuquerque.
Galgano, R. C. (2005): Feast of Souls: Indians and Spaniards in the Seventeenth-Century Missions of Florida and New Mexico. Albuquerque.
Gomez, L. E. (2005): Off-white in an Age of White Supremacy: Mexican Elites and the Rights of Whites and Blacks in Nineteenth-Century New Mexico. In: Chicano-Latin Law Review, 25 (Spring), 9 – 59.
Heaston, M. D. (1971): Whiskey Regulation and Indian Land Titles in New Mexico Territory: 1851-1861. In: Journal of the West, 10: 3, 474 – 483.
Ishii, I. (2003): Alcohol and Politics in the Cherokee Nation before Removal. In: Ethnohistory, 50: 4, 671 – 695. doi:Article.
Jacobs, M. D. (1996): Making Savages of Us All: White Women, Pueblo Indians, and the Controversy over Indian Dances in the 1920s. In: Frontiers: A Journal of Women Studies, 17: 3, 178 – 209.
Jacobs, M. D. (1999): Engendered Encounters: Feminism and Pueblo Cultures, 1879-1934. Lincoln, N.E.
Jacobs, M. D. (2002): Clara True and Female Moral Authority. Faculty Publications, Department of History. Online available at: http://digitalcommons.unl.edu/historyfacpub/24.

Jones, W. A.: Letter1900. Letter to Clinton J. Crandall from William A. Jones regarding transfer to the Santa Fe Indian School. Letter. January 16. National Archives and Records Administration, National Personnel Records Center.

Katanski, A. V. (2005): Learning to Write "Indian": The Boarding-School Experience and American Indian Literature. Norman.

Lawrence, A. (2011): Lessons from an Indian Day School: Negotiating Colonization in Northern New Mexico, 1902-1907. Lawrence, K.S. [in press].

Lomawaima, K. T. (1994): They Called It Prairie Light: The Story of Chilocco Indian School. Lincoln.

Mancall, P. C. (1995a): Deadly Medicine: Indians and Alcohol in Early America. Ithaca.

Mancall, P. C. (1995b): Men, Women, and Alcohol in Indian Villages in the Great Lakes Region in the Early Republic. In: Journal of the Early Republic, 15: 3 (Autumn), 425 – 448.

Mann, Ch. C. (2005): 1491: new revelations of the Americas before Columbus. New York.

Memmi, A. (1965): The Colonizer and the Colonized. Expanded. Boston.

Nieto-Phillips, J. M. (2004): The Language of Blood: The Making of Spanish-American Identity in New Mexico, 1880s-1930s. Illustrated edition. Albuquerque, N.M.

Noble, J. W. & Harrison, B. (2000): Civil Service Classifications in the Indian Service, April 13, 1891. In: Documents of United States Indian Policy, ed. F. P. Prucha (3rd ed.). Lincoln, N.E., 180.

O'Sullivan, J. L. (1845): Annexation. The United States Magazine and Democratic Review, August.

Ortiz, A. (1969): The Tewa World: Space, Time, Being, and Becoming in a Pueblo Society. Chicago.

Reel, E. (1901): Course of Study for the Indian Schools of the United States, Industrial and Literary. Washington, D.C.

Reyhner, J. A. & Oyawin Eder, J. M. (2006): American Indian Education: A History. Norman, OK.

Roberts, D. (2004): The Pueblo Revolt: The Secret Rebellion That Drove the Spaniards Out of the Southwest. New York.

Roosevelt, Th. (1905): Executive Order - Santa Clara Pueblo, New Mexico, July 29, 1905. Ed. J. T. Woolley & G. Peters. The American Presidency Project [online], July 29. http://www.presidency.ucsb.edu/ws/index.php?pid=76703.

Sando, J. S. (1992): Pueblo Nations: Eight Centuries of Pueblo Indian History. Santa Fe.

Singleton, S. M. (1911): Inspection Report, Clinton J. Crandall. June 20. RG 48, Entry 842, Inspection Division, Indian Jurisdiction Inspection Reports, 1907-1924, Box 7. National Archives and Records Administration, College Park, M.D.

Street, H. K. (1997): The History of Wine in New Mexico: 400 Years of Struggle. Ponderosa, N.M.

Stuart, P. (1985): Administrative Reform in Indian Affairs. In: The Western Historical Quarterly, 16: 2 (April), 133 – 146.

Stuart, P. (1987): Nations within a nation: historical statistics of American Indians. New York.

Szasz, M. C. (2007): Indian Education in the American Colonies, 1607-1783. Bison Books Ed. University of Nebraska Press, July 1.

Tafoya, L., Naranjo, F. & Cajete, P.: Letter to Rev. Father William Ketcham1910. Letter Regarding the Trespass of Hispano Livestock. April 10. Series 1-1: Correspondence, Reel 51. Bureau of Catholic Indian Missions, Marquette University, Milwaukee, Wisconsin.

Tipton, W. M. (1912): Inspection Report on Coggeshall and Wilson. Santa Fe, N.M., November 30. RG 48, Entry 842, Inspection Division, Indian Jurisdiction Inspection Reports, 1907-1924, Box 7. National Archives and Records Administration, College Park, M.D.

Trafzer, C. E., Keller, J. A. & Sisquoc, L. (2006): Boarding School Blues: Revisiting American Indian Educational Experiences. Lincoln, NE.

True, C. D. (1909): The Experiences of a Woman Indian Agent. In: Outlook (1893-1924) (June 5), 331.

U.S. Congress (2000a): Organization of the Department of Indian Affairs, June 30, 1834. In: Documents of United States Indian Policy, ed. F. P. Prucha, (3rd ed.). Lincoln, N.E., 68 – 70.

U.S. Congress (2000b): Modifications in the Indian Department, February 27, 1851. In: Documents of United States Indian Policy, ed. F. P. Prucha (3rd ed.). Lincoln, N.E., 83.

Wenger, T. (2009): We Have a Religion: The 1920s Pueblo Indian Dance Controversy and American Religious Freedom. The University of North Carolina Press.

‘No man is a man who does not discover something, be it a new star or an old manuscript’[1] – The Debate over New Education in Late Colonial India

Catriona Ellis, University of Edinburgh, UK

The aim of the new syllabus for elementary education in the Madras Presidency in 1940 was “to connect the school curriculum with the actual environment in which the pupils live and to make education more suitable to the needs of the rural population.”[2] This had been a continuing part of the rhetoric of the colonial government. For example, the government educational (Public Instruction) report of 1934 wanted “to make teaching and curricula progressively more scientific and more socially and culturally effective” (96).

Using the writings of colonial, missionary, and especially Indian educationists in pedagogic journals and in documentation of specific educational experiments, this chapter looks at the desired transition from pre-colonial and colonial ‘traditional’ teaching techniques towards what was viewed as a more progressive approach to teaching, particularly at elementary level. Elementary level teaching, which has been discussed less in the existing literature, was the only form of education received by the majority of the population in India during the colonial period. Of particular interest are the specific educational techniques these pedagogues wanted to establish as well as the inherent contradictions within this approach, particularly in a colonial setting. In addition, this essay queries the ambiguous notion of the ‘Indian child’ in these educational discourses. Since the objective (as stated in the 1934 report) was to make teaching more “culturally effective” with respect to the ‘Indian context’, we may ask in which ways the ‘Indian child’ was constructed as different from the Western norm, and how this relates to the simultaneous claim by many Indian educational experts that the ‘Indian child’ was ‘modern’ and therefore the same as the ‘normal’ child in the West. These questions lead us to explore the wider, and possibly even unintentional, epistemologies and power structures within these discourses and to examine the role of the notion of ‘culture’ in this context.

---

1 Patrick, G. T.W. (1893): “The Memory in Education”, New York Educational Review, quoted in Indian Journal of Education, p. 203, Indian Office Records, British Library (from now on IOR).

2 Elementary Education Manual, and Suggestions on Physical Activities for Elementary Schools quoted in Madras Presidency Public Instruction Report (DPI) 1939-40, p. 24, National Library of Scotland (from now on NLS)

1. Historical context of the Educational Debates

This study looks at the period of educational expansion between the 1882 Education Commission, which saw a commitment to the democratization of colonial education, until independence in 1947, although the decade of greatest debate and growth in elementary education was the 1930s. This educational expansion was generally funded through Grants-in-Aid (public funding for each individual school)[3], and money was given to a wide variety of local groups, including missionaries, religious groups and nationalists, who could promote their own, albeit secular, message within the boundaries established in the Grants-in-Aid scheme. These boundaries laid the schools open to inspection and meant that teachers were more likely to use the prescribed textbooks and focus on exam performance to maintain funding, meaning in practice a significant degree of homogeneity between schools. Administratively, after 1919 there was more direct Indian control of schools (Allender 2009) as education became decentralized among the new provincial assemblies, although British civil servants remained prominent in the educational bureaucracy. School attendance rates varied, but participation became gradually more widespread, especially among the higher castes. The figures from the 1931 Census in the Madras Presidency indicate that of all the castes included, there were 5.8 million boys between five and fifteen years, and 1.9 million of them were at school on 1 March 1932; in other words, 33% of school-age Indian boys, the highest figure ever reached, attended school.[4] While boys from the Depressed Castes[5] comprised 13.4% of the school-age population, only 26.13% of Depressed Caste boys went to school; the corresponding figures for high caste Brahmins were 4.6% of whom 57.32% attended school. In 1931, 12.4% of school-age girls (5-15 years, report does not give a caste breakdown) attended school.[6] Ultimately, there was a system of colonial rhetorical support for education, but a chronic shortage of funding.

Many colonial bureaucrats viewed this rhetorical support as an important part of their mission, and fitted it into the wider colonial narrative of improving Indian society. The Public Instruction Reports frequently discussed the introduction of education for girls and Depressed Castes as a gift from a "superior" and "more enlightened" civilization. As the literature has demonstrated, the British

3 This funding was administered at the local state level, for instance the Madras Presidency, but the schools had control over how this budget was then spent.

4 Madras Presidency Public Instruction Quinquennial Report IOR 1927-28 – 1931-32, p. 83.

5 Depressed castes was the name given for Untouchables. In the census reports they are also called Backward castes and Scheduled castes.

6 Madras Presidency Public Instruction Report 1931-32, p. 92, IOR.

sought to position themselves as the enlightened saviours of these oppressed groups; in the oft-quoted phrase, they saw themselves as 'white men saving brown women from brown men' (Spivak in Landry & Maclean 1996). The British colonial authority also sought to increase general participation in educational institutions, both in terms of student enrolment and in retention. The Indian Statutory Commission of 1928, which was to investigate political reform, dealt in detail with education and the raising of educational standards as an essential precursor to democracy and independence. Specifically, as stated by the Duke of York, education was important and had to be promoted in order to prepare Indians to "become the good citizens of the future in whose hands the destiny of our Empire can safely be left"[7] so that they were not led away in uprisings[8] and could become loyal citizens who understood the value of the rule of law. The rhetoric was always that of an enlightened and modern civilisation gifting its knowledge to the savage and backward Other, without any possibility of that Other attaining the true modernity of the coloniser (Bhabha 1984: 126).

By the 1920s, it was well established, however, that the education provided was generally unattractive and failed to retain pupils' interest, because the curriculum and school structure were alienated from Indian cultures, and were virtually worthless in rural areas, having little relation to prior spheres of competence and knowledge. In addition, the training of large numbers of clerks who had limited education but high ambitions produced fears of a subversive potential for the social order. These issues formed part of a continuing debate which began in the early nineteenth century about the nature and medium of Indian education and the relative worth of Eastern and Western knowledge and literature. By the 1920s, the debate again revolved around the use of the vernacular for teaching. In theory, then, the time seemed right for the emergence of an alternative form of education.

The type of documents considered here can be divided into two broad categories of 'educational discourse' (Goodman, McCulloch & Richardson 2009: 697). First, there is the programmatic educational rhetoric, which advocated new pedagogical techniques and described their benefits and proposed impact. Second, there is the documentation of actual classroom practice and discussions by headmasters who tried to implement the new ideas in their schools. These schools were experimental, such as the missionary-run Moga in the Punjab, and most of them were closely related to teacher training colleges, such as the Lady

7 Report of the Imperial Education Conference, 1923. Introduction by Duke of York (London, 1924), p. 10. IOR.

8 Educational Pamphlet 2. 'The Education of Factory Children in India' (Calcutta, Government Printing, India, 1918) p. 4, NLS.

Willingdon Training College in Madras. My analysis, therefore, deals with educational discourses and aspirations and does not claim to evaluate the empirical success or failure of these projects.

One source of evidence is writings by officials from Public Instruction Reports and other government publications, such as the Occasional Reports and Educational Pamphlets, which refer to new pedagogical techniques and advocate their expansion to all elementary schools. These texts are not specific to India, but reflect the global changes in educational discourse of the time under the label of "New Education". The fact that many Indian pedagogues also advocated these approaches might be proof of the close interests, affiliations and contacts between educational experts throughout the world, such as the New Education Fellowship and International Movement in Progressive Education (Kallaway 2007: 123). Many of these educational theorists published in monthly journals such as *Schoolmaster, Indian Journal of Education, Madras Journal of Education and Educational India* between 1880 and 1947, with particular frequency in the 1930s. The contributors to these journals were all well educated and had degrees and prominent jobs within the teaching profession. The purpose of their publications seems to have been to address and debate new educational ideas and to suggest ways of practically including them in the curriculum. The reading material for this group is interesting. For example, the main lending library (Connemarra) in Chennai still has an extensive collection of books published in the 1910s, 1920s and 1930s. These include all the well-recognised Western names such as Steiner, Piaget, Pestalozzi, and Vygotsky as well as Indian authors such as Gandhi or Tagore. This trend was repeated in the Adyar Research Centre of the Theosophical Institute, Chennai, where similar books exist. Kallaway (2007:124) has traced the changing nature of colonial debates about educational goals in conferences by education societies such as the New Education Fellowship, arguing that while in the 1920s theorists were strongly influenced by the progressive movement, by the 1930s, the goals were more pragmatically linked to the politics, economics and society of the different states. Although different theorists were added, most obviously a focus on Pestalozzi and Froebel in the 1880s and on Montessori in the 1930s, a similar change cannot be traced in the aforementioned educational journals.

Educational specialists were not the only ones interested in these debates, but it was also an era of educational experimentation within the nationalist cause. Prominent nationalists such as Tagore, Gandhi, Annie Besant, Syed Ahmed Khan, and others explored these ideas and often set up their own schools with more access to Hindu or Muslim literature and rituals as part of an attempt to wrest control from the British and portray themselves as the most forward-looking. Gandhi promoted a type of education which would not only lead to the spiritual, moral and physical uplift of the child, but also of the wider village and ultimately of the national community (Wardha Conference 1937: 43). Missionary theorists, many of whom had direct experience in education work or were involved in the Missionary Education Commission of 1920 (Humphrey Milford 1922: 20), played a similar role although it is unclear how much of this was fundraising propaganda and how much reflected a deep commitment to educational change on the subcontinent. Education, we may conclude, was a highly contested field.

2. Traditional Education

Progressive education set itself up, even in its name, as a modern invention that was inherently opposed to traditional education. It was called 'New Education' in the Indian context following international trends, and it implied an unequivocal condemnation of the 'old' education. However, in practice, there was no simple dichotomy as this label suggests because 'old' or 'traditional' applied to both colonial and pre-colonial educational approaches as I will briefly discuss.

It is generally accepted that the imposition of the British colonial education system largely wiped out the pre-colonial Indian systems of education. This is an overstatement, and many schools, particularly in rural areas, continued with their traditional pedagogies, but frequently went unreported because they did not fit the neat categories of the colonial system and the differences between the systems was probably less significant than previously thought (Kumar 2007: 37). The colonial system rejected traditional Indian education, especially teaching methods that focused memory and the rote-learning of ancient religious texts, such as the Upanishads, Vedas and classical Tamil works, both literary and ethical. These pedagogies comprised primarily the *apara vidya* or traditional brahmanical learning, taught by dedicated gurus to a select number of pupils. There was also the *laukic vidya* (Sarangapani 2003: 170), the pedagogies of which involved more practical training for the lower castes. For example, merchants or artisans (Kumar 2000: 69) were taught practical skills, basic arithmetic and literacy and were socialised into the business ethics of their caste. Pre-colonial learning was symbolised in the *pial* or *verandah* school, similar to many bush schools, and was directed by one teacher who emphasized oral tradition and often excessive discipline. While Gandhi lamented the demise of Indian education – the 'beautiful tree' – there was no real commitment to revive it and references to it are mainly nostalgic, in spite of attempts (Kumar 2000: 103) to re-introduce Sanskrit or Tamil religious and literary texts back into the curriculum.

However, the New Educationists also rejected traditional colonial education – as distinct from traditional Indian education. Historians and educationists such as Kumar (1991) and Crooks (1996) have shown how the transmission of knowledge through colonial education was used to reinforce colonial power relationships, both by prioritising the knowledge of the coloniser and by using that knowledge to impose a system of moral and social control. This is seen in the elevation of the Enlightenment values of scientific inquiry, rationality, and secularism (Srivastava 1998). These were perceived by the British colonial state to be in direct contrast to pre-colonial guru or *pial* led learning. The historian Viswanathan describes how English literature and history were used to strengthen students' attachment to the ideals of secular morality, reason and belief in "Western principles of law, order, justice and truth" (1989: 101). Despite the high ideal, at the elementary level, colonial education was associated with "poor pedagogic technology" (Kumar 2007: 300) such as cramming for excessive examinations, rote learning, overemphasis on literary education, and an all-powerful but low-status teacher. Few students enrolled, and for those who did, it was unclear whether they gained any practical skills or imbibed any moral values. By the 1920s, many colonial bureaucrats recognised that an alternative system was needed. The Indian Statutory Commission reemphasised that:

> Western methods and objectives have precluded the growth of an indigenous culture expressive of, and responsive to, the different types of native genius, and [the Commission] asked whether a re-orientation of the whole educational system is not required.[9]

Thus not only were pre-colonial pedagogies rejected, so too were the pedagogies of traditional colonial education. Moreover, the Indian Statutory Commission rejected traditional colonial education for the sake of "the growth of an indigenous culture" with "different types of native genius". At first glance, the above statement suggests that the "indigenous" and the "native" might be perceived as an anti-colonial stance by its mere acknowledgment. But the discursive structure is more ambivalent; the concept of the "native genius" is constructed in opposition to the coloniser's Western knowledge, which continued to be perceived as the highest form of knowledge. The "native genius", then, can be interpreted as a form of Othering of the 'Indian mindset' which was incompatible with "Western methods and objectives" (of education). At a time when the construction of racial difference was becoming increasingly prominent (Goodman, McCulloch & Richardson 2009: 703), this discourse inevitably alludes to the perception of an inherent backwardness in the 'Indian race'. The universal validity of Western

9 Indian Statutory Commission, Vol. 1, Report of the Indian Statutory Commission, Vol. 1 – Survey, (London, May 1930) p. 402, NLS.

knowledge is not questioned, but its applicability in the 'Indian context' is. Thus the suggested "re-orientation of the whole educational system" – in order to make education more accessible for 'Indian' learners – implies that 'Indians' needed a 'different' educational system which had, by definition, lower standards. The suggestion is not about questioning the hegemonic (colonisers') knowledge and values, but about 'educational engineering' in such a way to implant this education in a more "culturally effective" manner.

3. New Education

A growing rejection of both pre-colonial and colonial forms of traditional education led a number of Indian, colonial and missionary pedagogues to focus on 'progressive education'– or 'New Education'. Rather than the transfer of knowledge from the teacher to the student, the New Education emphasized the central role of the child, and thus encouraged learning through experience at a pace which suited the individual and stimulated the growth of his/her body and mind, rhythmic capabilities, and abstract intelligence (Karnataka 1937: 293). Correspondingly, the teacher was to take a less prominent role in the classroom; discipline was to be minimal, and freedom was paramount, with the child's interest being engaged in active learning through play and experimentation (Moga 1936: 416). The association with Western ideas of educational theory is evident, and in the journals there is frequent mention of global discourses centred on John Dewey (Van Doren 1928: 8) and Columbia University, Maria Montessori (Banerjee 1935: 129), Group Method (Swamikannu Paul 1936), Project Method (Siddalingaiya 1937: 405), Dalton Plan (Venkata Rao 1935: 297), and earlier ideas such as Froebel's Kindergarten movement. An example is the introduction of Pestalozzi's object lessons by missionaries in Bengal in the late nineteenth century, which involved the description of objects leading to categorisation and higher cognitive development. Reformers perceived this as demonstration of a new knowledge system and a new way of approaching education (Sengupta 2003: 115). Sengupta (2003: 100) argues the introduction of the object lesson was particularly important because it encouraged Indian children to move beyond objects, which they could describe and which were associated with India, and moved them towards formulating and expressing abstract ideas. This reflected missionaries' desire to convert the children from heathenism and the worship of objects to the intangible truths and ideas which they associated more with Protestant Christianity and a less physical form of deity. These abstract ideas were associated with a higher form of knowledge, which was perceived not so much as Western or colonial, but gained its *hegemonic power* through being *modern* and *enlightened* and therefore universal in application. Both Indian pedagogues, who, of course, had received this education themselves, and colonial officials welcomed this approach to education as a step towards the modern formation of knowledgeable citizens who understood and were committed to democracy. In embracing Western educational ideals as universally applicable and at the same time as a "higher form of knowledge", the tacit assumption seems to be that 'Indian education' was inferior and unable to produce abstract thoughts, and needed to be improved by the adoption of 'modern' and 'enlightened' approaches imported from the West.

3.1 Vocational Education

The most basic form of 'progressive' or 'modern education' discussed in the journals was the prioritising of vocational education within the curriculum, thereby allowing students to develop skills which would help them after they completed school, which, in turn, linked them to their communities. Important within vocational education was the establishment of the dignity of labour and hereditary occupations rather than a focus on secondary and tertiary education. These objectives were not entirely new. Vocational education had long been an obsession of colonial authorities[10] concerned about the high numbers of unemployed graduates, and making education more relevant to rural areas; but implementation was poor within the village schools. The 'progressive' approach, however, was to place vocational education on an equal footing with literacy and numeracy, particularly in time spent on task during the school day. This was implemented in a limited number of schools. Van Doren, for instance, mentions a particular focus on agriculture and the introduction of new European techniques and new livestock and poultry in the missionary Vocational Training School, Ankleswar (Van Doren 1928: 51). Closely related to this were industrial crafts such as blacksmithing, weaving and carpentry, taught at St Barnabas School in Manmad to supplement agricultural incomes (Van Doren 1928: 47). The Joint School at the Buckingham and Carnatic Mills was particularly commended for giving children a choice of vocation, while providing all students with introductory knowledge of a number of useful activities such as carpentry, tailoring, weaving, painting, whitewashing, and small repairs to property (Fleming 1921: 20). For girls at Ankleswar, the curriculum included subjects such as motherhood, childcare and nutrition, as well as gardening and housework (Van

10 Education Commission Report by the Madras Provincial Committee with evidence taken before the committee, and memorials addressed to the Education Commission (Calcutta, Government Printing Press, 1884), NLS.

Doren 1928: 93). The intended result was to produce useful citizens who could contribute to local society and progress themselves through the new techniques learned (Anon 1898: 66).

3.2 Learning through activity

Even more popular among theorists, however, was the engagement of the child-learner in structured activities rather than direct instruction in vocational skills. Children would learn through self-experimentation and a "scientific attitude of testing results and forming conclusions [which] is fatal to a blind belief in out-worn tradition" (Krishnayya 1934: 170), thereby rejecting the pedagogical techniques of rote learning and their associated traditions and knowledge. The Moga teacher training school in the Punjab was consistently held up as a model for progressive schools, being one of the first to pioneer these techniques. In an interview with another pedagogue, their principal claimed:

> At Moga we have broken away from the traditional methods of teaching, just because these methods train pupils to memorise and not to think for themselves; they teach pupils to accept the statements of others and not to question and find out for themselves; they encourage pupils to lean upon others, and not be self-reliant. We teach them responsibility by putting responsibility upon them. We train them in judgment by giving them many opportunities of choice. Moreover, we teach them to read intelligently by giving them many opportunities for reading. We teach practical arithmetic by introducing situations into the schoolroom which require the use of arithmetic. The principle of learning by doing controls our classroom work, and rules also the life of the school (Van Doren 1928: 7).

The article goes on to describe some of the activities pursued by students at Moga when the school was in its infancy (KT Paul in Van Doren 1928: xi). While the examples are important evidence of an idea being put into practice, albeit in a very limited way, what is interesting here is the implicit aim of constructing inquisitive, sceptical, and rationally thinking adults.

Thus through trying activities themselves, pupils were supposed to understand the foundations underlying the knowledge they were developing, and therefore remember it as they learned at their own individual pace. For example, a craft such as weaving could be studied practically, with each pupil participating. This in turn would lead to an explanation of its history, geography, and scientific and mathematical techniques, which could then be followed up by more extensive research in the school library (Dewey 1959: 42). This mirrored at a very basic level the methodologies – hypotheses, experiment, and conclusions – of experimental science. In a preliminary way, this is illustrated in Froebel's Kindergarten techniques, which encouraged learning through songs, dramas, gardening, and art, in addition to Pestalozzi's object lessons, which encouraged children to describe objects, move to categorisation, and then higher stages of reasoning and abstract thought by making comparisons between objects. Although such educational techniques had already been introduced in a very limited way in government-funded schools[11], their practical effect was minimal, and the progressives of the 1930s attempted to take the ideas much further by influencing the whole of the curriculum. The most famous example was Gandhi's Segaon Method promoted at the Wardha in 1937. Gandhi argued that Indian handicrafts such as spinning should not be taught mechanically, "but scientifically, that is the child should know the why and the wherefore of every process" (Wardha Conference 1937: 4), and this would lead to a further investigation of literacy, history, arithmetic needed for the successful completion of the process. His main argument – closely linked to the progressives in both nature and terminology – was that learning should take place by the scientific methods of observation and experimentation, which would help students develop their physical, rational and spiritual faculties (ibid.). Schools were not merely to become more attractive[12], and thus reduce stagnation and waste, but the intended end product was to be different: the usefully employed modern citizen who could act because he *understood* the reasons.

3.3 Curriculum and Teaching of Morality

Central to 'New Education' was the teaching of morality and civics and the placing of the rational individual in the context of the community. This implied a rejection of traditional morality taught through a catechism or through ancient religious texts, and of colonial morality taught through the study of literature or history (Viswanathan 1989). In the context of 'progressive education', morality was equated with citizenship for a modern nation (Srivastava 1998) and was to be taught through active cooperation and responsibility. Van Doren gives the example of students at Moga who visited a government hospital to find out about the treatment of disease and the practical administration of a major institution in order to start their own small dispensary. The project aim was to run the dispensary efficiently, learn about hygiene, and dispense basic medicine; the underlying intention of moral education was to teach the students pride in their work and cooperation (Van Doren 1928: 9). As is well established in other literature (Sen 2004), sport was traditionally favoured because it encouraged

11 For example every Madras Presidency Public Instruction Report on the 1890s and 1900s stressed the need for Kindergarten methods.

12 Progress of Education in India 1932-37, p. 147, IOR.

healthy competition and healthy bodies; progressive educators encouraged sports for similar reasons (von Marenholtz-Bulow 1885: 47). The missionaries at Ushagram argued, "good sportsmanship, from the give and take of competitive recreation, is teaching the boys to respect the rights of others and to trust those who play with or against them" (Van Doren 1928: 23). Other methods included giving children the monetary rewards of their work, from which they would be able to budget and pay for school fees, uniforms and treats (Van Doren 1928: 64), or encouraging trust by leaving cupboards unlocked at night (Van Doren 1928: 46). Boarding schools encouraged miniature government and community procedures, such as the panchayats (pupil committees) at the schools at Ankleswar (Van Doren 1928: 47) and the girls' school at Pakaur (Van Doren 1928: 93), whose students had the power to make community rules and enforce discipline. Interpersonal relationships were particularly important throughout. For example, girls were not only to learn how to prepare food for small families and keep budgets, but also to learn how to live peaceably in a group (Van Doren 1928: 80). Even though we have no empirical evidence as to whether these projects achieved the desired effect, the documentation of these practical examples illustrates how the educational rhetoric was put into practice and which objectives the educators pursued – the creation of trustworthy, self-aware citizens.

But moral teaching was more extensive, and the subjects themselves were important (Venkateswaran 1935), as examples by Van Doren and others writing about classroom practice illustrate. At Moga, basic literacy was taught through the group method. For example, we see an Indian adaption of the English story 'The House that Jack Built' for elementary Class 1:

> The teacher used flash cards with all the Hindi vowels, consonants and conjunctions used in the Government Primer and all the words in the story. A house was measured out, the class then discussed the materials for construction using the flash cards with Hindi words, then practiced writing the words in the sand. Finally the whole class dug the earth, carried the water and mixed them with the dry grass to form a proper mixture wherewith to make the house (Van Doren 1928: 31).

The Moga training course for teachers (Moga 1936: 416) also encouraged the teaching of literacy using the scientific method and included material relating to the children's home experiences, story-telling, careful use of phonetics and sounds, and variation in the types of literature used. Suggested ideas for other lessons were also incorporated, such as illustrations on the blackboards or making gifts and organizing excursions. The desired result was the formation of individuality (Moga 1936: 418), rather than merely making the classroom happier and thereby keeping children in school. Maths too was used to exercise and rationalise young minds through solving problems (Venkateswaran 1935). In addition, Ramchandra Rao argued that it was the *sciences* of biology, geography, and economics rather than, for example, a study of contemporary or comparative literature, that provided the citizen with the skills needed for the modern world (Ramchandra Rao 1935).

A detailed example of these ideas in practice is seen in Vekata Rae's (1935: 297ff.) suggestions for teaching Regional Geography. He advised teaching according to the terms of the Dalton Plan, in concentric circles widening out from the home to the wider world, but with a focus on 'a psychological plan' emphasising the consequences of geographical change. The idea was to cultivate an interest in people in different locations and establish that differences in habit were merely cultural. The example given is the Eskimo mother who licks dishes to wash them in the tundra region. Such comparisons were then extended to stories of explorers and stories centred on food, such as dates in Arabia. These stories were full of geographical facts, but also included moral lessons. Once again, the intended result was a child who was aware of themselves and their distinctive place in the world.

4. Pedagogy as science

The specific pedagogical ideas about 'New Education' fit into wider discourses of power and knowledge in late colonial India. Part of the association with modernity for these pedagogues and bureaucrats was the establishment of pedagogy as a scientific discipline as opposed to traditional pedagogy, which was perceived to be 'unmodern' and thus unscientific. The adherence to 'science' could be proclaimed in fairly general terms. For example, one author talks about teaching reading through methods based on (unspecified) "Western scientific research" (Van Doren 1928: 12). The scientific orientation in pedagogy was also closely linked to an overarching obsession with the pedagogical uses of psychology, as seen in the works of Freud, Piaget, and the natural development of the normal child. Krishnayya argued that

> ...time was when measurement was considered incompatible with mental activity, when it seemed sacrilegious to say that matters of the mind might be investigated with scientific precision and mathematical accuracy. But now larger and larger tracts are coming under the unsparing scrutiny of the psychologist and his tools are becoming more and more effective (Krishnayya 1937: 5),

making possible a scientific approach within the classroom.

A common argument was that an understanding of child psychology was even more important than knowledge of the curriculum (Anon 1934: 104) because of the tools it gave the teacher observing (Moga 1936: 420) and understanding the child, and even more importantly, providing a benchmark in 'normal' childhood development. Many of the articles described the mind in great detail. For example, Sakhare (1937) gave a lengthy discourse on different theories of the working of the mind, and Diddi (1937) looked at the Laws of Learning based on psychological studies. This included wide-ranging use of intelligence tests, for instance one author Swamikannu dealt extensively with the history and use of purported scientific tests in assessing the ability to acquire and process knowledge, and thereby assessing the mental age of the child, in comparison with the chronological age of the child. This was set against the 'normal' average of 100% for their age (Swamikannu 1935: 251).

The emphasis on child psychology marked the beginning of categorisation of children by intelligence, although there was a minority of researchers and psychologists who argued – based on 'scientific' arguments and experiments in California – that intelligence was linked to racial groups (Srinivasa Sarma 1936: 216). There is no study of the specific psychology of the 'Indian child' – contrary to the studies of the 'African child's psychology' in the Belgian Congo (Dapaepe 2009: 271). Montessori was quoted as arguing that 'Western children' had more capacity to enjoy art and literature because of longer exposure to the "civilising results of constructive science" (Montessori 1915: 883); another article by an Indian pedagogue argues that the children of civilised nations benefit from cumulative evolutionary knowledge and therefore have greater structural capacity to learn (Srinivasa Sarma 1936: 218). But these are isolated examples. A more general assumption was that intelligence was fixed at birth. This perception prompted an emphasis on the identification of 'laggards' who inhibited other students and were assumed to be unable to ever learn properly (Srinivasa Sarma 1936: 218). Even the missionaries at Ankleswar, who tended to work with lower caste converts, argued that "dullards and want-wits had better stay at home, for they will become none other than coolies" (Van Doren 1928: 76). Those who were perceived as inferior were to be ignored with little apparent regret (Anon 1890: 591). Not only were the 'feeble-minded' presumed to be incapable of learning, but they were assumed to be more likely to be socially deviant, too. Psychological techniques were advocated to exclude 'congenitally bad' children who were to be segregated from the rest of society (Anon 1934: 170), guaranteeing them a life of crime because of their presumed low intelligence. Educational expert Srinivasa Sarma even went so far as to argue that the drunkard, the criminal, the prostitute, and the insane individual were each a "positive menace to society", clearly referring to contemporary eugenics debates (Hodges 2001), but referring particularly to low intelligence levels: "imbeciles, idiots and morons" (Srinivasa Sarma 1936: 218).

By establishing education as a scientific discipline which informed and legitimised 'progressive' pedagogical methods, the pedagogues set themselves up as objective and rational experts (Gordon 1935: 327) who had control over knowledge and who operated under "the liberating force of the scientific spirit" (Bagshaw 1934: 165), whose expertise was, by definition, in no need of societal control. Education was 'the responsibility of the expert' in the same way as engineering or mathematics, and catastrophic results were to be predicted in case of any interference by lay people, who had no understanding of the scientific principles and the rational experimentation behind it (KT Paul in Van Doren 1928: xii). Because scientific knowledge was 'truth', it legitimised the power of the experts rather than holding them to be democratically responsible. Chronic deviance, or the regulation of the abnormal, was also to be controlled clinically through experts, who *understood* these things (Editorial, Educational India 1934: 102). Technological control was thus seen as the most legitimate form of power.

These experts were keen to establish themselves as partakers in a Western intellectual heritage of specialist pedagogues (Sen 2005: 27). While many of the articles from the 1880s and 1890s were copied from journals abroad, by the 1920s and 1930s the vast majority were written by Indians. Thus Indian educators could point to themselves as *equal* participants in a global discourse, and point to experiments, such as those at the Lady Willingdon College[13], as more progressive than the education system in both the United States and Great Britain. Additionally, although there were colonial bureaucrats involved, Indian experts could claim the monopoly of truth over education and over children's bodies. This stood in contrast to the negotiations in the mid-nineteenth century which, though involving prominent Indians such as Ram Mohan Roy, centred predominantly between different schools of colonial thought. This association with the 'modern' and rejection of colonial as 'traditional' is highly complicated (as demonstrated earlier), but supports Sen's (2005: 11) argument that children were not intrinsically important in this context, but were used both symbolically and in specific educational debates as objects of competition between colonial and Indian pedagogues. In this way, children's bodies became an important tool in which different elites could show and legitimise their power based on their scientific ability to know and to represent (Sen 2005: 5). Indian elites bolstered their own position through their monopoly over scientific truth, and sought to establish themselves as *more* expert, *more* enlightened and ultimately *more* modern than the colonial experts. This claim to a share in colonial epistemology

13 Madras Presidency Public Instruction Report 1931-32; Quinquennium 1927-28 to 1931-32, p. 96.

was deeply threatening to colonial power relationships (Bhabha 1984). While Western knowledge claims modernity 'for itself', as Chakrabarty (2002: 21) has shown in other contexts, this modernity is established and formed in dialogue with colonised elites, who established their own positions vis-à-vis both coloniser and their fellow nationals.

These discourses strengthened the claim of a middle class Indian elite to understand and know the culture of the colonisers as well as represent the Indian community. The discourse of education as science associated the Indian pedagogues with the colonisers as modern, in contrast to the traditional Indian home. The poor quality of Indian homes and community environment became a recurring theme which, according to historian Srivistava, helped explain the continued adherence of millions to 'non-modern' ideas and identities based on religion (Srivistava 1998: 197) and communal identity. For example, Chenciah argues that communal, class, and national divisions are "complexes that have developed in them by bad environment" (Chenciah 1936: 212). Thus deviance from normal development is interpreted as a result of an obstructive home environment. For example, Matthew sees parental attitudes as causing problems because there is not enough discipline in the home (Matthew 1936: 56), leading, as Masilamani argues, to moral degeneracy (Masilamani 1915: 427). Srinivasa Sarma argues that moral degeneracy was usually caused by mothers spoiling their children with excessive love, and by fathers, who were mostly disinterested in parenting, but were violent when they did interact with their children (Srinivasa Sarma 1936: 218). However, these experts affirm that while the home environment may be unsupportive, this did not prevent the child from accessing education, and did not affect his/her intrinsic plasticity. As Sen (2005: 49) argues, the middle class elite saw the 'Indian child' as having the same potential for development as any other child, despite being hampered by abnormal home circumstances. This position gave these middle class experts the power to represent, analyse, and control lower class children because of the 'non-modernity of subaltern parents' (Sen 2005: 49), which endangered the normal development of their children.

Kumar (2007: 12) describes "elite empowerment through elite intimacy with plural intellectual worlds"; in other words, middle class children had access to both colonial and Indian education with the continuing social advantages, or 'cultural capital', which would result. In contrast, lower caste children were to access education that was 'culturally specific'; this involved making a distinction between the epistemology of the higher castes (Balagopalan 2008) and that of non-elite children who were to be educated in rural knowledge and rural handicrafts. Vocational education was encouraged among low caste missionary converts and among those of Depressed Castes, limiting the potential of these children to progress out of their current social situation (ibid.). This caste-specific educational strategy reinforced the position of the elite as leaders of the community who had access to modern knowledge and colonial power, while maintaining the position of the non-elite as 'traditional'.

5. Constructing the 'normal' child

Underlying the idea of progressive and child-centred education were certain normative assumptions relating to what it meant to be a child and what form childhood development should take. At its most basic, child development was seen in terms of the psychological tests used, e.g. IQ tests and their results, on which children were categorised and educated in relation to the idea of the 'average child' (mental age = chronological age) (Swamikannu 1935: 251). There is frequent mention of the 'natural development' of the child (e.g., Gordon 1935: 328; Rao 1939: 110; also De Lissa 1924: 80), and descriptions of the quintessential child were characterised by 'self-activity' and imagination in which s/he becomes wholly engrossed (Venkateswaran 1935: 420). Within this discourse, the normal or natural activity of the young child was to play and this, too, received a great deal of attention in the literature. For example Srinivasa Sarma argues,

> play is the most valuable means to moral culture. Physical education is mental discipline. Play is the nursery of virtue […] it gives not only strength but courage and confidence, and contributes energy, decision and promptness to the will (Srinivasa Sarma 1935a: 342).

Cooperative play was seen as preparing the child for later life, as practice for cooperating with peers while satisfying an inherent love for experimentation (Krishnayya 1935: 218), spontaneity, and freedom (Vyas 1935: 334) in acting without adult control (Marenholtz-Bulow 1895: 46). Thus the main feature of the normal child was their desire to learn through activity and their active engagement with their environment. Venkateswaran writes that the "progress thereafter will be mainly one of exploration and conquest for the pupils, such exploration and conquest as would be impelled and captained by their own desire, venture and joy" which should be experienced in the classroom as "adventurous self-learning" (Venkateswaran 1935a: 257) and a gradual development in the rational understanding of the world. In another article, he argues that all spheres of life are expressed through action (Venkateswaran 1935b: 429). Chenciah (1936: 211), Nagaraja Rao (1939: 111) and Srinivasa Sarma (1935b: 129) all describe the child as characterised by activity, in addition to curiosity, creativity, and the constant active search for new experiences through which to develop.

5. 1 Discipline

Placing the 'normal child' as learning through play and self-discovery at the heart of education was the basis of the paradigm of New Education. However, the establishment of a system based on the normal or natural cognitive and language development of the child pathologises any deviance from this pattern (Walkerdine 1990: 203). This could be dealt with through discipline. Corporal punishment was rejected as an example of both colonial and pre-colonial barbarism (Venkateswaran 1935: 259; Anon 1898: 75), in the belief that discipline was only effective if "given in the spirit of sympathy and kindness", and that correction would come through reasoning and rational argument (Srinivasa Sarma 1937: 285), or "enlightened discipline".[14] The answer was, in the words of Lea Anderson, that "a certain atmosphere of freedom is essential for the growth of character. Too martinet a system does not produce men but machines" (Van Doren 1928: 46). The primary method of discipline was to be covert surveillance and self-regulation. This surveillance was intimately linked to the idea of 'love', in which teachers constantly watched, monitored and classified children as if in a laboratory (Walkerdine 1990: 22). The freedom of children was thus constrained, although they were granted the 'illusion of choice'. In her article, Chenciah argues both that mothers should observe the child's behaviour without the child's knowledge in order to guide behaviour subtly (Chenciah 1936: 212), and teachers should observe and categorise the child in order to facilitate development (ibid.: 213). Jenks (1996: 7) summarises Foucault's argument that through the nineteenth century, and with the rise of the bourgeois state which was heavily influenced by Western enlightenment ideals, "violence against the physical body is gradually transformed into a more subtle and intrusive correction and training of the very soul." In terms of children, the ultimate aim was to teach the child self-control (Krishnammah 1905: 341), allowing them to "evolve" themselves into "normal" adults (Jolly 1905: 212), although they should start life as "rebellious and unruly" rather than "infant saints" (Sitaraman 1907: 252). The individual was to become 'a responsible moral agent'[15] through "the internalising of the ruling sanctions and values of the community in such a manner that they become the individuals' own and receive his voluntary assent

14 Education in India, 1936-36, p. 12, IOR.

15 Education in India, United Provinces, 1936-36, p. 16.

and support."[16] This self-regulation was emphasised particularly in terms of the desired norms of behaviour (Anon 1889: 227). Srinivasa Sarma argues that "the problem of education thus becomes the problem of directing the *normal growth* of the desirable type of character" (Srinivasa Sarma 1937: 285). As the child develops rationally, s/he learns to understand his/her environment and can begin to practise self-control. This has the result of allowing the child to eventually gain control over his/her environment, but also generates new forms of social discipline aimed at controlling whole populations through the internal self-regulation of individuals (Seth 2007: 121).

5.2 Gender

Another example of this implicit normative idea is gender. Interestingly, particularly given the explosive nature of the topic, and its prominence in the debates of both nationalists and the colonial state, gender is not given much prominence in the journals (Chatterjee 1993). There is recognition of less physical strength (Anon 1934: 104) in women, although even that is disputed by some (Wallace 1922: 2). There is reference to the "ideal woman" who is intelligent (Keely 1890: 61) and "a social asset" (Ramchandra Rao 1935: 88), but also has womanly characteristics and spirituality, and serves as the keeper of all things spiritual (Chatterjee 1993). There is an article from a Girls' School on the scientific training of girls in housework, including human biology and botany, but the intention is that she can become a better mother and housewife (Ive 1895: 378). The most overtly political article is in opposition to the Child Marriage Act in 1890, but it is astonishing how little attention it receives, particularly given the prominence of girls as a category of student in the Public Instruction reports. This is one of the clearest examples of difference between theory and practice, for while girls were always referred to as being in girls' schools, in reality, consistently more girls attended mixed schools and would have followed the non gender-specific curriculum in place there.[17]

However, the normative features of activity and experimentation leading to the development of self-control are closely linked to the colonial masculine ideal. Mrinalini Sinha argues that the ideal of colonial masculinity was a "gendered identity based on a conviction that the status quo of Indian masculinity was fundamentally deficient in strength, courage, and self-control" (Sen 2005:61). The educational elite tried to establish this ideal through its writings,

16 Prof Clarke in Education in India, 1936-36, p. 17.

17 Madras Presidency Public Instruction Report 1931-32; Quinquennium 1927-28 to 1931-32, p. 92.

arguing that the 'Indian child' was no different from the 'universal' or 'normal' modern child, and that the primary ideal characteristics could be seen in masculine activities. Looking at the implementation of progressive education in 1970s Britain, Walkerdine (1990: 210) argues that this normality is based on a number of gendered assumptions, where reason and science are located in the normal development of the masculine body and its ability/power to control both itself and nature, while the (usually) female teacher's body produces reason through nurture, even as it manifested the emotional and passionate opposite of male reason. This means:

> The investment of reason in the sexed-body, as the foundation of modern western scientific rationality, not only locates self-control in rational argument, but also places it as the centre of an omnipotent fantasy of control over the workings of the universe. Mastery and control of the 'real' are centrally located in claims to truth and therefore to possess knowledge. In this sense mastery, control and bourgeois masculinity are conjoined in that uncertain pursuit of truth (Walkerdine 1990: 234).

Thus a particular form of male childhood was being advocated with an emphasis on activity, freedom, and control, which implicitly pathologises the 'female child'– constructed as passive and dependent. This is particularly important at a time when the symbolism of female education was such an important site of contestation (Seth 2007). Colonial educators, missionaries, nationalists and other indigenous educators all claimed that they were most modern because they promoted female education, and yet in their ideas of the modern child, they promoted a 'male' mode of accessing knowledge.

5.3 *Social Construction of Childhood*

The normative ideas surrounding the child and child development are clearly associated with discourses of modernity leading to the "idea of the rational independent autonomous child as a quasi-natural phenomenon who progresses through a universalised developmental sequence towards the possibility of rational argument" (Walkerdine 1990: 203). Indian pedagogues were trying to establish the Indian child as equal to and sharing in non-Indian, metropolitan forms of childhood development.

At the same time, recent research associated with the new sociology of childhood shows that childhood is a social construct rather than a natural development, and that "as such its status is constituted in particular socially located forms of discourse" (Jenks 1996: 29). While biological growth is the same, the significance of developmental stages varies according to the values of different cultures (Gupta 2006: 5). Pedagogue Banerjee (1935: 132) argues that New

Education "overemphasises the individual, whereas it was sadly missed in the past." This is important, because the underlying epistemological assumption is the development of the individual as a rational actor. This normative assumption can be linked to Western cultural and philosophical ideas, which tend to ignore the value of the community in everyday life. In contrast to this focus on individualism, Sadler (1905: 147) emphasises the need to place individuals in communities, whether church, nation and socio-economic relationships and activities. As Jenks (1996: 22) argues, modernist discourses of child development are based on Western conceptions of normality and individuality, which denies the child a role as an actor in a social space, and downplays his contribution to society. Through her contemporary work in a North Indian School, Sarangapani (2003: 257) agrees with this, and highlights the danger of modern universal truths about the growth of individuality/ rationality, which she argues are linked to Western cultural and philosophical ideas that de-skill children and take education out of its cultural context. As Nandy reminds us, "The West is now everywhere, within the West and outside; in structures and in minds" (1993: xi). As a result, the 'Indian elite' promoted the postcolonial construction of (traditional) 'Indian culture', which is associated with lower and Depressed Castes and in particular with the rural poor, as different (and inferior) to Western culture. Through this postcolonial Othering, they managed to set themselves up as 'modern' and 'normal' in accordance with Western universalism.

6. Conclusion

This paper delineates the discourses surrounding the introduction of New Education in late colonial India. This education was marked by a rejection of pre-colonial and colonial traditional pedagogies. Establishing progressive teaching methodologies was very much a global trend in the 1930s. My critical assessment of the discourses surrounding the adoption of these ideas in colonial India does not intend to discard these educational ideals as such. However, taking note of the fact that these educational discussions amongst experts had very little impact on educational practice in general – apart from a few 'experimental schools' – I set out to explore the functions these discourses may have served, produced as they were by a small Western oriented elite who operated within a colonial context.

The pedagogues' writings in educational journals and those who sought to put those writings into practice through specific educational experiments used the discourse to establish themselves at the pinnacle of a hierarchy of knowledge. They did this specifically by distancing themselves from 'traditional' India and proving their own credentials as modern scientists who alone could properly understand, and therefore could speak for, the 'Indian child'. Their power of definition and explanation was legitimised by their role as experts of a universal science of pedagogy in the use of scientific testing and categorisation. This discourse ultimately sought to establish the Indian pedagogues as equals in modernity, thereby, to some extent, 'subverting' the colonial subject formation through processes of Othering. As experts of educational science and of the according technologies, these pedagogues were on a par with Western pedagogical thinkers, thereby transcending 'culture' in a process of hegemonic subject formation; at the same time, as 'Indian pedagogues', they alone were in a position to understand and explain the 'Indian child' and to design a 'culturally adequate' system of education for the disadvantaged, thereby *Othering the non-elite children* and stabilising their own claims to 'normality' and universalism.

The aim of the colonial officials, missionaries, and Indian pedagogues was to improve educational performance through introducing a new system of education, which was more appropriate for the subcontinent. The curriculum was to be 'culturally specific', making education more attractive and more adapted to the home life of the children. The term 'culture' in these discourses, however, was linked to social stratification as well as to gender constructs. While the (urban) elite was associated with non-marked Western universalism and (Western ideals of) masculinity, the (rural) poor as well as females were 'culturalised' in terms of 'traditional Indian culture' as constructed within the colonial production of knowledge.

Moreover, as could be shown, the pedagogical techniques of the New Education were linked inherently to the epistemology of the colonisers. By promoting universal truths as modern, scientific views of what constituted normal childhood growth, development, and activity, the Indian pedagogues promoted Western ideas of individuality and citizenship. While attempting to establish a modern, culturally specific curriculum "expressive of, and responsive to" the Indian "native genius", the discourses surrounding the pedagogy and implementation of that curriculum implicitly reinforced Western knowledge as power and linked the universal with the West, which inevitably disenfranchised, Othered, and subordinated all other knowledges, including that which the curriculum was introduced to promote.

Literature and Sources

Allender, T. (2009): Learning Abroad: the Colonial Educational Experiment in India, 1813-1919. In: Paedagogica Historica, 45: 6, 707 – 722.

All India National Education Conference, Wardha (1937). Proceedings.

Anon (1885): The Early culture of the mind and its faculties. In: The Schoolmaster, 249 – 251.
Anon (1890): The Dull Boy. In: Madras Journal of Education, 591 – 592.
Anon (1898): Early education. In: The Schoolmaster (serialised), 183 – 187, 219 – 223, 245 – 253.
Anon (1898): Notes on Teaching. In: The Schoolmaster, 63 – 66.
Anon (1889): Discipline. Reprinted from The Private Schoolmaster. In: Educational Review, 227 – 229.
Anon (1934): Editorial Education and Environment. In: Educational India (September), 103 – 106.
Anon (1934): Question and Answer. In: Educational India (September), 102
Bagshaw, A. (1934): The place of beauty in education. In: Educational India (November), 165 – 167.
Balagopalan, S. (2008): Memories of Tomorrow: Children, Labor and the Panacea of Fomal Schooling. In: Journal of the History of Childhood and Youth, 1. 2, 267 – 285.
Banerjee, P. K. (1935): The Aim of Education. In: Educational India (October), 129 – 133.
Bhabha, H. K. (1984): Of mimicry and man: the ambivalence of colonial discourse. In: October, 28, 125 – 33.
Chakrabarty, D. (2002): Habitations of Modernity: Essays in the Wake of Subaltern Studies. Delhi.
Chatterjee, P. (1993): The Nation and its Fragments: Colonial and Postcolonial Histories. New Jersey.
Chaturvedi, V. (ed. 2000): Mapping Subaltern Studies and the Postcolonial. London/New York.
Chenciah, D. S. (1936): Right Training in the infant stage. In: Educational India (December) 210 – 213.
Crooks, N. (1996): The Transmission of Knowledge in South Asia: Essays on Education, Religion, History, and Politics. Delhi.
Dapaepe, M. (2009): Belgian images of the psycho-pedagogical potential of the Congolese during the Colonial Era, 1908-1960. In: Paedagogica Historica, 45: 6, 707 – 725.
De Lissa, L. (1924): Report of the Imperial Education Conference.
Diddi, S. R. (1937): General Methods of Teaching' in Educational India (February), 297 – 300.
Dworking, M. (ed. 1959): Dewey on Education: Selections with an Introduction and Notes. New York.
Fleming, D. J. (1921): Schools with a message in India. London/Edinburgh.
Goodman, J., McCulloch, G. & Richardson, W. (2009): 'Empires overseas' and 'empires at home': postcolonial and transnational perspectives on social change in the history of education. In: Paedagogica Historica, 45: 6, 695 – 706.
Gordon, D. S. (1935): New Education – What it means. In: Educational India (March), 327 – 332.
Gupta, A. (2006): Early Childhood Education, Postcolonial theory, and teaching practices in India: Balancing Vygotsky and the Veda. New York.
Hodges, S. (ed. 2001): Reproductive Health in India: History, Politics, Controversies. Hyderabad.

Ive, Miss (1895): Natural Science Teaching in Girls' Schools. In: Indian Journal of Education, 378 – 383.
Jenks, C. (1996): Childhood. London/New York.
Jolly, W. (1905): Etymology of the word 'education'. In: Educational Review, 209 – 212.
Landry, D. & Maclean, G. (1996): The Spivak reader: selected works of Gayatri Chakravorty Spivak. New York/London.
Kallaway, P. (2007): Conference Litmus: The Development of a Conference and Policy Culture in the Interwar Period with Special Reference to the New Education Fellowship and British Colonial Education in Southern Africa'. In: Tolley, K. (ed.): Transformations in Schooling: Historical and Comparative Perspectives. New York, 123 – 149.
Karnataka, S. R. (1937): Child-centred education. In: Educational India, February, 291 – 293.
Keely, M. (1890): Teaching – a noble calling. In: Madras Journal of Education, 164 – 165, 235 – 237.
Krishnayya, D. (1935): Infant Teaching. In: Educational India (October), 217 – 218.
Krishnayya, G. S. (1934): Some lessons from negro education. In: Educational India (November), 168 – 171.
Krishnayya, G. S. (1937): The Fine Art of Teaching. In: Educational India (September), 3 – 5.
Krishnammah, H. R. (1905): The Practice of Education. Part 2. In: Educational Review, 341 – 344.
Kumar, K. (1991): Political Agenda of Education: A Study of Colonialist and Nationalist ideas. New Delhi.
Kumar, N. (2000): Lessons from Schools: The History of Education in Banaras. New Delhi.
Kumar, N. (2007): The Politics of Gender, Community and Modernity: Essays on Education in India. New Delhi.
Masilamani, M. M. (1915): Home and School Influences. In: Educational Review, 425 – 430.
Matthew, A. V. (1936): Parental Attitude. In: Educational India, August, 55 – 57.
Milford, H. (1922): Village Education. In: India: the report of a commission of inquiry. London.
Moga Staff (1936): First Steps in Vernacular Education, Suggestions for Improvement. In: Educational India (May-June), 415 – 420.
Montessori, M. (1915): The Imagination in Childhood. In: Educational Review, 882 – 884.
Nagaraja Rao, K. (1939): The Individual Method. In: Handbook of the 30th Provincial Educational Conference, SITU Madras, 110 – 112.
Nandy, A. (1993): The Intimate Enemy: Loss and Recovery of Self Under Colonialism. Delhi.
Ramchandra Rao, B. (1935): The Need for a New Orientation in Education. In: Educational India (September), 83 – 88.
Sadler, M.E. (1905): The school in some of its relations to social organisation and to national life. In: Educational Review, 147 – 148.
Sakhare, M. R. (1937): Intelligence. In: Educational India (April), 367 – 368.
Sarangapani, P. (2003): Constructing School Knowledge: An ethnography of learning in an Indian village. New Delhi.
Sen, S. (2004): Schools, Athletes and Confrontation: The Student Body in Colonial India. In: Mills, J. & Sen, S. (eds.): Confronting the Body: The Politics of Physicality in Colonial and Post-Colonial India. London, 58 – 79.

Sen, S. (2006): Colonial Childhoods: the Juvenile Periphery of India 1850-1945, London.

Sengupta, P. (2003): An Object Lesson in Colonial Pedagogy. In: Society for Comparative Study of Society and History, 98 – 116.

Seth, S. (2007): Subject Lessons: The Western Education of Colonial India. New Delhi.

Siddalingaiya, M. (1937): Modern Developments in Educational Practice. In: Educational India (May-June), 402 – 407.

Sitaraman, P. (1907): Children and ethics. In: Educational Review, 251 – 252.

Srinivasa Sarma, M. S. (1935a): The Test of Educational Efficiency. In: Educational India (March), 340 – 342.

Srinivasa Sarma, M.S. (1935b): Attitudes – their Formation: the heart of the Educational Process. In: Educational India (October), 127 – 129.

Srinivasa Sarma, M.S (1936): The roots of educational reform: a study in pedagogical handicaps. In: Educational India (December), 214 – 218.

Srinivasa Sarma, MS (1937): Children's Misdeeds: their psychology. In: Educational India (February), 285 – 288.

Srivastava, S. (1998): Constructing Post-Colonial India: national character and the Doon School. London.

Swamikannu Paul, C. (1935): Intelligence Tests. In: Educational India (January), 241 – 252.

Swamikannu Paul, C. (1936): New Ideals in Education. In: Educational India (February), 293 – 395.

Van Doren, A. B. (ed. 1928): Fourteen Experiments in Rural Education: Some Indian Schools where new methods are being tested. Calcutta.

Venkata Rao, P. (1935): Pedagogies of Regional Geography. In: Educational India (February), 297 – 300.

Venkateswaran, N. K. (1935a): The three kinds of teaching. In: Educational India (January), 256 – 259.

Venkateswaran, N.K. (1935b): Three Axioms of Education. In: Educational India (May-June), 419 – 426.

Viswanathan, G. (1989): Masks of Conquest: Literary Study and British Rule in India. London.

Von Marenholtz-Bulow, B. (1885): Froebel's Fundamental Idea. In: The Schoolmaster, 44 – 48.

Vyas, T. (1935): Education and New Psychology. In: Educational India (March), 332 – 3 50.

Walkerdine, V. (1990): Schoolgirl Fictions. London.

Wallace, J. E. (1922): Three things for teachers to keep in mind. In: Village Teacher's Journal (April), 2 – 3.

‘The Others’ in the Turkish Education System and in Turkish Textbooks

Mustafa Çapar, Mustafa Kemal University, Turkey

Modern nation-states, in general, tend to assume that “internal homogeneity” is or should be the norm, and therefore, that heterogeneity – particularly in terms of ethnicity, culture, language, and also religion – constitutes a problem. Different strategies to deal with this “problem” can be observed in different national contexts. In the case of Turkey, a nationalist and essentialist ideology has particularly alarming effects because this nation-state has not as yet internalized democracy, so the nationalism that pervades the state means that the protection of minorities is tenuous.

Just like any other country, Turkey is a multi-ethnic society whose minority groups have been historically constructed and continue to be re-constructed as ‘the Other’ against the ‘Turkish norm’. In Turkey, these groups include non-Muslims (e.g. Armenians, Greeks, Jews, Yezidis, Assyrians), ethnic minorities (e.g. Kurds, Gypsies, Lazs), Alevis, street children, socialists, gays, to name but a few. However, non-Muslims and Kurds, in particular, are considered dangerous elements who threaten the integrity of the nation-state. This is reflected in their representation within the national education system.

Since the late 1800s, the content of textbooks used in schools has been heavily influenced by nationalist ideology. These books have contributed to raising children in a strict essentialist-nationalist ideology. When people educated in this ideology come to power, they consider this policy as natural, rightful and necessary. Therefore I argue that the Turkish national education system is a major agent of nationalist subject formation.

In fact, the Turkish education system is a veritable laboratory for strategies of *Othering*. While working as a school teacher in a primary school (*ilköğretim okulu*) and in high school (*lise*), I had many opportunities to observe the mechanism of constructing Turkish citizens as non-Turkish, either on grounds of ethnicity or religion, or both. When I asked students “What are the threats against Turkey?” the majority would respond that Armenians, Greeks and “separatists” (the Kurds demanding political and cultural rights) were a “great danger” for Turkey. Therefore, I decided to research these issues in more depth in my graduate dissertation. During my doctoral studies, I realized that processes of *Othering* “non-Turkish” ethnic minorities and non-Muslim communities by the Turkish education system are not limited to textbooks. The curriculum, official documents (law, regulations, notices etc.) and the discourses of statesmen have been systematically involved in these processes and strategies.

In the textbooks, minorities are dealt with in two ways: non-Muslims are depicted as harmful, dangerous and unreliable, whereas ethnically- and religiously-different groups like the Kurds and the Alevis seem not to exist at all. Accordingly, Turkish and Sunni/Hanafi students have no knowledge of Kurds and Alevis who form a significant part of the population of Turkey.[1] As all Muslims in Turkey are also tacitly assumed to be "ethnic Turks" and to practice Sunni/Hanafi beliefs, people with Kurdish and Alevi backgrounds are by definition outside of every Turkish norm(ality).

Since nationalism was popularized in Turkey more than a century ago, thousands of textbooks have been published grounded in this spirit. The authors of these books have changed, yet the content has remained the same. In particular, Social Studies textbooks have ignored differences, depicting the Turkish citizens as a homogenous collective, while at the same time warning students that minorities are dangerous. The combination of "warning" and ignorance has caused students to express a wide range of negative or ignorant statements ranging from doubt about their trustworthiness to hostility and hatred toward them to ignorance about their existence.

In the following essay, I will demonstrate the important role of historical narratives – from the late Ottoman Empire to the early days of the Turkish Republic – to the problem under consideration here. Contemporary constructions of minorities and the policies of ignorance and rejection can be traced to historical events involving "old minorities". History curricula and textbooks consistently emphasize the "evils" which Turkey and Turks suffered at the hands of non-Muslims in the past. By keeping alive the memory of rebellions which took place in the late 1890s and in the early 1900s, the school curricula teaches students that non-Muslims and other minorities are unfriendly and could turn on "us" at any moment.

After giving a brief historical account of the period from the late Ottoman Empire to the early 2000s, I will proceed to analyze how minorities have been constructed as non-Turkish Others in textbooks and other official documents in the Turkish education system.

1 For a detailed study on the subject of Othering of Armenians, Greeks and Jews, and Kurdish and Alevi groups in the Turkish education system from the late Ottoman Empire to the 1950s, see Education in Turkey and "Other Turks" (Çapar 2006). Moreover, regarding the Othering of non-Turks and non-Muslims, see Yıldız (2001), Kaplan (1999), Okutan (2004), Sadoğlu (2003).

1. "Us and the Others": from the Ottomans to the Republic

The Ottoman Empire, from the 16th until the early 20th century, was based on the "*millet* system", which regulated the status of non-Muslims and the autonomy of religious communities. The term "*millet*" denotes a religiously-defined, or 'confessional nation'.[2] Thus, the Ottoman Empire had two main confessional nations, Muslims and non-Muslims. The Muslims were recognized as the main or dominant nation. The non-Muslims were the 'other nation', subdivided into non-Muslims, Jews, Greeks and Armenians, the latter of which were further divided into three sub-groups: Gregorians, Catholics, and Protestants (Tunçay 2003: 2).

To a great extent, non-Muslims were free to determine their religious practices and education from 1839 until the First Constitutional Reform was launched in 1876, though they faced more restrictions compared to Muslims. Therefore, the claim that Ottoman rule was tolerant and treated all the ethnic and religious communities equally is debatable. Rather, it could be claimed that the *millet* system was based on specific strategies of *Othering*. For instance non-Muslims, unlike Muslims, were not allowed to bear arms or ride horses, and they had to wear clothes that represented their religion. A number of decrees and regulations promulgated in the late 1800s abolished these discriminatory rules. These new regulations, however, also placed the educational institutions of minority communities under the control of the government.

European nationalism spread rapidly in the late 1800s, affecting non-Muslim communities on the borders of the Ottoman Empire such that by the beginning of the 20th century some nations under Ottoman control began declaring independence. The sudden loss of territory under Ottoman rule moved Turkish intellectuals to consider new political approaches, and nationalist ideologies spread among Turkish intellectuals. At the same time, suspicions about and threats

2 Addition by editors: The Ottoman term millet specifically refers to the separate legal courts pertaining to personal law under which minorities were allowed to rule themselves (in cases not involving any Muslim) with little interference from the Ottoman government. People were bound to their millets by their religious affiliations (or their confessional communities), rather than their ethnic origins, according to the millet concept. Muslim communities prospered under the Ottoman Empire: Ottoman law did not recognize such notions as ethnicity or citizenship; thus, a Muslim of any ethnic background enjoyed precisely the same rights and privileges. In the 19th century, in the context of the rise of nationalism in the Ottoman Empire, the perception of the millet was altered. – Until the 19th century, there were (besides the Muslim millet) only three acknowledged millets in the Ottoman Empire: the Jewish millet, the Armenian millet, and the Greek Orthodox millet. But by 1914 their number had risen to 17. For further details see http://en.wikipedia.org/wiki/Millet_(28Ottoman_Empire); http://de.wikipedia.org/wiki/Millet-System

against minorities also intensified. These suspicions were compounded by the fact that non-Muslims cooperated with Christian European countries, and that separatist nationalist leaders were educated in minority schools.[3]

The 'non-Muslim problem' became more intense in the last decade of the Ottoman Empire and continued into the Republican Period, which began in 1924. In the modern Turkish Republic as well, minorities were perceived to be conspiring with outside forces trying to divide up Turkey. For this reason, non-Muslims and 'non-Turkish' Muslims (Kurds, Arabs, Circassians) were considered a threat to a unified Turkey. In short, official Turkish policy defined Muslim-Turkish identity against *non-Muslims* on the one hand, and the Turkish ethnicity against *non-Turkish ethnicity* on the other. Meanwhile, Turkish policy also emphasized the Hanefi-Sunni identity against other Muslims from different sects such as Nusairies (Alawi/Arab Alevis) and Alevis.[4]

As a result, an intense Turkification policy was initiated against those who were not perceived as ethnically 'Turkish', and schools were an important arena for this policy. With the exception of Jews, religious minorities were generally exempt from assimilation. The reason for this was the conviction, rooted in the *millet* system which conflated Turkish political and Muslim religious identities, that non-Muslims would never actually become Turks. Because of this, non-Muslims, no matter how they were referred to in official papers (as 'Turks' and 'citizens' holding equal rights with Turks), were never seen as Turks in practice. Especially since the beginning of the Republican period (1924), non-Muslims have not been seen as groups which should be assimilated into being Turkish and Muslim, but as a resisting force against those identities. They were perceived as people who wanted to demolish Turkey from within as accomplices of hostile outside forces – as my analysis of the official representation of these groups will demonstrate in detail.

3 Since the early 2000s, in order to comply with the rules of EU membership, some amendments to codes, the curriculum and textbooks have been made, though it has not been easy to remove all traces of the century-old images of minorities. As mentioned above, those in charge of such changes have themselves been raised within the nationalist-essentialist education system. Therefore, they often do not even recognise problematic ways that images and knowledge about minorities has been constructed; rather, these processes of Othering appear to them natural and adequate.

4 Wikipedia defines the Alevis as a religious, "sub-ethnic" and cultural minority community in Turkey. Wikipedia also classifies Alevis as a branch of Shia Islam; however, there are significant differences between Alevi beliefs and that of other Shia sects ("Alevi" http://en.wikipedia.org/wiki/Alevi [23.8.2010]). Turkish Alevis do not at all identify with the concept of Shia, which they consider to be an Iranian sect. Therefore, the definition of (Turkish) Alevism as a "branch of Shia Islam" is highly disputable.

As recently as 2009, Yusuf Halaçoğlu, Professor of Turkish history and chairman of the Turkish Historical Society, reflected a general attitude towards non-Muslims when he said that Alevis (see footnote 3) were actually Armenians. He supported his claim by referring to documents allegedly in his possession, but which he refused to share with the public. It has, of course, long been known that non-Muslims, in order to be exempt from non-Muslim taxes or to avoid oppression either individually or in groups, converted to Islam. But Halaçoğlu's claims clearly illustrate the perceptions that many Turks and Muslims have of Alevis and Armenians: neither Armenians nor Alevis (although Muslim) can be Turks. At the same time, by suggesting that most Alevis are not Muslims and Turks, but Armenians, Halaçoğlu alienates both Armenians and Alevis. From time to time, the declarations of officials working in important positions show that, despite pervasive discourses of anti-discrimination in Turkey, those who are not 'ethnically Turkish' *and* Muslim are seen as 'the internal Others'.[5] This perspective has consequences for education.

2. Turkish National Education – monolithic, nationalist perspectives

The objective of Turkish national education is to form nationalist teachers, nationalist students, and lastly, a nationalist society. To implement this ambition the curriculum and the school textbooks are full of essentialist and nationalist content. To quote from a school program:

> [Primary schools] have to teach national culture to children. National education is assigned to teach all of its citizens the same national ideals and the same national objectives, information, habits, interests and the will to serve in an effective way.

---

5 Another recent example of this perspective can be found in the following statement by the State Minister and the deputy Prime Minister, Cemil Çiçek, who in 2010 repeated the words of Kenan Evren, the leader of the 1980 military coup: "[...] ideological terror before the 1980s, rightist-leftist terror after the 1980s... Not only Armenian terror, there is a close relationship between the Armenian terror and the PKK terror, these are 'blood relatives'. When one of them is passive, the mission was given to the other. Actually, pardon me but, that some of the terrorists haven't been circumcised, means a lot. It's not a myth; we know who is what very well.' ("Çiçek'ten Ermeni PKK'lılar İması") http://www.radikal.com.tr/Radikal.aspx?aType=RadikalDetayV3&ArticleID=1014804&Date=11.05.2011&CategoryID=77 (date: 21.08.2010); emphasis added MÇ). The minister is 'killing two birds with one stone' by Othering both Armenians and the Kurds who have had problems with the government.

> [...] Every course at school should be considered as a medium to help reach national targets (quoted by Esen, 2003: 11-14).[6]

H. Nihat Bilgen, coming from a Turkish National Education background, uses phrases quite reminiscent of the above in his article 'Nationalism in Contemporary Education' in the textbook *Citizenship and Human Rights* (Yurttaşlık ve Vatandaşlık Hakları):

> Education is to make our people adopt a Turkish identity. This identity should involve our flag, our land watered with martyrs' blood, and our dear nation, and the unchanging features of our national and spiritual values. The priority of all areas of education should be to teach our students this value (quoted in Çiftçi et al. 2002: 101f.).

The monolithic nationalist ideology is taught in many textbooks, either directly or indirectly. In *National Security Information* (Milli Güvenlik Bilgisi), this objective is dealt with quite specifically. According to this book, the central task of schools is not so much to teach scientific information, but to equip students with militaristic views and abilities:

> Schools' endeavours in education and teaching should serve to equip the youth with the love of country and nation, raise them as a component of the military force [...]. To this end, with the help of physical education the wartime power is enforced. National sensitivity is motivated through national and military anthems. In national ceremonies young age groups attend as the audience, later ages attend as participators to enhance the development of military skills. [...] Military units are visited to show students that in the army such responsibilities progress in a certain order and discipline. In this way, the notion of national security is renewed (Milli Güvenlik Bilgisi I II III 1980: 5).

This militarist tendency is implied in other courses, too. Sometimes a discourse that refers to dying and killing is used to enforce militarist motives, e.g., it is said that Turks are soldiers who would never hesitate to fight, shed blood, or die for their country. Through such nationalistic and militaristic discourse, 'non-Turkish' students are effectively alienated in the Turkish education system.

Nationalism pervades all relevant documents, from the Constitution to national education laws, regulations, curriculum and textbooks in the form of 'Atatürk's nationalism'. According to this, all Turkish citizens are Turks, and thus everyone in Turkey is implicitly a Turkish/ Atatürk nationalist. This approach, which prevailed since the 1920s, became even more intense after a military coup in 1980.

---

6 All quotations from Turkish documents and textbooks were translated into English for this publication.

'Atatürk's nationalism' is first mentioned in the 'Introduction' of the 1982 Constitution. It is repeated in the second article of the Constitution and all regulations are designed accordingly. Referencing the Constitution, the Foundations of the National Education Laws, for instance, state the main objective of national education as follows:

> ...to raise citizens devoted to Atatürk's reforms and principles, and devoted to Kemalist nationalism in the constitution, adopting the national, moral, humanistic, spiritual and cultural values, preserving and developing them; loving their family, homeland, nation and trying to advance them.[7]

Another method to promote ethnocentric forms of Turkish nationalism that constructs minorities as 'Others' is to refer to Mustafa Kemal Atatürk's ideas on nation and nationalism. From primary schools to universities, these ideas are visible in many textbooks. In one of the books used in primary schools, nationalism is promoted by referring to statements by Atatürk: "We are explicit patriots and Turkish nationalists. The foundation of our Republic is the Turkish community, the more the people of this community are full of Turkish culture, the stronger the republic will be" (Çiftçi et al. 2002: 75). According to another textbook, nationalism is so important that denying it means the termination of Turkish existence (Mumcu & Su 2002: 260). And in a textbook for 'Turkish' (as school subject) published in 2009, it is claimed that nationalism is a beneficial ideology for the Turkish nation: "The principle of nationalism is very beneficial in many ways. It strengthens our country against internal and external threats. It prioritizes the unity of our country above anything else" (Çetin et al. 2009a: 45). This quotation is representative of many textbooks. Official discourse employs nationalism as a 'protective wall' against (construed) internal and external threats.

One of the claims of nationalism, which can also be traced back to Atatürk's words, is that Turks are an ancient and superior nation. One civics textbook written by Mithat Sadullah in the late 1920s claims that Turks are the world's oldest nation, and that, when other nations were still in a 'barbaric period', Turks already had a strong administration and law system. Allen (1968) suggests that Turks are portrayed as the world's most courageous and most benevolent nation. The hypothesis that Turks were the leaders of all other civilizations and spread civilization to the world emerged in the 1920s, and peaked in popularity in the 1930s.[8] It is, explicitly or implicitly, still expressed in today's textbooks,

---

7 "Milli Eğitim Kanunu" http://mevzuat.meb.gov.tr/html/88.html (date: 19.08.2009).

8 In the 1930s, the Turkish Language Institute and the Turkish History Institute were founded to prove this hypothesis. The Turkish History Institute focused on proving the 'Turkish History Hypothesis' and the Turkish Language Institute was tasked with dem-

as the following extract from the teacher's manual for the Grade 4 social sciences textbook of 2009 illustrates:

> Clothing such as trousers, shirts or jackets, were first used by the Turks. The decimal system used in the military today belongs to the Turks. Similarly, Turks were the first to play sports, such as polo, to do skiing, fencing, etc. The Turkish nation has, throughout history, helped advance world civilization.
>
> The writers of the manual instruct the teacher as follows: 'You can cover the contribution of the Turks to world civilization by having the pupils do research on the topic' (Tekerek et al. 2009a: 69).

Interestingly, the authors of these texts express no doubts about the reliability of this 'information' and as these passages indicate, reproduce it without any hesitation.

2.1 Teacher Education and Training: Forming the Nationalist Teacher

Most universities train teachers in their education faculties (and other faculties) to be nationalist and militant. From primary schools through universities, students are taught that their system is based in 'Atatürk nationalism' and 'the unconditional unity of their country'. Teacher candidates who graduate from these faculties transfer the nationalist academic education which they received onto the educational institutions in which they started their own education. In other words, the Turkish education system leaves no room for critical questions or other points of view, and effectively reproduces the monolithic perspective in a complete and comprehensive manner to new generations.

The nationalist curriculum found in the 1948 *Primary School Syllabus*, for example, has changed little in the last sixty years, and is substantially the same in *The Latest Primary School Syllabus* published in 2002. Teachers cover issues related to the Turkish nation, Turkish homeland, and national issues not only in Turkish and Social Sciences classes, but also in Sciences, Arts, Physical Education and Music courses. For instance, teachers are supposed to use real-world examples to explain that the Turkish nation has spread its culture and has been a good model in all walks of life, and that the Turks have sacrificed a lot to be able to spread the superior Turkish culture. Even in arithmetic class, the teacher is expected to advance a nationalist perspective in the choice of problems for arithmetical calculation (Esen, 2003: 14; Copeaux 2000: 93).

---

onstrating the 'Sun Language Theory'. To this end several international language and history congresses were held. They tried to prove that the origin of all civilizations (Sumerian, Egyptian, and Indian) as well as the origin of all languages was Turkish. All the while, Turkish anthropologists tried to prove that the Turks were a superior 'race'.

Teachers in Turkey are required to follow The National Education Regulations, but it is assumed they have the flexibility to decide on specific content and on the methods within their own classrooms. It is questionable, however, whether teachers have the background or training to actually teach content that differs from national standards, considering the academic training that is available. Furthermore, the Ministry of Education has taken steps against serious 'deviations' by publishing 'teachers' manuals' with content very similar to the ethnocentric student textbooks. These books, too, repeat the 'facts' that the Turks are a superior nation and leaders of world civilization, and Atatürk's principles of nationalism as the foundation of national unity and solidarity (Erol et al. 2008b: 44; Çetin et al. 2009b: 90-91; Tekerek at al. 2009b: 69). Teachers are expected to talk about these 'facts'. Having been raised with similar 'information', most teachers repeatedly transfer this to their students without critical reflection, continuing the closed circle of nationalist knowledge.

2.2 The Essentialist Student Oath

For years, one of the most controversial issues in the Turkish education system has been the 'Student Oath'.[9] The oath that starts with the words "I am Turkish, I am honest, I am hardworking", and ends with the phrase "I am dedicating myself to my nation. Happy is the one who can say 'I am Turkish'". The oath is recited every morning in schools except in non-Muslim minority schools and foreign schools, implying that all citizens, without exception, are ethnic Turks, and thus denying all affiliations and identities except the Turkish ethnic background. In particular, the last two sentences of the oath have been criticized. Many ethnic groups, especially Kurds, are opposed to their children's having to recite an oath that erases their ethnic identity.

The Student Oath is a fundamental enactment of Turkish state ideology through the Turkish education system. Therefore, from the state's perspective, questioning the Oath simultaneously questions the state-developed ideology of 'Turkishness', and that is a taboo. However, recent developments in Turkey,

9 The words of this oath were written by Reşit Galip who was the Minister of education in the 1930s: "I am Turkish, I am honest, I am hardworking. My principle is to protect the young, and to respect my elders, and to love my country more than myself. My aim is to advance, and go forward. The Great Ataturk, I swear that I will follow the path you opened, and walk towards the target you showed us without a halt. I devote myself to the existence of Turks. Happy is the one who can say 'I am Turkish!'" ("Andımız" http://okulweb.meb.gov.tr/60/08/622036/andimiz.html [date: 02.8.2010]).The oath is recited by a student word by word, and the students standing in a military order repeat each sentence.

such as the country's candidate status in the European Union, the influence of international agreements, other internal and external developments, and social-political dynamics have created space to debate the Student Oath. In May 2009, under pressure from non-governmental organizations, then-Minister of National Education Nimet Çubukçu stated his openness to discussing the recitation of the Student Oath in schools. Though he later stepped back from this statement, the fact that such a public admission could take place can be seen as a step forward. At the same time a human rights organization called Mazlum-Der started a campaign against the Oath[10], and put up posters on billboards in the city of Diyarbakır. This campaign, which reflected the attitudes of many Kurdish residents of the city, drew negative reaction of the government institutions and nationalist circles, and the posters were immediately removed.[11] Still, this initiative did promote a critical discussion of the monolithic nationalist ideology.

3. Laws and Regulations: The Unidentified Others

Ethnic minorities, especially Armenians and Greeks, have long been portrayed within the Turkish education system as an existential threat, a kind of Trojan horse trying to destroy the country. This approach can be observed from the late Ottoman Empire continuing into the first years of the Republic, and it can be traced through the curriculum, school books, as well as in minority education regulations published by the National Education Ministry.

Political reorganizations in the 19th Century, such as the 1839 Rescript of Gulhane, the 1856 Reform Decree, and the 1869 National Education Regulations, also reformed public education, with special regulations and expanded inspections of educational institutions for non-Muslims. Inspection of non-Muslim schools intensified with the Special School Regulations (SSR) or 'Mekatip-i Hususiye Talimatnamesi' of 1915. Educational historian Yahya Akyüz (1999: 240) claims that the SSR were instituted after a decrease in the non-Muslim population due to the Balkan Wars and the Armenian Relocation. The most important rearrangement in the SSR was that courses in 'Turkish', 'Turkish history' and 'Turkish geography' became compulsory, and had to be taught in the medium of Turkish (1915). This reorganization foreshadowed future even more restrictive measures by the government. In the revised regulations published in 1923, school inspection was made more explicit. In the 6th

10 "Öğrenci Andı Tartışması" http://www.ntvmsnbc.com/id/24968646/, date: 12.9.2009

11 "'Andımız Kaldırılsın' Kampanyasının Afişleri Kaldırıldı" http://www.radikal.com.tr/Radikal.aspx?aType=RadikalDetay&Date=13.7.2009&ArticleID=944876, date: 3.9.2009

article in the new SSR, courses in Turkish language, history and geography were required to be taught "by Turkish teachers in the Turkish language" (SSR, 1331/1923: 1f.). What is noticeable in this article is the stipulation *"by Turkish teachers"*. The implication of this statement was that ethnic Turks, and not minority teachers, were the only ones recognized as Turks. Even today, SSR require that that these courses must be taught by a "Turkish teacher", and that all first deputy principals must be [ethnically] Turkish. This means that even if a member of a minority community is a legal citizen, s/he cannot serve as the first deputy principal of the school, nor teach the aforementioned courses. This regulation contradicts several constitutional provisions, including the 8th article of the 1876 constitution, the 54th and 88th articles of the 1961 constitution, and the 66th article of the 1982 constitution. These articles inclusively define 'Turkish citizens', regardless of their religion or 'race' (Kili & Gözübüyük 2000). It follows that the SSR and similar laws and regulations discriminate against minorities in violation of the relevant articles of the constitution.

One important document defining education of non-Muslims is the 1923 Treaty of Lausanne[12]. Because this treaty is the basis of the independence of the Republic of Turkey, it supersedes the Turkish Constitution, and the Turkish Republic has to comply with its articles. Articles 38-44 are about the social and cultural rights of minorities. According to Baskın Oran (2001) of the University of Ankara, article 41 ensures that non-Muslim minorities as well as minorities of other ethnic groups can teach and be taught in their own languages. According to the treaty, schooling costs for minority students are to be paid out of municipal, state, or other budgets. In practice, this obligation is ignored, as seen in the increasing financial pressure on minority schools. Instead of being financed and subsidized by public funds, non-Muslim schools have been subjected to high tax rates under the 1942 Property Tax Law (Varlık Vergisi Kanunu). Conducted under the mantra of "Turkification of the economy", this policy helped drive non-

12 The peace treaty ended the Turkish War of Independence. It was signed in Lausanne, Switzerland, on July 24, 1923, between the Allies of World War I and the Ankara-based Grand National Assembly of Turkey (Turkish national movement) led by Mustafa Kemal Ataturk. It settled the Anatolian and East Thracian parts of the partitioning of the Ottoman Empire, and was registered in the League of Nations Treaty Series in September 1924. The Treaty of Lausanne superseded the Treaty of Sèvres, which was signed by representatives of the Ottoman Empire, and it led to the international recognition of the sovereignty of the new Republic of Turkey as the successor state of the defunct Ottoman Empire.

Muslim minorities away from commercial activities, assuring that commerce and trade were controlled by Turkish Muslims (Bali, 2000).[13]

Another document that illustrates that minorities are not perceived as belonging to the "national We" are regulations published in 1938 entitled *Administrative Issues in Turkish Special and Minority Schools*. Under these regulations it became obligatory to have a Turkish (meaning 'ethnically Turkish' *and* Muslim) chief assistant head master in minority schools, who was appointed by the Cultural Affairs Minister and whose duty it was to monitor minority schools and inform the government about any 'anti-Turkish' acts (Çapar 2006).

4. The "Other" in Textbooks: the Internal and External Enemies

In general, books about the Turkish nation include conflicting views about the existence of 'the Others'. While some mention their existence, some of them also claim that there are no minorities in Turkey.

In one 2002 textbook, *National Security Information* (Milli Güvenlik Bilgisi) minorities in Turkey is acknowledged as follows:

> According to the Lausanne Treaty signed 24 July 1923, there are no minorities in Turkey except for non-Muslims. In Turkey, over 95% of the population, and over thousands of years, citizens have been sharing the same destiny, living in the same culture, having the same objectives (2002: 97).

The information in the book both directly and indirectly leads students to form certain misconceptions. Among these are that 5% of the population does not share the same destiny, same culture, and same objectives; therefore, non-Muslim minorities are explicitly defined as non-Turkish. Another implied 'fact' is that all Muslims in Turkey are 'ethnic Turks'. According to this text, being Turkish is equated with being Muslim and vice versa. In *New Geography* published in 1933-34, there are similar claims, as well as assertions that minorities are detrimental to the Turkish state:

> Almost all people living in Turkey are Turks. ... Until recently in Turkey there were a lot of Greeks and Armenians. Given the opportunity, some of these people tried to harm Turkey. After the Independence War they abandoned Turkey. Today, in Turkey, there is only one nation whose heart beats for the rise of the Turkish homeland, speaking the same language, believing in the same religion, and it is the Turkish nation (quoted by Kahyaoğlu 2003: 182).

---

13 These taxes have so far not been collected, but the fact that such a policy was accepted in principle shows the attitude of the state towards non-Muslims.

These ideas have continued to be expressed using very similar language more recently. One history book published in 1986 stated that "[a]ll minorities are of Turkish descent", while claiming in subsequent passages that "[t]here is no discrimination against them" (Su & Mumcu 1986: 169). Implicit in this statement is that minorities have no unique rights, thereby closing the discussion off. In a more recent textbook, the following passage follows a definition of citizenship in the Constitution:

> It cannot be said that only people from Turkish descent are citizens, or only the Muslims are citizens. Any person who lives in Turkey and is officially accepted as a Turkish citizen is entitled to all the rights that the Turkish state provides (Çiftçi et al. 2002: 99).

This statement clearly claims that all citizens in Turkey are entitled to equal rights. However, limits on these rights are clear in relation to any critical position towards the official ideology:

> What is common in groups that are destructive, separatist and reactionary is that they are against Atatürk's principles. Because of this the claim that 'we are against the official ideology', signals that they are against the main principles of the country that Atatürk established (Çiftçi et al. 2002: 35).

It is as if these conflicting sentences went unnoticed by the authors. Although they do not see 'race' or religion as a reason for discrimination, they still claim that it is necessary to speak the same language, to have common emotions, objectives and history, culture and benefits (Çiftçi et al. 2002: 35), and according to them everybody should believe in the same official ideology.

4.1 Internal and External Enemies

The perception of a threat posed by internal and external enemies is the most common argument of Turkish discourses to bolster nationalism. According to this argument, Turkey's neighbours, especially Greece, Russia, recently Iraq, and the Federated State of Kurdistan, as well as the USA and the European Union (EU) are characterized as external enemies wanting to divide and weaken Turkey. Those portrayed as internal enemies are the minorities in Turkey, separatist groups (especially Kurds), cosmopolitans, socialists, communists, the opportunist extremists. These two "types of enemies" are embedded within each other, and are portrayed as supporting and 'feeding' each other. According to school textbooks, since the time of the Ottoman Empire, minorities and 'separatists' have been cooperating with external enemies in order to precipitate internal division within the Empire and later within the Republic of Turkey. In history textbooks especially, it has frequently been claimed that minorities in the Ottoman Empire were provoked to hostile actions by non-Muslim nations, and that the Greeks and the Armenians, after 'The Armistice of Mondoros' of 1918 that ended World War I, cooperated with the Allied Powers in the attempt to divide up the country which had been their home and had always allowed them to live peacefully (Kopraman et al. 2002: 68; Başol et al. 2009: 39). Therefore the Turkish State and the Turkish public are called upon to be alert to these internal and external enemies. By presenting the Turkish Armed Forces as the protector of Turkey from these internal traitors and external enemies (Milli Güvenlik Bilgisi I II III 1980: 24), both the internal intervention of the army as well as a military intervention abroad is legitimized.

While the alleged threats of 'internal traitors' imply the heterogeneity of the population of Turkey, the *National Security Information* (Milli Güvenlik Bilgisi) textbook explicitly emphasizes a "homogenous structure" of the Turkish population, even though the phrase "in general" does suggest that exceptions from this general rule are tacitly acknowledged:

> Turkey's population displays a homogenous structure in general. This physical structure shows itself in social life, too, and ensures our national unity. The fact that the attacks on Turkish existence are directed against our national unity proves that our enemies have understood the value and importance of this homogenous structure" (Milli Güvenlik Bilgisi I II III 1986: 289).

In essence, the claim reinforces the ethnic and religious homogeneity of Turkey. It is an obvious contradiction: on the one hand, the claim underscores that Turkey is an ethnically homogenous country and that the bonds of nationhood are unbreakable, while on the other hand warns it against the internal-external enemy that keeps the fear of 'division' alive. One might conclude that essentialist nation states are in part held together, despite of all these obvious contradictions, by the manipulative discourse of the hegemonic group which stabilises the existing structures of power by keeping its members, particularly its young, 'on the alert' to fearful and threatening scenarios.

4.2 Depiction of Particular Groups in Turkish Textbooks

The Armenians

Ever since the Republic was established, Armenians have been an ethnic group that has been frequently constructed in textbooks as the 'enemy' and as potential traitors under both the Ottoman Empire and the Republic. When dealing with 'the Armenians', textbooks as a rule refer to 'the Armenian riots' that took place before the Republic was founded, to their cooperation with the Russians in trying to found a country in the east and south of Turkey in the 'Çukurova, Maraş Erzurum, Bitlis, Elazığ and Diyarbakir area', and to this end, "their slaughtering innocent Turks, even women, the old and children" (Kara 2006: 57). The Ottoman Empire's actions, particularly the 1915 Armenian Relocation, are presented as rightful precautions.

In general, Armenians were depicted as 'the loyal nation' who lived freely in the Ottoman Empire, until they cooperated with external forces, and with the provocations of the external forces, betrayed the Ottoman state (see Kara 2006: 129, Kopraman 1993: 60; Başol et al. 2009: 58; Tekerek et al. 2009b: 79). In a textbook entitled *Turkish Republic Reform History and Kemalism*, however, the loyalty of Armenians is questioned by stating that, contrary to what had been believed, they were neither loyal nor innocent:

> The declaration of the authorities in the Ottoman Empire about the Armenian loyalty and innocence spoiled the Armenians, yet Armenians were neither innocent nor loyal to the state. What they did to the state they were affiliated with was nothing short of betrayal and hostility (quoted by Gemalmaz 2003: 50).

Until the 1980s, Armenians were only mentioned in textbooks with respect to the problems they caused in the Ottoman Empire, and to their cooperation with the Russians. Little if any information about Armenians and Armenia itself were given. But after the 1980s, the place of Armenians in Turkish textbooks changed suddenly. Medieval Armenian history disappeared, and the 'Armenian conflict' was dealt with more explicitly (Copeaux 2000: 296). One reason for the change were the attacks of an Armenian terrorist group ASALA on Turkish Embassies that killed numerous ambassadors. Another reason for the change was an increasingly critical discussion about the 1915 Relocation, first in the United States, and then by governments around the world. In reaction to this worldwide criticism, the Turkish government became defensive, and this response was quickly reflected in the national education system. As a 'counter argument', Turkish textbooks began to propagandize how Armenians 'slaughtered the Turks'. Many such historical accounts can be found in textbooks, of which I will only give a few examples.

One history book published in 1992 repeated what official histories had preached for a century, and concluded in their assessment of the 1915 events that blame lay with the Armenians:

> [After 1914] tens of thousands of Turks were slaughtered savagely. With the provocation of Western countries Armenian gangs slaughtered the people of innocent Turkish villages. They barricaded the army supply roads, and plundered towns. With the spread of such activities, the Ottoman Empire, to enable peace in the war territories, relocated the Armenians in Anatolia, to Syria and Iraq. The relocation was

> mainly via train, boats and trucks. During the migration, food and medical needs were met by the government and precautions were taken against bandit attacks. Still, this relocation was considered to be a slaughter by the Europeans. On the other hand, the Armenians in the Anatolian land occupied by the Russians in World War I, retreated with the Russians (Merçil et al. 1992: 218).

This text claims that the government provided vehicles to ease the migration. But another book by the same author, Yusuf Halaçoğlu (2008: 68f.), explains that the rise in Armenian casualties was due to insufficient medicine and availability of vehicles, shortages caused by wartime allocation of material to the Ottoman Army and military shippers. In yet another publication, Halaçoğlu justifies the relocation and the casualties during the relocation by stating that hundreds of people both in European and in the Ottoman armies died due to an epidemic.

Similar discourse structures can be found in many schoolbooks. One history book, after narrating Armenian cruelties against the Turks, claimed that Armenians in the eastern region of Turkey were forced to migrate and that this was a 'proper decision':

> During the migration some of the Armenians died because of harsh weather conditions and disorder. It should not be forgotten that due to natural conditions and lack of good care about 100.000 Turkish soldiers died in Sarıkamış. Turks are not responsible for what happened to the Armenians. In fact thousands of Armenians could reach Syria and survived there under the protection of the Turkish state (Su & Mumcu 1986: 118).

In one high school second grade history textbook published by Faruk Sümer in 1993, it is claimed that more Turks died during the relocation than Armenians. Some writers promote the view that only Armenians who had been fighting were relocated. Another widespread position is that "if Turks wanted to kill Armenians, they would have done it in their prime time"; and school book authors defend the righteousness of the relocation and killing of Armenians by stating that "we had to defend ourselves when the Armenians started killing Turks because of the Western provocations" (quoted by Copeaux 2000: 301). According to a history textbook for third year high school students:

> From the middle of the 19th century to the early 20th century, Armenians who believed in the existence of an Armenian conflict were misled by the provocations of some European countries to betray their homeland and state; they acted in a way which led to suspicion towards all Armenians. Because of this they caused the innocent Armenians incredible pain and suffering. In fact, the number of Armenians who were not misled by these despicable forces, and who assumed Turkish citizenship, is not little (quoted by Copeaux 2000: 303).

The propaganda against Armenians remains in place today. According to the Publications Journal, an official Ministry of Education journal (Tebliğler Dergisi, July 2002, n. 2538), three secondary courses: History 1, History 2, and Turkish Republic History of Reforms and Kemalism, were to cover content related to Armenians, Greek-Pontus and Assyrians, while fifth and seventh graders in primary school were to cover the Armenian Conflict. Teachers are given step-by-step instructions to teach about how Armenians cooperated first with the Russians, and later with other foreign nations, as well as how their cruel treatment of Turks precipitated their relocation in 1915, and what they experienced during the move. The textbook based on this program explains to students that Turkish policy was justified in the Armenian conflict. Teachers are expected to explain that the brunt of guilt falls on the foreign countries cooperating with the Armenians. Additionally, a documentary film was prepared by the Turkish General Staff in 2008 on the 'Armenian atrocity', and in 2009 it was suggested that the film be sent to all National Education Ministry schools. When Armenian minority schools complained about the film, distribution was stopped. Yet by that time, the film had arrived at most schools, and many students had already seen the brutal scenes.[14] Though both Turkey and Armenia declared that they would revise course content related to these historical issues, no such revision has been undertaken yet.

The Greeks

Until the above mentioned changes to the portrayal of Armenians in the 1980s, Greeks had been the most frequently mentioned ethnicity and nation in Turkish textbooks. Like the Armenians, Greeks are portrayed with negative adjectives in textbooks. It is frequently emphasized that Greeks played a role in the fragmentation of the Ottoman Empire. The characterization of Greeks as enemies, however, dates back to the early 19th century, when Greeks rebelled against the Ottomans for their independence. According to Adamantios Polyzoides (Lengerli 2006: 70), after the 1821 Greek revolution and the declaration of independence in 1929, Turks perceived Greeks as suspect. Firstly, the separation from the Ottoman Empire alone was sufficient to generate these negative portrayals. In addition, there is a strong belief among Turks that Greeks, similar to the Armenians, played a decisive role in the dissolution of the Ottoman Empire (Efiloğlu

---

14 "Sarı Gelin'in Özrü Kabahatinden Büyük" http://www.tumgazeteler.com/?a=4708313&cache=1 (date: 11.7.2010). "Ermenilere Yönelik İfadeler Kitaplardan Çıktı DVD'ye Girdi" http://www.bianet.org/bianet/azinliklar/112627-ermenilere-yonelik-ayrimci-ifadeler-kitaptan-cikti-dvdye-girdi, date: 11.7.2010

2007: vii). Therefore Greeks in general, and especially the Greek minority in Turkey, are perceived as potentially threatening.

In contrast to these portrayals of suspicious and malevolent activities by Armenians and Greeks, Turks are depicted as an overwhelmingly tolerant nation. According to official sources, they have never persecuted another nation, the rights of ethnic and religious groups were always granted, and minorities were free to practice their religion and live according to their ethnic background. Therefore, the Greeks were also free to learn their own language, and practice their religion and culture (see Boztemur 2003: 233). But according to these texts, Greeks and the Armenians abused this tolerance and 'stabbed the Turks in the back'. A textbook by Su & Mumcu elaborates on this idea:

> Some misguided Turks rose against the patriots in order to save themselves. The victorious occupying nations were highly interested in the division of the country, and the Armenians and the Greeks who lived outside of those parts of the country which were under the control of the victorious powers started to attack as well. While the Armenian Revenge troops entered Adana with the support of the French, on July 10, 1920, and persecuted the people dramatically, the Armenians in neighbouring Eastern cities both directly attacked us and provoked everybody against the Anatolian action (Su & Mumcu 1986: 104).

Here the authors not only refer to the Greek and Armenian betrayal, but also that of 'some misguided Turks', which serves as an implicit warning to students against possible future betrayal against the state. It remains vague, however, whether 'some Turks' in this case implies 'ethnic Turks' or the Kurds and other ethnic groups accepted as Turks because they are Muslims.

Textbooks also compare, unfavourably, the historical knowledge and awareness of Greeks and Turks. According to a textbook written in 1929, the Greeks neither know about their origins nor about the first periods of their history. Their knowledge on their ancestors depends merely on myths. According to this text, Greek history dates back to only 2000 BC, and they led a half savage life (see Çapar 2006: 416). In contrast to this, as emphasized above, Turks are depicted as the 'superior race' and the 'superior nation': "The Turkish race we are proud to be a member of has a distinguished status as one of the best, soundest, smartest and most skillful races of the world" (Yıldız 2001: 233f.). Herkül Millas points out that it is possible to come across similar sentences, with the actors reversed, in Greek textbooks as well. According to Greek textbooks, the Greeks are the 'super nation', and the Turks do not have 'any' civilization, they suffer from an inferiority complex and resort to barbarity to deal with it (Oran 1991: 339). It is remarkable how these judgments mirror each other. Millas' quotes display the fact that in the Greek education system, too, there is an attitude that nourishes the concept of 'the Others' as the enemies (Millas 1995).[15]

The Jews

Unlike Armenians and Greeks, Jews are not referred to in textbooks, hence negative judgments are also absent, even though in colloquial language, 'Jewish' – just like 'Armenian' – is a swear word. It might then be assumed that because Jews are generally not judged negatively in textbooks, this could be seen as advantageous. Yet, this also implies that they are not part of Turkish society. For this reason, they are 'the invisible Others' in national education. Outside the educational arena, the Jewish community suffered diverse forms of oppression. In particular, they were pushed to speak Turkish, an aim supported by Jewish intellectuals (Bali 2000). Since the Jewish community diligently avoided trouble with the government, they did their best to comply with all its demands.

Among the books analyzed for this article, there is only one story – in an 8th grade Turkish textbook – in which Jews are mentioned. The story 'The Inherited Mat' is about two Jewish merchants who come to buy something at a certain house, but cannot agree on the price with the household. Except for being shown as a little cunning, negative characteristics are not expressly attributed to these Jews. However, the 'features of Jews' and other minorities were frequently reproduced in newspapers and magazines during the first half of the 20th Century. Jews have been caricatured as stingy, greedy merchants (Bali 2000). Therefore, even a minor allusion to these negative characteristics may be enough to reinforce such stereotypes.

The Kurds

Like Jews or Alevis, Kurds are not referred to as an ethnic group in Turkish textbooks. Until the 1980s, Kurds were only referred to with respect to the role they played in the dissolution of the Ottoman Empire, as the 'Kurdish Group', and in the Republican Period with respect to the 'Sheikh Said Uprising'. However, in both cases the word 'Kurd' is used cautiously, not connoting the ethnic group of Kurds. The key word in the 'Kurdish problem' is generally 'separatism', a concept frequently used after 1980. In one history textbook published in 1986, the Sheikh Said Uprising, its reasons and causes are analyzed:

---

15 Oran observed that the practices of Othering in Turkish national education are similar to those in Greece against the Turkish Muslim minorities, and the laws are enacted accordingly (1991: 117-130).

> In the Ottoman period, the Eastern regions were not developed because they had been neglected for many years. In an underdeveloped region, it is easy to abuse religious beliefs. Agents in the Progressive Republican Party started to use the party for separatist goals, and to spread the belief that religion was neglected. This resulted in the Sheikh Said Uprising in the east on February 13, 1925 (Su & Mumcu 1986:187).

In all the textbooks analyzed for this chapter, Sheikh Said is presented as leading extremist activities, and as a traitor who cooperated with the British. In History IV, published in 1934, the uprising is depicted as follows:

> The uprising could take place instigated by an ignorant and extremist sheikh as well as some traitorous politicians who were used by external enemies, and supported by a crowd ignorant of world events who lived on the mountains and in villages and wished to ruin the cities (1934: 192).

A much more recent textbook, states that the Sheikh Said Uprising bears features that set it apart from other uprisings. According to the writers,

> they tried to spread the rebellion all over the country, and this is an act against the Turkish reforms. The main factor that triggered this uprising was the intention to bring back the sultanate and caliphate by demolishing the modern, democratic, and secular Turkey (Başol et al., 2009: 107).

Su & Mumcu depict the end of the uprising in their history book as follows: "Sheikh Said, the leader of a religious sect, and other rebels were caught. They were charged and given penalties they *well deserved*" (Su & Mumcu 1986: 188; emphasis added). The Sheikh Said Uprising is presented in a similar fashion in other textbooks. However, some extra-curricular books claim that the Sheikh Said Uprising was in fact a Kurdish uprising. In reports not written and approved by the government, other Kurdish uprisings that have occurred are mainly interpreted as ethnic uprisings, rather than religious rebellions. But the government, and therefore Turkish national education, does not acknowledge 'Kurds' as an ethnic minority, and therefore with few exceptions avoids the use of the word 'Kurd' in official texts.

In the *National Security Information* textbook, Kurds are referred to only within the context of 'separatism':

> Separatism denotes the intention of some citizens in our nation to found a new country within the borders of Turkey based on a so-called different racial origin, and on books written to serve foreign ideals" (Milli Güvenlik Bilgisi I II III 1986: 261).

In the same book, an extensive list of Muslim ethnic groups in Turkey is included[16], and it is claimed that diversity is a weakness that can be leveraged by

16 These include the Turks, Zazas, Chechnians, Abazias, Circassians, Lazs, Yoruks, Turkmens, Karakecilis, Karakoyunlus, Kayıs, Bozoks, Avsars.

internal and external forces that try to divide up Turkey, given the country's strategic geopolitical importance:

> One should keep in mind that these are the different branches of the Turkish tree. The aim of giving different names to the branches of the same tree as if they came from different nations is to divide up Turkey" (Milli Güvenlik Bilgisi I I III 1986:261).

With these words the students are warned about the potential of internal division. At the same time, the textbook's inclusion of the extensive list of Turkish peoples does hint at the country's diversity. But they are made to 'vanish' by being perceived as branches of the same national tree. It should also be noted that the list of ethnic groups ignores non-Muslims.

The Alevis

Like Jews and Kurds, Alevis are not mentioned in Turkish textbooks. Their invisibility is not limited to textbooks, and stems from conflicts that date to the Ottoman Empire. During that time, there were attempts to convert the Alevis (see footnote 3) into Sunnis. To this end, some (very basic) primary schools were established. Imams who were appointed by an organization affiliated with the Sheikhulislam (Somel 2001: 22f.) were responsible for the supervision of these schools so that these schools were effectively '*Sunni*-Muslimized'.

The Turkish national education system is monolithic in the context of religion as well. Except for non-Muslims and their schools, it is assumed and accepted that all Turks living in Turkey are Sunni-Muslims. "There are four different sects in Islam. We belong to the Hanefis. Each sect has an imam. Ours is Imam-I Ebu Hanefi" (Din Dersleri 1927:39). Turks (Muslims) belong to the Hanefis, in particular to Maturidis" (Mızraklı Köy İlmihali 1931: 100f.).

In the 1940s, Minister of Education Hasan Ali Yücel who served from 1938 to 1946, criticized the fact that only the Hanefi and Matrudi sects are officially perceived as part of the Ottoman Empire. He complained that this definition excluded millions of people in Turkey, and claimed that the government did not have the right to impose the practices of one sect on its citizens (Yücel 1993: 120-21). However, these warnings and criticisms had no effect on the prevailing attitudes. National education focused only on Sunnis and Hanefis, and it tried to convert Alevis to Sunni Islam.

This push to convert Alevis intensified after a military coup in 1980, when the government initiated a project to construct Sunni mosques in Alevi villages so that they could be converted to Turkey's "national" religion (Çakır 1999: 80). This was rationalized by officials by claiming that there were no clergymen to conduct funerals in Alevi villages (Bozkurt 1999: 113). Many Alevis reacted against this move, but in the tense conditions in the aftermath of the coup, resistance was ineffective, even though the effort to convert Alevis through Sunni mosques was also ineffective. Through the attempted conversion of Alevis, their existence was at least acknowledged by Turkish authorities, though only to the degree that their religious traditions were seen as standing outside the Sunni-Muslim definition of a Turk and thus in need of conversion.

Since the 1990s, the Alevi Bektashi organizations have asked that the current compulsory education in Sunni Islam be made optional, and they have requested that education for Alevis be made truly secular (see Schüler 2001: 142-47). Other Alevi organizations agree with religious education, as long as the belief of the Alevi sect is covered as well. One of these organizations, the Cem Institute, has even tried to write a religious education textbook about the Alevi sect for Alevi students.[17] After much time and effort on this project, the Cem Institute finally succeeded in drawing the attention of the government to the need for secular education. In recent years the government, in cooperation with many non-governmental organizations, has organized a number of Alevi Workshops. However, Alevi organizations claim that these workshops maintain the government's mission of assimilating Alevis. In a review of the preliminary report of the 7th Alevi Workshop, the Alevi-Bektashi Federation called the report "a document of assimilation":

> In the report, the demand is that the already existing 'applied religion education' should continue. In addition to this course 'a new field' can be integrated, and this new field refers to elective religion courses. In fact, the government is increasing the assimilation medium and systematic torture, and proposing two religion courses instead of one, which is unacceptable. This effort means turning primary schools and high schools into Imam Hatip Schools.[18]

The Alevi-Bektashi Federation requested the abolition of compulsory religious education in schools because these courses focused solely on Sunni Islam. The federation also asked for the revision of textbooks, dictionaries, encyclopaedias and other reference books advised by the Ministry of Education, and demanded that humiliating definitions be removed.[19]

---

17 "Alevi Ders Kitabı Hazır" http://www.ogretmenlersitesi.com/haber/3608 (date: 22.6.2009)

18 "Alevi Çalıştayı Ön Raporu Bir Asimilasyon Belgesidir" http://www.alevifederasyonu.org.tr/index.php?option=com_content&view=article&id=415:alevi-ly-raporu-bir-asimilasyon-belgesidir&catid=13:abf-baslamalar&Itemid=259 (date: 23.08.2010)

19 "ABF'nin Talepleri" http://www.alevifederasyonu.org.tr/index.php?option=com_content&view=article&id=255&Itemid=264 (date: 23.08.2010).

Today, Turkey's ten million Alevis are not referred to at any level of national education, neither as a religious nor as a cultural group. In a recently-published religion textbook for 12th graders, there is a three-page unit on Alevism-Bektashism with incorrect and misleading information: Alevism is said to be not a religion, but a way of thinking, and that the Cem service was not a religious practice but a ceremony (Kılıç 2010). Alevis are depicted as a mystic branch of Sunnis. This is further evidence that Alevis and their religion are only assigned a place in the national education system if they are assimilated, in other words 'diminished'.

5. Conclusion

Dominique Schnapper depicts the period of colonization by the Spanish and their endeavour to assimilate the 'Indians', comparing this situation to the conversion of Muslims to Christianity. He points out the tension between the universalistic attitude of Christianity and the church policy:

> Although all Christians have been created as an image of God, the Church discriminates between the 'pureblood old Christians' and the 'non-pureblood ones' [...] According to theologians the blood of converts was spoiled because of their wrong beliefs. They were condemned till eternity for denying Jesus, and this stain, impossible to erase, was inherited by their children and grandchildren; even baptism wouldn't erase this stain. The Church, by violating its own principle, formed categories that depended on races (Schnapper 2005: 62f.).

This definition of religious discrimination and exclusionary *Othering* can be applied to the secular Turkish Republic as well. It is ironic that in a nation-state founded in part on a principle of secularism, discrimination and Othering were and continue to be based on religious background. However, in Turkey, non-Muslims are not only discriminated against because they are not Muslims, but also because they are not 'ethnic Turks'.

Drawing on Schnapper's discussion of the racialized discrimination in the Roman Catholic Church, it can also be said that non-Muslims who are not 'pureblood' Turks, no matter how hard they try to be Turks, will never be perceived as 'real Turks'. Like Schnapper's Catholic Indians, non-Muslim Turks "will remain dirty till eternity, and have contaminated their successors". Today, the minorities within the borders of Turkey, the Greeks, the Armenians, and the Jews, Kurds and Alevis "bear all the evil they have inherited from their ancestors" (for cited in quotes see Schnapper 2005: 62f.).

Within the Turkish education system, ethnic and religious "Others" are ignored, marginalized and/or misrepresented across a wide spectrum, from national education laws, curriculum down to language within Turkey's nationalist textbooks. In recent years, internal and external political pressure has led to some changes in the content of textbooks. Some books have been revised and some content that promotes alienation, and constructs minoritised Others as the enemies is slowly being removed. However, because Turkey's education system and the laws which govern it remain rooted in exclusionary notions of nationalism, these revisions are resisted and do not come easy. As Harald Seufert claims: "Despite some changes, nationalism has been the essential feature of being a Republic and the determining factor of official discourse" (2001: 29). Minorities with different ethnic and religious backgrounds continue to be portrayed as non-belonging 'Other' in all public areas including education. The effects of this nationalist ideology can be observed in the attitudes towards those from different ethnic and religious background living in Turkey, including physical attacks and informal disparaging discourse.

To sum up, the Turkish national education system does not embrace differences. On the contrary, it effectively attempts to raise individuals who bear hatred and animosity towards those perceived as 'Others'. Even though the education system strives to erase differences, those educated within this system are well aware that different ethnic and religious groups exist. Many nationalist individuals thus formed may be prepared to act, on little provocation, against their compatriots who have either been constructed as 'the non-Turkish Other' or else ignored, and they might even be prepared to turn this reaction to violence. There are many examples for gruesome atrocities in Turkish history, such as the pogrom against Jews in Thrace (1934), the pogrom against Jews, Armenians and Greeks in Istanbul (1955), the right-wing attack against Alevis in Kahramanmaraş (1978), and the arson attack at a cultural event of left-liberal artists and intellectuals in Sivas (1993); most recently the murderous attack against Kurds living in western Turkey. Naturally, it is not fair to blame solely the official national education system for this intolerance and these attacks, and to suspect everybody who passes through the imposing education system as a racist nationalist. It is a fact, however, that the Turkish national education and curriculum has an aggressive attitude towards differences. In September 2010, Hanefi Avcı, who held important positions in the Turkish national intelligence service, gave a remarkable interview to a journalist about the discriminating and alienating education system:

> The government used the public for its own ideologies. Certain issues were imposed on them. Hatred of the minorities was always nourished in Turkey. Even laymen have prejudices against the minorities. Because this has been going on for years, the youth is ready to cause unpleasant events. You cannot call them provocations, because the context was created to lend itself to such events (Taraf 2010).

Just as this intelligence officer states, the hatred towards minorities, 'the Others' such as Kurds, women, gypsies, gays, homeless children, socialists, etc., is the 'fruit' of a discourse about 'the Others' as the enemy.

Translated from Turkish by a PhD-student, University of Istanbul, who wishes to remain anonymous, in cooperation with Prof. Dr. İnci Dirim, University of Vienna.

Literature

"ABF'nin Talepleri" http://www.alevifederasyonu.org.tr/index.php?option=com_content&view=article&id=255&Itemid=264 (date: 23.08.2010).

"Alavi" http://en.wikipedia.org/wiki/Alevi (date: 23.8.2010).

"Alevi Çalıştayı Ön Raporu Bir Asimilasyon Belgesidir" http://www.alevifederasyonu.org.tr/index.php?option=com_content&view=article&id=415:alevi-ly-raporu-bir-asimilasyon-belgesidir&catid=13:abf-baslamalar&Itemid=259 (date: 23.08.2010).

"Alevi Ders Kitabı Hazır" http://www.ogretmenlersitesi.com/haber/3608 (date: 22.6.2009) "Andımız" http://okulweb.meb.gov.tr/60/08/622036/andimiz.html (date: 02.8.2010).

"'Andımız Kaldırılsın' Kampanyasının Afişleri Kaldırıldı" http://www.radikal.com.tr/Radikal.aspx?aType=RadikalDetay&Date= 13.7.2009&ArticleID=944876 (date: 03.9.2009).

Akyüz, Y. (1999 [1982]): Türk Eğitim Tarihi (Başlangıçtan 1999'a). İstanbul.

Allen, H. E. (1968 [1935]): The Turkish Transformation: A Study in Social and Religious Development. New York.

Bali, R. N. (2000 [1999]): Bir Türkleştirme Serüveni. İstanbul.

Başol, S. et al. (2009 [2008]): İlköğretim Türkiye Cumhuriyeti İnkılap Tarihi ve Atatürkçülük 8. Ankara.

Bozkurt, F. (1999): Aleviliğin Yeniden Yapılanma Sürecinde Toplum-Devlet İlişkisi. in: Olsson, T., Özdalga, E. & Raudvere, C. (eds.): Alevi Kimliği. İstanbul, 104-114.

Boztemur, R. (2003): Tarih Ders Kitapları ve İnsan Hakları. in: Çotuksöken, B., Erzan, A. & Silier, O. (eds.): Ders Kitaplarında İnsan Hakları: Tarama Sonuçları. İstanbul, 207-239.

Copeaux, E. (2000 [1998]): Tarih Ders Kitaplarında (1931-1993) Türk Tarih Tezinden Türk-İslam Sentezine. (Trans. Ali Berktay), İstanbul.

Çakır, R. (1999): "Politik 'Alevilik' ile Politik 'Sünnilik': Benzerlikler ve Zıtlıklar. in: Olsson, T., Özdalga, E. & Raudvere, C. (eds.): Alevi Kimliği. İstanbul, 79-83.

Çapar, M. (2006): Türkiye'de Eğitim ve "Öteki Türkler". Ankara.

Çetin, A. et al. (2009a [2006]): İlköğretim Sosyal Bilgiler 5. İstanbul.

Çetin, A. et al. (2009b [2006]): İlköğretim Sosyal Bilgiler 5: Öğretmen Kılavuz Kitabı. İstanbul.

"Çiçek'ten Ermeni PKK'lılar İması" http://www.radikal.com.tr/Radikal.aspx?aType=RadikalDetayV3&ArticleID=1014804&Date=11.05.2011&CategoryID=77, (date: 21.08.2010).

Çiftçi, F. et al. (2002 [1999]): İlköğretim Vatandaşlık ve İnsan Hakları Eğitimi. İstanbul.

Din Dersleri (1927): İstanbul. [Is this the title of the work? Is there any other information?]

Efiloğlu, A. (2007): İttihat ve Terakki'nin Azınlıklar Politikası. (Unpublished Doctorate Thesis), İstanbul Üniversitesi, Sosyal Bilimler Enstitüsü.

"Ermenilere Yönelik İfadeler Kitaplardan Çıktı DVD'ye Girdi" http://www.bianet.org/bianet/azinliklar/112627-ermenilere-yonelik-ayrimci-ifadeler-kitaptan-cikti-dvdye-girdi (date: 11.7.2010).
Erol, A. et al. (2008b): İlköğretim Türkçe 6 Öğretmen Kılavuz Kitabı. İstanbul.
Esen, Y. (2003): Okul Bilgisi ve Ders Kitapları. Bağlı M. T. & Esen, Y. (eds.): Ders Kitaplarında İnsan Hakları: İnsan Haklarına Duyarlı Ders Kitapları İçin. İstanbul, 1-19.
Gemalmaz, M. S. (2003): Ders Kitaplarında İnsan Hakları Ölçütleri Açısından Taranmasıyla Elde Edilen Verilerin Değerlendirilmesi. in: Çotuksöken, B., Erzan, A. & Silier, O. (eds.), Ders Kitaplarında İnsan Hakları: Tarama Sonuçları. İstanbul 23-64.
Halaçoğlu, Y. (2008): The History of 1915: What Happened to the Ottoman Armenians? Ankara.
Kahyaoğlu, D. (2003): Ders Kitaplarında İnsan Hakları Projesi Çerçevesinde Coğrafya Ders Kitapları. in: Çotuksöken, B., Erzan, A. Ve Silier, O. (eds.): Ders Kitaplarında İnsan Hakları: Tarama Sonuçları. İstanbul, 172-206.
Kaplan, İ. (1999): Türkiye'de Milli Eğitimin İdeolojisi. İstanbul.
Kara, K. (2006): Türkiye Cumhuriyeti İnkılap Tarihi ve Atatürkçülük: Lise. İstanbul.
Kılıç, M. C. (2010): Din Kültürü Dersi kitapları mı, Sünnileştirilmiş Alevilik kitapları mı? http://www.aleviten.or.at/cms/menuleft/newsdetail/article/din-kueltuerue-dersi-kitaplari-mi-suennilestirilmis-alevilik-kitaplari-mi.html (date: 24.5.2010).
Kili, S. & Gözübüyük, Ş. (2000 [1957]): Türk Anayasa Metinleri (Sened-i İttifaktan Günümüze). İstanbul.
Kopraman, K. Y. et al. (1993): Tarih 2. Ankara.
Kopraman, K. Y. et al. (2002 [1993]): Tarih 2. Ankara.
Lengerli, S. (2006): National Identity and the Other: The Otherisation of 'the Greek' in Turkish Nationalist Discourse. (Unpublished Ph.D. dissertation), Ankara: Atılım Üniversitesi, Sosyal Bilimler Enstitüsü.
Mekâtib-i Husûsiye Talimatnâmesi (1339AH/1923): İstanbul.
Merçil, E., Miroğlu, İ. & Halaçoğlu, Y. (1992): Lise İçin Tarih II.
Mızraklı Köy İlmihali: En Yeni ve En Sade Din Dersleri (1931): İstanbul.
"Milli Eğitim Kanunu" http://mevzuat.meb.gov.tr/html/88.html (date: 19.08.2009).
Millî Güvenlik Bilgisi I II III (1980 [1973]): İstanbul.
Milli Güvenlik Bilgisi (2002): İstanbul.
Mumcu, A. & Su, M. K. (2002 [2000]): Lise ve Dengi Okullar için Türkiye Cumhuriyeti İnkılâp Tarihi ve Atatürkçülük. Ankara.
Okutan, M. Ç. (2004): Tek Parti Döneminde Azınlık Politikaları. İstanbul.
Oran, B. (1991): Türk-Yunan İlişkilerinde Batı Trakya Sorunu. Ankara.
Oran, B. (2001): Küreselleşme ve Azınlıklar. Ankara.
"Öğrenci Andı Tartışması" http://www.ntvmsnbc.com/id/24968646/ (date: 12.9.2009).
Sadoğlu, H. (2003): Türkiye'de Ulusçuluk ve Dil Politikaları. İstanbul.
"Sarı Gelin'in Özrü Kabahatinden Büyük" http://www.tumgazeteler.com/?a=4708313&cache=1 (date: 11.7.2010).
Schnapper, D. (2005): Sosyolojik Düşüncenin Özünde Öteki ile İlişki. (Trans. Ayşegül Sönmezay), İstanbul.
Schüler, Harald (2001): Aleviler ve Sosyal Demokratların İttifak Arayışı: Dilsel ve Dinsel Olarak Tanımlanmış Sosyal Demokrat-Laik Ortam ve Partilerdeki Rolü. (Trans. Nihat

Ülner). in: Yerasimos, S. et al. (eds): Türkiye'de Sivil Toplum ve Milliyetçilik. İstanbul, 133-183.
Seufert, G. (2001): Milliyetçi Söylemlerin Sivil Toplum Üzerindeki Etkisi. (Trans. İsmet Akça). in: Yerasimos, S. ve diğ (eds): Türkiye'de Sivil Toplum ve Milliyetçilik. İstanbul, 25-44.
Somel, S. A. (2001): The Modernization of Public Education in the Ottoman Empire 1839-1908: Islamization, Autocracy and Discipline. Leiden, Boston, Köln.
Su, M. K. & Mumcu, A. (1986): Lise ve Dengi Okullar için Türkiye Cumhuriyeti İnkılâp Tarihi ve Atatürkçülük. İstanbul.
Taraf (2010): Taraf Gazetesi. 1 Eylül 2010.
Tebliğler Dergisi. (Haziran/June 2007/2597): http://mevzuat.meb.gov.tr/html/2597_0.html (date: 12.9.2009).
Tebliğler Dergisi (Temmuz/July 2002/2538): http://yayim.meb.gov.tr/dergiler/pdf/2538.pdf (date: 05.11.2009).
Tekerek, M. ve diğ. (2009a): İlköğretim Sosyal Bilgiler 4. Öğretmen Kılavuz Kitabı. İstanbul.
Tekerek, M. et al. (2009b): *İlköğretim Sosyal Bilgiler* 4. İstanbul.
Tunçay, M. (2003): Çokkültürlülük Persfektifleri. http://stk.bilgi.edu.tr/docs/tuncay_std_2.pdf (date: 3 Ağustos 2010).
Yıldız, A. (2001): "Ne Mutlu Türküm Diyebilene" Türk Ulusal Kimliğinin Etno-Seküler Sınırları (1919-1938). İstanbul.
Yücel, Hasan-Âli (1993): Millî Eğitimle İlgili Söylev ve Demeçler. İçel.

Education, recognition and the Sami people of Norway

Jonas Jakobsen, University of Tromsø, Norway

In this article I present and discuss selected aspects of the case of the Sami people in Norway, their struggle for influence over their own education institutions, and for equal as well as special rights in the Norwegian education system. Compared to many other Indigenous peoples, the case of the Sami in Norway appears to be "a story of success" (Stordahl 2008: 249). For example, the Norwegian Sami have their own education institutions, and they are among the most educated Indigenous peoples in the world (Eiheim 1995; Stordahl 2008). I also use the Sami case to reflect upon the relation between education and the self-identity of cultural minorities, here drawing upon (and discussing) the work of German social philosopher Axel Honneth.

1. The Sami in Norway

The word "Sami" is used to identify an Indigenous people living in Northern Europe, in the northwest of Russia and in the northern reaches of Sweden, Finland and Norway. Since the definitions of ethnicity vary, it is difficult to determine the exact number of Samis today, but official sources estimate the number to be between 50,000 and 80,000, out of which the largest part, approximately 40,000, are living in Norway, primarily in the northern regions. The International Labor Organization Convention 169 on Indigenous and Tribal peoples (ILO 1989), which Norway has ratified with 17 other countries worldwide, defines "indigenous peoples" as:

> […] peoples in independent countries who are regarded as indigenous on account of their descent from the populations which inhabited the country, or a geographical region to which the country belongs, at the time of conquest or colonization or the establishment of present state boundaries and who, irrespective of their legal status, retain some or all of their own social, economic, cultural and political institutions (ILO 1989).

Until World War II, the official policy in Norway was to assimilate the Sami, that is, to make them discard their Indigenous identity in favor of an ethno-national Norwegian identity and state citizenship (Gaski 2008: 220). As a result of an intensive and long lasting policy of assimilation from the 17th century onwards, a radical decline in people who identify themselves as Sami can be witnessed, as well as extensive impoverishment, political powerlessness and a lack of knowledge about Sami history and culture. Many Sami parents, for example, did not teach their children the Sami language (ibid.).

A turning point for the political organization of Sami interests came in the 1950s, where a revitalization movement focused on the Sami identity led to a new Sami self-image. Crucial for this new movement was to create "a self-concept of the Sami as being a distinct people who had lived in the area before the present state came into existence and drew its national borders" (ibid). Based on this new self-understanding, the Sami have increasingly made the political claim to *self-determination*, which includes the rights of self-government, autonomy, territorial integrity and exclusive enjoyment of their own lands and resources (Weigaard 2008). Norwegian authorities have to some extent acknowledged this. Thus, in his 1997 speech to the Sami Parliament, HM King Harald said that the Norwegian State was built on the territories of two peoples, the Norwegians and the Sami (Weigaard 2008: 189). By this, the King openly expressed some sort of symmetry between the two peoples based on historical possession of territories, and he clearly put the Sami in a different category than other national minorities, such as immigrants.

Even though the basis of the Sami movement was political, the drive towards ethnic revitalization was also expressed through art, music, education and popular culture. In the 1970s and 80s, this process expanded toward *nation-building* that included creation of Sami maps and a flag. Through this process, the Sami movement tried to transform the negative stigma associated with Sami culture into a positive marker of Sami identity (Stordahl 2008; Gaski 2008).

In 1989, the Constitution of Norway was changed in order to recognize the Samis, and the obligations of the Norwegian state towards the Sami people: "It is the responsibility of the authorities of the State to create conditions enabling the Sami people to preserve and develop its language, culture and way of life" (The Constitution of Norway, article 110a). In the same year, and partly as a result of a long controversy between the Sami community and the Norwegian state over the decision to build a power dam across the Alta River in the Sami core areas, the Sami Parliament was established. This parliament, which is financed by the Norwegian state and has been granted authority over specific areas, works to promote a viable Sami culture, and to make sure that the indigenous rights of the Samis, as expressed in ILO 1989, but also in the article 27 of the International Covenant on Civil and Political Rights (1966) and the UN Declaration on the Rights of Persons Belonging to National or Ethnic, Religious or Linguistic Minorities (1992), are effectively protected and realized.

To be recognized as a Sami in Norway today, which includes the right to elect members of the Sami Parliament, one must both self-identify as Sami and have at least one grandparent whose primary language is Sami. For many Sami living outside the traditional areas, however, the ethnic borders between Sami and Norwegian is blurred; they do not bear visible cultural traits or possess knowledge that is traditionally seen as an expression of "Saminess", and many can not speak the Sami language (Gaski 2008: 219). For others, the assertion of a strong Sami identity is part of an ongoing struggle for national self-determination and cultural recognition within the Norwegian society.

2. From being objects of assimilation to being subjects in control of their own education institutions

Since the 17th century, the Sami's way of live underwent great changes as a result of nation building among the four nations of Russia, Denmark, Sweden and Finland. Each of these nations was fighting for territory and wanted to include the Sami as part of their population. As a result, the Sami where sometimes taxed by several governments. Since they needed additional reindeer to pay taxes, the Sami developed large-scale reindeer herding. Thus, the Sami in (what is today) Northern Norway where pushed more or less violently to assimilate: linguistically (from Sami to Norwegian), religiously (from shamanism and animism to official Christianity) and as subjects of state administration. In 1717, the first educational initiative towards Sami society, the so-called *Seminarum Scholasticum*, was established in Trondheim. The task of this college was to teach educators, clergymen, and missionaries the Sami language in order to prepare them for missionary work among the Sami (Stordahl 2008: 252). The head of college, the missionary Thomas Westen, also called the "apostle of the Sami", was influenced by Luther's view on the importance of one's mother tongue for adopting the message of Christianity. However, in the 19th century, when Norway was liberated from Danish control and a new romantic nationalism flourished, a new linguistic policy emerged (Stordahl 2008: 253). Education and language were now seen more directly as central means of assimilation: Norwegian was established as the primary language also in Sami schools by the new Norwegian state. Sami culture was expelled from all curricula or even said to be "non-existing", and there where no longer translations of schoolbooks into Sami. In addition, extra pay was awarded to teachers who could demonstrate good results in teaching Norwegian to their Sami pupils (Hirvonen 2004). Some Sami children were sent to dormitories or boarding schools, far away from their parents, to learn how to become "Norwegian". As the Norwegian scholar on Sami culture and history Harald Eidheim writes, the Sami were "forced into a school system designed to promote competence in the language and culture of the majority population" (Eidheim 1995). This assimilation led to "feelings of inferiority" resulting in "shame, self-contempt and unreleased aggression" (ibid.). As I will argue with Axel Honneth in section three, such feelings are the result of experienced disrespect, that is, a fundamental lack of recognition, which violates the possibility of developing and maintaining a positive self-relation.

According to the Norwegian scholar Vigdis Stordahl, the change in Norway's assimilation policy after the Second World War should be seen in relation to a general loss of credibility of the ideologies of Social Darwinism and nationalism (Stordahl 2008: 253). Furthermore, she continues, "The commitment that Norway made to the United Nations work with the Declaration of Human rights was another nail in the coffin for assimilationist ideologies" (ibid.). In other words, the Norwegians increasingly understood themselves as a democratic and humanistic nation, in which discrimination, racism and second class citizenship could not be tolerated. The northern areas therefore had to be brought to the same social and economic standards as the rest of the country – they had to become a part of the Norwegian welfare state. Thus, over a few decades the northernmost region was redeveloped after the destruction of WWII, when Norway was under German occupation, into modern towns and townships and "the welfare state reached the smallest of out-of-the-way-places" (ibid.).

Therefore, we have witnessed two interdependent processes since World War II: (1) a planned integration of the Sami society into the Norwegian society on behalf of the nation state, and (2) a political Sami revitalization *on ethnic grounds* (Stordahl 2008: 255):

> The Sami organizations, as well as local Sami politicians, use the arguments of the welfare state for what it was worth. The result being that Sami communities not only kept track with the general social and economic development of the state, but also managed to build an infrastructure of Sami institutions like museums, a radio and TV station, healthcare institutions, secondary high schools, a research institution and eventually a University College (ibid.).

A central part of this process was the decision to expand and reform the primary educational system in Finnmark. The training of Sami teachers for primary school has been going on for a long time, but only since the 1970s have the views of the Sami themselves on what such training should consist of been taken into account (Hirvonen 2004: 8). A Sami teacher training department was established at the college of higher education in Alta (in Northern Norway) in 1974, though it was not until 1989 that the Sami have been able to organize the training of their teachers, with the founding of the Sami University College in Kautokeino. Here, pre-school and primary school teachers are trained in Sami language, culture and history (Hirvonen 2004).

Sami culture and history is now an obligatory part of national curricula in all elementary schools in Norway. Furthermore, the Sami have a legally enacted right to education "based on Sami language and culture", which is recognized as a precondition for a "viable Sami culture in the future".[1] This means that children in the core Sami areas have a right to primary school education in the Sami language, and that in municipalities outside these areas, a minimum of ten Sami speaking pupils have the same right. National Universities have also integrated Indigenous themes and research in their curricula, as well as quotas for indigenous students in specific studies. In addition, annual public reports on Indigenous issues help shape state government policies for Indigenous research and education (Stordahl 2008: 253).

Generally speaking, the success of the Sami struggle for rights – both as Norwegian citizens and as Indigenous people – as well as for influence and cultural recognition within Norwegian society has benefitted from the development of the welfare state, coupled with a serious movement to overcome earlier assimilation policies of the past, and recognition of Sami self-determination. Harald Eidheim writes:

> This Sami project has, of course, benefitted from the fact that it originated and gained momentum in welfare states which also to a certain degree have developed liberal views on the position of ethnic minorities and indigenous peoples. The Sami have had access to elementary and higher education and to material welfare in general to an extent which indigenous peoples in the greater part of the world can hardly dream of attaining (Eidheim 1995).

This is not to suggest that the struggle is over or that Sami-Norwegian relations are always harmonious. Mutual distrust on both sides still exists, and disagreements over rights, land, economy, culture, and Indigenous rights are still on the political agenda, both nationally and locally. But I concur that the overall process is correctly moving towards what Jürgen Habermas has called a "difference-sensible" inclusion of the Other (Habermas 1999).

3. Axel Honneth, recognition, and Sami education

In this section I will give a brief overview of Axel Honneth's work on the concept of recognition (Honneth 1995; 1996; 2007), focusing on those aspects I deem useful for a theoretical reflection of the Sami struggle for *rights*, *influence*

1 Translated from a document from the Norwegian ministry of labor: http://www.regjeringen.no/nb/dep/ad/dok/regpubl/stmeld/19961997/stmeld-nr-41-1996-97-/9.html?id=191245

and *positive self-image*. All three aspects of the Sami struggle are visible in the field of education. Though Honneth has not elaborated specifically on the implications of his theory for the field of education, other authors are beginning to do that (e.g. Huttunen & Heikkinen 2004; Huttunen 2008; Straume 2011). In my opinion, education is relevant for all three "spheres" of modern societies which are analyzed by Honneth: (a) the private sphere and its face-to-face relations, (b) the legal sphere, and (c) the social sphere or "society".

Since the publication of Honneth's *Struggle for Recognition* (1996), his work has been taken up by sociologists, philosophers, psychologists, social workers and others. This illustrates the breadth of his theory and its relevance for understanding tendencies and problems in modern societies. After Jürgen Habermas, Honneth is said to be the most influential living representative of the so-called "Frankfurt School" of critical philosophy. For Honneth, what is viable in the tradition of the Frankfurt school – sometimes described as "critical theory"– are three obligations: (1) to produce critical research on the social reality of modern capitalist societies; (2) to focus on different areas of society, including the workplace, family, culture, the welfare state and so on, since alienation and inequality occur in all areas of society, not just in the state or in the economic sphere; and (3) to engage in interdisciplinary work and draw on insights from, for example, political science, law, sociology, cultural studies and philosophy.

Honneth is probably best known for combining a theory of *self-realization* with a critical theory of modern *society*. The idea that human beings do not only *exist*, like plants and animals, but are confronted with the task of *realizing themselves* by developing the potentials of their humanity is not new of course; it goes back at least to Plato and Aristotle, and can be found in different variants within the great world religions. Honneth claims that successful human self-realization amounts to the development of three positive forms of self-relation, which he calls (a) *self-confidence*, (b) *self-respect* and (c) *self-esteem* (Honneth 1996: 129). According to Honneth, self-confidence is an emotional self-relation, which can be developed only in personal relations such as family, love relations or friendship. Self-respect, by contrast, is developed through the experience of counting as a bearer of equal rights, that is, as a person with the same legal status as all others. Finally, self-esteem is the result of being seen as an important contributor to society, typically through one's *work*, but also more broadly through one's way of life, knowledge or cultural tradition. Honneth is of course aware that different cultures and life-forms have very different views on human self-realization, but he nevertheless claims to have formulated a basic philosophical anthropology that is permeable and open enough to different cultural interpretations that it does not presuppose or bias any particular culture or world-view (Honneth 1996).

According to Honneth, the three aspects of self-realization correspond to three spheres of modern societies, namely – as mentioned above – the (a) private sphere, (b) the legal or juridical sphere, and (c) the social sphere (sometimes called the sphere of solidarity). Participation in all three spheres, he claims, is a minimum condition for living a free and non-pathological human life. Societies in which some citizens are systematically prevented from participating in one or more of these spheres, therefore, are *unjust* societies: Why should only some, and not all citizens, be able to realize themselves in this basic or minimal sense? Common for all three spheres, Honneth continues, is that their moral "grammar" or infrastructure consist of intersubjective relations of recognition; in each sphere, a central aspect of our humanness is recognized: our particular emotional and bodily needs in the private sphere, our moral dignity and autonomy qua human persons in the legal sphere, and our concrete capabilities and contributions to society in the social sphere. Recognition is therefore not about polite behavior or etiquette, it is as Charles Taylor (1992) puts it, "a vital human need" (26). In the following, agreeing with Huttunen & Heikkinen who claim that "[e]ducational practices are in many ways associated with the process of recognition" (2004: 163), I will take a closer look at the three forms of recognition analyzed by Honneth, and relate them to the case of Sami education, and the Sami struggle for recognition in Norway.

3.1 Love and self-confidence

The first form of recognition, Honneth calls "love". Ontogenetically speaking – that is, seen from the perspective of the individual's historical self-development – this is the first sphere of recognition in which we participate: We all begin our existence as members of a family or a child-parent relation. Using the concept of "love", therefore, Honneth refers to something more than romantic love-relations between adults, namely our fundamental dependency on care and positive feedback from "significant others". As infants and small children, of course, we are completely delivered to the emotional and physical care of our parent(s). Honneth here draws upon the psychoanalytic research of Donald Winnicot to show that an infant's and small child's early experience of love is a precondition for developing the amount of emotional self-confidence, which allows it, later in life, to engage in healthy personal and intimate relations with others, and to manage the precarious balance between *independence* from the other and *dependency* on the other, which good personal relations demand. In addition, our ability to participate as *citizens* in public and political life "without shame"

(Honneth 1996: 164) is conditioned by our participation in successful interpersonal relations; that is, relations in which our emotional life, our inner drives and needs, are recognized as worthy of articulation and consideration by others.

Education – at least in the most common usages of the word – is an institutionalized and public phenomenon, typically organized by the state, and not a "personal" or "emotional" matter. Nevertheless, Honneth's analysis of the ways in which emotional care influences our basic self-trust and self-confidence is relevant to the field of education. After all, education is not just about curricula and accumulation of knowledge, but also (some would say *primarily*) about the meetings between pupils or students and their educators, teachers or supervisors. For many young pupils and students, the teacher is one of the first adults, apart from their own parents, with whom they enter a long lasting relation that demands some degree of mutual trust and sympathy to work well. Therefore, recognition in form of care at a personal level is important for the pupil's development of the basic form of self-confidence, which Honneth locates in the "private sphere":

> This relation of recognition thus also depends on the concrete physical existence of other persons who acknowledge each other with special feelings of appreciation. The positive attitude which the individual is capable of assuming towards himself if he experiences this type of emotional recognition is that of self-confidence (Honneth 1995: 253).

In the 19th century, as mentioned above, Sami children were systematically separated from their families at a young age and sent to boarding schools, administered by the Lutheran Church, with the explicit goal of assimilating them into the majority "in language, culture, and in their overall view of themselves" (Todal 1998: 357). Honneth does not discuss such examples himself, but in my view, his theory would estimate that such separation would pose a clear threat to the child's development of emotional self-trust, at least if the recognition by family members is not replaced with a similar recognition by other close persons, e.g., teachers or pupils. But our knowledge of these schools tells us that the atmosphere there was not an atmosphere of recognition and emotional bonding. Many Sami describe their experiences in the boarding schools as traumatic. Thus, in an interview in the book *No Beginning, No End: The Sami Speak Up*, Kerttu Vuolab (1999) states that the Sami children's feelings of self-worth and their knowledge of their mother tongue were destroyed by the assimilation process and by being torn away from their families and homes. She also goes on to describe how the children felt awkward going home after having been all the time speaking some other language than Sami, and after having eaten other types of foods. According to Vuolab, the experience of being removed from home at an early age and subjected to forced assimilation was traumatic and confusing on a *personal* level. In the short story, *The Boarding School* (1996), by Ellen Marie Vars, we get a similar impression of what many Sami children experienced in the boarding schools. Like Vuolab's description, the main character in the story (Katja) must live in the boarding school and cannot visit her family except during Christmas and summer vacations. Katja is constantly told that she is "dirty", and she has a trubled relation to the other children (Vars 1997).

3.2 Equal rights and self-respect

Most often, the political demands of the Sami movement have been formulated as demands for rights; sometimes for *equal* rights, sometimes for *special* rights (that is, rights not granted to other citizens). This is also the case in the Sami struggle for education. In the following, I discuss aspects of this struggle in the light of Honneth's understanding of legal recognition and its relation to the practical self-relation that he calls "self-respect" (Honneth 1996: 80).

The idea of equal rights – regardless of gender, sexual orientations, social status, ethnicity, religious belief and so on – is a historical formation of western modernity. This link between human rights and the "Western" project of modernity has made some postcolonial theorists very skeptical of the idea of human rights as such. For example, the influential anthropologist Talal Asad (2003: 127-158) sees human rights as (a) bound to "Western" ideas of individualism and autonomy, which are alien to most non-western traditions, and (b) ideological tools with which the nation state can discipline, and legitimize violence against, its own citizens: "The state has the power to use human rights discourse to coerce its own citizens – just as colonial rulers had the power to use it against their own subjects" (Asad 2003: 135). Since nation states, according to Asad, are free to interpret and use human rights as they please, he has no hope that appeal to such rights can be of help for suppressed minorities; such minorities are rather "governed" and "disciplined" (in the sense of Foucault's "governmentality") by adopting the majority's view of a "true" human being and its rights. However, as touched upon in section 1 of this article, the Sami struggle for recognition and influence has been closely linked to the vocabulary of human rights; it has referred extensively – and often successfully – to global human rights declarations ratified by the Norwegian state, such as the ILO. In contrast to Asad's misgivings, therefore, the Sami case seems to confirm Honneth's view that there is a universalistic potential inherent in the very idea of equal rights, which, no matter how poorly this idea is realized in a given society, can be used by disadvantaged groups in their struggle for inclusion in the legal order as equals.[2] The idea of equality exhibits what Honneth calls a "normative surplus of validity" (Honneth & Fraser 2003: 186-87, 263-64), which means that the normative *idea* always transcends the way we have *institutionalized* this idea in a particular legal order; if it did not, marginalized groups like women, workers, gays and lesbians, or ethnic minorities would not have been able to use human rights vocabulary to delegitimize ideologies and practices that previously excluded them from the group of people who has a "right to have rights", as Hannah Arendt has put it. Today, the idea of legal equality has become a part of the standard normative framework of Western societies, which means that those groups who struggle within this framework can use a normative principle *already recognized by the majority population*, namely formal equality in the legal system, to show that social reality does not match the norm. However, to show this often calls for redefinitions of the culturally hegemonic interpretations of legal equality, which means that some sort of conflict or social struggle is unavoidable.

When groups or individuals struggle for inclusion in the legal system as equals, what kind of recognition are they struggling for? What is it that we recognize in other persons when we recognize them as bearers of equal rights? Honneth's reply to these questions is influenced by Kant: When we recognize others as equal addressees of the law, we recognize their fundamental status as morally autonomous beings, that is, as "ends in themselves", who should never be used purely as means for others' purposes (Honneth 1996: 111). Legal recognition, in other words, is bound to a universal respect for the freedom and dignity of the human person. To deny anyone an equal status in the legal system, by contrast, means to disrespect – or misrecognize – the shared dignity that makes us human. According to Honneth's strong intersubjectivism, therefore, it is only through the experience of being recognized as an equal bearer of rights that the subject learns to respect itself. Or put negatively, the experience of being structurally disadvantaged in the legal system violates the ability to relate to oneself with self-respect.

In the course of Western legal history, Honneth writes, not only the *amount* of people who count as bearers of rights has been expanded (quantity), but also the *meaning* of the concept of equal rights (quality). Following T.H. Marshall's classic distinction (Honneth 1996: 115), Honneth here mentions three paradigmatic changes in the conception of human rights. First, in the 18th century, human rights were understood as "negative freedoms" or *civil rights*, such as freedom of speech, freedom of conscience, freedom of movement and so on; secondly, in the 19th century, these freedoms where supplemented with the "posi-

2 See also my critique of Asad in Jakobsen 2011.

tive" right to *political participation*, that is, with democratic and political rights; thirdly, in the 20th century, a new understanding of *social rights* emerged according to which the two other types of rights are seen to be little worth for the citizen without a certain amount of economic security, general welfare and *education*. It is clear that the explicit interest in the field of education by both Sami and non-Sami scholars as well as politicians is due to the growing recognition that, in order for this group to use their civil and political rights on an equal footing with non-Sami Norwegians, their access to elementary and higher education is crucial.

The field of education, however, is a good example of the fact that *different* treatment sometime is necessary to create *equal opportunities*. To recognize the Sami as equals in the education system does not mean to give them the exact same elementary education as everyone else; this would clearly disadvantage Sami, whose language and culture has historically been marginalized within the Norwegian education system. The right to receive elementary education in Sami language, and in accordance with Sami culture and values, it can be argued, is necessary if the ideal of equality is to be taken seriously. Agreeing with authors such as Jürgen Habermas (1999), Seyla Benhabib (2002) and Will Kymlika (1995), Honneth has in fact argued that "cultural" rights are legitimate in some cases, not in order to protect the culture as such, but in order to secure formal equality between people who are different. The right to eat Halal-slaughtered meat can, for example, be granted to Muslim children in schools in order to secure their equal participation in the education system (Honneth & Fraser 2003).

Nevertheless, since Honneth's model is still focused on equality among citizens of a modern nation state, it has difficulties explaining and justifying the extensive use of special rights granted to the Sami – and *not* to other minorities, such as immigrants or religious minorities – in the Norwegian case. Why should not Russians or Muslims have their own universities and be taught in their mother language? Here, it makes sense to differentiate with Will Kymlika between "national minorities" and "ethnic groups". National minorities are defined by Kymlicka as "previously self-governing, territorially concentrated cultures" (Kymlicka 1995: 10) that have been incorporated into a larger state through conquest or federation. By contrast, "ethnic groups" are defined as voluntary immigrants who do not occupy homeland. Thus, Alaska Natives, Native Americans or Sami can be called national minorities, whereas Italians or Afghans (living in Norway) will be ethnic groups. For Kymlicka, national minorities have more substantive entitlements to certain group-differentiated rights because they have been forcefully incorporated through colonization, war and purchase of territories. Even though this differentiation (as all group differentiations) can be questioned in a number of ways, it still points to the importance of including the colonial history as normatively significant for the Sami, and other postcolonial subjects, when it comes to balancing difference and equality within the legal framework of the nation state. From that perspective, I believe, the poststructuralist position of Talal Asad (2003) correctly reminds us that the nation state has a history, a violent history, and that its legitimacy is not self-evident. Honneth, by contrast, seems to regard the nation state as an unproblematic starting point for social theory and critique.

3.3 Contribution and social esteem

According to Honneth, humans have a basic need not only for love (in the private sphere) and equal respect (in the legal sphere), but also for recognition of their concrete capabilities and achievements. By this he means that the human subject needs to develop those personal strengths and skills, which separates it positively from others. By doing just that, typically through one's work, one can experience the importance of one's own skills and capabilities for the reproduction of society; through the recognition of one's positive contribution to society, one is able to *esteem oneself* as a unique and important individual (Honneth 1996: 133, 173). For Honneth, therefore, self-esteem is something we develop in the "social" sphere, which he sometimes calls "solidarity" and sometimes the sphere of "contribution" (Honneth 1996: 130). Thus, the large percentage of Sami in higher education suggests that this group is well equipped to participate in social life as recognized contributors to Norwegian society.

Even though Honneth's focus is on *work*, the struggle for social esteem also plays a major role in other contexts, such as minor groups and subcultures, or at an institutional level. According to Huttunen & Heikkinen (2004), Honneth's concept of social esteem, which he has not applied to the field of education himself, is especially relevant for this field. First of all, they write, "a teacher's work is a process of giving and receiving recognition" (2004: 164); and secondly, the dialectics of recognition is "at the heart of the process of education (Bildung)" (ibid.). In both cases, what is at stake is the students or pupils contributions to the learning process, the active effort he or she makes, and the response from the teacher, which can be, but is not always, a form of recognition.

The teacher's evaluation of the pupil, of course, and the teacher's *way* of evaluating, play a major role in the development of a fruitful learning environment, and therefore is a process of learning itself. In addition, it can, at an early stage in the pupil's life, further or inhibit his or her development of self-esteem, that is, the development of a positive view of ones own abilities and skills. According to Huttunen & Heikkinen, therefore:

> The teacher should be discreet when giving negative feedback to a student. Refraining from giving any negative feedback is of course no solution. That could lead to false self-esteem, and have even worse consequences. In giving feedback, it is essential the recognition be genuinely based on the work. Critical feedback is very important, but it must be given in a discreet way without any humiliation. Even when the student's work is a total failure, the teacher should tacitly point out where the student has gone wrong, and how he or she can proceed toward an acceptable performance. The student should always be given a new chance to earn respect with his or her work, and the student should be encouraged to go on with the work. […] When a strong solidarity is established, the learning community is guided by something higher than an individual consciousness: by a collectively constructed culture and spirit (2004: 172).

In practice, however, positive circles of recognition and learning are not always easy or unproblematic to establish. When it comes to education of national minorities, for example, there might be substantial disagreement between teachers, schools, parents, pupils, national curricula or minority representatives about "correct" knowledge and methods of teaching. Vuokku Hirvonen's study *Sami Culture and School* (2004), for example, provides numerous examples of discrepancies between national curricula and established teaching methods on the one hand, and experiences of Sami teachers in Sami schools on the other. Even though the Sami curricula open up for the integration of Sami culture and knowledge, the school system in the Sami areas still has to adapt to a Norwegian and Western context, which, in some respects, contradicts the teachers' ideas of effective learning and Sami culture. Piera, a teacher who works at a combined primary and lower secondary school, for example, expresses the view that the ideal Sami school would be outdoor, and that the curricula would have to focus on more practical issues and less on theoretical ones (Hirvonen 2004: 117). This implies, of course, that some of the skills and achievements of the pupils could be recognized in a way that classroom teaching and a theoretical focus do not allow for. Generally, Hirvonens study show that Sami teachers focus on practical ways of learning as better suited for Sami children, as expressed by the teacher Niillas:

> The Sami way of learning often means learning by doing things in practice. And we also use a lot of stories and narratives when teaching. That's the first thing that comes to my mind when talking about Sami ways of learning. […] Theoretical knowledge should be based on practical training (ibid.).

According to Niilas, not only would adopting educational methods that are suitable for the Sami produce better learning results, it would also help to make the local culture more visible in the educational plans:

> If, again, you wanted to adopt a conception of learning that you could call Sami pedagogy, it would involve having a closer connection between the schools and the local community. The culture of the community would be visible in all the planning done in the school (ibid.)

For Sárá, another Sami teacher, the local aspect is important since those who have knowledge of Sami culture often are the older people and people outside the school system:

> It is the older people and institutions that have the knowledge. However, we are used to thinking that all knowledge can be found within inside the school walls. The teacher is the one who is supposed to do the teaching. In the Sami world nowadays, it is very often the older people and people working in other occupations who know about things and know the proper Sami words. What I mean is that we should have a lot more resources to use this knowledge. At the moment, we are restricted to the school building and the usual sources of information (ibid. 121).

To the extent that Sárá wishes to challenge the hegemonic view of "learning" in the Norwegian school system, and the majority view of "knowledge", she participates in a struggle for recognition in Honneth's sense. This struggle is also a struggle for social esteem at the level of national discourse and politics: like other social or cultural groups, the Sami make demands on "society" and argue why their "contribution" or "way of life" deserve to be esteemed more, for example through institutional changes of the school system, or in form of more state resources (e.g. resources to bring in local elders or bring teaching out in the nature).

Only in this last sense can we speak of a struggle for *cultural recognition*, and not just for equal or extended rights. Such struggles may lead to redefinitions of the cultural infrastructure of society, but Honneth sharply refuses that his theory can be used as an argument to secure anyone a *direct guarantee* of cultural recognition (Honneth & Fraser 2003: 160-170). For one, we never know with certainty what a culture *is* – the borders that define a culture, and separate it from others, are always a matter of contestation or conflict, first and foremost for those who are associated with it or said to be its "members". Honneth would therefore agree with Seyla Benhabib who claims that

> Any view of cultures as clearly delineable wholes is a view from the outside that generates coherence for the purpose of understanding and control. Participants in the culture, by contrast, experience their traditions, stories, rituals and symbols, tools and material living conditions through shared, albeit contested and contestable, narrative accounts (Benhabib 2002: 5).

Thus, Sami also disagree on the question of "Saminess"; some wish to distance themselves from this label, others to defend it, still others to redefine it. For some, an official recognition as "Sami", e.g., a pupil who can learn better "outside" in the nature than inside the classroom, may be just as much a stigma, a reifying identification, as liberation.

A critical, social theory can criticize the structural asymmetries that condition contemporary struggles for cultural recognition, such as political practices or ideologies that exclude certain groups from influence and respect, but it should not – according to Honneth – try to decide the substantial outcome of such struggles. It is up to the cultural subjects themselves to do that. To present Sami culture in a worthy way in national curricula, and in general in national media and discourse, is not to recognize it as such, but to give the Sami a more fair chance of struggling for recognition.

4. Concluding remarks

I have argued that recognition is an important aspect of learning and education and that Honneth's critical theory of recognition has explanatory force when analyzing the postcolonial situation of the Sami people of Norway. The Sami struggle for inclusion and influence over their own situation has to a large extent been fought as a struggle for rights and for cultural recognition. However, I also pointed to some problems in Honneth's focus on the nation state as a given analytic entity; the legitimacy of the Norwegian nation state and its territorial claims, for example, have always been called into question by (some of) the Sami.

Honneth's refusal to deal directly with "thick" cultural identities and questions of cultural recognition can be seen both as strength and as weakness. It is a strength because it avoids a homogenizing and essentialising concept of "cultures" that define their members in static or rigid ways, and also because it avoids taking a political stance to specific demands for cultural recognition in a given society. For Honneth, as we saw, only the *formal conditions* for a fair struggle for recognition, such as the absence of stigmatizing or demonizing portrayals of certain groups in national discourse or media, can be evaluated with his theory, not specific demands for cultural recognition: No one can be criticized for not liking (or even disliking) a cultural tradition. However, this formalism could also be seen as a weakness in the sense that it does not take the problem of cultural difference and marginalization seriously enough.[3] Honneth's fo-

3 See Niedrig's contribution Multicultural Education and Apartheid – Educational Discourses in South Africa in this anthology for a more detailed discussion of the ambivalences of multiculturalism and cultural identity.

cus on "work" as the prime sphere of social esteem (see also Jakobsen & Lysaker 2010) ignores a range of contemporary struggles for recognition, and experiences of misrecognition, that are related more to cultural stigma than to work in any traditional sense.

Acknowledgements

The author would like to thank Heike Niedrig, Christian Ydesen, Adrea Lawrence and Chris Frey for helpful comments, critiques and suggestions.

Literature

Asad, T. (2003): Formations of The Secular. Stanford

Benhabib, S. (2002): The Claims of Culture. Equality and Diversity in the Global Era. Princeton.

Eidheim, H. (1995): On the Organisation of Knowledge in Sami Ethno-Politics. In: Brantenberg, T., Hansen, J. & Minde, H. (eds.): Becoming Visible – Indigenous Politics and Self-Government. Online vailable at: http://www.sami.uit.no/girji/n02/en/106eidhh.html, date 01-06-2011

Gaski, L. (2008): Sami identity as a Discursive Formation: Essentialism and ambivalence. In: Minde, H. (ed.): Indigenous Peoples: Se Self-determination, Knowledge, Indigenity. Delft, 219 – 236.

Habermas, J. (1999): The Inclusion of the Other: Studies in Political Theory. Massachusetts.

Hirvonen, V. (2004): Sami Culture and the School. Reflections by Sami Teachers and the Realization of the Sami School. An Evaluation Study of Reform 97. Karasjok.

Honneth, A. (1995): Integrity and Disrespect: Principles of a Conception of Morality based on a Theory of Recognition. In: Wright, C.W. (ed.): The Fragmented World of The Social: Essays in social and political philosophy. New York, 247 – 260.

Honneth, A. (1996): Struggle for Recognition. The Moral Grammar of Social Conflicts. Oxford.

Honneth, A. (2007): Disrespect: The Normative Foundations of Critical Theory. Cambridge.

Honneth, A. & Fraser, N. (2003): Redistribution or Recognition? A Political-Philosophical Exchange. New York.

Huttunen, R. (2008): Habermas, Honneth and Education. The Significance of Habermas' and Honneth's Critical Theories to Education. Köln.

Huttunen, R. & Heikkinen, H.L.T. (2004): Teaching and the Dialectics of Recognition. In: Pedagogy, Culture & Society, 12: 2, 163 – 174.

Jakobsen, J. (2011): Habermas, Asad and the Arab Spring. Online available at: http://modernandreligion.blogspot.com/2011/06/habermas-asad-and-arab-spring.html, date 15-06-2011

Jakobsen, J. & Lysaker, O. (2010): Social Critique Between Anthropology and Reconstruction: An Interview With Axel Honneth. In: Norsk Filosofisk Tidskskrift, 3, 162 – 174.

Kymlika, W. (1995): Multicultural Citizenship. A liberal Theory of Minority Rights. Oxford.

Stordahl, V. (2008): Nation building through Knowledge Building. The discourse of Sami Higher Education and Research in Norway. In: Minde, H. (ed.): Indigenous Peoples: Se Self-determination, Knowledge, Indigeneity. Delft, 249 – 265

Straume, I. S. (2011): Danning i en flerkulturell lærerutdanning. In: Norsk pedagogisk Tidsskrift, 1, 5 – 15.

Todal, J. (1998): Minorities With a Minority: Language and the School in the Sami Areas of Norway. In: *Language, Culture and Curriculum*, 11, 354 – 366.

Vars, E. M. (1997): Boarding School. In: Gaski, H. (ed.): *In the Shadow of the Midnight Sun: Contemporary Sami Prose and Poetry.* Seattle, 217 – 226.

Vuolab, K. (1999): All Situations were Occasions for Stories. In: Helander, E. & Kailo, K. (eds.): No Beginning, No End: The Sami Speak Up. Alberta, 41 – 57

Weigård, J. (2008): Is there a Special Justification for Indigenous Rights? In: Minde, H. (ed): Indigenous Peoples: Se Self-determination, Knowledge, Indigeneity. Delft, 177 – 192.

The Constitution of Norway. Online available at: http://www.stortinget.no/en/In-English/About-the-Storting/The-Constitution/The-Constitution/, date 01-06-2011

The International Labor Organization Convention 169 on Indigenous and Tribal peoples (ILO 1989). Online available at: http://www.ilo.org/ilolex/cgi-lex/convde.pl?C169, date 01-06-2011

Educating Greenlanders and Germans – Minority Education in the Danish Commonwealth, 1945 – 1970

Christian Ydesen, University of Aalborg, Denmark

The first German schools were established in Southern Jutland/Nordschleswig in 1920 in connection with the transference of Southern Jutland/Nordschleswig to Denmark after Germany was defeated in World War I. These schools received subsidies from the Danish state; but in 1945, following the end of German occupation of Denmark, all 89 schools were closed. However, as early as in 1946 German private schools re-opened in Southern Jutland/Nordschleswig and in March 1955 the Bonn declaration was signed by the German federal chancellor Konrad Adenauer and the Danish prime minister H.C. Hansen. This declaration guaranteed the Danish and German minorities of the border region the right to cultural and linguistic development.

A very different picture concerning education presents itself in Greenland. With the passing of the 1950 education act, schooling in Greenland was headed by a newly established School Directorate consisting of the Danish procurator in Greenland [landshøvdingen], a highly placed church official [provsten] and the School Director of Greenland [skoledirektøren]. With the revision of the Danish constitution in 1953, Greenland ceased to be a colony and it was formally granted status as a Danish county. This meant that the newly established Ministry for Greenland (MfG) in Copenhagen governed Greenland. During the 1960s, Greenland's educational system developed into a structure very similar to the Danish system. In fact, there was a political decision to create as much identity between the Danish school and the Greenlandic school as possible.

The purpose of this article is to conduct a historical comparative analysis of these two parallel but very different educational fields within the Danish Commonwealth. Working with ethnic minorities in the history of education makes it useful to take a closer look at the construction, negotiation and application of identities in the two cases. These processes hold the key to understanding the definition and maintenance of alterity and thus the ability to deconstruct the historical naturalisation of practices and hierarchies. Moreover, this approach potentially transcends the traditional retention of the national category as the dominant mode of historical research because it focuses explicitly on the reciprocal and dynamic relationship between ethnic minority groups and the Danish educational authorities, which means that practices and processes are elevated as analytical focus areas.

1. Inuit Education within the Danish Commonwealth after 1945

> "[...] everything comes at a price. That goes for the Greenlanders as well. The new they get must partly be paid with old that is lost." (Gam 1968: 48)[1]

This quotation by Mikael Gam (1901-1982), who was Danish Minister for Greenland between 1960 and 1964, is indicative of a significant shift in the Danish approach to Greenland in evidence after World War II.

Greenland had been in contact with Scandinavia since the early Middle Ages and from the early 18th century Danish colonies were established in Greenland. Apart from the introduction of Christianity and the teaching of Danish history, however, Denmark long pursued a policy of shielding and protecting the Greenlandic people and preserving their indigenous culture (DIIS 2007: 11; Rud 2006: 502ff.). This protective policy was partly because Danish decision makers saw Greenland as a vulnerable and unique country and partly because they did not want to cause a stir if the Danish language was forced too quickly upon the Inuit population (Ebbesen 1961: 282; Petersen 1921: 30). However, after World War II this approach was replaced with initiatives of social engineering and social experiments that were often launched in response to difficult situations and at moments of pressure.

The new policy line was reflected in the 1961 report from the Committee for Social Science Research in Greenland:

> "Defining the need of Greenlanders for education, it is decided above all to assume educational 'equality' with the remaining parts of Denmark. This is so because the desire for 'equality' is considered to be an increasingly crucial factor in the relation between Greenlanders and Danes" (Henriksen 1970: 85).

And Christian Berthelsen, who was Inuit School Director between 1960 and 1971, makes it abundantly clear: "Time and time again, I was expressly told that my most important task was to teach the Danish language to the youth growing up" (Berthelsen 2008: 13). And in a 1966 letter, Berthelsen wrote: "The road to further education for the young Greenlander goes [...] through a certain mastering of the Danish language [...]".[2]

This rupture in the Danish approach towards Greenland – to a large extent instigated by prominent Greenlanders themselves working toward decolonisation and emancipation – also meant that Greenlandic children de facto were faced with the challenge of coping with a neo-colonial culture, expressive of

1 All quotations from Danish documents are translated into English by the author.

2 Kultureqarnermut, Ilinniartitaanermut, Ilisimatusarnermut, Ilageeqarnermullu Naalakkersuisoqarfik (KIIIN) [Department for Culture, Education, Research, and Church] Archive, j.nr. [Record no.] 0670-05-01, 1966/67, læg [Sheet] 4.

Danish middle-class values of modernisation, progress, industrialisation, economic growth, and prosperity but applied in a Greenlandic context that focussed on industrial and commercial development. The Danish government regarded the Greenlandic system as less developed, and thus its inhabitants were in need of a knowledge transfer from Denmark to Greenland.

From a Danish perspective, the economic growth and social welfare programmes that Denmark enjoyed came to function as an ideological carrot for Greenlanders; in the most basic terms, Greenlanders were promised wealth and prosperity if they would learn Danish and follow in Denmark's footsteps. It was felt that Danish industrial society should be the yardstick against which Greenlandic progress and modernisation was to be measured. A hierarchy was therefore established between traditional Greenlandic society and Danish industrial society – at least among administrators and decision makers. In other words, a change occurred from dissimilation and protection of the indigenous culture to assimilation in the name of economic prosperity, progress, and equality.

As such, a neo-colonial culture took root as a paradigm in the administrative echelons of Greenland and thus shaped the imaginations of decision makers when they were faced with challenges and problems. One significant challenge in the educational field in the post-war period was the dramatic drop in the infant mortality rate in Greenland in the 1950s, which put tremendous pressure on the logistics of the educational system in the 1960s as the number of pupils rose accordingly (Berthelsen 2008: 17). In fact, the number of pupils in compulsory education more than doubled between 1950 and 1970 (Berthelsen 1972: 16).[3] The marriage of these logistical problems, the transition to Danish norms and values, and the increased interest among Greenlanders in education prompted the Ministry of Greenland (MfG) and the School Directorate to send children who were candidates for lower secondary school to Denmark to relieve the pressure on the often dilapidated and inadequate Greenlandic schools (Jensen 1997: 153). A systemic collapse of the Greenlandic educational system seemed imminent, and the window for new educational practices was thrown open.

1.1 The Preparation Scheme

The 'preparation scheme' saw the light of day in 1961 with the professed 'home sending' of 26 ethnic Greenlandic children (13 girls and 13 boys) for one year of

3 As of December 31, 1951 the number of pupils in compulsory education in Greenland was 4,328. As of December 31, 1969 the number had risen to 10,502.

schooling in Denmark.[4] During the course of the preparation scheme that lasted from 1961 to 1976, a total of 1,530 children from grades five, six, and seven were sent to Denmark.

The purpose of the scheme was to improve the Greenlandic children's Danish language skills to enable them to pass the lower secondary school exam faster than children who went to school in Greenland.[5] Because of the language barriers between Greenlandic and Danish, it took two to three years more to produce a lower secondary school graduate in Greenland than in Denmark.[6]

The first preparation classes were initially located in both Greenland and Denmark. There were, however, serious concerns that too many pupils would be allowed into the first preparation classes in Greenland and that the admission criteria would be set too low. Thus, the School Directorate called for a more meticulous selection of all preparation pupils, which sparked a more systematic screening process containing various tests – tests that were to be employed to select students for a one-year school trip to Denmark (the preparation classes in Denmark).[7]

From 1967, the one-year school trips to Denmark were formalised as the first preparation class for the lower secondary school. Between 1965 and 1971 there were no meaningful alternatives to the preparation scheme and the trips to Denmark (Egede 1971; Henriksen 1970: 90). As Kirsten Gynther, the teacher supervising the preparation scheme in Denmark, wrote in a 1967 letter to the school director: "If parents in Greenland want their child to have an academic education, they are forced to send their child on a one-year school trip to Denmark and during that stay, let their child be in the care of complete strangers".[8] As a result of the much-improved Danish language skills acquired by the children who had been schooled in Denmark, this usually guaranteed them a place in the lower secondary school, an outcome that made the trips to Denmark very popular among parents.[9]

---

4 KIIIN Archive, j.nr. [Record no.] 949.3, læg [Sheet] 2, 1961: Minutes from a MfG Meeting on June 19, 1961.

5 Rigsarkivet (RA) [Danish National Archive), MfG, journalsager [Records] 1957-89, nr. 1203-07-00 and KIIIN Archive, j.nr. 949.3, 1961.

6 KIIIN Archive, j.nr. 949.3, læg 2, 1961: Minutes from a MfG Meeting on June 19, 1961.

7 RA, MfG, journalsager [Records], nr. 1200-01-03: Minutes from a Meeting in the School Directorate on December 11, 1963.

8 KIIIN Archive, j.nr. 0670-05-01, 67/68: Letter dated December 20, 1967.

9 KIIIN Archive, j.nr. 949.3, læg 2, 1961: Telegram from the school director to the MfG dated June 27, 1961: "[…] many parents want to send their children on a school trip to Denmark […]".

The intake for the lower secondary school happened formally based on school recommendations of suitable pupils from the sixth and seventh grades and the boarding schools, but gradually the intake occurred almost solely from the preparation classes. In the case of too many pupils being recommended, the lower secondary school in the capital of Godthåb [Nuuk][10] would hold attainment and intelligence tests, and those results would then become the decisive factors in the selection of pupils.[11]

However, during the later years of the scheme, its raison d'être and aim changed significantly, as a result of improved schooling conditions in Greenland that made it possible to recruit pupils for the lower secondary school without them having to go to Denmark. Thus, the trips to Denmark were increasingly reserved for pupils from small settlements and remote areas where no advanced schooling was available.[12] This shift to an explicit focus on children least exposed to hegemonic cultural practices and values is a strong reminder of the neo-colonial context of the educational project; it also indicates that Greenland was not a homogeneous entity. Hence, there were at least two centre-periphery relations at play: Denmark - Greenland and urban Greenland - rural Greenland.

The preparation scheme was finally abandoned in 1976. By then the "[...] political, pedagogical, technical and economic conditions of the scheme [had] changed fundamentally. The learning and relief factors which led to the stays in Denmark [were] no longer present".[13] This development reflected that the position of the Greenlandic language was strengthened among Greenlanders during the 1970s, since new political winds blew with an aim of making the Greenlandic educational system less dependent on the Danish language and prolonged stays in Denmark. This development culminated with the introduction of Greenlandic home rule in 1979.

1.1.1 The Selection Process

The selection process of the preparation scheme is very telling about the construction, negotiation and application of identities in Greenlandic education. The preparation scheme called for rigorous uses of selection technologies. From its

10 'Godthåb' is the Danish name for the Greenlandic capital. The official Inuit name is 'Nuuk'. I have chosen to use the Danish name in this article because it was the official name before 1979 when home rule was introduced in Greenland.

11 Beretning om det grønlandske skolevæsen [Account about the Greenlandic Educational System] 1960-61, Nuuk 1962: 20.

12 KIIIN Archive, j.nr. [Record no.] 0670-05-01, IX, 1972-1976, læg [Sheet] 3: MfG draft about one-year school stays in Denmark dated January 13, 1976.

13 Ibid.

outset, the selection process of the Greenlandic children in the preparation scheme was rather complex consisting of several elements and incorporating many dimensions:

> In the announcement for the school leaders about the selection of suitable pupils for schooling in Denmark [...] the School Directorate has put particular emphasis on the following issues:
>
> The giftedness of the pupils, Danish language skills, the unambiguous consent of the parents to the scheme, last but not least: the physical and psychological stability of the child.[14]

The evaluation of a child's giftedness was based solely on its academic achievements. Due to the vast number of Danish teachers in Greenland described above, this evaluation was most often conducted by Danish teachers, making Danish language skills a major factor in the evaluation (Jensen 2001: 198). Physical abilities were measured by a medical examination and attested to in the ensuing doctor's note that also contained a tuberculosis certificate. The psychological abilities of the child were not measured based on psychological tests but were merely founded in the evaluating teachers' guesstimates.

The comprehensive nature of the preparation scheme is also reflected in the long list of documents the children had to bring on their trip to Denmark: moving certificate, birth certificate, smallpox certificate, immunisation certificate, medical statement about the child's state of health, and a confidential statement about the personal situation of the child's home environment.[15]

As such, the overall selection process can best be characterised as a tripartite process consisting of a centrally devised standardised testing battery, a teacher evaluation of each individual child accompanied by a prioritised school recommendation list, and a final decision on the fate of the child by the school director taking numerous aspects into account (e.g., the financial situation and the number of Danish foster homes available).[16] The ambition was to handpick the children with the highest academic potential as well as the necessary psychological robustness and stamina. Upon arrival in Denmark they would follow the curriculum in a normal Danish class. Under all circumstances the Greenlandic children

---

14 KIIIN Archive, j.nr. [Record no.] 949.3, 1961: Minutes from a MfG Meeting on June 19, 1961.

15 KIIIN Archive, j.nr. 0670-05-01: Letter from the school director to All School Leaders in Greenland, dated June 29, 1965.

16 The MfG, journalsager 1957-89, nr. 1203-22-07 (found in KIIIN Archive, j.nr. 0670-05-01, 68/69).

would be placed in a Danish 6th grade, because they had not been taught English, and because it was deemed best for the sake of language adjustment.[17]

This tripartite selection process is in itself an interesting construction and in the following paragraph I will take a closer look at the construction, negotiation and application of identities employed in the selection process of the preparation scheme.

1.1.2 Constructing the Greenlandic other – teacher evaluations

As already mentioned, the teacher evaluations consisted of the following information: the student's giftedness, Danish language skills, psychological stability, grades, and a general evaluation as well as the stance of the student's parents.[18] What is particularly striking is that giftedness and psychological stability were entirely based on teachers' opinions/guesstimates.[19] Apart from teacher evaluations, the school recommendations also contained comprehensive information on the children's home environment, medical status, and even if the child was a bed-wetter.[20]

The sources contain an abundance of teacher evaluations of individual children. In the following table[21], I have selected a few of them to indicate the range of aspects that were evaluated as well as the construction of identities that stand out distinctly. The following captures the type of information recorded about different children recommended from different school districts over different years. I have categorised the evaluating statements by general headlines in order to provide an idea and an overview of the aspects covered in the reports.

17 The MfG, journalsager 1957-89, number 1203-22-07 (found in KIIIN Archive, j.nr. 0670-05-01, 68/69).

18 KIIIN Archive, j.nr. [Record no.] 949.3, 1961.

19 Ibid. In a recommendation from the school in Sukkertoppen to the school director of Greenland, it is stated: "[The pupils] are recommended in numerical order according to giftedness, according to the opinion of the school." May 29, 1961.

20 RA, MfG, journalsager [Records] 1957-89, nr. 1203-22-07 (found in KIIIN Archive, j.nr. 0670-05-01, 68/69).

21 The information in the table was found in KIIIN Archive: j.nr. [Record no.] 949.3, læg [Sheet] 1, 1961; j.nr. 949.3, læg 11, 1962; j.nr. 949.3, læg 1, 1964/65; j.nr. 0670-05-00, læg 1, 1964-1969; j.nr. 0670-05-01, læg 2, 1965-1966.

Table 1: Evaluating statements about Greenlandic children

School district	Year	Giftedness	Body and appearance
Julianehåb	1961	Mediocre giftedness, smart, above average giftedness, possibly very gifted	Decent appearance, physically robust.
Holsteinsborg	1962	Gifted, Very good abilities, bright, very gifted, probably very gifted.	Could be used in a commercial for both toothpaste and oatmeal.
Sarqaq and Narssak	1964	Very good abilities.	Clean, bodily development not beyond 6th grade.
Sukkertoppen	1965	Gifted, very gifted, moderately gifted.	Clean and neatly dressed.
Claushavn [*Ilimanaq*]	1965	Bright, gifted.	Sense of hygiene and dressing.

Home environment	**Work ethic**	**Traits**
A bad home, drunken dad.	Always decent in his work, hard-working.	Independent, reliable, a quiet leader boy, nervous, self-assertive, independent mature, independent.
Spoiled by parents, reasonable home.	Hard-working, careful.	Shy, timid, sulky, charming, pleasant, cheerful, well-prepared, stable.
Average home, very bad home, the father is a fisher but ill and unable to work. Both parents are unable to work and drunkards, father is still "unable" to go sealing.	Hard-working, likes to work.	Careful, girly, giddy, very rest-less, lazy, modest, honest, probably homesick, phlegmatic, exceptionally decent and well-behaved for a boy, conscien-tious, timid.
Good home, six siblings, very good home, financial difficulties, drunken father, parents do not have the sense to put the right pieces of clothing together, good upbringing, home very well-kept.	Hard-working, careful with his work, careless in his work.	Good behaviour, decent and nice, talented and nice, talented, timid, nice and friendly, shy, a little too cheeky, nice, skilled, a pretty nice girl but sometimes a bit grumpy.
Small house with only one room.	Hard-working, stable.	Very shy, good temper, grateful, honest, reliable.

This selection of teacher evaluations demonstrates the comprehensive nature of the teacher evaluations and their focus on a number of cultural aspects related to the children's home lives. It is not an overstatement to say that teachers aimed at a "holistic evaluation" of their pupils.

A closer look at the different categories and their taxonomic logic reveals how the evaluative grid provided by the authorities (see announcement by the School Directorate above) was applied in practice. The first category concerning "giftedness" is clearly a central aspect of each individual evaluation. The terms recurrently used in the recommendations of children suggest that this category is well-defined, allowing teachers to order the children in an almost objective order: "Very gifted" is better than "gifted", which again is better than "moderately gifted". However, it remains unclear how different teachers in different schools employed these designations. In the second category regarding body and appearance, hygiene, the ability to dress neatly and to some extent, robustness, and general appearance are of value in the recommendations. The third category about home environment is rather peculiar. It is striking how both coming from a "bad home" and coming from a "good home" are used as arguments for recommending children to the preparation scheme. This demonstrates that teachers had different agendas and emphasised different values in their recommendations. Quite often, teachers would recommend their pupils to the preparation scheme based on social problems. One example stems from the 1965 Sukkertoppen evaluation in which it reads: "The father is a drunkard and it is a major boon, from an educational and human point of view, that the son can get away from home". On the other hand, the value of being a good ambassador for Greenland may have been decisive in the weighting of a good home and social background in some evaluations. The fourth category about work ethic is quite unambiguous. "Hard-working" is a recurring value, which testifies to the inherent values of an industrial society. On the other hand, the fifth and last category is quite ambiguous. The subjectivity, values, and to some extent, the prejudices of the teachers are very striking in this category. For instance, we learn that boys are normally not very well-behaved and girls are not supposed to be grumpy. However, it should be mentioned that when a child is evaluated with numerous negative character traits, they are normally compensated by virtues in other categories, which indicates a hierarchy between the categories – but a hierarchy completely subject to the whim of each school or teacher. For instance, some schools seem to place little emphasis on the giftedness of the children and strongly emphasise the character traits of the child, whereas others do the exact opposite. Moreover, the adjectives employed clearly reveal a very vague definition throughout all categories. For instance, what is the exact difference between "very gifted", "gifted", and "moderately gifted" and how do these terms relate to "talented", "bright", and "very good abilities"? The subjective elements in the evaluations are palpable.

The evaluation of children in a neo-colonial context also sparked definitions of otherness. Some of the teachers' comments seem to be informed by a post-colonial cultural knowledge base. Not only the Greenlandic language, but also character traits like "shyness", and "timidity" appear to function as markers of otherness in this context since these traits were very often accompanied by statements such as " […] like most Greenlandic children […]". Thus, these markers express "racialisation", which means transforming an attribute into an identity, and thus makes meaningful the category of race (Green 1997: 907). As such, Greenlandic children were met with expectations rooted in notions of race. It is striking that a large proportion of the Greenlandic children, according to Head Teacher Holger Henriksen, were characterised as "retarded" among Danish teachers (Henriksen 1970: 92). This indicates that the neo-colonial mind-set also played into a question revolving around the category of race most explicitly present in teacher expectations and evaluations.

Given the comprehensive nature of the evaluations, it is fair to say that teachers set themselves up in a position where they could pass judgment on the very life and existence of their pupils – often with the best intentions within the framework of the neo-colonial culture prevalent in Greenland. In this connection, the teacher evaluations and the processes of othering and racialisation testify to the aforementioned point that Greenlandic children de facto were faced with the challenge of coping with a neo-colonial culture wherein complexes of inferiority and superiority played a leading role.

1.1.3 Constructing the Greenlandic other – tests

The test battery of the preparation scheme consisted of the following achievement tests[22]:

1. Dictation in the Greenlandic language,
2. Greenlandic picture essay,
3. Dictation in the Danish language,
4. Danish question essay,
5. Danish picture essay (introduced in 1968 to replace Danish reading essay), and
6. Arithmetic 1-4.

---

22 KIIIN Archive, j.nr. [Record no.] 0670-05-01: Letter from teacher David Sommer to the school director dated April 30, 1969.

From an analytical point of view, the norms and values of this test battery centred on the following abilities: abstract thinking, logical reasoning, grammatical understanding, creativity, consistency, and comprehension – abilities that are in no way culturally neutral but are in good harmony with the values of an industrialised society which needs citizens who could perform such tasks one day in their jobs as adults. The Danish values of modernisation, industrialisation, economic growth, and prosperity described earlier permeated the test battery and as such affected the construction and application of identities. Such a link becomes very clear in a late 1960s ministerial memorandum on education concerning the 8th and 9th grades that stated: "The aim is to provide a curriculum which will enable the pupil to live up to the demands of the test and thus the demands of society".[23]

A Greenlandic (G) version of the Danish professor Kaj Spelling's Non-Verbal Test Battery (GNVTB-test) developed in Malaysia, was included in the test battery from the school year 1969/70. The GNVTB-test was standardised on 375 representative Greenlandic pupils from ten towns and eight villages in western Greenland (Jensen 2001: 205). It was characterised as a culturally neutral non-verbal ability test and was constructed to give an impression of the intellectual capacity of the children, resulting in an IQ score. It is important to note about the use of the GNVTB-test that

> the test will not be decisive for a pupil's participation in 1st prep. in such a way that a poor test score will bar the pupil from being accepted. On the other hand, a good test score will indicate that a pupil whose performance in the attainment tests is less convincing still might be accepted into 1st prep.[24]

The GNVTB-test took one hour and its validity was based on a correlation with John C. Raven's norms for group and individual tests, as well as a relatively high correlation between the GNVTB-test and the Danish 1943 revision of the Binet-Simon intelligence test (0.71) and the Danish military psychological intelligence test (0.78) (Spelling 1963: 151).

When trying to analyse the implications of identity constructions, negotiations, and applications in a test battery used in an intercultural context, it is useful to focus on certain central characteristics of testing. First, testing per se is based on the traditional psychometric view that everything is measurable in some way. In this way, testing uses a sample of items to represent performance across the entire domain that the test is intended to measure. This implies that testing subscribes to the idea of objective and well-defined knowledge domains – e.g., reading comprehension ability and mathematics problem-solving ability –

23 RA, MfG, Journalsager [Records] 1957-89, nr. 1253-22.

24 Private Archive, contemporary GNVTB-test Instruction.

or more abstract traits – e.g., intelligence, competence, or aptitude – as particular and well-defined areas of knowledge (Madaus, Russell, & Higgins 2009: 38ff.). These underlying assumptions are decisive in relation to the test design, and they encourage a certain way of sorting the world both ontologically and epistemologically. For instance, such assumptions force a division between language and mathematical skills that is conducive to the composition of the test battery, the evaluation of the test scores, and the weighting of the test components in the overall evaluation. In this case, it becomes obvious that the arithmetic tests, which were perceived to be culture- and language-neutral, were imported from the Copenhagen school system. The language tests, on the other hand, were seen as bound to the Greenlandic context; consequently, they were produced in Godthåb. However, it is noteworthy that these tests were still designed predominantly by Danish teachers.

Thus, the notion of knowledge domains that prevails in the test battery of the preparation scheme refers to the societal division of labour in which certain skills are useful in one area of the labour force and other skills are useful in another. This is not culturally neutral, and it is certainly in stark contrast with the habits of Greenlandic society where the need for skills did not necessarily follow the division of adult labour in Denmark. This point is reflected in a 1963 letter from a western Greenland settlement: "Please observe that the tests are very difficult for a pupil from a settlement".[25] The quotation points to the fact that knowledge domains are historically and socially constructed. Certainly, educational testing has special importance in an intercultural context because the non-native test taker often does not have the same frame of reference as a native test taker (Gundara 2000; Shohamy 2004).

Although Spelling generally subscribed to a paradigm emphasizing the role of the environment in intelligence measuring, it is striking that the GNVTB-test claims to be able to transcend exactly these cultural biases and artificial variances in knowledge domains by probing the inherent intelligence level of the children. In other words, the GNVTB-test sought to transcend culture and knowledge domains of attainment with a knowledge domain of intelligence perceived to be even more fundamental and overarching than the one it replaced. The GNVTB-test conceptualises and anticipates precisely the existence of an invariant or path-dependent unique characteristic – intelligence – in the individual, that is, an essence that can be identified accurately in relation to a preconstructed notion of a knowledge domain. The circumstance that the GNVTB-test correlates with other similar tests does not prove the validity of the instru-

25 KIIIN Archive, j.nr. [Record no.] 943.3, 1963/64, læg [Sheet] 3: letter from Qoornoq school to the deputy school inspector in Nuuk dated May 23, 1963.

ments because they are based on the same assumptions and hypotheses regarding knowledge domains, correlations, causal effects, society, and human nature (Mogensen, Lange, & Fenger 1960: 106). It is thus a circular argument bound to the norms and values of psychometrics.

Instead, this analysis points to the existence of a problematic aspect of any test that systematises and denies the test takers their uniqueness, because they must live up to the preconceived logic of the one-size-fits-all test.[26] Testing canonises mediocrity, because it is pre-structured to incorporate a scale of values – a field of tension between genius (good) and idiocy (bad) – but only as certain forms. The test designer must be able to anticipate all manifestations of genius in order for genius answers to be credited. Because this is impossible, there is only limited room for deviation, and none at all for spontaneity and surprise; testing evaluates only one kind of genius and one kind of idiocy. This holds for the GNVTB-test as well, and when it is used as a selection technology, it is necessarily rooted in the past (retrospect), whereas it prescribes actions directed towards the future (prospect) (Gerberich 1963: 191).[27] Instead, the test taker is merely assimilated based on the test and his/her own past.

Thus, it becomes clear that none of the tests of the preparation scheme test battery can be purged of cultural norms and values. Even the GNVTB-test cannot escape this critique, and the analysis shows that the GNVTB-test, to a significant extent, subscribes to norms and values of abstract thinking and logical reasoning, such as the arithmetic tests. However, there seems to be a significant difference in relation to the essay language tests, which retain certain qualitative characteristics. These tests were not formally standardised, and they were evaluated not by a rigid binary true/false dichotomy but by a teacher evaluation. This made it possible to take into consideration creativity although it would open up to socially pre-formed prejudices and racialisations. And although the language tests were evaluated from a more holistic point of view, they still canonised the taxonomic values of abstract thinking, logical reasoning, grammatical understanding, consistency, and comprehension.

---

26 This is so, even though leading proponents of high-stakes educational tests often state that tests are fair and objective because they are standardised and they are administered under the same conditions for all test takers (Phelps 2009). The point in this connection is that test takers inevitably are different and therefore a standard test cannot incorporate their differences. Instead, the test is at imminent risk of stifling and suspending the test taker's particularities. It is important to note that the test taker's score is dependent on both his/her performance and performance of the norm-group to which he/she is compared, i.e. the standardisation.

27 This 'Janus-face' of testing is expressed in a commonly used definition of evaluation (Vedung 1991: 20; Boyd 1930: 279).

The testing component of the selection process thus forced children to adopt an identity made up of one or more of the preconceived knowledge domains of the test battery.

1.2 Concluding remarks

This analysis of educational selection practices and technologies in neo-colonial Greenland has revealed that Danish values of modernisation, industrialisation, economic growth, and prosperity permeated the Greenlandic educational system and the selection technologies themselves.

The high-stakes selection technologies were used as gate-keepers for academic education; hence the inherent values of the selection technologies were imposed upon the children with consequences for the construction of their identities.

The asymmetric relation between Greenlandic and Danish values in the Greenlandic educational system took place within a system aimed at assimilation. At the same time, the educational system contained marked processes of a paradoxical and contradictionary nature which might be explained from a postcolonial perspective.

The aim of Greenlandic education – supported and advocated by both Danish and Inuit administrators and politicians – was assimilation to 'the Danish way' in order to achieve modernisation. As has been analysed in other colonial contexts, the educational project of "civilizing the Inuits" depended on constructing the targets of the assimilation efforts as "Others", who were in some significant way deficient. These processes of othering, as visible in the teacher evaluations, however, tend to construct the Other as essentially different (and inferior) and thus contradict the goal of assimilation. At the same time these perceptions reinforced the asymmetry of the educational relation between Danes and Inuits in the educational system by affirming essentialised and racialised cultural identities.

However, the line of differentiation between Danes and Inuits and the identification of the Other was blurred since Inuit civil servants and politicians functioned as administrators and leaders in many areas of the educational system. The "Inuit" were not a homogeneous group in terms of "cultural background" or in terms of power positions, economic interests, and political agendas. Greenlandic education after 1945, therefore, clearly mirrors the complexities and ambiguities of non-binary postcolonial relations in other parts of the globalised world. This assessment of the Greenland case gains even more evidence when contrasted with another case of "ethnic minority education" in Denmark.

2. German Minority Education within the Danish Commonwealth after 1945

Following the end of the German occupation of Denmark in May 1945, the Danish Ministry of Education issued a circular in June 1945 ordering the closure of all German minority schools, the abolition of the German school inspector's office, and the suspension of German schools' right to conduct examinations (Becker-Christensen 2009: 409). Moreover, the existing private German schools were confiscated as economic compensation for the money spent on expanding German education in Denmark during the occupation. At the same time, a criminal investigation of German teachers and their wartime collaboration with NS Germany was conducted (Nørr 2003: 404).

All German schools in Denmark remained closed pending an investigation of German schoolbooks containing NS ideology and alignment. And for the future, the Danish school directorate had to approve all books likely to be used in German schools.[28]

In 1946, German public education was officially abolished, the special German classes at Danish public schools were eliminated, and the only option open for German ethnic education was to establish private or home-schooling (Thaler 2007: 153).[29]

Thus, German schooling in the Danish part of the border region between Denmark and Germany, called "Southern Jutland" in Danish and "Nordschleswig" in German, lay in ruins. In the spring of 1945, almost 4,000 children attended German minority schools. In 1947 that number had decreased to a mere 200 (Becker-Christensen 2009: 409).

The border region between Denmark and Germany had been a disputed area since The Schleswig Wars of 1848-1850 and 1864. In 1864 the combined armies of Prussia and Austria effectively defeated the Danish army and the region was under German rule for 56 years until the northern part of the region was transferred to Denmark in 1920 after a referendum in the wake of German defeat in World War I. Following the events of 1920 many German industrial workers and civil servants immigrated to Germany, which meant that farmers and rural

---

28 Landsarkivet for Sønderjylland (LAS) [The Provincial Archive for Southern Jutland], Hans Novrup, amtsskolekonsulent [County School Inspector] 1938-1961, materiale angående sønderjyske skoleforhold – tysk mindretal [Material regarding education in Southern Jutland – German minority].

29 LAS, Hans Novrup, amtsskolekonsulent 1938-1961, betænkninger redegørelser – det tyske mindretals skolevæsen [Reports – German minority education], 'Det tyske skolevæsen i Nordschleswig i 1945-1946' [German minority education in Nordschleswig] dated December 1946.

workers were overrepresented in the German minority (Thaler 2007: 149). The region, however, was governed according to a principle of self-identification, meaning that classification as a minority was left to individuals, families, and communities. The Danish authorities in the interwar years pursued a flexible and non-intrusive policy for German minority education in both public and private education. This policy line was precipitated by the existence of a Danish minority in the southern part of the region, which remained under German rule. This created a situation of reciprocity between Denmark and Germany as well as between the two minorities.

But this benevolent and reciprocally-promoted climate changed abruptly in 1945 when the German occupation of Denmark ended. The Danish authorities imprisoned almost 3,000 members of the German minority deemed to have been involved in suspicious and hostile activities during the German occupations. The prisoners were placed in a camp formerly used by the German Wehrmacht to incarcerate Danish political dissidents. Indeed, the tides had changed.

Apart from popular hostility towards Germany and Germans in general, an underlying issue in this change of policy was the cleansing of the Danish self-perception from any stain of NS-collaboration. If any trait reminiscent of NS (authoritarian character, racism, etc.) was projected on the "Germans", then Danish society had no need for critical self-inspection. It is, however, noteworthy that the leader of the Danish NS party, Frits Clausen (1893-1947), was in fact born and raised in Southern Jutland. The Danish resistance movement emerged as heroes in public after the German occupation ended, and keenly persecuted the German minority and Danes with known or rumoured German sympathies.

However, in the summer of 1946, four German private schools were re-established, and within the next five years, the number of German private schools in Southern Jutland/Nordschleswig had risen to 25 schools with 825 pupils.[30]

This gradual re-establishment of German education took place in a climate of deep animosity against the German minority. Danish politicians even pursued a policy of pushing the border further south, although these plans were effectively abandoned in 1946. Once German private schools were allowed to reopen in 1946, German teachers received severe threats, which caused at least one

30 LAS, Hans Novrup, amtsskolekonsulent 1938-1961, betænkninger redegørelser – det tyske mindretals skolevæsen, 'Ændring af lov nr. 412 af 12/7 1946 vedr. private tysksprogede skoler' [Change of act no. 412 dated July 12, 1946 regarding German private schools].

school not to open.[31] Moreover, there were serious problems with housing and the supply of building materials for the construction of German private schools.[32]

These problems reflect the on-going debates about the position of German education in post-war Denmark. Clearly German education evoked strong feelings among the Danish majority and the German minority. There was a clear realisation on both sides that the continued existence of the German minority depended on its schools. From a Danish perspective, Southern Jutland/ Nordschleswig was an icon for Danish nationalism because of a national inferiority complex in relation to Germany, which was intimately connected with its military defeat in 1864. To this end, the region was a cultural outpost that had been subjected to Danish "re-colonisation" following the end of German occupation. As documented by historian of education Erik Nørr, Danish educational policies were subject to national interests focused on limiting and curbing the German minority influence on education, thus precipitating the assimilation of the German minority to Danishness (Nørr 2003).

The German minority on the other side argued – as a subtle threat - that Denmark's control over Southern Jutland was not assured in perpetuity (Christensen 2004: 92). The German minority filed complaints that it was barred from establishing schools under the liberal Danish Free School Act of 1855, which stipulated the right of anyone to establish a free school and receive government funding. Hence, the German minority argued, it was subject to an inferior position of discrimination compared to other citizens.

Their argument was backed by the fact that the establishment of German education was subject to a number of additional stipulations and criteria compared to the Danish Free School Act:[33]

- All teachers and school books had to be approved by the Danish authorities,
- the curriculum had to be approved by the school directorate,
- the right to home schooling was – as a rule - limited to only the children of the parents undertaking the home schooling,
- the Minister of Education decided whether other children would be able to attend home schools,
- teaching materials used for home schooling had to be approved by the School Directorate, and

31 LAS, Hans Novrup, amtsskolekonsulent 1938-1961, betænkninger redegørelser – det tyske mindretals skolevæsen, 'Det tyske skolevæsen i Nordschleswig i 1945-1946' dated December 1946.

32 Ibid.

33 Lov nummer 412 af 12/7 1946 [Act no. 412 dated July 12, 1946].

- private German schools and German home schooling were subject to School Commission inspections.

Furthermore, German teachers could be removed from a private German school at the whim of the Danish School Directorate: in addition to a rule of non-collaboration with NS organisations during the German occupation, the key criteria in evaluating German teachers were whether the teacher in question would be completely loyal to Danish interests and whether s/he had a faultless reputation.[34] Hence, it was often more than difficult to find qualified, suitable, and acceptable teachers.

2.1 Thawing the antagonism – the reciprocity of majority-minority-relations

A unique and crucial factor working for the return to a benevolent climate and an unmistakeable thaw in this rather antagonistic climate was the element of reciprocity as a consequence of the Danish minority in Germany. As with the inter-war years, the parallel existence of German minorities in Denmark and Danish minorities in Germany—a kin-state—created a symmetric, reciprocal situation. Although the German and Danish minorities in Denmark and Germany, respectively, were not mirror images in respect to numbers and composition, they still found themselves in comparable situations of struggling for minority rights, in general, and the right to independent education, in particular.

The position of the German minority suffered from the absence of a German kin-state until the establishment of West Germany in 1949 (Christensen 2004: 87), although the 1946 emergence of the German regional government in Kiel was an important step in re-establishing the delicate balance between kin-states and minorities.

This gradual thaw is reflected by the fact that in 1948 the German minority was given the option to reacquire 13 of the former private schools (Becker-Christensen 2009: 409). And in June 1952, the 1946 act was revised stipulating that German teachers and schoolbooks no longer had to be approved by the Danish School Directorate. However, the limitations on German minority schools' right to conduct exams and the Danish authorities' inspection of German schools and German home schooling continued (§ 3-4).

Another important precondition for the thawing process was the existence of the 'Haderslev Circle' [Haderslebener Kreis] formed in November 1943 by a bank director, an industrialist, a lawyer, and a reverend. This group of former

34 LAS, Hans Novrup, amtsskolekonsulent 1938-1961, betænkninger redegørelser – det tyske mindretals skolevæsen, 'Det tyske skolevæsen under nyordningen' af Hans Novrup [German education during the restructuring], page 3.

dissidents of NS Germany provided the post-war German minority with much-desired credibility after the occupation and became the nucleus of the German minority just after the war. The Haderslev Circle reorganised itself on democratic terms, based on loyalty towards Denmark and unconditional acceptance of the international border between Denmark and Germany (Kühl 2005: 41). Although the rather conservative Haderslev Circle did not enjoy the full support of the German minority, it was very well connected to Danish politicians and administrators, and it pursued a policy of dialogue with the Danish majority in order to avoid legal persecution of German minority members (Lessow 1995; Christensen 2004: 94, 106).

However, the Haderslev Circle opposed another faction within the German minority, namely that of the imprisoned group of nearly 3,000 German minority members mentioned above. This faction was called "the Fårhus-people" named after the name of the prison camp "Fårhus" (Christensen 2004: 92ff.). The "Fårhus-people" found the policies of the Haderslev Circle much too lenient, and they sought to give the minority's affiliation with Germany pride of place rather than the expression of loyalty towards Denmark.

Thus, internal division haunted the German minority with the publication of two opposing declarations for the future policies of the German minority towards Denmark. But with the formation of the German minority organisation, Bund deutscher Nordschleswiger (BdN), in November 1945 the Haderslev Circle's declaration was passed with very few changes providing the Circle with a significant political victory. However, the continued Danish majority support for the policies of the Haderslev Circle was dependent on the successful effects of the loyalty declaration for the imprisoned Germans (Christensen 2004: 113f.).

The policies of the BdN following the line of the Haderslev Circle, however, proved to be unsuccessful since the Danish authorities refused to release the incarcerated Germans. Thus, the loyalist policies shifted toward a nationalist political course, downplaying the role of the German minority during the occupation and emphasizing the unjust policies of Danish society towards the post-war German minority. This change in political course was precipitated by the emergence of the German regional government in Kiel, which provided moral support for the new course (Christensen 2004: 122). Furthermore, the release of the detained Germans in 1947 also facilitated the decline of influence suffered by the Haderslev Circle since the now former prisoners did not trust in the abilities of the Haderslev Circle to lead the minority. However, the formerly detained members of the German minority endorsed the declaration of loyalty towards Denmark. Their nationalist policies proved to be purely rooted in a sense of national belonging without any hidden ideological preferences (Christensen 2004: 125).

High on the Danish political agenda in 1947 was the improvement of the conditions for the Danish minority in Germany; this issue became linked with the detained members of the German minority in Denmark (Christensen 2004: 127). With the establishment of the Federal Republic of Germany[35] in 1949, Denmark and "West Germany" found common ground in the European space where economic and defence policies took pride of place and this helped generating an amenable climate sparking the Copenhagen-Bonn declaration in 1955.

Thus, the major breakthrough of the thaw came in 1955 with the Copenhagen-Bonn declarations, which have been described as "[...] a 'Magna Carta' [...] for the national minorities in the region" (Kühl 2005: 31). The declarations ensured that both minorities were bestowed the right to establish private minority schools with the right to offer recognised exams (Kühl 2005: 16; Becker-Christensen 2009: 379). Examinations conducted by German schools gained recognition from Danish authorities, provided that they were comparable with similar Danish examinations. From an analytical perspective, the Copenhagen-Bonn declarations did not result in any changes in the possibilities for primary and secondary education in German compared to the period 1920-1945, but did represent a marked change from the previous decade (Pedersen 2005: 103).

The long-sought aim of the German minority was to establish a German high school, and in 1964, this pinnacle of German education in Southern Jutland/Nordschleswig opened its doors. By then, the German minority had some 28 schools with approximately 1,550 pupils (Becker-Christensen 2009: 409). In 1965, a formally established liaison committee between the Danish government and the German minority was established (Kühl 2005: 58).

Within the European Union, the minority policies and relations in the area bordering the Danish-German border have been identified as a role model for minority situations (Buch 2004: 281). At the same time, it is clear that significant processes of constructing, negotiating and applying identities were at play during the formative years of the contemporary situation.

35 After the war, the western sectors of Germany, controlled by France, the United Kingdom, and the United States, were merged (23 May 1949) to form the Federal Republic of Germany (Bundesrepublik Deutschland) with Bonn as its provisional capital; the Soviet Zone became the German Democratic Republic (Deutsche Demokratische Republik, or DDR, on 7 October 1949), its capital was East Berlin. They were, mainly outside of Germany, informally known as "West Germany" and "East Germany".

2.2 *Constructing the German Self and Other – the criterion of self-identification*

As with the interwar period, official policy allowed both sets of minorities in the border region to self-identify as German or Danish after 1945 (Kühl 2005: 50; Pedersen 2005: 91). This policy change occurred in order to avoid forcing identities on individuals, but it also made it difficult to gain an exact statistical overview of the size and composition of the German minority in Southern Jutland. People who identified as "German" did not necessarily speak any German. In fact, there was nothing "objectively" German about them. However, people in the local communities would often have distinct ideas about the preferences and values of their peers, which suggests that constructions of alterity and dissimilation played a central part in everyday life. For instance, it was common knowledge among local inhabitants which shops and businesses were owned or run by Germans or Danes with German preferences and sympathies. On the other hand, the German minority also put a limit on who could actually join the minority by granting or denying recognition in daily activities. As a result of these observations, the existence and reproduction of the German minority were the result of negotiations in several fields. In other words, the German minority was dynamic and heterogeneous, making it more than difficult to precisely establish the boundaries and demarcations of the minority.

Following from the antagonistic climate permeated by feelings of animosity, it is clear that there was a difference between the official policies – often dictated by the Copenhagen administration and executive – and the local climate in which people lived their lives. This is evidenced by the sabotage attempts against German minority schools.

Thus, the construction, negotiation, and application of identities in Southern Jutland/Nordschleswig served different functions and different purposes. First and foremost, it served the purpose of retaining and reproducing ethno-national identities and sense of national belonging. In a Danish context this encapsulated the paradox of being in power to govern the German minority, and at the same time, being by far the smaller nation bordering an economic power. Second, it functioned as a way of reproducing the existing order by constructing the other group as exemplar for certain character and cultural traits. From a Danish point of view, Germans were seen as diligent, structured, and disciplined but lacking in creativity, flexibility and humour; this provided the Danes with a hidden superiority. Third, it provided an element of meaning in everyday life through the construction of binary opposites and a resulting struggle rooted in power relations and national characters.

In other words, a struggle of identities unfolded in Southern Jutland/Nordschleswig. Given the criterion of self-identification of belonging to the German minority, a major battleground was in school curricula, particularly in the subjects of history, geography, and Danish. Hence, Danish fears of a waning cultural position resulted in specific Danish curricular demands for German minority schools. In the eastern counties of the region, the Danish educational authorities demanded six Danish language classes, one Danish history class, and one Danish Geography class per week, while in the city of Tonder, just some five kilometres from the border, only one additional Danish language class and one Danish ancient history class per week were prescribed.[36]

But in order to take a closer look at the construction, negotiation, and application of identities in Southern Jutland/Nordschleswig it is fruitful to treat the inspection reports filed by Danish county school inspectors following their visits to German minority schools.

2.3 Constructing the German Other – school inspections

As already discussed, German minority schools in Southern Jutland/Nordschleswig were met by regular inspections performed by Danish county school inspectors. In the Western counties of Aabenraa/Apenrade and Sonderborg, German minority schools were subject to 30 inspections by Danish county school inspector Hans Novrup (1889-1970) between 1947 and 1955.[37] The Danish county school inspectors were tasked with recurring inspections of all schools under their jurisdiction – both Danish and German – to control and guide the teaching undertaken in the county schools. In 1950, Novrup had 122 schools to inspect out of which 11 were German minority schools.

Novrup was a very productive and diligent inspector and his reports are highly interesting archival sources that bring into the question the construction, negotiation, and application of identities in Southern Jutland/Nordschleswig. Interpreting Novrup's 30 reports generates a telling picture of the central educational and cultural issues at stake, the self-image of the Danish educational system, and how a central Danish civil servant perceived the German minority.

The policy picture of a Danish focus on history and geography is confirmed in the reports. Following an inspection visit in January 1950, Novrup noted:

---

36 LAS, Hans Novrup, amtsskolekonsulent 1938-1961, betænkninger redegørelser – det tyske mindretals skolevæsen, 'Ændring af lov nr. 412 af 12/7 1946 vedr. private tysksprogede skoler'.

37 LAS, Sønderborg Amtsskoledirektion 1920-1959, Tilsynsprotokol [Inspection reports] & LAS, Åbenrå Amt skoledirektion 1920-1958, Tilsynsprotokoller.

"The teacher had to be enlightened about Danish history and Nordic Geography due to misconceptions". In the same report Novrup also made a note about the female teacher: "the teacher had a very appealing appearance". Thus, apart from searching for school books with NS content – of which there were several reports in the period - the county school inspector aimed at evaluating the children, the teaching and the teacher in terms of character, personality, ability, and appearance. Apparently, there was no strict pattern or criteria for this evaluation. To some extent, the reports reflect whatever popped into Novrup's mind although emphasis was placed on curriculum and proficiency.

It is noteworthy that Novrup in his descriptions of German teaching used words such as "meticulous", "diligent", "rational", "strict", "skilful", "disciplined", "sensible", and "precise". While these adjectives at a first glance are liable to bear positive connotations among many educators, the other side of the coin is that they also categorised and connected German education with traits that did not exhaustively describe Danish educational and pedagogical ideals. Danish educational ideals were centred on creativity, independent thinking, and a democratic mind-set. Thus, something was perceived to be missing in German education, which made Danish educational practices progressive and superior. In Novrup's reports the apparently positive descriptions were very often joined by words like "uninspired", "old-fashioned", and "naive". Unequivocally, these accompanying descriptions of negative observations served the purpose of positioning German and Danish educational ideals and practices in relation to each other and reproducing close-knit perceptions and ideas about the qualities and drawbacks of each educational system. While there was an image of Danish education as progressive when compared to old-fashioned and traditional German education among Danish teachers and parents, German education maintained a reputation for being well disciplined and rational.

Since the 1920s these positions and perceptions are tellingly reflected in a saying among Danish parents in Southern Jutland/Nordschleswig:

If you are faced with the choice of choosing between a good German and a good Danish teacher you should choose the Danish teacher because your child will learn creativity and independent thinking. But if you are faced with the choice of choosing between a bad German and a bad Danish teacher you should choose the German teacher because at least s/he will accomplish to educate your child rationally and systematically.

Thus, even a bad German teacher was perceived to be able to live up to the constructed "German educational ideals" implicating that they were easier to meet and thus implicitly lacking in advance compared to the more advanced Danish educational ideals calling for a skilled teacher.

When evaluating German minority school children, Novrup used descriptions such as: "well taught", "attentive", and "interested". But again, there was a fly in the ointment. German minority children were also described as "not very bright" and "tardy".

Obviously, these negative remarks need not be associated with Germanness per se. After all, Novrup would use similar descriptions about certain Danish children. But when applied in an explicit majority-minority environment, the descriptions inevitably spill into the construction of Germanness among the Danish majority. Novrup - as the Danish civil servant with legal rights to conduct inspections of German minority schools – had the power of definition at his disposal.

2.4 Concluding remarks

This analysis of Danish post-war educational policies towards the German minority in Southern Jutland/Nordschleswig clearly reveals that something was at stake in the majority/minority interplay of the Danish-German border region.

From a Danish perspective, the border region was a cultural outpost in which constructions of national character and national sentiment were prevalent. The hostile popular feelings towards Germany and Germans following the occupation made these processes especially pronounced. "Germans" and "Germanness" were constructed by Danes to be everything that "Danes" and "Danishness" was not. These mechanisms of dissimilation were paired with a paradoxical and ambivalent set of policies aimed at curbing and diluting German culture and Germanness in order to promote assimilation. This paradox is very much in evidence in schools where German education was severely undermined with every means possible immediately after the German occupation ended in May 1945. But within a few years, the climate thawed, and Danish policies towards the German minority gradually became more lenient and constructive. However, the analysis revealed significant discrepancies existed between official Danish policies and everyday lives and practices in the region.

From a German perspective, opposing strategies for dealing with the new climate and Danish minority policies surfaced. Should loyalty to Denmark or to Germany take pride of place? Clearly, the very existence of the German minority in Denmark was at stake. With almost 3,000 minority members incarcerated, blatant Danish hostility, and internal divisions and disagreements, the situation was dire. The re-establishment of ethnic education was high on the Germans' agenda since this was seen as the very precondition for the nesting and reproduction of the German minority. The decisive remedy to this situation came from the Danish desire to improve the situation of the Danish minority in Germany and the reign of international politics with the establishment of the regional government in Kiel and later the formation of West Germany.

Thus, the symmetric relations due to the special case of reciprocity in the region were re-established. The emergence of the Cold War and the gradual formation of a European space in which Denmark and Germany would share economic and military interests, paved the way for the Copenhagen-Bonn declarations, effectively guaranteeing the rights of both minorities in the border region.

3. Conclusion

Analysing the two cases from a post-colonial perspective illustrates how Danishness was constructed in very different ways with respect to the two "groups" treated in the analysis.

In the neo-colonial Greenlandic context, Danish politicians and administrators took the role of the colonisers. The educational practices reveal significant discursive forms and patterns of "Othering" in which Inuit children were portrayed with certain character traits such as timidity, shyness, use of the Greenlandic language, and sometimes, even lack of mental abilities. This pattern of "Othering" happened within a context where Danish values of economic development, progress, and industrialisation took pride of place. The Inuit children were evaluated from an outsider perspective. This evaluation took place in written teacher evaluations and in the employed selection technologies, i.e., tests of various kinds, and it bore significant consequences for the future of each individual child.

The case of post-war German minority education in Denmark generates a picture where national rivalry and a complex history of border conflicts played important roles. Germans and Germanness were constructed and functioned as forms of alterity for the Danish national character and national sentiment. The Danish authorities were tasked with the delicate situation of governing a potentially powerful German minority, which played into a national inferiority complex towards Germany since the military defeat of 1864. The German minority in Denmark was, unlike the Greenlanders, a possibly powerful group, which the Danish authorities, after the German occupation had ended, saw as potentially dangerous. Thus, the German minority needed to be curbed and controlled.

Both cases illustrate the presence of asymmetric relations, in which Danes strived to maintain authority. But in the German case, that asymmetry was gradually suspended due to the emergence of a reciprocal balance rooted in the conditions of the Danish minority in Germany and the establishment of the German regional government in Kiel and the federal Government in Bonn.

At the same time, because of the criterion of self-identification, the German minority was dynamic and heterogeneous making it more than difficult to precisely establish the boundaries and demarcations of the minority. To some extent, this also seems to have been the case in Greenland where the Inuit elite took active part in promoting assimilation to 'the Danish way' in order to achieve modernisation and equality with the rest of Denmark apart from maintaining some of their authority and status by mediating between the Danish government and their fellow Greenlanders.

However, a significant difference between the two cases is that Greenlanders could not choose whether they wanted to belong to a minority, whereas the German minority, to a certain extent, could. The point here is that the analysis indicates a difference between "racialised" identities (which cannot be chosen) and other identity constructions in which a marked element of negotiation takes place.

Danish educational policies in both cases were characterised by assimilative ends. In the Greenlandic case, this policy was endorsed and supported by the Inuit elite seeking equality with Denmark. In the German case, the assimilation policy took place in opposition to the German minority seeking to secure as much independence for itself as possible. However, it is noteworthy that significant and contradictory processes of dissimilation shadowed these seemingly clear assimilation policies. In Greenland, Otherings and racialisations permeated the educational practices ensuring that complete assimilation was unobtainable. In the case of the German minority, dissimilation processes were rooted in the very construction of Danish national identity.

These paradoxical and contradictory processes demonstrate that Danish educational policies served very different functions and different purposes in the two cases.

Literature and Sources

Becker-Christensen, H. (2009): Fra "mod hinanden" til "med hinanden". In: Hansen, H.S., Henningsen, L. N. & Rasmussen, L. P. (eds.): Sønderjyllands historie (Vol. II, pp. 241-472). Aabenraa: Historisk Samfund for Sønderjylland.

Berthelsen, C. (1972): Den grønlandske skole gennem 20 år. Skoledirektøren for Grønland.

Berthelsen, C. (2008): Ønsker om at lære dansk. In: Grønland 4-5, 1 – 19.

Boyd, W. (1930): Towards a new education – a record and synthesis of the discussions on the new psychology and curriculum at the fifth world conference of the New Education Fellowship at Elsinore, Denmark, in August 1929. London.

Buch, J. (2004): Review of: Kühl, Jørgen: Den dansk-tyske mindretalsmodel og Europa. Nationale mindretal og minoritetsordninger i det dansk-tyske grænseland belyst i en eu-

ropæisk sammenhæng. In: Sønderjyske Årbøger. Vojens: Historisk Samfund for Sønderjylland, 281 – 284.
Byram, M. (1986): Minority Education and Ethnic Survival - Case Study of a German School in Denmark. Clevedon.
Christensen, J. H. (2004): "Die neue Entwicklung in Dänemark hat begonnen". Det tyske mindretal i Nordslesvig 1945-47. In: Sønderjyske Årbøger. Vojens: Historisk Samfund for Sønderjylland, 87 – 132.
DIIS (2007): Afvikling af Grønlands kolonistatus 1945-54 – en historisk udredning. Copenhagen.
Egede, I. (1971, November 11): En grønlandsk folkeskole eksisterer ikke. Information.
Ebbesen, H. (1961): Den grønlandske skole er stadig dobbeltsproget. In: Grønland 8, 281 – 288.
Gam, M. (1968): Den grønlandske skoles udvikling. In V. Skovgaard-Petersen, Årbog for dansk skolehistorie, 32 – 48.
Gerberich, J. R. (1963, October): The development of educational testing. In: Theory into Practice, 2: 4, 184 – 191.
Green, M. (1997): Making Subjects: History-Writing, Education, and Race Categories. In: Paedagogica Historica, 33: 3, 882 – 908.
Gundara, J. S. (2000): Interculturalism, Education and Inclusion. London.
Henriksen, H. (1970): Skole og kulturmøde i Grønland II. In: Grønland 3, 85 – 96.
Jensen, E. (1997): Langt hjemmefra – grønlandske skolebørn i Danmark i 1960'erne og 1970'erne. In: Grønland 4, 150 – 154.
Jensen, E. (2001): Langt hjemmefra – grønlandske børn på skoleophold i Danmark i 1960'erne og 1970'erne. Nuuk.
Kühl, J. (2003): Den dansk-tyske mindretalsmodel og Europa. Nationale mindretal og minoritetsordninger i det dansk-tyske grænseland belyst i en europæisk sammenhæng. Aabenraa: Institut for Grænseregionsforskning.
Kühl, J. (2005): The Bonn-Copenhagen Declarations of 1955: Background, Context and Impact of the Danish-German Minority Regulations. In: Kühl, J., Weller, M. & Lloydd, M. (eds.): Minority Policy in Action: The Bonn-Copenhagen Declarations in a European Context 1955-2005. Haderslev: European Centre for Minority Issues, 31 – 89.
Lessow, A. (1995): Der Haderslebener Kreis und seine Bedeutung für den Neubeginn der deutschen Arbeit in Nordschleswig 1945. Schriften der Heimatkundlichen Arbeitsgemeinschaft für Nordschleswig 70, 88 – 95.
Mogensen, A., Lange, B. & Fenger, G. (1960): Om Binet-Simon-systemet. Copenhagen.
Nørr, E. (2003): Genforeningens bedste gave. Aabenraa: Historisk Samfund for Sønderjylland.
Pedersen, K. M. (2005): Languages and Identities in the National Minorities in the Danish-German Border Region and in the Bonn-Copenhagen Declarations. In: Kühl, J., Weller, M. & Lloydd, M. (eds.): Minority Policy in Action: The Bonn-Copenhagen Declarations in a European Context. Haderslev: European Centre for Minority Issues, 91 – 137.
Petersen, S. (1921): Den grønlandske skole. In: Vor Ungdom, 25 – 32.
Phelps, R.P. (2009)(Ed.): Correcting Fallacies about Educational and Psychological Testing. Washington: American Psychological Association.

Rud, S. (2006): Erobringen af Grønland: Opdagelsesrejser, etnologi og forstanderskab i attenhundredetallet. In: Historisk Tidsskrift, 106: 2, 488 – 520.
Shohamy, E. (2004): Assessment in multicultural societies: Applying democratic principles and practices to language testing. In: B. e. Norton: Critical Pedagogies and Language Learning. Cambridge, 72 – 92.
Spelling, K. (1963): Miljøets indflydelse på intelligensudviklingen – specielt med henblik på "racemæssige" forskelle. Copenhagen.
Thaler: (2007): A Tale of Three Communities. In: Scandinavian Journal of History, 32: 2, 141 – 166.
Vedung, E. (1991): Utvärdering i politik och förvaltning. Lund.
Ydesen, C. (2010): The Rise of High-Stakes Educational Testing in Denmark, 1920-1970. PhD Dissertation: Danish School of Education.

Post-Colonial Education in West Africa: The Relevance of Local Cultural Teachings for Understanding School, Community, and Society Interface

George J. Sefa Dei, University of Toronto, Canada

A contemporary challenge for African education is how schooling can respond to the needs and challenges of a diverse student body (Dei et al. 2006). How we are to deal with the systemic fragmentation that dislocates and alienates African learners from their own histories, cultures, knowledge, languages, and sense of place is an equally critical concern. 'Coloniality' and colonial relations of power dissociate many learners from their own local cultural and experiential knowledge and the authenticity of local voice. When I speak of 'coloniality' I am not referring to the Eurocentric theorizations of colonialisms. Rather I speak of the colonial as anything that is imposed or dominating – not simply alien or foreign (Dei 2000, Dei & Asgharzadeh 2001). It is important to see coloniality and colonial power relations as a process mediated through the hierarchization of the notion of social difference. The concept of difference is about knowing selves, cultures and histories, as much as about our spiritual, racial, gender, class, sexual identities, etc. The making of difference should also be seen as a historical signifying process tied to the idea of identity. However, there is a limitation when identity is simply understood as a signifier of difference. We must understand social difference as a process of thought as well as a mode of being.

Dealing with social difference in schooling implies both, a consideration of how we create 'communities of learners' as well as reflections on how we may affirm multiple ways of knowing emanating from local culture, history and politics. To understand post-colonial education in Africa, it is important that we examine those moments and spaces in which educators are bridging different systems of knowledge to educate contemporary learners. How do educators try to help their students to develop a sense of ownership in their own learning? How may students be enabled to identify with the learning process and to articulate a sense of connectedness and belonging in their schools? To identify such local teaching approaches may also help to develop teaching strategies that create a sense of moral and civic responsibility, community belonging and identification.

As noted in another publication (Dei 2011), informal Indigenous education was a prevalent aspect of pre-colonial education. Today, it still plays a role in the socialization of youth. Through Indigenous education the individual is socialized to be a member of the community. Parents, elders and the family were central figures shaping and educating the child. Indigenous forms of education involved the entire community as educators. Education as conveyed through local cultural resource knowledge was passed on from one generation to another, and in a manner that assisted the youth to practically and intellectually not only understand their natural environment, but also, their particular social function in society. Traditional African education focused on the molding of character and morality and the development of skills necessary for active participation in social life. Unfortunately, colonial education was not very interested in such Indigenous forms of education. This is evident by the fact that colonial schools emphasized the training of personnel to fit the requirements of colonial administration and governance which was very much connected to Western systems and ideas of development. African Indigenous cultures and traditions were either devalued or denigrated. African history was that constructed from the European presence rather than understanding history as a totality of lived experiences of African peoples encompassing many years of Indigenous cultural and historical development, as well as struggles and resistances to design our[1] own futures. Colonial schooling emphasized literacy as skills in reading, writing and mathematics. It downplayed local knowledge systems in science, technology mathematics, culture, vocation and the arts (see Foster 1965; Fafunwa 1974, 1982; Fafunwa & Aisiku 1982; Sifuna 1990, 1992; White 1996; Quist 2003). Indeed, the ills of colonial education have been commented upon by many critical African writers. Shizha (2005), for example, discusses the challenges of post-colonial African education as it seeks to shed itself from the tentacles of colonial education. She points out that "colonial education corrupted the thinking and sensibilities of Africans" being filled with abnormal complexes which "de-Africanized and alienated them from their socio-cultural milieu. . . Africans were denied their cultural development. By denying Indigenous people their self-expression and historical memories, colonialism then denies their cultural process" (p. 69).

Nonetheless, despite the deep impacts of European colonial schooling in Africa, Indigenous forms of learning and socialization have persisted and are being transformed to offer knowledge, skills and capabilities to youth in many communities. African parents and Elders have continued to socialize and instruct the young with teachings about Indigenous cultures, traditions, cosmologies, songs, myths and mythologies, folktales and proverbs. The understanding is that there is a wealth of knowledge to be gained by critically learning about Indigenous cultures, traditions, histories and cosmologies as a way of human survival in a rapidly changing world. The challenge is for post-colonial African education and schooling to tap into such wealth of traditional and Indigenous forms of education in the service of educating the contemporary learner. One possible

1 I employ "we/our" in this paper to implicate myself as African-Canadian educator in the discussion.

area for such integration of Indigenous local cultural resource knowledge into the schooling, education and socialization of youth is through proverbs, folktales and other forms of folkloric production. These are important sites and sources of knowledge that offer critical teachings about everyday living and coping with challenges in life.

Within every community there are well-established cultural resource knowledge systems that guide social interactions and moral conduct. Such teachings are embedded in everyday and longstanding cultural practices. Since the production and validation of knowledge is always about the exercise of power relations, I also emphasize the need to disentangle the colonial forms of knowing and "schooling" from forms of education that teach local culture, history and traditions in ways that critically address the colonization of the African citizen.

1. Research context, objectives, literature review, methods of empiric research

This article is based on the preliminary findings of a longitudinal research project conducted in Ghana and Nigeria between 2007-9 examining the pedagogic and instructional relevance of African proverbs and folktales in youth education, specifically in the areas of character and moral development of the young learner.

These African case studies contribute to a growing body of research on the role of Indigenous education in moral and character education and violence prevention. A major objective of the research project as a whole was to understand youth violence from the vantage points of learners and educators as well as to understand how a local cultural resource base can contribute to violence prevention amongst youth by developing a strong character through the adherence to locally-generated moral and civic responsibilities.

After a brief outline of the objectives of the research project, I will summarize some of the most relevant insights gained from our literature review and then proceed to detail the methods employed in the African case studies.

1.1 Research objectives

The overarching interest of the case study was guided by five research objectives:

a) to examine the existing literature on what is known about the impact of teaching character/values education in general, and the implications for Canadian, North American and African schooling;

b) to understand the teaching of discipline, punishment and respect for authority from the perspectives of youth, teachers, school administrators, parents and communities;
c) to document past, current and long-term institutional approaches for dealing with youth discipline and punishment, and respect for authority in educational settings;
d) to examine the instructional, pedagogic and communicative values and challenges in local Indigenous teachings (proverbs, fables, folktales, myths, etc.) about the lack of discipline, and respect for self, peers and authority; and,
e) to suggest ways this study can enhance learning for African and North American youth by working with educators to develop learning and instructional materials and to develop strategies to implement character/values education in Ontario schools.

1.2 Literature review – a brief summary

As already touched upon, many communities utilize proverbs, parables, folktales and mythologies to convey meanings of society, nature and cultural interactions (e.g. Abrahams 1967, 1968a, 1968b, 1972; Dorson 1972; Taylor 1934; Wolfgang and Dundas 1981). We know that a number of Indigenous traditions focus more on storytelling than proverbs and fables. Yet, in Indigenous epistemologies we see how story telling conveys powerful meanings similar to those encoded in proverbs, parables, fables, and tales in other Indigenous contexts (Firth 1926). Within the stories a critical learner can get a powerful sense of the pedagogic, instructional and communicative relevance of such cultural knowledge. For example, Johnson (1993, 2003) shows North American Ojibwa mythology as rich, complex, densely meaningful, and mysterious. His works provide readers with a succinct understanding of Ojibwa peoples' lives, legends, and beliefs. Like stories and mythologies, proverbs when told often evoke an act of self-reflection from the learner/listener. As powerful knowledge forms, proverbs, folktales, and stories offer a deeper level of understanding and appreciation of the community's place in the larger social, physical, and cultural realm of life.

In African contexts, as in those of North America, there is a growing body of works dealing with the broad theme of 'Indigenous knowledge' (Dei 2011). There are also a number of texts documenting African proverbs and their cultural meanings and interpretations (see, for example, Kudadjie 1996, Yankah 1989; 1995; Opoku 1997, 1975; Ogede 1993; Kalu 1991; Pachocinshi 1996; Abubakre & Reichmuth 1997). So far much of the focus has been on proverbs. Arguably, the issue of local cultural resource knowledge as contained in proverbs, parables, fables, myths, mythologies, and folklore and their specific pedagogic, instructional, and communicative significance in enhancing learning outcomes for youth in contemporary school settings has not received adequate critical exploration (e.g. Boateng 1990, Bascom 1965). Yet this local cultural knowledge is relevant for the lessons they offer in promoting the goals of collective responsibility, community building, mutual interdependence, and the rights and responsibilities of citizenship. It also affirms the importance of multiple sources of knowledge in schooling and education.

The epistemic saliency of local subjects is embedded in an awareness of the self and one's place within a collective. Knowing the self, community and culture is important in order to appreciate the challenges and how we respond. Since indigeneity and issues of identity are powerfully linked, we cannot dismiss the power of Indigenous and local cultural knowledge. In fact, as Friedman (1992) also notes struggles over identity have serious implications when local peoples lose both their ontological and epistemological foundations. While culture may be negotiated, questions and issues of identity, history and the politics of affirming local knowledge are not negotiable for local peoples. Local knowledge contained in proverbs and parables are significant for expressing the intellectual agency of communities. Local cultural resource knowledge that allows for a critical reflection on past experiences and histories to respond to everyday problems and find solutions to problems is very relevant. Claiming such knowledge does not mean taking recourse to a mythic or romanticized past. Arguably, what is reclaimed in living memory has never been lost; it has always been there as competing history. The recourse to the past, culture, history and tradition has become a question of emphasis and recognition of the relevance of such bodies and systems of knowledge. The claim to a past is not to romanticize this past. Claiming knowledge of the past, history and cultures is an awareness and understanding that all communities have their own systems of thought and practices that need to be uncovered, examined, scrutinized, understood, and disseminated as a necessary exercise in collective knowledge production. The past is still much with us. It is living present. It is neither a fossilized, static nor a period without blemish. Furthermore, no tradition is immune to criticism. The present is constitutive of what it is not, namely, the past (see also Lattas 1993). Therefore, we must understand the past and present if we are to carve out a successful path or direction to the future. Reclaiming knowledge about past histories and cultural experiences calls for a critical interrogation of knowledge in order to understand the sites of empowerment as well as disempowerment for groups. Such intellectual exercises calls for understanding the successes, failures and challenges people have encountered in their lives and communities. The past, culture, history and traditions are thus not simply reclaimed for glorification or mere celebration. While celebrating a past is important, it is through the recognition of important sites and sources of knowledge depicting past actions and events that are key to decolonization projects. This is a realization that the past, a people's history and local cultural resource base have roles to play in the search for answers to daily concerns and problems.

1.3 The case studies in Ghana and Nigeria

African schools, like schools in North America and elsewhere, continue to search for educational approaches that are adequate for a diverse group of learners. Of specific pedagogic interest in this study of African proverbs is to examine the practices and measures educators, school administrators, parents and communities institute to address forms of youth discipline and character education and how local Indigenous knowledge facilitates school teaching and learning. The broader goal of this study is to articulate an Indigenous philosophy for understanding questions of character, values, discipline and punishment, respect for oneself, peers, authority and the wider community that can be relevant to classroom teaching and learning for youth in the educational system.

1.3.1 Gathering data: The voices of African educators

Throughout the entire research period, 2007-9, a dozen focus group discussions had been organized together as workshop session with teacher students, teacher trainers, and other educational specialists. In addition to the focus groups, a total of eighty-five (85) individual interviews were conducted with twenty-five (25) educators; twenty (20) Elders / parents and forty (40) students drawn from the local universities, secondary schools and community colleges, as well local communities in Ghana and for a brief period in Nigeria. The focus of the interviews was the use and meanings of local proverbs and African Indigenous philosophies, as well as the instructional, pedagogic and communicative values and challenges in local teaching using proverbs, fables, folktales, myths, etc. about discipline, and respect for self, peers and authority.[2]

1.3.2 Analysing the data

The interviews were tape-recorded in face-to-face individual and group discussion sessions; the recordings were later transcribed. The interviews were conducted largely in English except for discussions with some Elders and parents where the local language was used for later translation into English. Transcribed

2 There is currently an on-going major study that extends the educational research sites to other regions in Ghana, Kenya and Nigeria for in-depth comparative analysis.

data were analyzed using a program for qualitative data analysis (Ethnograph). All files of the tape transcriptions were coded and names of people replaced by pseudonyms before entry into the qualitative data analysis program. There were various stages of revising the codes in order to systematically enter them into the Ethnograph. Throughout the data analysis we made notes in the transcripts highlighting issues of theoretical and practical significance. New codes were developed along the way as new information emerged. Relevant themes of the taped transcriptions and discussions have been selected for further interpretation and analysis for this paper. The focus in this article is specifically on the narratives of college educators and teacher students at the university. The research data has revealed rich material for analysis and understanding of the issues of the relevance of local cultural resource knowledge for the education of the contemporary learner.

The analysis of the data from the two case studies in Ghana and Nigeria is still a work-in-progress, but one of the most important preliminary findings so far is an overwhelming confirmation of my basic research assumption that a number of African educators employ proverbs in class on a regular basis, both directly and indirectly, and attribute important functions to their use in the education of the young.

For the following section I have selected a number of quotations from the data to indicate:

a) the spectrum of functions accorded to proverbs in education by African educators; and,
b) the important issues of contestation in the employment of traditional proverbs in modern, post-colonial social contexts as will be illustrated in particular with regard to gender issues.

2. Preliminary study findings

In this section, I present some of the narrative accounts of Ghanaian and Nigerian educators, who in this paper comprise college educators and student teachers at universities, as they speak of the significance of local cultural knowledge (specifically proverbs) to offer directions for the ways of rethinking schooling and education in African contexts. The narratives also highlight ways of approaching the education and socialization of the contemporary young learner grounded in more critical ways of looking at local culture, traditions, values, norms and practices as dynamic forms of knowledge to be reclaimed for positive (solution-oriented) ends.

2.1 Functions and problems in the educational use of proverbs

Many of my informants claim that proverbs can assist in the task of educating youth. In particular, they argue that proverbs can teach youth to be responsible and act in an appropriate manner to address problems of disrespect, the lack of discipline and anomie. Family head and Senior School Administrator of Academics in Ghana, Nana Bodine (pseudonym), is well-known for his knowledge of local proverbs. He explains the uses of proverbs and why he uses proverbs in his teachings:

> I use them to illustrate points. Now, when you are in a situation and you are able to use examples or illustrations it actually throws more light on it. And, the listener is firmly grounded in the knowledge of the expression that you are giving the person. It is just like writing an essay or English composition or composition in any language and then you use examples or illustrations. [File 09: Text Units 19 - 41]

School as well as college teachers who utilize proverbs in their teaching contend that they reach the students more directly because it gets them to think and to use their analytical skills to solve problems. This may be a shift away from rote learning and regurgitation, which have been the standard pedagogical practices in most traditional African education contexts. It was apparent in our interview that proverbs have served Nana Bodine well in his role as a traditional Elder, i.e. family head. African society, in Ghana and Nigeria alike, expects their Elders to be embodiments of rich cultural knowledge. Bodine wants to continue this tradition and to impact such local cultural knowledge to the youth he teaches at school. In placing the knowledge and use of proverbs in the school system, Nana Bodine is emphatic in his disappointment about the way local languages are being handled:

> It is unfortunate we are not promoting proverbs because simply because even we are dropping the main language at a cost. So, I would wish that we try to bring the various languages back. Now even though English has been the medium of expression because most of the books we are using are written in English, it should go side by side with our language. We should not throw them away completely. So that there should even be times that maybe just like some of the eastern nations we can go all out with our own language. You see it is more meaningful, that is our first language. And, it is more meaningful and we understand things better in that language. So I think if we are able to incorporate the language in the school syllabus, the proverbs are part of our language and we will develop them. And it will help. [File 09: Text Units 320 - 335]

Nana Bodine's colleague, Bafoah who teaches core and elective mathematics at the senior high school level in Ghana, insists proverbs do teach about responsibility. Notwithstanding the language issue, Bafoah also sees the relevance of proverbs in the school system now. Proverbs can be convenient for everyday conversations once a learner is well-versed in such cultural knowledge. Additionally, Bafoah sees some differences in teaching proverbs to students in secondary school as opposed to those in the elementary school, particularly in terms of pedagogical approach:

> I think in the secondary school you will not have many problems because with the teenagers, a lot of them are intelligent. And they can reason through what you say. But at the lower forms, I think some of them . . . in terms of maturity – they are not matured [*sic*] enough sometimes to understand some of these proverbs. Because some of the proverbs are heavy and they carry a lot of weight. So, I think at the lower level there will be that problem of breaking it down for them to understand. [File 04: Text Units 213 - 227]

There must be a different pedagogical approach to teaching proverbs in schools depending on the grade level. With maturity comes a deeper appreciation of proverbs. From Bafoah we learn that proverbs are more than mere "illustrations" of lessons. Thus, an adequate understanding of the proverbs cannot be taken for granted. Proverbs call for sophisticated reading, analysis, interpretation and understanding. A critical examination of proverbs requires deeper level of analysis, interpretation as well as critical discussions that may possibly involve broaching controversial issues and contentions.

2.2 Proverbs as educational tool in character development and moral education

Master of Arts in Library studies student Danny, who hails from the Upper West region of Ghana and had taught at the primary school level for five years prior to enrolling in graduate school, also sees proverbs contributing to the character development about questions of morality.

> Yes . . . on the character development of morality. As I said, it helps us when you hear of proverbs it doesn't come out unnecessarily from the elders or from any other body. An incident normally happens and out of it the proverb comes to correct it. So, it is some sort of trying to remind us that what is happening now or what we are going through has happened before and therefore it is coded in such a statement. So maybe, the elder will tell them look at things this way. So when the proverb is given it reawakens you. It puts you back in a frame of mind that "no, what I have done maybe is not good." Because at the end of every action that you do and the proverb comes, somebody is suffering and it is not meant to be like that. That is what I see as the impact that it is creating on character formation. [File 18: Text Units 25 - 38]

In a focus group discussion with a group of College of Education student teachers in Nigeria, it was a unanimous view that as far as youth character development is concerned both, the home and the school, have important roles to play. But it was also noted that times are changing and traditional roles of the home, family and educators have also changed. As two student teacher participants echoed such views:

> A: Even apart from that charity begins at home. Even if the parent or the mother is imparting that morality into the children and she herself is not practicing it, I think the child or the children will not accept it because they will be looking at the parent and will ask what my parents are teaching me or what they want me to emulate – are they doing the right thing?
>
> B: But I don't want to accept that because most of our parents.... you know we are in a different age. Okay, consider a mother that was not trained very well, how you want that mother to impart good morals to her children. It is because this is in schools. [File 12: Text Units 196 - 208]

Both respondents believe in the importance of moral education to instill discipline and sense of responsibility in youth. Youth learn by example. The student teachers see the combined responsibilities of the home and school in the socialization of the learner. Role modeling is as critical and just as relevant as what is learned in a textbook. Teachers have many avenues and teachable moments to make an impact of their students. In a focus group discussion with some University teachers, when asked how each promotes character development in a learner, one participant duly noted:

> Most often what we do is . . . most of us we do write, too. So we mentioned something here about modeling. Most often what we do is we create models that these young ones can actually emulate in our plays; in our productions and I think this is the best way we have been doing this. [File 13: Text Units 884 - 928]

By showcasing positive role models through texts they produce, teachers can help young people lead exemplary lives. Young people learn by example, and they are influenced by what they see around them. Teachers influence students through their actions as well as what they teach students through the text.

2.3 Issues of contest and power: the gendering of proverbs

Gender divisions and demarcations in society can sometimes receive currency in local proverbs and cultural traditions, and for the educator, they can be important pedagogic sites that raise questions of gender relations in society. Nana Bodine, a senior high school administrator for academics and family head, brings a gender-based interpretation of the proverbs. As an expert of local proverbs and their role in school teachings, his analysis is interesting:

> You know our society is such that it has been male dominated. And most of the rules that exist in our society have been done by men. But, I believe that even this . . . female sexual mutilation has been initiated by men because they just wanted to stifle the freedom of these women. . . . Yes, in fact there are some expressions which actually do not encourage women to come out. Another one is "Obaa yen oguan a ne mma woton won." [A female who rears a sheep does not sell its offspring] Or "Abofra bo nwa onbo akyekyere." [A child catches a snail not the porcupine] This is just to control the young ones [and women] so that we don't give them the freedom to express themselves. It is there but maybe there are reasons for that. We have to dig for the meaning and know the reason why they were doing that. You see, how eh . . . especially among the Akans, inheritance was matrilineal. We are criticizing it so much but we do not know its origin. So we rather have to try and seek the meaning and then refine them instead of criticizing them entirely. [File 09: Text Units 184 - 201]

He admits to the patriarchal nature of society and how certain local proverbs simply reinforce that. But he also exercises some caution for first understanding why certain proverbs persist in the first place. This may call for a critical gender analysis to understand and expose how patriarchy works in society to subordinate women and children to men and adults. Such critical analysis cannot simply be read as a critique of culture. Ghanaian high school teacher Akua Asantewaah also points to the way some proverbs privilege more the status of the man in the society. She offers some suggestions for the teacher who is working with proverbs to use proverbs that highlight and elevate the status of all groups:

> Most of our people they used to . . . It is like most of our proverbs were not that fair to women. So, most of them were like trying to put down the woman and then raise the man. But, I think that maybe we should try to get other proverbs that will bring a balance between the genders male and female. . . . I think we are still on the proverbs that were maybe there before we were born. So, maybe in future like language students and teachers and other people we should try to see if we can also come out with our own proverbs. And such proverbs shouldn't be against the women. It should try to bring about unity and those things. [File 11: Text Units 135 - 156]

Such exercise may entail examining the whole repertoire of local proverbs available and to teach the ones that have valuable lessons for learners. Engaging both genders in education around local proverbs might well be beneficial for the wider society. Tamipiah is a student teacher studying human rights education at university in Ghana. When asked about who are the custodians of proverbs, he brings a gender-based observation about the teaching and use of proverbs in homes, schools or within communities:

> As for the usage, I will say that they [proverbs] are mostly used by the elders and the elderly males but when it comes to the teaching of proverbs, sometimes it is the women who stay with the children more at home. And, they tend to teach the chil-

> dren more than the male adult will teach. As for the usage, I will go more for the males. As for the teaching, it is the females who do it more than the males. [File 17: Text Units 163 - 174]

Tamipiah recognizes the special place and standing of women in communities and their knowledge on local issues and affairs. Males may speak in proverbs far more habitually than women, possibly to lend authority to their speech, but when it comes to teaching and socializing children in the homes, families and communities, it is women who as a rule bear the brunt of such undertaking. Danny who hails from Lawra in Upper West region in Ghana, and is studying Master of Arts in Library Studies student agrees there are important gender dimensions in proverbs:

> ...there are gender dimensions. Men (in my language; the Dagati language) speak in a certain way and it is generally accepted by all but there are certain type of language or certain types of words that a woman cannot even mention. Like, for instance, a woman cannot just sit down and just start talking about, let's say, sex in the open. But men can just sit down and just talk about sex even in the presence of the woman. But if a woman should speak that way, the community will take such a lady to be a spoilt child. When a man speaks the same thing, in the same obscene way, it is accepted by society. So I will say that yes, in the gender dimension the women cannot speak certain languages and bring out their ideas in a certain way. Even during teaching, a woman cannot even talk about sex but the man can easily talk about sex and feel free. So there are gender dimensions which we need to discard [File 18: Text Units 129 - 142]

Tamipiah emphasizes that the gendered aspects of proverbs can be found not only in who is teaching or saying what, but whose speech is usually sanctioned. This societal sanction does not always help in the socialization of children and he argues some of these sanctions against women must be abandoned. The importance of bringing a critical gender perspective must be cautioned by the ways proverbs are culturally bound and contested. Proverbs call for deep conceptual thinking and if one fails to understand the local culture one may equally misunderstand some aspect of their proverbs. A critical teaching of culture, tradition and local proverbs calls for examining the sites of empowerment and disempowerment in various cultures and traditions. While proverbs offer useful instructional lessons of moral and character building, social responsibility, community belonging, understanding of culture, history, identity and sense of place, proverbs should also be subjected to critical analysis to uncover how such knowledge sources can also continue to disempower ethnic minorities, women and disadvantaged groups. This is particularly the case when tradition is taken at face value and is either misinterpreted or discussed out of context.

3. Concluding discussion

Judging from the views expressed in the above quotations, African proverbs form an important part in the education of the young in the postcolonial African schools, even though it has not been acknowledged in the past, let alone researched. This presentation of preliminary results from the two case studies only hints at the complexities involved with regard to social diversity and power structures when cultural resource knowledge in the form of proverbs is taken up in schools. The following discussion outlines a variety of issues to be addressed in the ongoing analysis and interpretation of the qualitative data as well as in future research.

How do we connect teachings of community, social responsibility, moral and character education to local cultural resource knowledge and, more particularly, to the question of re-visioning schooling and education in the African context of equity? The growing literature of the interrelated subjects of character/moral and citizenship education suggest these consist of knowledge, skills, and dispositions that can ensure effective learning outcomes for youth in terms of the acquisition and application of knowledge for social change. The studies of Kohlberg (1981, 1984) and McClellan (1999) show that the question of moral education is not simply about teaching "right and wrong", but teaching youth to engage in critical thinking to make independent and informed decisions about their lives and their worlds. While it has long been observed that moral education cannot be separated from the school curriculum (Dewey 1909/1975), sufficient attention has not been paid to all levels of the school system. Similarly, when equity has been under consideration, its conceptualization has been limited to the question of access, usually in terms of gender and class (e.g. Bloch et al. 1998) and in terms of unequal allocation of resources across the respective societies. Equity in African education milieus is under-researched and under-theorized, particularly as it concerns the pluralistic contexts of social difference in relation to schooling experiences and the impact of educational outcomes. In pluralistic contexts, educators have to confront questions about whose values and what values are taught in schools with an eye toward developing a *caring community* of learners. Not surprisingly, the vital issue how teachers themselves understand moral and character education needs further exploration. Ryan and Bohlin's (2000) examinations of character education in North American teacher preparation programs raises the possibility of enhanced teacher preparation curricula. But teacher education needs to take into account the actual practices and views of pre-service and in-service educators. The case studies above give voice to the views of Ghanaian and Nigerian educators and student teachers, provide a first insight into the current perspectives of (future) African teachers.

Two key questions that need further research are:

1) In pluralistic contexts, what do we know of moral education that focuses on the relationships between and among individuals, groups, schools and civil society?
2) How are the public issues of citizenship and belonging reflected in teaching respect and discipline for oneself, one's peers and one's authority in a variety of contexts?

If character education is viewed as a vital tool for preparing youth for effective learning outcomes, then we must respond to other political and contextual issues and challenges that confront education in pluralistic contexts. Within the Ghanaian and Nigerian contexts, for example, this study has documented communicative approaches in which teachers sought to instill traditional values and virtues in youth to ensure discipline, respect for self, peers and authority. But how are such localized education efforts, as contained in Indigenous philosophies and concepts, relevant in helping confront some of the challenges of modernity across space and time? Character and values education can only proceed from a multi-centric place that is reflective of the community of learners. This means that teachers need to know more about the diversity of pedagogical and content approaches to character education in schools.

Arguably, schooling and formal education in Africa has been about technological development. But in emphasizing the goal of national consciousness, this popularized 'postmodern' education in Africa has denied heterogeneity among local populations as if difference itself was a problem. With this orientation, as argued elsewhere (Dei 2004a, b; Dei et al. 2006), formal education at one level has undoubtedly helped create and maintain the glaring disparities and inequities structured along the lines of ethnicity, culture, language, religion, gender and class, which persist and grow. At another level, differences, as it can be discerned from the varied and multiple pedagogic and instructional approaches in pluralistic contexts, have been glossed over. This pattern, however, can be disrupted. Formal education can acknowledge difference and diversity in student populations, teaching and instructional methods, sources of knowledge etc., while, at the same time, highlighting commonalities of pedagogic and content approaches among learners with conflicting interests. Ultimately, it is such holistic education that can contribute to both national integration and social reconstruction. To do so, though, transformative educational change must encompass more than the reform of existing curricular and pedagogical practices. It must respond to problems of knowledge production, interrogation, validation and dissemination as well as address schooling practices that discriminate and alienate some learners. Learners must own their knowledge. They must identify with school knowledge, teaching and instructional practices. Learners must be emboldened to tap into their local cultural resource base. Education that focuses on the social and cultural values which address conflict and encourage reciprocity and peace is most likely to succeed. To promote the democratic participation of all citizens in a project of nation-building and to provide lasting solutions to human problems, education in Africa must acknowledge and affirm difference in the sites and sources of knowledge production within the context of pursuing equity and social justice.

Teachers within post-colonial African schools contend with many challenges as they search for ways to educate the contemporary learner to be grounded in her or his history, culture, ancestry, language, identity and sense of place. Because colonial education was primarily interested in the 'end product', or trained personnel ready to assist in colonial governance and administration, African learners were simply taught in schools to master prescribed content and skills with little attention to teaching strategies beyond rote learning and regurgitation. Indeed, rote learning and regurgitation became – and still are – the standard educational practices in most traditional African schools. In many ways this form of education is more about schooling than education, or the acquisition of knowledge – rather than skills – for individual and collective social action. It is education which allows people to know about their worlds and to act and live meaningful in such worlds. It is important for us to acknowledge the historical roots of the colonial developments regarding African education while we think through creative ways of transforming schooling and education to serve the needs of African peoples (Abdi & Cleghorn 2005).

Contemporary African schooling and education has a large responsibility to prepare the current generation of learners not only to claim their own identity, sense of place and history, but also, to continue to write history by finding lasting solutions to the many challenges that confront communities today. The African learner must be strengthened to imagine, design and create new futures of which we can collectively be proud. We need a transformed education that helps learners acquire new competencies, skills, critical knowledge base and learning processes for civic engagement and responsibility that are rooted firmly in African history, culture, tradition, identity and politics. Education should be about building a sustainable environment as 'communities' and 'communities of learners' for enhancing collective work. Our institutions of learning have the challenge of cultivating multiple and Indigenous, cultural ways of knowing in positive, solution-oriented ways. In effect, schooling and education in Africa cannot abandon African culture, knowledge system and Indigenous languages. These are essential aspects of our African identity and personality, and self/collective respect. Schools have a responsibility not only to teach these ideals and ideas/knowledge, but also to uphold them.

There is more that can be learned from traditional Indigenous knowledge systems. For example, knowledge about traditional pharmacology, traditional systems of farming, oral literature, traditional agro-forestry, soils, climate and vegetation classification, folkloric production all add to our rich repertoire of intellectual tradition of science, technological arts and literature. Such knowledge, when engaged, is local, contextualized learning that can assist in the contemporary education of the young African learner in his/her community's rich historical experience with local science, technology, language, arts and culture. Indigenous knowledge systems, as embedded in local religions, folklore, celebrations, healing practices, food preparation, oral tradition, pageantry, and work activities, all reveal local understandings of the connections of society, culture and nature. Indigenous African cultural media, such as folk music and dance, can serve as useful tools for teachers. Folklore and proverbs contain a profound richness of the thought processes and language of Indigenous peoples. They constitute important communicative tools by reinforcing the epistemic saliency of peoples whose ways of knowing are often devalued or negated in the formal educational arena. If our institutions of higher learning cannot teach and uphold these local knowledge systems, they are bound to be lost. When those systems are lost, we also lose our identities. A people without culture, history and language are de-rooted souls!

In claiming local cultural resource knowledge that herald issues of the past, culture, ancestral knowledge, history and heritage and language, the question of post-colonial identities become relevant. A number of postcolonial writers (e.g., Gilroy 1993, 2000; Appiah 1992, 2005; Gates 1992, 2010; Hall 2005, 2007a, 2007b) have often criticized the evocation of the past as problematic because of the implied claim to an "authentic", unmediated past. Stuart Hall's discussion of the problems of "postcolonial cultural identities" (2005, 2007a, 2007b) reinforces the assertion that reclaiming local cultural knowledge does not mean taking recourse to a mythic or romanticized past. However, Hall (2005) is rather skeptical about any attempts to recover an "authentic" pre-colonial African identity, undamaged by the experience of colonial dominance and oppression, as much as he recognizes that such attempts and their politics may serve as psychological resources for resistance. Hall discusses the complexities involved in the negotiation and the re-invention of "postcolonial identities." I share such concerns to an extent. My point of departure is that the re-assertion of identities at any time in a people's history always recognizes the complexities of identity and the fact that all identities are metaphorically in constant flux. Therefore, "authentic" does, in my reading, not imply "pure", "unfettered" or "uncontaminated". In this sense, I appreciate the importance of (re)claiming African identities as an exercise of decolonization that recognizes the authenticity of African voices and experiences. Such identities stand in contrast to a singular identity which is often constructed within Euro-American hegemony and ideology.

In this paper, I have written from an anti-colonial perspective inspired by Fanonian thinking that recognizes the importance of history, culture, place, language and local [Indigenous] knowledge as conferring and emblematic of particular identities. Such identities when constructed from ancestral experience, history and local cultural resource knowledge should be seen as 'authentic' and valid in their own right and yet subjected to interrogations without dismissal. The issues raised by Nana Bodine, Akua Asantewaah, Tamipiah, and Danny, as quoted above, provide important clues as to how this challenge might be taken up.

The construction of such identities accord power as well as subject intellectual agency to the colonized body and marginalized voice. The colonial encounter has been marked by resistance through the assertion of the discursive power of the colonized peoples who were determined to assert local voice and experience. These resistance efforts were carried out through individual and collective action as well as subjective politics of the colonized subject. Through the Fanonian and anti-colonial prism we come to understand embodied Indigenous epistèmes as experienced through the socio-cultural and political field of the African experiences. The intellectual interest in claiming authenticity rests in the experience of the African identity today which has been historically shaped through many cultural formations and spaces. An understanding of the Indigenous African experiences constitutes a form of valid/ legitimate knowing. The post-colonial African identity is about relations to particular histories, cultures, places and identities that also symbolize particular ways of knowing. Explicating the Indigenous African presence and experience as sites of knowing entails raising highly relevant theoretical and philosophical questions about how we come to know the African identity. For example, how does Indigenous African culture as a way of knowing form integrative spaces for the African identity? What are the responsibilities, consequences and/or implications for African voices when the politics of identification and the politics of identity work erode the voices of shared colonial histories? How might we speak about ethnicity, difference and culture without diluting the responsibility of those speaking about Indigenous African identity or identities? Where does knowledge reside (e.g., in bodies and cultural memories)? What counts as knowledge about a people's experience, who constructs such knowledge and how do they do so? How do we come to know and understand such knowledge? To reiterate then, one of the challenges for contemporary African education is to take culture, history, and ancestral experience as significant sites of knowledge and work with these in the education of the contemporary African learner.

Acknowledgements

I would like to acknowledge the assistance of Dr. Meredith Lordan, Munya Kabba, Jaggiet Gill, Camille Logan, Rosina Agyepong, Paul Adjei, Dr. Anthony Kola-Olusanya and Marlon Simmons all of the Ontario Institute for Studies in Education at the University of Toronto (OISE/UT) who, at various times, worked as graduate researchers with me on various aspects of the project. I am forever grateful to Professor Kola Raheem and the staff of the Centre For School and Community Science and Technology Studies (SACOST), University of Education, Winneba, Ghana, as well as Mr. Paul Akom, former Dean of Students at the University of Education at Winneba for their invaluable assistance on my research project. My Visiting Professorship for the 2007-8 school year at SACOST and Winneba afforded me the opportunities to make contacts which ensured success for my study. Similarly, I am indebted to Mr. Tola Olujuwon and the Provost, faculty, staff and students of the Adeniran Ogunsanya College of Education, Otto/Ijanikin, Lagos State, Nigeria where I was a Visiting Scholar for a short period in the fall of 2007. Also, many thanks to Messrs Ebenezer Aggrey, Andrew Osei-Poku, Alfred Agyarko, Martin Duodo, Kwaku Nii, and Dickson K. Darko, all who served as my local research assistants on various aspects of the project. My sincere gratitude goes to the many Ghanaian and Nigerian educators, students and parents who gave their time for the interviews during my fieldwork. The Literacy and Numeracy Secretariat of the Ontario Ministry of Education and the Social Sciences and Humanities Research Council of Canada (SSHRC) have provided funding for this study at various stages. I thank the anonymous reviewers of the paper for their comments and suggestions which helped strengthen the discussion.

Literature

Abdi, A. & Cleghorn, A. (eds. 2005): Issues in African Education: Sociological Perspectives. New York.

Abrahams, R. (1967): On Proverb Collecting and Proverb Collection. In: Proverbium, 8, 181 – 184.

Abrahams, R. (1968a): A Rhetoric of Everyday Life: Traditional Conversational Genres. In: Southern Folklore Quarterly, 32, 44 – 59.

Abrahams R. (1968b): Introductory Remarks in a Rhetorical Theory of Folklore. In: Journal of American Folklore, 81, 143 – 158.

Abrahams, R. (1972): Proverbs and Proverbial Expression. In: Dorson, R. (ed): Folklore and Folklife. Chicago, 117 – 127.

Abubakre, R. D & Reichmuth, S. (1997): Arabic Writing between Global and Local Culture: Scholars and Poets in Yorubaland. Research in African Literatures, 28: 3, 183 – 209.

Appiah, K.A. (1992): In My Father's House: Africa in the Philosophy of Culture. New York.

Appiah, K.A. (2005): The Ethics of Identity. Online available at: <http://www.pupress.princeton.edu/titles/7806.html> Princeton University Press http://www.worldlingo.com/ma/enwiki/en/Princeton_University_Press [no access date given.]

Bascom, W. (1965): The Forms of Folklore: Prose Narratives. In: Journal of American Folklore, 78: 307, 3 – 20.

Bloch, M. J., Beoku-Betts, J. & Tabachnick, B. (eds. 1998): Women and Education in Sub-Saharan Africa: Power, Opportunities and Constraints. Boulder.

Boateng, F. (1990): African Traditional Education: A Tool for Intergenerational Communication. In: Asante, M. K. & Asante, K. W. (eds.): African Culture: The Rhythms of Unity. Trenton, NJ, 109 – 122.

Dei, G. J. S. (2000): The Role of Indigenous Knowledges in the Academy. In: International Journal of Inclusive Education, 4: 2, 39 – 56.

Dei, G. J. S. (2004a): Dealing with Difference: Ethnicity and Gender in the Context of Schooling in Ghana. In: International Journal of Educational Development, 24, 343 – 359.

Dei, G. J. S. (2004b): Schooling and Education in Africa: The Case of Ghana. Trenton, NJ.

Dei, G. J. S. (2011): Education and Socialization: A Ghanaian Case Study of Local Cultural Knowledge as Formal and Informal Education for Learners. In: Canadian and International Education [under review for publication].

Dei, G. J. S. & Asgharzadeh, A. (2001): The Power of Social Theory: Towards an Anti-Colonial Discursive Framework. In: Journal of Educational Thought, 353, 297 – 323.

Dei, G. J. S., Asgharzadeh, A., Shahjahan, R. & Eblaghie-Bahador, S. (2006): Power, Knowledge and Social Difference in African Schooling. Toronto: University of Toronto Press.

Dewey, J. (1909/1975): Moral Principles in Education. Carbondale, IL.

Dorson, R. (ed. 1972): Folklore and Folklife. Chicago.

Fafunwa, A. B. (1974): History of Education in Nigeria. London.

Fafunwa, A. B. (1982): African Education in Perspective. In A. B. Fafunwa & Aisiku, J. (eds.): Education in Africa: A Comparative Study. London.

Fafunwa, A. B. & Aisiku, J. (eds. 1982): Education in Africa: A Comparative Study. London/Boston.

Fanon, F. (1967): Black Skin, White Masks. (Translated from French by C.L. Markmann). New York. (Original work published in 1952, Paris: Editions du Seuil).

Firth, R. (1926): Proverbs in the Native Life with Particular Reference to those of the Maori. In: Folklore, 32.

Foster, P. (1965): Education and Social Change in Ghana. London.

Friedman, J. (1992): The Past in the Future: History and the Politics of Identity. In: American Anthropologist, 94: 4, 837 – 859.

Gates, H. L, Jr. (1992): Loose Canons: Notes on the Culture Wars. New York.

Gates, H. L, Jr. (2010): Tradition and the Black Atlantic: Critical Theory in the African Diaspora. New York.

Gilroy, P. (1993): The Black Atlantic: Modernity and Double Consciousness. Cambridge, Massachusetts.

Gilroy, P. (2000): Against Race: Imagining Political Culture Beyond the Color Line. Cambridge, Massachusetts.

Hall, S. (2005): New Ethnicities. In: Morley, D. & Chen, K. (eds.): Stuart Hall: Critical Dialogues in Cultural Studies. New York, 441 – 449.

Hall, S. (2007a): The Global, the Local, and the Return of Ethnicity. In: Hall, S., Held, D., Hubert, D. & Thompson, K. (eds): Modernity: An Introduction to Modern Societies. Oxford, 623 – 629.

Hall, S. (2007b): Fundamentalism, Diaspora and Hybridity. In: Hall, S., Held, D., Hubert, D. & Thompson, K. (eds.): Modernity: An Introduction to Modern Societies. Oxford, 629 – 632.

Johnson, B. (1993): Ojibway Tales. Lincoln.

Johnson, B. (2003): Ojibway Heritage. Toronto.

Kalu, O. U. (1991): Gender Ideology in Igbo Religion: The Changing Religious Role of Women in Igboland. In: Africa / Istituto Italo-Africano, 46: 2, 184 – 202.

Kohlberg, L. (1981): Essays on Moral Development. Vol. I: The Philosophy of Moral Development. San Francisco.

Kohlberg, L. (1984): Essays on Moral Development. Vol. II: The Psychology of Moral Development. San Francisco.

Kudadjie J. N. (1996): Ga and Dangme Proverbs: For Preaching and Teaching. Accra: Asempa Publishers. Online available at: www.afriprov.org/ebooks/gadangme.htm, date: May 20, 2005.

Lattas, A. (1993): Essentialism, Memory and Resistance: Aboriginality and the Politics of Authenticity. In: Oceania, 63, 2 – 67.

McClellan, B. E. (1999): Moral Education in America: Schools and the Shaping of Character from Colonial Times to the Present. New York.

Ogede, O. S. (1993): The Role of the Igede poet Micah Ichegbeh's 'Adiyah' Songs in the Political and Moral Education of his Local Audiences. In: African Languages and Cultures, 6: 1, 49 – 68.

Opoku, K. A. (1975): Speak to the Winds: Proverbs from Africa. New York.

Opoku, K. A. (1997): Hearing and Keeping: Akan Proverbs. Accra.

Pachocinshi, R. (1996): Proverbs of Africa: Human Nature in the Nigerian Oral Tradition: An Exposition and Analysis of 2,600 Proverbs from 64 Peoples. Continuum International Publishing. Available online at: http://www.paragonhouse.com/catalog/product_info.php?cPath=23_46&products_id=155 [no access date given]

Quist, H. (2003): Secondary Education—A 'Tool' for National Development in Ghana. A Critical Appraisal of the Post-Colonial Context. In: Africa Development, 28: 3-4, 186 – 210.

Ryan, K. & Bohlin, K. (2000): Teacher Education's Empty Suit. In: Education Week on the WEB. Available online at: http://www.edweek.org/ew/ewstory.cfm?slug=26ryan.h19, date: March 29, 2000.

Shizha, E. (2005): Reclaiming Our Memories: The Education Dilemma in Postcolonial African School Curricula. In: Abdi, A. & Cleghorn, A. (eds.): Issues in African Education: Sociological Perspectives. New York.

Sifuna, D. N. (1990): Development of Education in Africa: The Kenyan Experience. Nairobi.

Sifuna, D. N. (1992). Diversifying the Secondary School Curriculum: The African Experience. In: International Review of Education, 38: 1, 5 – 20.

Taylor, A. (1934): Problems in the Study of Proverbs. In: Journal of American Folklore, 47, 1 – 21.

White, B. (1996): Talk About School: Education and the Colonial Project in French and British West Africa. In: Comparative Education, 32: 1, 9 – 20.

Wolfgang, M. & Dundas, A. (1981): The Wisdom of Many: Essays on the Proverb. New York.

Yankah, K. (1989): The Proverb in the Content of Akan Rhetoric: A Theory Proverb Praxis. Bern & Frankfurt/Main.

Yankah, K. (1995): Speaking for the Chief: Okyeame and the Politics of Akan Oratory. Bloomington/Indianapolis.

Multicultural Education and Apartheid – Educational Discourses in South Africa

Heike Niedrig, University of Hamburg, Germany

Multiculturalism, the new name for apartheid! (Collins & Gillespie 1992)

Apartheid curriculum policy may be regarded as an extreme form of 'multiculturalism'. (NEPI 1992: Curriculum report)

During my research on the discourses around 'multilingualism' and on concepts for multilingual education in the Post-Apartheid-schools (1995-97), I was continuously confronted with issues concerning the relationship between language and culture. In the South African context, these issues were highly charged emotionally; and while some of my informants were adamant that there was a strong connection between language and cultural identity, others would fiercely reject the notion of an innate linkage between the two and question the concept of 'cultural identity' altogether. My two quotes (above) indicate the historical and political frame for the heated debate as does the following interview statement of a South African educational researcher:

> Apartheid is a negative benchmark for our debates about the appropriate educational response to difference. [...] And since apartheid education used cultural difference as its ideological foundation, it is not at all surprising that South Africans are both at home in talking about education and cultural difference and repelled by it (Joe Muller, interviewed in Moore, 1993).

As a researcher in Comparative and Multicultural Education, I studied the South African educational discourse in order to contrast it with similar discourses in Germany. Basil Moore, an Australian based educational researcher and South African émigré, claims that the historical context of South Africa in which questions of 'multiculturalism' and 'multicultural education'[1] are so obviously politically charged is particularly suitable "*to explore some of the significant theoretical issues within the concept of multicultural education which may be just as relevant, if not so obvious, in other contexts*" (Moore 1993: 30). I agree with this assessment, and by outlining the particularities of the South African case, its specific historical and socio-political context, I intend to explore the ambivalence inherent in any discourse on multiculturalism.

---

1 At the time of my research, the term "multicultural education" was the established term in South African discourse whereas in Germany the term "intercultural education" was more common. As my comparative discourse analysis could show, however, these terms were used to convey, essentially, the same ideas, including all the inherent ambivalences as discussed by Baquero Torres (in this volume).

My contribution is based on findings from my research in South Africa during the mid-1990s, a crucial time of social transformation and negotiation. This context made visible not only how 'cultural identities' are formed through powerful discourses, but also how they are challenged and contested in counter-discourses, as suggested by postcolonial theory. These issues surfaced in my interviews even though my research objective was to explore the *educational consequences of the official multilingual policy* since 1993: The new South African Constitution acknowledges 11 official languages[2] and obliges the government to promote multilingualism. My core material consists of 76 expert interviews with members of educational NGOs, representatives of government organisations, and 'language and culture activists' from Afrikaner as well as South African Indian cultural organisations. In addition, I visited twelve schools with very different apartheid-history backgrounds and current ethnic and linguistic compositions, and I analysed all major discussion documents produced in the context of the constitutional and educational negotiations.

In the following essay, I will briefly outline my theoretic perspective, which is based on central ideas of postcolonial thinkers like Stuart Hall and Homi K. Bhabha. For readers less familiar with South Africa, some general information about South African history will then be introduced, before I put the above quotations into their historical context, and I will trace some aspects of the history of cultural discourse that contributes to the perceived equivalence of apartheid education and multicultural education. Against this background, I will come back to the time of transformation and analyse, from a postcolonial theoretical perspective, the impact of the colonial and apartheid heritage on post-apartheid educational conflicts in order to formulate a number of general conclusions.

1. Postcolonial theory and the discursive construction of 'cultural identity'

Only recently, with the end of the apartheid regime, South Africa seems to have entered the phase of *postcolonialism* – and clearly this implies the polyvalence of every 'post'-terminology (Bhabha 1990, Hall 2006). I prefer the term "Post-Apartheid South Africa" to the label "New South Africa", which was very popular in the time of transformation, conveying as it does all the enthusiasm and optimism attached to the start of something completely 'new'. The term 'Post-Apartheid', however, can only in a superficial understanding be interpreted as

2 These languages are (in order of number of L1-speakers): Zulu, Xhosa, Afrikaans, Northern Sotho, English, Tswana, Southern Sotho, Tsonga, Swati, Venda, and Ndebele.

meaning that the times of apartheid are over and done with. The prefix 'post' always refers back to the term that it qualifies in an ambivalent manner, implying both – change, but also continuity. So as much as the abolition of the apartheid laws and the new Constitution indicate a significant rupture, it is also obvious that in the post-apartheid society, no social positioning is possible that does not relate to the old order of apartheid. Terminology designed to express detachment from apartheid categories such as "so-called Coloureds" or "formerly classified as…" as well as the avoidance of racialised terms and their replacement by reference to language ("African Languages-Speaking South Africans") are abundant in the new discourses about social inequalities and struggles. These discourse strategies are marked attempts to overcome the racist ideology and at the same time confirm its ongoing relevance.

As has often been pointed out, colonialism (and thus postcolonialism) does not merely refer to a system of political domination and economic exploitation, but also to a system of knowledge and representation linked to relations of power. This is highly relevant for the question of 'cultural identity' which cannot be separated from the concept of 'multicultural education'. According to Stuart Hall, we should think of 'cultural identity' not as a given (an essential core, a sort of collective 'one true self'), but "as a 'production', which is never complete, always in process, and always constituted within, not outside, representation" (Hall 1990: 222). The first implication of this view is that cultural identities have a history, and as anything historical, they undergo constant transformation, and are "subject to the continuous 'play' of history, culture and power" (ibid. 225). There is, however, more to this notion of 'cultural identity' than the acknowledgment of historical change. To delve into the theoretic depths of this approach, Hall refers to the French poststructuralist linguist Jacques Derrida and his central term *différance*. By inserting an inaudible 'a' in the place of an 'e', Derrida plays with the French grammar as well as with the double meaning of *différer* which means both: to differ and to defer (postpone). Thus Derrida challenges linguistic thinking which perceives 'language' as representation of pre-lingual meaning: There is no meaning without relations of difference; and 'difference' is not an identity, but a process, always deferring meaning in an incessant play of signification. Meaning is then the *subsequent effect* of the "play of difference" in the process of signification – not something which is "already there" to be merely "expressed" in speech; and it is something which is never "fixed", but always shifting (Derrida 1998 [1967]).

Where precisely do 'identities' appear in this never-ending process? At this point, Hall finds Derrida and his disciples guilty of a "celebration of formal 'playfulness'" which tends to evacuate the profound theoretical insights of their political implications. According to Hall, however, it is possible to understand "identity" as a contingent and arbitrary stop, as a necessary, but always only temporary 'break' in the infinite semiosis of language. This 'cut' or rather this discursive positioning, which makes meaning possible, must not be mistaken as natural or permanent (the essentialist interpretation of identity), rather every such position is – in Hall's interpretation – an arbitrary and 'strategic' closure. In other words, there is no pre-discursive 'cultural identity' which could then be *re*presented in the different genres of narrative and visual representation – speech, text, film; but 'cultural identity' is the effect of those modes of representation. "[I]dentities are the names we give to the different ways we are positioned by, and position ourselves within, the narratives of the past" (Hall 1990: 225). From this theoretic viewpoint, it follows that we cannot examine identities and their 'representation' in terms of their 'falsity/genuineness', but solely with respect to the style or modality of their discursive production – and of course with regard to their strategic function in the 'politics of identity'.

What does this mean with respect to the 'cultural identity' of the 'Black subject', which is the focal issue of Hall's reflection? In Hall's postcolonial reading, the "African" is an effect of the dominant regimes of representation and knowledge: "...the colonial discourse, the literature of adventure and exploration, the romance of the exotic, the ethnographic and travelling eye, the tropical languages of tourism, travel brochure and Hollywood..." (Hall 1990: 233). That is, the "African" is the effect of a process of forceful positioning which has been labelled as Othering in postcolonial discourse (see Thomas-Olalde & Velho in this volume for a detailed discussion of this term). The focus of this chapter, then, is to discuss the implications of the 'politics of identities' for the educational reforms in the time of transition from Apartheid- to Post-Apartheid-society and how these impact the discourse on "multicultural education".

2. South African history – a brief general outline

I will start, though, with a few historical pieces of data (cp. Davenport 1991, Worden 1994) to provide readers with a general orientation with respect to the subsequent presentation and analyses.

Table 1: South African History – A Selection of Key Data

1652	Dutch East Indian Company (Cape); official language: Dutch
1815	Cape as British Colony; since 1822 official language: English
1834-1838	Official abolition of slavery in the Cape colony
1836-1838	Great Trek and founding of so-called “Boer Republics” in the North, official language: Dutch (emancipatory struggle towards recognition of Afrikaans)
1860	First indentured labourers from India arrived to work on the Natal sugar plantations
1899-1902	South African War (or “Second Anglo-Boer-War”) – British victory
1910	Union of South Africa: official bilingualism; tentative balance of power
1948	Election: Victory of the National Party (NP) with apartheid policy programme
1950	Population Registration Act and other apartheid (segregation) laws
1953	Bantu Education Act
1976	Soweto uprising: Students protested against “Bantu Education”, sparked off by the unyielding imposition of Afrikaans as medium of instruction for 50% of the subjects in “Black Secondary Schools”. At least 176 students were killed by police. But the NP government eventually backed down on the language medium requirement. So in hindsight many historians qualify the event as a turning point in the struggle against apartheid education.
1990	Release of Nelson Mandela by President F. W. de Klerk after 26 years of imprisonment
1991	Start of CODESA (Convention for a Democratic South Africa) negotiations in preparation for interim constitution; Interrupted by violent conflicts between members of Inkatha Freedom Party (IFP) and African National Congress (ANC), depicted in the media as “ethnic conflicts” or “black-on-black violence”.
1993	Interim Constitution
1994	First free, general, democratic elections; victory of ANC; Government of National Unity under President Mandela
1995	Desegregation of all schools
1996	Constitution of South Africa

I may be accused of adopting a Eurocentric view in my brief summary of South African history. However, since I agree with Stuart Hall’s assessment that it is not possible to resume a pre-colonial African history untarnished by colonial and racist oppression, I may as well choose 1652 as the starting point, when the Dutch East Indian Company established a small trading post at the Cape to provide fresh food for the Company’s ships that travelled to India via the Cape of Good Hope. Of course, at that time the Southern part of Africa was by no means a place devoid of human inhabitants, as has been claimed by historians in the service of legitimizing “White rule” in South Africa. Archaeological evidence shows that at least from the Late Stone Age the region was widely inhabited by hunting and gathering San people (Worden 1994: 6). The first pastorals (today called Khoikhoi) with herds of sheep and cattle began roaming the Cape around 2000 years ago. And between 300 and 1000 CE, African farmers from the north migrated and settled in what is now South Africa. According to historical documents, the first Dutch settlers were soon involved in relations of trade and conflict with members of Khoikhoi groups. Later people from Indonesia, Malaysia as well as East Africa were forcibly brought to the Cape colony and enslaved as labourers. At that time, the Cape settlement was under the rule of the Dutch East Indian Company, and Dutch was the official language of the multi-ethnic community. Historical linguists argue that the Khoi-languages as well as Portuguese-Malay spoken by many slaves greatly influenced the development of the Dutch dialects of the Cape which in this process were ‘creolised’ into a distinct new language form: Cape Dutch, later known as Afrikaans.

Thus, when the Cape became a British colony in the early 19th century, the British colonialists inherited a long-established Dutch (Afrikaans) speaking settler community. The relation between the British and the ‘Boere’ (White Afrikaans-speaking farmers) were fraught, leading to, among other things, the mass emigration of Afrikaans-speaking settlers to the north (1936-38). The so-called “Great Trek”, commemorated in 1938 in a spectacular centennial celebration, became one of the foundation myths of Afrikaner nationalism.

The second “Anglo-Boer-War” (1899-1902) resulted in the foundation of the Union of South Africa (1910), though South Africa remained in the British Commonwealth until 1961. In the 1948 elections, a conservative nationalist Afrikaner faction of the all-White-electorate finally prevailed, implementing the infamous apartheid policy which lasted until 1990 with the release of Nelson Mandela and the unbanning (legalization) of all opposition parties. In the four years leading up to the first general, free and equal elections in April 1994, intense negotiations around an interim Convention for a Democratic South Africa (CODESA) constitution were conducted by representatives of the major political parties. The quotations at the top of this paper come from this time of transition and intense debate. The following section will introduce some of the relevant questions surrounding issues of “multiculturalism” and “multicultural education” as South Africa’s future was negotiated in the early 1990s,

3. Educational policy issues at stake in the time of transformation

The first quote – *"Multiculturalism, the new name for apartheid!"* – is the provocative title of Collins and Gillespie's contribution to the curriculum-discussion during that time of transition. In this article they accuse the de Klerk government still in place during the CODESA negotiations of not working towards the abolition of the political and social realities of apartheid. Instead, the authors claim it was busy modernising its own political discourse: "This discourse used by the white elite is couched in terms acceptable to the international community such as 'protection of minority rights'" (Collins & Gillespie 1992: 55).

This strategy by representatives of the 'old order' is, indeed, evident in many statements quoted in the media such as the following: "We feel strong enough about this matter not to accept anything less than internationally agreed rights for minorities" (quoted in "The Citizen", March 29th, 1996). The matter referred to is the future of (all-White) Afrikaans-schools. Against the backdrop of apartheid history, it is obvious that "protection of minority rights" meant the protection of White privileges. The concept of "minority" as employed in this context is thus a perversion of the sociological concept of 'minority' which is less about numbers, but rather about social dominance and relations of power.

The idea of the protection of minority rights, however, found its way into the Constitution of South Africa in the form of the establishment of a "Commission for the Promotion and Protection of the Rights of Cultural, Religious and Linguistic Communities" (Constitution of 1996, Chapter 9, §181 (1) and §§185-186). The inclusion of this section demonstrates the success of the conservative forces involved in the constitutional negotiations. The establishment of such a "group based" Commission was met with concern by many multilingual activists, as it was set up in undefined rivalry to another institution equally anchored in the new Constitution, the Pan South African Language Board (PanSALB). In contrast to the "Commission", the PanSALB is not tasked to protect "group rights", but to prevent open or hidden discrimination with respect to language competencies in general; in other words to ensure that laws and official practices do not infringe upon the equal rights and access to government services of all South Africans, no matter which of the official language(s) they speak. These two not quite compatible views of protection of language rights both left their mark on the Education-Section of the Interim Constitution resulting in conflicts about the interpretation of this law.

Education-Section in the Interim Constitution (1993, § 32)
Every person shall have the right –
a) to basic education and equal access to educational institutions;
b) to *instruction in the language of his or her choice* where this is reasonably practicable; and
c) to establish, where practicable, *educational institutions based on a common culture, language or religion*, provided that there shall be no discrimination on the ground of race [emphasis added].

Subsection (b) reflects the PanSALB vision of equality with regard to language rights; subsection (c) in contrast corresponds with the Commission's task to protect group rights, translated into educational policy as the right of communities to establish exclusive schools. The practical relevance of this legal provision is evident in several conflicts around the admission of Black children into historically White schools as will be discussed in detail later. Here, I might only add that the Education paragraph was thoroughly amended in the Final Constitution as result of these conflicts.

The second quotation – *"Apartheid curriculum policy may be regarded as an extreme form of 'multiculturalism'"* – is from the National Educational Policy Investigation curriculum report (NEPI 1992). NEPI was the response to the work of a commission appointed by the de-Klerk-government in 1991 called Educational Renewal Strategies (ESR). ESR's task was to work out (technical rather than political) solutions to the problems and tensions in the segregated school system. The NEPI researchers, on the other hand, represented the opposition to the apartheid-school-policy and set for themselves the goal to work out educational alternatives in preparation for the time after the end of apartheid. One of the seven NEPI reports dealt with questions of the curriculum, focusing on the relationship between cultural diversity and a common identity for South African citizens. The above quotation, which is the first sentence of this report, indicates that from the NEPI researchers' perspective the apartheid educational policy was *always* rooted in an educational philosophy compatible with the discourse of multiculturalism. The following section will trace some of the historical discourse structures that gave rise to this perception.

4. The concept of "culture" in apartheid policy and education discourse

It is well known that the system of apartheid was based on the categorisation of the South African population into so-called population groups (Population Registration Act 1950), namely White, Indian, Coloured and Native[3]. The racist categorization was not an invention of the National Party which came to power in 1948 with its programme of apartheid; rather, these categories were, at that time, already firmly in place. They had been established during the period of colonialism, largely based on the discourse of 19th century scientific racism. By 1948, the global sense of outrage at the racism of NS-Germany probably facilitated a rapid switch from the discourse of "race" to a discourse of "culture" in South Africa to make the institutionalised policy of racism more palatable to the international community.

What is often overlooked in this context is the fact that the discourse of apartheid was always internally contested, even among the White ruling faction of the South African population that represented apartheid ideology. One of the central challenges of the discourse around group identities was in fact the difficult question of how to define the "White Afrikaner" (Cross 1992). The propagation of an *Afrikaner Volkskultur* was the basis for the mobilisation of resistance against British hegemony in South Africa since the 19th century. The central defining feature of the emerging Afrikaner-identity was the Afrikaans language. This perception is echoed in a complaint about the marginalization of Afrikaans in the public sector in my interviews 1996. Beverly Malan was a curriculum expert in service of the late apartheid government. The following statement was made in defence of the White Afrikaner parents in the school conflicts which I will discuss in depth later:

> Because the Afrikaans people feel that they are the **only** ones who have been expected to make sacrifices after election. They have given up everything. And now they are expected to give up their **language**, and their language is **them**. Because they grew together with the language. And English has taken all the gaps. Everywhere (Beverly Malan, Curriculum expert of the late apartheid government, interview March 1996).

The suggestion that the common bond defining a *Volk* is its language ("their language is **them**") was largely influenced by the philosophy of the German Romantic movement. Aletta Norval (1996), in her thorough analysis of apartheid discourse, points out that this discourse evolved from competing sources, such as different streams of Calvinist thinking. But notions borrowed from the philosophy of Johann Gottlieb Fichte were particularly influential in the design of the "Grand Apartheid" and its homeland policy.

> Was dieselbe Sprache redet, das ist schon vor aller menschlichen Kunst vorher durch die bloße Natur mit einer Menge von unsichtbaren Banden aneinander ge-

3 The term "Native" was first replaced by "Bantu" and later by "African".

knüpft, [...] es gehört zusammen und ist natürlich eins und ein unzertrennlich Ganzes. Ein solches kann kein Volk anderer Abkunft und Sprache in sich aufnehmen und mit sich vermischen wollen, ohne wenigstens fürs erste sich zu verwirren, und den gleichmäßigen Fortgang seiner Bildung mächtig zu stören (Dreizehnte Rede, Fichte (2008), orig. 1808).[4]

A number of South African scholars who were later to occupy political positions in the South African government had studied in Germany in the 1920s and brought back nationalist notions which have been labelled "neo-Fichtean" because of their preoccupation with the idea of the *Volk* as an organic body held together by a common historical culture and language (Davenport 1991: 288). Two such influential apartheid politicians are H.F. Verwoerd, Minister of Native Affairs (1950-1958) and Prime Minister (1958-1966), and Dr. W.W.M. Eiselen, Secretary of Native Affairs in the 1950s, and Chairman of the Bantu Education Commission (1949-1951).

South African politicians like Verwoerd and Eiselen propagated a "multinational" policy and "separate cultural development" of these distinct "nations"; this policy assumed the existence of separable, linguistic-culturally homogeneous "ethnic groups". Under this philosophy, these groups were to live apart from each other in separate territories in order to develop according to their own cultural tradition and heritage. This thinking was the basis for, among other things, the delineation of a Homeland for each African language group.

Neville Alexander, probably the most renowned apartheid opponent dealing with language policy issues, commented the Eiselen-Verwoerd policy on the language question as follows:

> High sounding rationalisations about the dignity of each and every human (i.e. 'ethnic') group and their right to promote their own language and culture, and all the philosophical trappings borrowed from the German Romantic movement of the late 18th century – especially from the philosophers Herder and Fichte – were used to explain this policy. But in fact, it was the possibility of breaking up the Black people into a large number of conflicting and competing so-called ethnic groups that really gave rise to this policy. [...] Using classical Central European social theory, the ideologues of Afrikaner nationalism proceeded to identify some 10 specific ethnic or national groups among the African people of South Africa as well as the (highly problematical) 'Coloured nation-to-be' and (eventually) the 'Indian' nation (Alexander 1989: 21f.).

4 Translation by author: "What speaks the same language, has already been bound together before all human arts by mere nature through a multitude of invisible bonds, [...] it belongs together and is naturally one and an indivisible whole. As such it cannot wish to incorporate a people of different descent and language and to blend together, without first confusing and powerfully interrupting the regular progress of its formation" (13th speech by J.G. Fichte, notes from 13th of April 1808).

As Alexander points out, the underlying aim and the objective effect of the revitalisation of "Bantu cultures" was a divisive retribalisation of Black South Africans; thus it was an attempt to prevent a unified postcolonial Black identity. I certainly agree with Alexander's concise assessment. But I believe that in order to reflect the ambivalences inherent in the discourse on "Bantu cultures" that bolstered apartheid policy, it is important to note that a number of people like Eiselen were, in fact, driven by a genuine concern for the protection of African "cultures" which were, in their view, on the point of being "destroyed" by the advance of "White civilisation". Separation seemed imperative in order to intervene into the "drama of culture conflict" and to protect African cultures from the pernicious effects of urbanisation (see Kros 2002). Eiselen, the chairperson of the Native Education Commission (1949-1951), was a German-trained anthropologist with family roots in the Berlin Mission Society. Cultural Anthropology discourse in Eiselen's time was inspired by the Boas-Benedict-concept of culture that prepared the ground for "cultural relativist" thinking, or the position that "cultures" are different but equal, and that the value of each "cultural item/practice" can only be judged with respect to its function within a particular "culture". This concept of culture is equally opposed to the notion of different stages of civilisation in the development of one universal form of culture and to the assumptions of scientific race theory, which Franz Boas, in fact, refuted with his empirical data. Eiselen, too, explicitly distanced himself from theories about racial intelligence which were en vogue at his time. Instead, he insisted that the *Bantu culture* provided a particular social environment that predisposed its members to learn in particular ways from which they should not be alienated, which implied amongst other things, that education should be delivered in the "mother tongue". The according educational philosophy is strikingly reminiscent of contemporary "multicultural education" discourses:

> The Bantu child comes to school with a basic physical and psychological endowment which differs so slightly, if at all, from that of the European child, that no special provision has to be made in education theory or basic aims ... But education practice must recognise that it has to deal with a Bantu child i.e. a child trained and conditioned in Bantu culture, endowed with a knowledge of a Bantu language and imbued with values, interests and behaviour patterns learned at the knee of a Bantu mother. These facts must dictate to a large extent the content and methods of his early education (The Eiselen Report 1951, cf. Christie & Collins 1984: 175).

The educational preoccupation with the "cultural background" of children, based on the concept of "culture" as defined by European Cultural Anthropology, is integral to different approaches in "multicultural education". Applied in the colonial apartheid-policy context, however, the "different, but equal" axiom could hardly conceal the underlying convictions about the relation of superiority and inferiority, which are perhaps less visible in other contexts. As postcolonial theory, going back to the seminal work of Edward Said's *Orientalism*, has been able to dissect, the construct of the Others and their "culture" is based on "knowledge" largely produced by anthropology, a scientific discipline rooted in colonialism, and thus embedded in a power-knowledge complex (cp. Thomas-Olalde & Velho in this volume). The image of the "African" just like the construct of the "Oriental" has shaped the "Western White" self-image as inherently superior, while these "Others" are set up in particular relations of "difference":

> The distinction between 'savage Negro and civil Mohometan' and the commentaries on the African's indolence, their unbridled passions and their cruelty or mental retardation [...] formed part of the series of oppositions and of the levels of classification of humans demanded by the logic of the chain of being and the stages of progress and social development (Mudimbe 1988: 12f.).

Therefore, "protection of Bantu cultures", no matter how benevolent the intent, cannot be separated from the reification of colonial knowledge and the stabilising of power relations.

5. Post-Apartheid education – the difficult heritage

With the end of educational segregation emerged the discussion about "multicultural education". In practice, the desegregation of schools meant, of course, not that White parents sent their offspring to homeland or township schools, but that children from underprivileged sectors of education started to migrate to the historically privileged schools that were soon labelled "multicultural schools".

In this situation, the concept of "multicultural/intercultural education" was eagerly adopted from European and US-American contexts to be applied to these schools. 'Black children' who entered the historically 'White schools' were perceived in a position usually accorded to 'immigrant children', that is as 'strangers' who needed to be integrated into an already established structure. Accordingly, training-programmes embodied in publications like "Multicultural Education: A teachers' manual" by Lemmer & Squelch (1993) or the comprehensive programme by the Open Schools Association[5]: "Open Schools. A Professional Growth Programme for Teachers" were widely distributed among the teaching staff of newly desegregated schools. The general thrust of these programmes was rather similar to approaches labelled "pedagogy for foreigners" in

5 Open schools: the label for (mostly Catholic) private schools that opened their doors to limited numbers of 'non-White' children in the 1980s when, after the Soweto uprising, some cautious reforms permitted 'multiracial schools' in the private school sector.

the German context (cp. Baquero Torres in this volume) – they aimed, on the one hand, at arousing sympathy and understanding among the White teachers about the difficulties of their new students who had been raised and continued to live in the townships; on the other hand, they guided teachers in addressing the linguistic and socialisation "deficiencies" of the so-called LEP (Limited English Proficient) students. The Open Schools training programme was fiercely attacked in a scathing review by Ruth Versfeld, herself a teacher at a Catholic open school, on the grounds that its compensatory approach focused on spreading stereotyped images, albeit "benevolent" in intent, about Black children and township life, while ignoring any need to restructure the schools' organisation and curriculum in order to reflect the new student population.

Concurrent with the quick adoption of concepts designed to assimilate Black children into a 'White school culture', a more sophisticated debate on adequate approaches to 'cultural diversity' took place, particularly within the NEPI[6] process mentioned earlier. The NEPI report on "curriculum" issues discussed the relationship between "multiculturalism and citizenship" (NEPI 1992: 22), and specifically posed the question of how diversity can be dealt with in the curriculum without reifying once more the apartheid categories around "cultural differences" (ibid. 77ff.). The authors of the NEPI report finally suggested the development of a "procedural approach" as a "policy option", meaning that the curriculum should be about the development of procedures for the negotiation of differences, rather than about the teaching of certain content (ibid. 81). This recommendation implies a particular concept of 'culture':

> As far as possible, concepts such as culture, citizenship, commonality, and diversity need to be understood as historically produced and changing, rather than as static categories. Teaching this could well be one of the goals of the curriculum (ibid. 81).

The common denominator on which the apartheid opponents could agree vis-à-vis the "negative benchmark" of the apartheid curriculum and its essentialist concept of culture was to highlight process, dynamism and historical variability of 'culture'.

So far I have summarised some important aspects of the conceptual debates which by nature remain rather abstract. Two different case studies[7] around "mul-

6 NEPI: National Education Policy Investigation (see section 3).

7 Due to editorial limitations, I cannot include a third case, the language and cultural policy of the South African Indian minority, which would add a different dimension and even more complexity to the discussion, and – most importantly – undermine the binary Black-White-perspective of the two case studies presented here (cp. Niedrig 2000: 278-296).

ticultural schools" conflicts in South Africa serve to illustrate the relevance of the conceptual debates.

5.1 The Afrikaans school conflict

In spite of all the misgivings and fears, the integration of children from underprivileged sectors into formerly 'White schools' was, in the vast majority of cases, surprisingly smooth, at least on an organisational level. The process was probably facilitated by the fact that 1) the first contingent of new-comers was predominantly children from Black middle class families who could afford the cost of transportation, and 2) that many White schools were under threat of being closed down due to a declining White student population.

In a couple of White Afrikaans-medium schools, however, parent communities reacted with great indignation and hostility towards the Black children desiring entry into "their" school. Newspapers around the world reported on the case of Potgietersrus Primary school in the Northern Province. Here, the school administration and parents' representatives took legal action against the admission of Black students. The core argument of the plaintiffs referred to the protection of the linguistic and cultural identity of the school. The Black children demanded to be taught in English, thereby making use of their right "to instruction in the language of their choice" as granted in the Interim Constitution of 1993 (§ 32b). According to the plaintiffs, however, this demand undermined the right to linguistic self-determination of the school community. Their legal reasoning was based on the same paragraph of the Interim Constitution, which also guaranteed the right "to establish [...] educational institutions based on a common culture, language or religion" (§ 32c).

While they pursued legal action, the parents of the 200 White students at Potgietersrus Primary removed their children from the school and taught them in makeshift classrooms outside of the school building. Very likely, in their historical interpretation, this action resumed the Afrikaner resistance against the British colonisers who forced English as medium of instruction on Dutch schools in the early 19th century. In 1995, of course, the issues at stake had significantly shifted – nobody compelled the Afrikaans-speaking children to be taught in English.

The Potgietersrus case was brought up in many of my interviews on the Language-in-Education policy issues. The following extracts illustrate the spectrum of perceptions.

Paul Musker, director of ELTIC[8], a small Johannesburg-based NGO committed to promoting multilingual education, had gained substantial insight into the court proceedings as expert of the defence for the government. Musker does not completely condemn the wish for "common language schools", but he insists that the most urgent need after the abolition of the segregated school system was to redress the very unequal access to educational resources. Eighteen out of 20 schools in the Potgietersrus region, he argues, are in an "appalling condition", whereas two of these schools, quite in contrast to the others, are among the best equipped schools in the country. "So if you have a school like Potgietersrus Primary, it would be a travesty of the Constitution if you were to in any way exclude Black children from it" (Paul Musker, director of ELTIC, Johannesburg, interview March 1996).

One central aspect of Musker's analysis is the observation that the demand of the Potgietersrus Primary school governing body that their school was to be based on "common language", "common culture" *and* "common religion" was not – as implied by the argument – due to an equivalence of linguistic, cultural and religious affiliation; quite to the contrary, 'culture' and 'religion' had to be introduced as additional arguments because the criterion of 'language' alone would not have guaranteed the desired 'racial' (so-called 'cultural') exclusivity of the school:

> [W]hat was happening at Potgietersrus, if you read the court transcripts, you see, what was happening was pure racism. Absolutely racism. – As a matter of fact, some of the kids who want to get into the school do speak Afrikaans. Afrikaans is a very widely spoken language, it is not only spoken by white people. That's why you have to add 'Eurocentric' because it is not enough to say Afrikaans. Because if you only say Afrikaans, you get coloured kids, Black kids, Indian kids who speak Afrikaans, especially in the Northern Province. That's why they had to give three criteria for selection of pupils: Language: Afrikaans; culture: Eurocentric; religion: Christian. – Common language, common culture, common religion (Paul Musker, ibid.).

This critical statement has implications beyond the particular case at stake; it demonstrates ELTIC's general strategy of *deconstructing essentialising discourse*. Musker's assertion aims at undermining the neo-Fichtean notion of 'language' as the natural unifying bond of a 'Volk': "It's been a strong position of the previous government as well, that one language equals one culture equals one race" (Paul Musker, ibid.). Against such a racialisation of "culture" and "language", Musker puts the ELTIC view that "even an individual can have a multiplicity of cultures, very comfortably" (ibid.).

8 ELTIC (English Language Teaching Information Centre) team members: Paul Musker (director); Sebolelo Nomvete, Dodds Pule, Thomas Maligavhada, Charles Cooper.

Not surprisingly, a completely different view of the problem was put forward by Beverley Malan, the curriculum expert in the service of the late apartheid administration during the time of transition and reform preparations who was already quoted ("their language is **them**"). She claims to be in favour of multilingualism, but is very critical about the language-policy developments because in her opinion, it is all about driving out Afrikaans:

> It is not just a perception, I can back it up with many facts, that there is a concerted effort to get rid of Afrikaans and Afrikaners, to pretend that we were never here: They break down our monuments, they take our language off television. – Now black pupils go to white Afrikaans schools, they **demand** to be enrolled in that school and then they **demand** to be taught in English. And if the school says: No, we are an Afrikaans school, you can come in provided you are willing to be instructed in the medium of Afrikaans, we will give you extra support, then they call them racist. They say schools refuse to teach them in English because they don't want them in schools (Beverly Malan, Deputy Director for Languages at the Department of National Education until 1994, Pretoria, interview March 1996).

Malan puts forward three arguments to support the Potgietersrus Afrikaner parents' stance. Firstly, the demand to be instructed in English was unfair towards the Afrikaans-speaking teachers who – even though as a rule fluent in English – were not trained to teach in English. Secondly, as a consequence the Black students actually obstructed their own access to the high quality education they expected at that school. Thirdly, the demand for parallel classes in English led to an unjust distribution of educational resources:

> And thirdly, there is a ration laid down by law in terms of teacher: pupil. – One teacher for each 40 pupils. Now what happens, all those Black pupils who are coming in are not necessarily in the same class, which means that there won't be 40, 40, 40 of them. So **their** classes are small, 5 or 10, because special concessions have to be made for them, whereas the other classes are now much larger (Beverley Malan, ibid.).

In this perspective, therefore, the problem of unequal access to educational resources raised by Musker is fundamentally converted: Here it is "all those Black pupils" who are unfairly privileged because for them special concessions are being made. Malan conjures up the historically founded fear of many Afrikaners who feel threatened by any attempt to Anglicize the education system. But in no instance does she mention the rejection of Afrikaans as medium of instruction by large parts of the Black population, which is equally founded in history (e.g. the Soweto uprising 1976). In her way of thinking, the Black pupils demand more than they can reasonably expect. If they demand to be enrolled in Afrikaans-medium schools, then they must bow to the existing school community's rules – because they are, as implied in the argument, merely 'guests' in that school. Her message is that the conflict around the protection of single-medium Afrikaans-schools is not about racism, but about the dominance of English. In this interpretation, Black children act as 'Trojan horse' of British imperialism when they enter Afrikaans-medium-schools and then demand to be taught in English.

This reasoning, however, was not the only response of the Afrikaans-lobby to the events at Potgietersrus, as the following two statements by Johan Combrink and Gerard Schuring demonstrate. Both essentially agree with Musker's conviction that the conflict is a case of racism, and that 'linguistic and cultural identity' is no more than a pretext to justify racist ends. Combrink, chairman of the "Foundation for Afrikaans, the friendly language", accordingly regrets that the turmoil caused by the Afrikaans parents in Potgietersrus has caused damage to the interests of the Afrikaans movement.

> It seems to me like the Potgietersrus Afrikaans people did the cause of Afrikaans more harm than good. [...] I doubt very much whether it is about English, I think it is about colour. It just so happens that the African people also want to be taught in English. What would have happened if a contingent of white children had moved in and wanted to be taught in English? Would they have had the same stand, those Potgietersrus people? I doubt it. I doubt it very much (Johan Combrink, Director of the "Foundation for Afrikaans, the friendly language", Stellenbosch, interview April 1996).

Schuring is a senior researcher at the Human Science Research Centre in Pretoria, a partly state-run research organisation. He specialises in language statistics and language planning, and his defence of an important role for Afrikaans in the New South Africa is backed up by an intricate argument based on his language data which show that Afrikaans first language speakers are the largest 'multiracial' language community in South Africa, and that Afrikaans is the predominant lingua franca in the *lower* strata of the economy (Schuring 1993). In the Potgietersrus case he identifies three layers of problems that are interwoven with each other, but he also believes that the "race question" plays a central role in the apparent language-in-education conflict in the subtext of the argument:

> So you have three problems: One is that some of them really do not believe in this bilingual education. They think it is bad. Mother tongue education is best. Two: There is a change of culture, if you bring in lots of pupils. [...] So that's the cultural difference. And the third one is the question of 'race'. And I personally believe that the question of race is underlying a lot of the conflicts: Only a small minority will really use that as an argument, and then they try and use 'language' and 'culture' as a way of justifying themselves (Gerard Schuring, Chief Researcher of the HSRC, Pretoria, interview March 1996).

We might conclude that the conflict around the admission policy of (some) Afrikaans-schools is basically about safeguarding "racial exclusivity" and material privileges under the guise of the protection of "language identity" and "cultural identity". Nevertheless, the shifting of the conflict into the realm of language rivalry between Afrikaans and English, as has been illustrated in the Malan quotation, is not merely a discursive tactic. The fear of identity loss due to "forced Anglicisation" is real, and the Afrikaans conflict, therefore, demonstrates that any discourse that strengthens local or particularistic identities (*modality of ethnocentrism*) is inherently Janus-headed because it can bolster both rightwing racist projects as well as the opposition of oppressed minorities (Hall 1996: 300; Hewitt 2003: 189).

Another pertinent point in Schuring's response is his reference to a "change of culture". He elaborates that if "they" (meaning Black children) are in the majority, "then we are in the minority. Then **their** ways of doing things dominate **our** way of doing things. So at the moment, **we** dominate, **our** culture is still there, and **they**'ve got to adapt. But when it is the other way round, things are difficult" (Gerard Schuring, ibid.). One of the most striking features of this discourse around "culture" is the emphasis on a racialising We-They dichotomy, which once again shows that in the South African context, the notions of culture and language are inevitably racialised, and the discourse on "culture" is always potentially a "language hideout" for the concept of "race". However, this is a feature of "culture discourses" in other contexts as well, as postcolonial discourse analysis has been able to show. Schuring's interpretation of the conflict seems like an illustration of Bhabha's (1990) critical assessment. In Bhabha's view, the endorsement of "cultural diversity" as foundation of multicultural education policy is paradoxically a form of "containment of difference" because the "other cultures" must always fit into the "grid" of the dominant culture (Bhabha 1990: 208), or as Schuring in his comment above openly admits, cultural dominance of the privileged group is the precondition for the "toleration" of the "Others".

To deconstruct the racialised "cultural identity" discourse, Afrikaner identity is an interesting starting point, because here the construction efforts are particularly obvious. This identity is constantly (re-)produced via dichotomous oppositions and projections, involving language policy in particular. Johan van Wyk, a professor of South African literature and languages, describes the development of a Standard Afrikaans, strongly promoted by the apartheid government and its Language Board, as it were, as a process of deleting all "Black traces", and as intimately intertwined with the discursive construction of a (White) Afrikaner identity. He interprets the focus on the "racial purity" of Afrikaans as a compensatory strategy to deal with the inferiority complex of the (White) Afrikaans speakers, which resulted from the defaming of Afrikaans as a "hotnot's language" and as a "bastardised language of Malay scullery maids" in the 19th and early 20th century. In a social context that treated everything African with contempt and that took the European model of civilisation as the pinnacle of evolution, aspects of the stigmatised Other within the Self were repressed and racism became a constitutive part of the own identity: "The racism which was made an element of the identity speaks of the way in which the African aspects of the identity was socially traumatised" (van Wyk 1991: 85).

Based on Hall's (1990) analysis of the concept of "Black identity", it is possible to read the issues at stake in the process of Afrikaans language development as an attempt to deal with the relationship between *présence européenne* and *présence africaine*, in which the European presence marks dominance and oppression, and the African presence represents the stigmatised and subjected. The apartheid-era Language Board which was commissioned with the development of a Standard Afrikaans after 1948 not only embarked to remove all traces of "Black influences" on the language, but also insisted on a complete rejection of all English loan words in order to reinforce the perception that Afrikaans had "originated on African soil" (as opposed to the master code of British colonialism), and thus to identify Afrikaans speakers as "native to Africa" and legitimate inhabitants of South Africa, in contrast to the British invaders. The identity construction of the "Afrikaner", therefore, managed to project "dominance and oppression" onto English language and culture, while simultaneously erasing the stigmatised Black aspects from their 'own' language and cultural identity so that Afrikaans, as a supposedly "civilized" language with a European heritage, also served to distinguish the White Afrikaners from the Black Africans and their "primitive" languages.

Predictably, in post-Apartheid South Africa, the unresolved relationship with the "African aspects" of one's own identity will return in differing ways. A good example is the *sangoma* conflict, which will be presented in the second case study.

5.2 How to "Africanise" the curriculum?

Africanising a curriculum which has rightly been criticised as "Eurocentric" might be easy enough with respect to some uncontested subjects: the inclusion of the African fauna and flora into the biology curriculum, for instance, or the addition of renowned African writers to the literature curriculum. In the first case, the shift seems 'culturally neutral', in the second, one may argue that African writers like the Nobel prize laureate Chinua Achebe, who as a rule write their texts in the ex-colonial languages, are part of world literature and easily connect with the universalist claims of Western education. A rather different dynamic can be observed, however, as soon as elements of "traditional African culture" come into play.

Illustration: The Creative Arts Project[9] of the NLP and the "sangoma-incident"

The "Creative Arts Project" was developed by the National Language Project (NLP), an NGO in Cape Town. The project was introduced into some of the newly desegregated 'White' and 'Coloured' primary schools in Cape Town as part of *Environmental Studies*, an area of the Junior Primary School curriculum that encompasses elements of history, geography, social studies, and science. The NLP team pursued a number of objectives with this project. First, they used it as a new form of in-service teacher training, because the project was designed to explore new teaching approaches – using songs, drama, and arts – in cooperation with the teaching staff of the selected schools. Second, the project incorporated elements of "multilingual education" for linguistically-diverse classrooms, aiming to validate low-status African languages. Third, closely linked to the language issue, the project tried to integrate the different cultural backgrounds, experiences, and traditions of the children and their families, in particular the often 'invisible' contexts of the African children.

The framework story of the project is a fictional journey from the rural Transkei (a former Xhosa-Homeland) via the Eastern and Western Cape to Cape Town. On this journey, the children meet different groups of people and are compelled to speak the three main languages of the Cape region – Afrikaans, Xhosa and English. The different 'adventures' of the children during this journey take up topics of Xhosa-songs as well as the content of stories by a traditional Xhosa storyteller from Transkei and short stories by a well-known Afrikaans writer about the *Boere*. The starting point of the journey is a wedding celebration in a Transkei village at which a *sangoma* (a traditional healer) takes part; her medicine does not work anymore because one important ingredient is lacking, so the children are sent off on a quest for this item. In my interviews with members of the NLP team, after watching a number of the project lessons, many complex issues were raised, of which I will take up only *one* for the purpose of this article: the tensions around the *sangoma*-figure.

According to Athalie Crawford from the NLP, the *sangoma*-figure was a fascinating element of the project for the 6- to 9-year old children, since *sango-*

---

9 My presentation of the „Creative Arts Project" is a summary of the information obtained in interviews with several NLP-members: Noxolo Mgudla, Tholakele Maphalala, Somikazi Deyi, Andrew Kruger and Athalie Crawford. I also refer to Crawford's article "Get that sangoma out of this classroom!", published in the NLP-magazine "Bua" (1995).

mas are not merely fictional creatures to be encountered in fairy-tales, but rather they embody the connection between everyday life and the supernatural. In particular the Xhosa-speaking children contributed much information about *sangomas* based on their own experiences. Therefore the NLP team was taken aback by the extremely negative reactions of several adults. One White teacher explained that from a Christian point of view the introduction of such a figure into the lessons was inacceptable because it promoted "devil worship". Some Black teachers rejected *sangomas* as elements of a primitive and backward culture that did not belong into the school context. And one Black mother complained saying, "she did not send her child to a model C [ie, a formerly White] school to learn about *sangomas*" (Crawford 1995: 27f.).

This situation posed a dilemma to the NLP team. On the one hand, they interpreted the conflict as an expression of exactly the kind of cultural marginalisation that the "Creative Arts Project" was meant to counteract. On the other hand, they felt that missionary fervour in the defence of 'noble African traditions' was not an adequate response to the conflict. So, they decided to embark on a small internal 'research project', which, in my view, is an interesting attempt at searching for a concrete procedure to "negotiate" controversial issues around "cultural differences", as suggested in the NEPI curriculum report (1992). They invited Xhosa-speaking teachers to a group interview, the topic of discussion being their own experiences and attitudes as well as the attitudes of their families with regard to *sangomas* and ancestor worship. In the beginning, the topic aroused embarrassment and distancing. But after about half an hour of discussion, the "ice was broken", and all participants started to freely offer their experiences with the "supernatural". It became clear that all participants were familiar with *sangomas* from early childhood, and that *sangomas* had in fact always been an accepted part of their communities. Nobody had ever perceived them as dangerous or remarkable, but simply as elders who deserved respect like any other elders. And even though the validation of and participation in "traditional culture", as evoked by the *sangoma*-incident, might not be socially acceptable in the modern, culturally dominant White contexts, such traditions were still very much alive just underneath the surface of officially recognised cultural life. The group concluded, therefore, "that issues of culture necessarily involve negotiating relations of dominance and subordination" (Crawford 1995: 28).

The *sangoma* incident mirrors the pattern in the debate around language issues: just as their own multilingual everyday practice is partly denied and partly criticised by speakers of African languages (in favour of "English only"), we see how a natural part of the own everyday life is met with denial and rejection. This division between everyday practice and the denial and defamation in official contexts is an expression of the immanent ambivalence of "African identity".

The diverse reactions of rejection and detachment signal to which extent the mere suggestion to (openly) identify with the inferior, marginalised Other of Western rationality and enlightenment is an intolerable imposition.

Athalie Crawford insists, therefore, that it is of utmost importance to explore educational approaches to address issues of racism, racialised identity constructions and inherent hierarchies even with young children.

> Because it came up at one point in one small group activity we had with the kids. There was an explosion of bad feelings with some of the White little boys saying to a Black girl in their group: 'We wouldn´t play with girls like you.' The girl said: 'It is because you are full of apartheid, that´s why!' – And there was a very sharp, very angry exchange. […] So my feeling is that we have to discuss this issue, to find a way of saying: It is not your fault that you are feeling these things. It comes from another context. To contain it, so that the kids can feel all right about each other again. And feel right towards themselves […] Many of the children have no idea of the history of the country. They don´t really have that age. They´ve been brought up in a culture where the feelings are very strong that Whites are both on top of things and got the power, and are often very horrible. And that Blacks have got no power, and they´ve got nothing, and they are very stupid, but they are good. That´s the feeling. And I think somehow that has to be addressed (Athalie Crawford, project development, NLP, Cape Town, interview May 1996).

Crawford succinctly summarises the dichotomous positioning of "Black" and "White" in the Post-Apartheid South African narrative: "Blacks" are stupid and without power, but they are good. "Whites", on the other hand, are on top of things, they do have all the power, but they are evil. This quote from the South African context gives a glimpse into the general (post)colonial repertoire of images, as has been analysed in depths by Stuart Hall who points out that there is simply no place *outside* of the discourses and imaginations in which the "European presence" has already located the "Black subject". The European gaze, which constructs and fixates the "African" as the "Other", is no external force, but rather a constitutive element of "African identity":

> The ways in which Black people, Black experiences, were positioned and subject-ed in the dominant regimes of representation were the effects of a critical exercise of cultural power and normalisation. Not only, in Said's 'Orientalist' sense, were we constructed as different and other within the categories of knowledge of the West by those regimes. They had the power to make us see and experience **ourselves** as 'Other'. […] It is one thing to position a subject or set of people as the Other of a dominant discourse. It is quite another thing to subject them to that 'knowledge', not only as a matter of imposed will and domination, [but] by the power of inner compulsion and subjective con-formation to the norm. That is the lesson – the sombre majesty – of Fanon's insight into the colonising experience in 'Black Skin White

> Masks'. This inner expropriation of cultural identity cripples and deforms (Hall 1990: 226, emphasis in the original).

These reflections highlight a general problem with regard to Africanising the curriculum as long as "traditional African culture" is, as Athalie Crawford put it, a "suspect category". Nevertheless, the solution cannot be to exclude these experiences from the formal curriculum. Quite to the contrary, the question must be raised to what extent its inclusion into the official curriculum for all South African children can contribute to turn such aspects of everyday life into "legitimate knowledge":

> There is clearly a great deal of cultural knowledge that is seen as inappropriate to the school context, or as likely to be censured, but the children will pour it out if it is validated by people with the status of teachers. So children are constantly having to distinguish between what can and cannot be spoken about in the Model C [formerly White] school context. The rule of thumb is, probably the closer it is to white society the more likely it is to be approved, and the more it is at odds with the dominant ethos the more likely it is to be seen as disreputable in some way. This is a heavy burden for young children to carry (Crawford 1995: 29).

Conclusion

The discourse around multiculturalism in South Africa is complex and contradictory. In giving some insight into my findings, I have tried to illustrate the inherent ambivalence of the discourse of "multicultural education", an ambivalence that is likely not restricted to the South African context.

On the one hand, as the Afrikaans school conflict demonstrates, the protection of "cultural identity" implies a potentially problematic reification of collective identity constructions and can be employed to stabilise relations of power and hegemonic structures. On the other hand, educators throughout the world who deal with the educational situation of children from disadvantaged minority communities easily agree that the acknowledgment of the child's cultural and linguistic resources – the resources of her family and community – is an important potential means of empowerment. Again, as the *sangoma* incident illustrates, it does not suffice to merely include elements of the "minority culture" into the school context without addressing questions of power relations and cultural hegemony.

The dilemma that seems so far nearly impossible to resolve is how to address these issues in a manner that does not confirm, but dislodges the underlying power structures: There is a real danger of unwittingly reproducing these structures by presenting "Blacks" merely as the "victims" of White colonialism, imperialism and cultural hegemony. To be asked to identify with the position of the "victim" is just as much of an imposition as any other positioning in forceful discourses of Othering. But even the evident alternative, the discourse of "heroic resistance" in the retelling of the past, however much it might provide a symbolic and psychological resource, still mimics in its reversal the dominant discourse structure and reproduces the (apartheid) Black-White dichotomy.

The question of how to deal with dominance and repression inherent to any such representation is central in Hall's analysis of the "Black identity" which he discusses in relation to cinematic representation:

> The dialogue of power and resistance, of refusal and recognition, with and against Présence Européenne is almost as complex as the 'dialogue' with Africa. [...] How can we stage this dialogue so that, finally, we can place it, without terror or violence, rather than being forever placed by it? Can we ever recognise its irreversible influence, whilst resisting its imperialising eye? The enigma is impossible, so far, to be resolved. It requires the most complex of cultural strategies (Hall 1990: 233f.).

Even though there is, apparently, no ready-made 'solution', two suggestions emerge from my South African material, which are compatible with approaches to be found in postcolonial theory: deconstruction and hybridity. Firstly, there is the suggestion to fundamentally dislodge the categories of cultural identity rather than attempt to re-evaluate them. Rob Morell, a South African historian involved in history education, elaborates on how to deconstruct the notion of "Zulu identity" which has been highly politicised since Mangosuthu Buthelezi (chief of a Zulu clan by inheritance, and Chief Minister of the Homeland KwaZulu) founded the Inkatha Freedom Party (IFP) in 1975. The IFP mobilises its members on the basis of "Zulu ethnicity", and since 1979, in rivalry to the ANC resulting in violent clashes between members during the CODESA negotiations. Apartheid policy certainly encouraged such conflicts, which could be interpreted as based in "ethnic conflict":

> If I accept the apartheid apologist's theory of culture, then I can teach, for example, Zulu 'culture'. I can even include elements of Zulu 'culture' across the whole range of subjects. But, if I accept that 'culture' is a social construct, then there is no such 'thing' as Zulu culture that I can teach. All I can study is a whole range of people who in various ways call themselves Zulu and try to figure out how they construct and contest and use what it is to be a Zulu. I can also study how people who do not call themselves Zulu construct and contest and use what it is to be Zulu. And I can try to figure out what is the range of political purposes in the way in which Zulus and non-Zulus construct what it means to be Zulu. I can use all of that to ask 'what is going on when people talk about Zulu culture?' [...] So we send students off to interview Zulus and non-Zulus in different social and political locations to find out what, for them, it means to be a Zulu and what, for them, Zulu culture is. Then they

> can come back and share with each other what they have found out and recognise that it is a value-laden, political, problematic and contested concept at this very experiential, first-hand level. [...] It is around these sorts of notions, I believe, that we should construct learning experiences for students to come to terms more critically with the concepts of 'culture' and 'cultural difference' as inalienably political (Rob Morrell, Historian at the University of Natal, Durban, quoted in Moore 1994: 259f.).

The second suggestion steers us away from the "protection of cultural identity" in terms of "purity", which implies exclusivity and segregation, in order to acknowledge and promote mixture and 'impurity'. Athalie Crawford, who is not only an educator, but also a Jazz singer, draws a comparison to the development of new styles of music when speaking about her vision of a new "mixed culture":

> And what we want is for the actual different ways of thinking to be able to merge with each other so that we do come out with a South African way of thinking. The same as there is a South African music, African styles of music and Jazz now merged (Athalie Crawford, NLP, Cape Town, interview May 1996).

Essentially, the incontrovertible lesson to draw from the "South African case" is the disillusionment of a simple enrichment approach to "multicultural education". When Crawford argues in favour of forging a common new culture, she by no means imagines such a process as a harmonious combination and merging of different elements, but rather as a process of struggle and conflict. Based on her presentation of the *sangoma* conflict, she concludes:

> If we are serious about redressing cultural domination, and if multiculturalism in schools is to be more than a buzzword, we cannot avoid tackling the discomfort and edginess that the discourse around other less validated belief systems generates (Crawford 1995: 29).

> And it is not a question that we are all forging one new culture together. Hopefully we would like to do that, but it's out of these kinds of struggles that one would (Crawford, interview May 1996).

The first and basic condition for this process would be, therefore, the willingness to enter into such conflicts and struggles, into open-ended "negotiations" in the interpretation of the term by Bhabha, without guarantee of the outcome, with no control whatsoever from a position of cultural dominance, a process of negotiation where at any time the "own identity" may be called into question.

Literature

Alexander, N. (1989): Language Policy and National Unity in South Africa/Azania. Cape Town.

Benedict, R. (1934): Patterns of culture. Boston, MA.

Bhabha, H. K. (1990): The Third Space. In: J. Rutherford (ed.): Identity, Community, Culture, Difference. London, 207 – 221.

Boas, F. (1912/2001): Changes in Bodily Form of Descendants of Immigrants. Elibron Classics. Boston. [Replica of 1912 edition by Columbia University Press, New York.]

Christie, P. & Collins, C. (1984): Bantu Education: Apartheid Ideology and Labour Reproduction. In: Kallaway, P. (ed.): Apartheid and Education. The Education of Black South Africans. Johannesburg, 160 – 183.

Collins, B.C. & Gillespie, R.R. (1992): Multiculturalism, the new name for apartheid: A study of school curricula in the new South Africa. In: Journal of Intercultural Studies, 13: 1, 55 – 66.

Cross, M. (1992): Resistance and Transformation. Education, Culture and Reconstruction in South Africa. Johannesburg.

Crawford, A. (1995): Get that *sangoma* out of this classroom! In: Bua, 10: 1, 27 – 29.

Davenport, T.R.H. (1991): South Africa. A modern history (4th edition). London.

Derrida, J. (1998): Of Grammatology. Corrected edition, trans. G.C. Spivak [French 1967]. Baltimore & London.

Fichte, J.G. (1807-08/2008): Reden an die deutsche Nation. Edited by A. Aichele. Hamburg.

Hall, S. (1990): Cultural Identity and Diaspora. In: Rutherford, J. (ed.): Identity, Community, Culture, Difference. London, 222 – 237.

Hall, S. (1996): The Question of Cultural Identity. In: Hall, S., Held, D. & McGrew, T. (eds.): Modernity and its Futures. Cambridge, 274 – 325.

Hall, S. (2006): When was 'the postcolonial'? Thinking at the limit (orig. 1996). In: Chambers, I. & Curti, L. (eds.): The Postcolonial Question: Common Skies, Divided Horizons. London, 242 – 260.

Hewitt, R. (2003): Language, Youth and the Destabilisation of Ethnicity. In: Harris, R. & Rampton, B. (eds.): The Language, Ethnicity and Race Reader. London/New York, 188 – 198.

Kallaway, P. (ed. 2002): The History of Education under Apartheid 1948-1994. The Doors of Learning Shall be Opened. New York.

Kros, C. (2002): W.W.M. Eiselen: Architect of Apartheid Education. In: Kallaway, P. (ed.): The History of Education under Apartheid 1948-1994. The Doors of Learning Shall be Opened. New York, 53 – 73.

Lemmer, E. & Squelch, J. (1993): Multicultural Education. A teachers' manual. Halfway House.

Moore, B. (1993): Multicultural Education in South Africa: Some Theoretical and Political Issues. University of South Australia. Unpubl. mimeo.

Moore, B. (1994): Multicultural Education in South Africa: Some Theoretical and Political Issues. In: Perspectives in Education, 15: 2, 237 – 263.

Mudimbe, Y. V. (1988): The invention of Africa. Gnosis, Philosophy, and the Order of Knowledge. Bloomington/Indianapolis.

National Education Policy Investigation (NEPI) (1992): Curriculum. Cape Town.
Niedrig, H. (2000): Sprache – Macht – Kultur. Multilinguale Erziehung im Post-Apartheid-Südafrika. Münster/New York.
Norval, A.J. (1996): Deconstructing Apartheid Discourse. London/New York.
Open Schools Association (ed. 1994): Open Schools. A Professional Growth Programme for Teachers. Developed by the Centre of Educational Development of the University of Stellenbosch in Co-operation with the Open Schools Association. (incl. video and projector transparencies). Cape Town.
Schuring, G. (1993): Bilingual and trilingual language policies for South Africa. In: Prinsloo, K., Peeters, Y., Turi, J. & v. Rensburg, C. (eds.): Language, Law and Equality. Proceedings of the Third International Conference of the International Academy of Language Law (IALL) held in South Africa, April 1992. Pretoria, 239 – 246.
Worden, N. (1994): The making of modern South Africa. Conquest, Segregation and Apartheid. Oxford.
Wyk, J. van (1991): Afrikaans language, literature and identity. In: Theoria, 77, 79 – 89.

Notes on Contributors

Patricia Baquero Torres, born 1965, M. A. in Philosophy and Education, Ph.D. in Education. Academic Lecturer at the University of Education, Freiburg, Germany.

Mustafa Çapar, born 1962, Teaching Diploma, M. A. and Ph.D. in Anthropology. Assistant Professor at the Department of Anthropology, Mustafa Kemal University, Hatay, Turkey.

George J. Sefa Dei, born 1954, B. A. in Sociology and Archaeology (University of Ghana), M. A. and Ph.D. in Social Anthropology (University of Toronto). Professor of Sociology and Equity Studies, Ontario Institute for Studies in Education, University of Toronto, Canada.

Catriona Ellis, born 1982, M. A. in History. Ph.D. fellow at the University of Edinburgh, Scotland.

Rosa Fava, born 1971, M. A. in History, incl. Teaching Degree. Ph.D. Fellow at the University of Hamburg, Germany. Scholar at the Hans-Böckler-Foundation.

Christopher J. Frey, born 1972. M. A. in East Asian Studies, Ph.D. in History, Philosophy and Policy Studies. Assistant Professor of Historical and Comparative Foundations of Education at Bowling Green State University, USA.

Jonas Jakobsen, born 1975, M. A. in Philosophy and German. Ph.D. fellow at the University of Tromsø, Norway.

Adrea Lawrence, born 1973. B. A. in American Studies, M. A. in Social Studies Instruction and Curriculum, Ph.D. in Educational Leadership and Policy Studies. Assistant Professor at American University, United States.

Astrid Messerschmidt, born 1965, M. A., Ph.D. and Habilitation (postdoctoral thesis) in Education. Professor of Education and Intercultural Learning at the University of Education in Karlsruhe, Germany.

Heike Niedrig, born 1963, B. A. in African Languages, M. A. in German Literature and Sociology, incl. Teaching Degree, Further Diploma in Multilingual Education, Ph.D. in Education. Associated Researcher at the Institute for Intercultural Education, University of Hamburg, Germany.

Oscar Thomas-Olalde, born 1973, B. A. in Philosophy (University of Mexico), M. A. in Theology, Ph.D. fellow (Political Sciences) and Research Assistant at the Department of Educational Sciences, University of Innsbruck, Austria.

Astride Velho, born 1968, M. A. in Psychology, Ph.D. fellow at the University of Innsbruck, Austria. Scholar at the Hans-Böckler-Foundation.

Christian Ydesen, born 1974, M. A. in History and Philosophy, Ph.D. in History of Education. Associated Researcher at the Department of Education, University of Aalborg, Denmark.

Interkulturelle Pädagogik und postkoloniale Theorie

Herausgegeben von Heike Niedrig und Louis Henri Seukwa

Band 1 Patricia Baquero Torres: Kultur und Geschlecht in der Interkulturellen Pädagogik. Eine postkoloniale Re-Lektüre. 2009.

Band 2 Heike Niedrig / Christian Ydesen (eds.): Writing Postcolonial Histories of Intercultural Education. 2011.

www.peterlang.de